The Panama Route, 1848–1869

Eldredge Collection, Mariners' Museum, Newport News, Va.

The "Steam Clipper" *Golden Gate* of the Pacific Mail Steamship Company, 1851

The Panama Route
1848–1869

John Haskell Kemble

University of South Carolina Press

Published in Columbia, South Carolina, by the
University of South Carolina Press

Manufactured in the United States of America

First Published by the University of California Press,
Berkeley, 1943

Library of Congress Cataloging-in-Publication Data

Kemble, John Haskell, 1912–
  The Panama route, 1848–1869 / John Haskell Kemble.
    p. cm. — (Classics in maritime history)
  Reprint. Originally published: Berkeley : University of California
Press, 1943. Originally published in series: University of
California publications in history, v. 29.
  Revision of the author's thesis.
  Includes bibliographical references (p.).
  ISBN 0-87249-697-X
  1. Voyages to the Pacific coast. 2. Pacific Mail Steamship
Company—History—19th century. 3. Postal service—United States—
History—19th century. I. Title. II. Series.
F865.K32 1990
383'.142'091641—dc20   89-28560
                                                                  CIP

TO
CAROLINE HASKELL KEMBLE

William N. Still, Jr., Series Editor

Classics in Maritime History

*What Finer Tradition: The Memoirs of Thomas O. Selfridge, Jr.,
Rear Admiral, U.S.N.*
by Thomas O. Selfridge, Jr.
A Year on a Monitor and the Destruction of Fort Sumter
by Alvah F. Hunter
Confederate Navy Chief: Stephen R. Mallory
by Joseph T. Durkin
*Admiral of the New Empire:
The Life and Career of George Dewey*
by Ronald Spector
Sloops & Shallops
by William A. Baker
The Confederate Privateers
by William Morrison Robinson, Jr.
The Panama Route, 1848–1869
by John Haskell Kemble

Studies in Maritime History

*Stoddert's War: Naval Operations During the Quasi-War with
France, 1798–1801*
by Michael A. Palmer
The British Navy and the American Revolution
by John A. Tilley
*A Maritime History of the United States: The Role of America's
Seas and Waterways*
by K. Jack Bauer
Confederate Shipbuilding
by William N. Still, Jr.
Raid on America: The Dutch Naval Campaign of 1672–1674
by Donald G. Shomette and Robert D. Haslach
*Lifeline of the Confederacy:
Blockade Running During the Civil War*
by Stephen R. Wise
Admiral Harold R. Stark: Architect of Victory, 1939–1945
by B. Mitchell Simpson, III
History and the Sea: Essays on Maritime Strategies
by Clark G. Reynolds

PREFACE TO THE 1990 EDITION

When it comes to preparing a new preface for a book written a half century ago, there is a real problem as to what to say. Something regarding the history of the making of the book may be of interest. I believe that I first heard the name of the Pacific Mail Steamship Company in 1921 when my parents and I arrived at the Ferry Building in San Francisco having come north from Los Angeles on the Southern Pacific "Owl," and were told that there was no "hack" from the Whitcomb Hotel to meet us because it was at the Pacific Mail wharf where the steamer *Venezuela* had just arrived. In 1925 I was in San Francisco again and was greatly impressed by the lithographs of Pacific Mail steamers in the Schwerin Collection at the De Young Museum. In 1928 I was casting about for a topic for a high school term paper, and lighted on the Pacific Mail as a possibility. My interest in the company's history never flagged after that, and as I went on to college I became aware that no adequate history of the company existed. I determined to try to fill the gap, and when I went to graduate school at the University of California, Berkeley, I set out to write such a history. It became quickly apparent that the history of the Pacific Mail from 1848 until 1869 was almost entirely concerned with the Panama Route. (It did not enter the trans-Pacific trade until 1867.) It therefore seemed logical to write an account of the route as a whole during those years with the Pacific Mail and its competitors fitted within it. The result was a doctoral dissertation completed in 1937.

I revised the manuscript taking into account materials newly encountered, especially the surviving papers of the Pacific Mail itself which came to the Huntington Library in 1937. This manuscript I submitted to the University of California Press in 1939, and it was accepted for publication the next year. On the very day in 1942 when I left Claremont for active duty in the Navy, I received the copy-edited manuscript to go over, correct, and check. Galley proofs came in the summer of 1942, and the page proofs were ready in the summer of 1943. By that time I was on duty in the Pacific Ocean Areas, and could "beg off" the task of indexing. The completed book reached me at Pearl Harbor in the autumn of 1943.

The University of California Press issued the book as Volume

29 of the University of California Publications in History. The edition was small—the number of 300 copies sticks in my memory. In any event it went out of print fairly quickly. Since the Press had not copyrighted it, probably demand from the newly sprouting college and university libraries encouraged the appearance of a reprint. One was issued by Library Editions, Ltd. in 1970, another by the De Capo Press in 1972, and a third by the Kraus Reprint Co. in 1974. There may have been others. Of course the absence of a copyright rendered them legal. The University Press may have been asked informally for its permission. I certainly never was. These must have been small press runs, and over the years I have almost never seen one offered for sale in a catalog or from the shelves of a bookstore.

In the half century since the book was written, I have encountered from time to time materials which might have been incorporated in it, but none of them seemed to be of such moment as would call for a complete rewriting. Therefore the text and bibliography have been left unchanged. I have corrected a few errors and misprints in the original edition, but in the main it is reissued as originally published. I am glad that the University of South Carolina Press has seen fit to produce this new edition, and I trust that the book will be of interest and use to those who are drawn to the reading and study of the history of the Pacific Coast and to the maritime history of the United States.

John Haskell Kemble
Claremont, California

PREFACE

FOR TWO DECADES, the Panama route was the best way of travel and communication between the Atlantic and Pacific coasts of the United States. Annually, thousands of passengers went over it eastward and westward, as well as vast volumes of mail and treasure. Its paddle wheelers and dugout canoes, its mule trains and snorting locomotives formed a vital part of the communication system of the United States. The Overland route and the voyage 'round the Horn could not be compared with it for speed or dependability. When the initial novelty of 1849 had worn off, travel by Panama came to be taken as a matter of course. It has therefore received less attention than other more picturesque but less really significant phases in the history of American transportation.

The present study has grown from a lifelong interest in maritime history and particularly from an early concern with the history of the Pacific Mail Steamship Company. It has taken shape with the discovery of materials and has therefore given the author the joy of exploration in little-charted seas. Many individuals and institutions have been generous of their experience, time, and facilities in assisting in its completion, and the brief mention which they may receive can do little more than acknowledge a very real debt of gratitude. My mother and father, Caroline Haskell Kemble and Ira Oscar Kemble, have unstintingly given encouragement and intelligent interest and have been willing and able assistants in the work of preparing tables, arranging the text in final form, and reading proof. To a high-school teacher, Miss Mayo Elizabeth Wheeler, I am grateful for initial stimulation and direction. Professor Edgar Eugene Robinson of Stanford University was a wise mentor in my undergraduate days. To Professor Herbert Eugene Bolton of the University of California, who was my guide in graduate study, I owe much, not only for his direction and suggestions, but also and even more for the inspiration and enthusiasm of his example. Professor Frederic Logan Paxson was an unsparing but kindly critic, and I am grateful for his generosity of time and interest in my behalf. Mr. Robert Ernest Cowan discussed the subject with me on many occasions and gave generously of his vast knowledge of the bibliography of California. For access to his unrivaled collection relating to American steam navigation, as well as for the generous sharing of his intimate knowledge of the field, I am grateful to my friend Elwin Martin Eldredge. J. Porter Shaw has shown constant interest and has been of great assistance through his familiarity with naval architecture and Pacific-coast shipping. Mr. Joseph Gartland, Assistant Inspector General of the Post Office Department, Captain Dudley W. Knox, U.S.N. (Retired), and Dr. Charles Oscar Paullin of the Carnegie Institution of Washington have all contributed significantly of the time, knowledge, and resources at their disposal. Miss Dorothy O. Johansen and Miss Doris Marion Wright have generously placed materials from their research at my disposal.

The Native Sons of the Golden West, through grants of a Resident Fellowship at the University of California and a Traveling Fellowship, made it possible to place this study on the basis of materials gathered not only on the Pacific coast, but also in the eastern United States and at Panama. A research grant from Claremont Colleges provided the means for further research in the National Archives at a later stage in the work.

It is possible only to name the institutions which have made their resources available to me and the members of their staffs, who have been invariably helpful and courteous: the Bancroft Library, the Stanford University Library, the Henry E. Huntington Library, the Pomona College Library, the State Library of California, and the M. H. de Young Memorial Museum in California; the Provincial Library and Archives of British Columbia at Victoria; the New York Public Library, the New York Historical Society, the United States Custom House, and the Webb Institute of Naval Architecture in New York; the Harvard University Library at Cambridge; the Essex Institute and the Peabody Museum at Salem; the Department of State, the Library of Congress, the Library of the Post Office Department, the National Archives and the Office of Naval Records and Library in Washington; the Panama Railroad Company, the Canal Zone Library, the Archivo de Panamá and the *Panama Star and Herald* on the Isthmus of Panama. To these, as well as to many others, I wish to express my gratitude.

J. H. K.

Claremont, California
October 31, 1940

CONTENTS

ILLUSTRATIONS

MAPS

A RIPPING TRIP

AIR—"POP GOES THE WEASEL"

You go aboard of a leaky boat,
    And sail for San Francisco;
You've got to pump to keep her afloat,
    You have *that*, by jingo.
The engine soon begins to squeak,
    But nary thing to oil her;
Impossible to stop the leak—
    Rip goes the boiler!

"Pork and beans" they can't afford
    To second cabin passengers;
The cook has tumbled overboard
    With forty pounds of "sassengers";
The engineer, a little tight,
    Bragging on the Mail Line,
Finally gets into a fight—
    Rip goes the engine!

When home, you'll tell an awful tale,
    And always will be thinking
How long you had to pump and bail,
    To keep the tub from sinking.
Of course you'll take a glass of gin,
    'Twill make you feel so funny;
Some city sharp will rope you in—
    Rip goes your money!

—*Put's Golden Songster*, 1858

The Panama Route, 1848–1869

CHAPTER I

OPENING THE PANAMA ROUTE

FOR TWENTY YEARS after the establishment of American dominion on the shores of the Pacific, the lines of contact with the eastern United States led chiefly over the Isthmus of Panama. The steamships which plied up and down both coasts of North America carried important intelligence, mail, newspapers, express freight, and passengers. In the strong rooms of the ships leaving San Francisco for Panama went the gold mined in the foothills of the Sierra Nevada. A railroad was pushed through the jungles and over the torrents of the Isthmus, so that after 1855 the crossing could be made from ocean to ocean in less than half a day. Great steamers were built, factories for boilers and machinery established, and supplies of coal and provisions gathered to make possible swift and efficient operation. The individuals and corporations concerned in the operation of the Panama route between 1848 and 1869 were often bitterly hostile to one another, but the combination of their efforts, however directed for the moment, resulted in the development and maintenance of a vital artery in the transportation system of the United States. Until the completion of the transcontinental railroad, the ordinary person or message could not travel between the Atlantic and Pacific coasts more swiftly or surely than by way of Panama.

Long before the advent of the United States and the emergence of Alta California to a place of importance in world affairs the Isthmus had been a center of activity and interest. It had enjoyed a great era of prosperity for nearly three centuries after the coming of Spanish colonists to the Americas. The cities of Panama and Porto Bello flourished, for the whole trade of the Viceroyalty of Peru passed through their warehouses and harbors, while the great fairs of Porto Bello became famous for the amount of business transacted there. As Spain's hold on her American empire relaxed in the second decade of the nineteenth century, the prosperity of the Isthmus declined. The laws of trade were disregarded, and goods came and went from the west coast of South America by way of Cape Horn rather than crossing the Isthmus at Panama. When speed was not a requisite, this was much more economical than the transshipments at the Isthmus, and therefore the Bay of Panama harbored fewer ships each year, and the paved road to Porto Bello fell a prey to the encroaching jungle and the floods of the rainy season.

Although trade languished, the Isthmus was not forgotten. The potentialities of the region could not be overlooked by the enterprising British and American merchants and official representatives who grew increasingly familiar in these parts during the Hispanic-American wars of independence. In 1826, the centuries-old project of an isthmian canal was revived by a company of New Yorkers, who organized the Atlantic and Pacific Ocean Company and obtained the sanction of the Guatemalan government for a canal in the Lake Nicaragua region. This project gained the attention of British diplomatic agents, but was not carried into execution.[1] In 1829, Silas Burrows, a Connecticut Yankee, organized a line of packet brigs to connect New York with Cartagena and the Isthmus of Panama. He advertised his willingness to carry letters to Panama at monthly intervals and announced that it was his plan to establish a line between Panama and Callao within the year 1830. It was his expectation that this line would be of particular importance to whalers and sealers in the Pacific, as well as to merchants. Burrows withdrew from the business in 1835, and the line did not survive him long, but his activity gave evidence of a recognition in the United States of the significance of the isthmian route for communication with the Pacific.[2]

Diplomatic and naval officers traveling to or from stations in the Pacific commonly went by way of Panama if connections could be arranged. News from the Pacific sometimes reached the United States by way of Panama, though as often it crossed Mexico and was sent north from Vera Cruz. In the summer of 1847, the Postmaster General wrote to the Secretary of the Navy, asking that homeward-bound warships call at Panama for mail, and to the Secretary of State, requesting that the consul there be instructed to forward mail whenever the opportunity might present itself.[3] The volume of this traffic was small, though its nature often made it highly important.

The western shore of the Americas came finally within the purview of the industrial revolution when a regular steamship

---

[1] For notes to chap. i, see pp. 261–264.

service along the Pacific coast of South America was proposed
by William Wheelwright, an American mariner who had entered
business in South America and was United States consul at Guayaquil. When he failed to obtain support in the United States, Wheelwright crossed to England and there met with greater success. The
Pacific Steam Navigation Company was chartered on February
17, 1840, and at the close of that year two steamers, the *Peru* and
the *Chile,* were dispatched from England to South America.
Although they received a mail subsidy from the British government, the limited business offered and the expense of obtaining
coal on such a distant station caused the steamers to lose money
during the first five years of their operation.[4] On the Atlantic, the
Royal Mail Steam Packet Company, chartered in 1839, began mail
service in steamers between England and the West Indies in 1842.
The line was extended to the Isthmus of Panama in 1846, and a
canoe-and-mule line across to the Pacific was organized, connecting
with the steamers of the Pacific Steam Navigation Company. In
the same year an agreement was reached with the admiralty which
provided for a through mail service over the Isthmus and as far
south as Valparaiso.[5] Mules were purchased to transport specie
from Pacific to Atlantic, and in 1848 the first merchandise left
England for the west coast of South America by this route.[6]

Although the British were pioneers in the operation of steamships to the Isthmus, they were not alone in the field. The importance of Panama was recognized in the United States as well.
At the same time that English steamers were making their first
calls there, diplomatic steps were being taken to secure permission
for Americans also to use the transit. In a treaty entered by the
Republic of New Granada, of which Panama was a state, and by
the United States on December 12, 1846, the latter was promised
the right of way and transit across the Isthmus by any means then
existing or which might come to exist in the future. In return,
New Granada received from the United States a guarantee of the
neutrality of the Isthmus, and of her rights of sovereignty and
property over it.[7]

The Pacific coast of North America did not offer the inducement
to merchants for the establishment of regular lines of communication which the growing republics of South America held forth.
As long as Alta California was held by Spain and Mexico, its

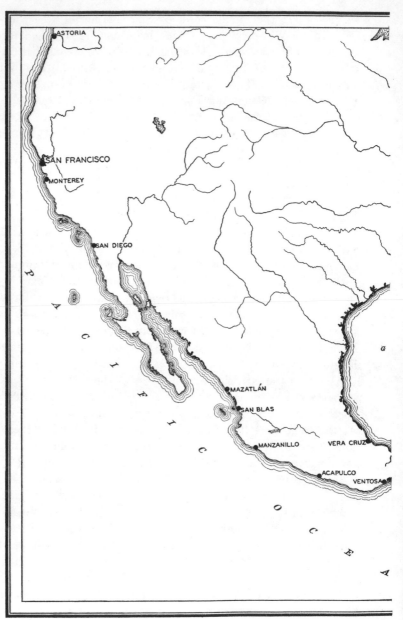

ASTORIA

SAN FRANCISCO

MONTEREY

SAN DIEGO

P
A
C
I
F
I
C

O
C
E
A

MAZATLÁN

SAN BLAS

MANZANILLO

VERA CRUZ

G

ACAPULCO

VENTOSA

Map of North America, Showing

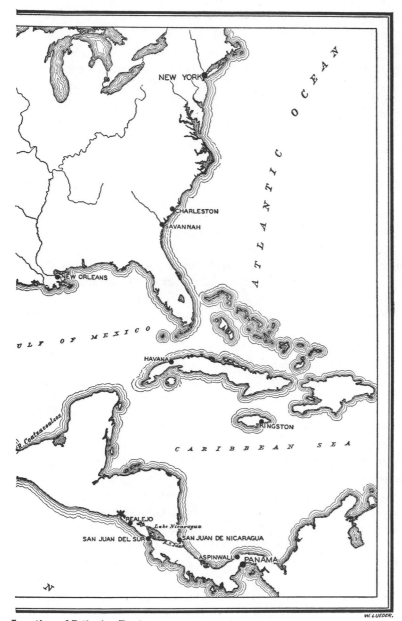

Location of Isthmian Routes

official connection with the outside world was chiefly through the
supply ships which came north from San Blas. Even these ceased
to sail regularly after Mexico became independent. The hides and
tallow of California's missions and ranches were traded for manufactured articles and went directly to the ports of South America,
England, or New England in the British and American ships which
came for them. North of California, the Russians drew back to
Alaska in the second quarter of the nineteenth century, while
British and American fur traders carried on a lively commerce
among the Indians of the coast. The furs were shipped directly to
Canton, England, or the United States in the ships which brought
manufactured articles to trade for them. In 1835, the Hudson's Bay
Company sent out from England the steamer *Beaver,* which was
designed to ply along the coast and collect furs. This was the only
steam vessel constantly in operation north of Panama prior to the
coming of the American mail steamers in 1849. As long as the
Pacific coastline of North America was sparsely populated by
persons interested chiefly in trapping and cattle raising, there was
no need for rapid or regular communication with the rest of the
world.

The North Pacific region had been known by Americans since
John Ledyard accompanied Captain James Cook on his third and
last voyage into the Pacific in the years 1776–1780, and Robert
Gray had explored the mouth of the Columbia River on his cruise
of 1787–1792. Traders from New England came almost to monopo-
lize the maritime fur trade in the area. In 1811 a New York
merchant, John Jacob Astor, sent out expeditions to establish a
fur post at the mouth of the Columbia, which resulted in the
founding of Astoria. The post was sold in 1813 under pressure of
war to the Northwest Company, a Canadian organization; American
traders nevertheless remained on the coast. Official interest of the
United States in the region was indicated by the expedition of
Meriwether Lewis, sent out by President Jefferson in 1804, which
crossed the continent and spent the winter of 1805–1806 near the
mouth of the Columbia River. The rival claims of Britain and the
United States to Oregon were not sufficiently clear to allow a
sharp division of the territory, and the question was temporarily
settled by the Joint Occupation Treaty of 1827. A final decision
was foreshadowed in 1832, when agricultural settlers from the

Missouri frontier of the United States set out on the overland journey to Oregon. Farming and fur trading could not exist side by side, and as the land was cleared and the wild animals killed by the American immigrants, the Hudson's Bay Company withdrew north of the Columbia and prepared to move its Pacific-coast base to Vancouver Island. By 1843 there were enough Americans in the Willamette Valley to put aside the government of the Hudson's Bay Company over the area. Finally, the Oregon Boundary Treaty of 1846 extended the international boundary to the Pacific along the forty-ninth parallel, and the territory south of it became the undisputed possession of the United States.

In the same year the United States declared war on the Mexican Republic, and by the early months of 1847 the province of Alta California had been conquered by American forces. In this region also, there had been an increasingly large and influential body of residents who had come from the United States for purposes of trade and agriculture and who gladly aided in bringing it under American rule. By the treaty of Guadalupe Hidalgo, in 1848, the United States acquired not only Alta California, but also the great mountain and desert area of the Southwest, and the western boundary of the nation was brought to the Pacific Ocean from Puget Sound to San Diego.

When Oregon became a part of the American Republic in 1846, the whole character of the problem of transportation to the Pacific was changed. Having acquired territory on the Pacific, the United States became responsible for providing some regular means of communication with the region. There were three routes by which this could be carried out: by way of Cape Horn in sailing vessels, overland from the Missouri River by road, or by way of the Isthmus of Panama in sailing ship or steamer. The first of these was the easiest, involving no great outlay of money and traversing seas which had been known to American sailormen for over half a century. It was made impracticable by the matter of time, however, for a passage of six months between New York and the northwest coast was usual, and this was too slow for the transportation of mail. Since 1819 there had been proposals to establish wagon roads across the continent, and in 1845 Asa Whitney asked for a land grant to aid him in the construction of a railroad to the mouth of the Columbia. Whitney's scheme was considered fantastic, how-

ever, for even a good wagon road would be closed by the snows of
winter a considerable part of the year, as well as being constantly
exposed to the attacks of Indians. Therefore, in 1846, there was
little question that the most practicable means of transportation
between the coasts was by way of the Isthmus of Panama. This
involved a voyage from some Atlantic or Gulf port of the United
States to the mouth of the Chagres River, on the Atlantic side of
the Isthmus. Thence the route followed the river to the head of
navigation and overland to the city of Panama on the Pacific side.
From Panama, it continued by sea up the coast to Oregon. Although
the expense involved in the establishment of this line was greater
than by way of Cape Horn, it cost much less than an overland
road or railroad and offered greater speed and regularity than
the others, with the exception of the rather distant prospect of a
railroad. When the matter of establishing regular mail and passenger service to the Pacific was seriously discussed, there was
united opinion in favor of the route across the Isthmus of Panama.

Under the act of Congress of March 3, 1845, providing for foreign
mail service, an attempt was made to open a line to the North
Pacific. The Postmaster General invited proposals for ships to
carry the mail between New York and Chagres by way of Havana
or Kingston, and for a joint or separate offer of service from
Panama to the Hawaiian Islands, with a call en route at the mouth
of the Columbia River. In the offers it was to be stated whether
steam or sailing vessels would be employed and whether or not a
mail agent would be carried. Although there was no requirement
with respect to the frequency of voyages, it was suggested that
sailings be once every two months. Ships accepted for this mail
service were to be available for delivery to the government for naval
service upon demand. Persons interested were asked to submit bids
by January 15, 1846, so that decisions could be made by the end of
the month and the line might commence operation about May 1,
1846. Since the contracts were to run for four years, they would
expire about June 30, 1850.[8] There was only one offer for the performance of the entire service. This came from Amos Kendall, who
had been an important member of President Jackson's "Kitchen
Cabinet" and had held the office of Postmaster General under both
Jackson and Van Buren. He proposed to operate sailing vessels on
the run between New York and Chagres, and also between Panama

and the Columbia River by way of the Hawaiian Islands. The service was to be at bimonthly intervals and at an annual cost to the government of $58,000, if the United States would provide transportation for the mails across the Isthmus at its own expense.[9]

Albert G. Sloo offered to carry the mail monthly between New Orleans and Chagres in 700-ton steamships for $90,000 a year, provided the United States would supply him with the funds with which to construct the steamers. He also offered to carry the mails for the postage alone if the government would provide the money to build steamers of 1,500 tons burden with 1,500-horsepower engines. At the same time, Sloo was bidding for the New York–Havana–New Orleans service at $100,000 or $200,000 a year, depending on whether the voyages were to be performed weekly or fortnightly.[10]

On March 9, 1846, the Postmaster General reported to the House of Representatives that Kendall's offer for the Pacific portion of the service was very reasonable and that the only reason for not accepting it was that steamer service on the Atlantic side could not be arranged on suitable terms. If this were the only objection, Kendall was ready to remove it; in a letter of June 24, 1846, he offered to carry out the whole service for $42,000 a year. The ships would sail every two months, would go from Panama to the mouth of the Columbia by way of the Hawaiian Islands, and call at San Francisco or Monterey on the southbound trip.[11] Again Cave Johnson, the Postmaster General, urged the advantages of the offer and stated his willingness to accept it if Congress would give its approval and make the necessary appropriation.[12] The proposal to carry out the service in sailing vessels was not satisfactory to Congress. It was a day in which the superior speed and dependability of the steamer had become perfectly evident, and for the important mail line to the Pacific steamers were desired. Consideration of Kendall's offer was therefore abandoned.

Interest in the project did not wane, however, and from the beginning of 1846 there were bills constantly before both houses of Congress which provided for regular mail service to the coast of Oregon by way of the Isthmus of Panama. When President Polk announced the settlement of the Oregon boundary controversy in a message to Congress on August 6, 1846, he not only recommended that some government for the territory be instituted and that trade with the Indians be regulated, but also declared : "it is likewise important that mail facilities, so indispensable for the diffusion of information and for building together the different portions of our extended Confederacy, should be afforded to our citizens west of the Rocky Mountains."[13] Discussion of the matter was protracted, however, and Congress found it difficult to agree on its terms.[14] Provision for the Oregon mail service was finally made in "An Act to establish certain Post Routes and for other Purposes," which became law on March 3, 1847. A through service was authorized in steamers, with sailings from an Atlantic or Gulf port at least every two months. Between Panama and Oregon, the steamers were required to call at Monterey and San Francisco, which were then in the hands of American forces. For this line, the Postmaster General was limited to a maximum payment of $100,000 a year.[15]

On April 21, 1847, an advertisement for bids under this law was issued, with the announcement that they would be received until July 15 and that the decision would be announced on August 1. The Atlantic service was divided from that on the Pacific, and bids were received separately for each part. Jabez M. Woodward offered to operate steamers between New York and Chagres at bimonthly intervals for $45,000 a year, the steamers to be of not less than 500 tons. James M. Stocker proposed a monthly service from Charleston to Chagres by way of Indian Key, Key West, and Havana in a first-rate steamer of 500 to 700 tons for $100,000 annually. On the Pacific, a route was outlined from Astoria to Panama, with calls at San Francisco and Monterey and with an overland extension from Panama to Chagres. Woodward also tendered an offer for this service at $55,000 a year between Astoria and Chagres, or $50,000 from Astoria to Panama and $5,000 from Panama to Chagres. The total of Woodward's offer fell within the limitation of $100,000 set by Congress. The other tender of service on the Pacific was made by William Kelly, John J. Sullivan, John McField, and James L. Fowler. They proposed to carry on monthly service between Panama and Astoria in five copper-fastened pilot-boat-built schooners of 100 to 120 tons for $65,000 a year. A single bid for the transportation of mail across the Isthmus was received from O. H. Throop, who offered monthly service for $2,492, or fortnightly service for $3,968 a year.[16]

Bidding for the Post Office contract was complicated by the fact that the Navy Department had simultaneously been authorized to provide a similar service and had at its disposal an unlimited supply of funds to pay for it. The Secretary of the Navy had been directed by Congress to contract with Albert G. Sloo for the line from New York to Chagres, and he believed that he was required to accept bids for the Pacific portion. With this competition between governmental agencies, the Post Office Department was unable to make contracts for the route, and the Postmaster General estimated that the whole service from the Atlantic coast to Oregon would cost more than $200,000, or double the amount available to him.[17] In spite of efforts extending over a period of three years, the Post Office Department failed to establish regular communication with the Pacific coast.

The decade between 1835 and 1845 had witnessed the successful application of steam to the operation of ocean-going vessels. It had been finally demonstrated that a steamer was practicable for a long sea voyage, and that it was possible for her to make such a voyage with greater speed and regularity than a sailing vessel. The supremacy of sail for the transportation of heavy cargoes was not challenged, but mail, express matter, and passengers, which paid a comparatively high tariff, were carried increasingly by steamers. These ten years saw the foundation of the great network of British mail lines: the Peninsular and Oriental Steam Navigation Company from England to Egypt, India, and the East in 1837, the Cunard Line between England and North America in 1839, the Royal Mail Steam Packet Company from England to the West Indies and South America in 1839, and the Pacific Steam Navigation Company on the west coast of South America in 1840.

The navies of Great Britain and the United States were interested in the opening of steam mail lines not only because of the traditional concern of the navy with ocean mail service, but also because of the expectation that the mail steamers would be useful for naval purposes. The difference between the steam and sailing warship in the middle nineteenth century amounted to little more than varying methods of propulsion, and since the sailing merchant ship had always formed an effective auxiliary naval vessel in time of war, it was expected that the steam merchantman would be as useful. The subsidizing of lines of ocean steamers by the navy was therefore not unreasonable, for by this means the mails would be carried and additional naval units for service in time of war would also be provided. The vulnerability of the engines of an unarmored ship had yet to be clearly demonstrated, and even long after it had, the theory that a merchant steamer might be useful for fighting purposes persisted, forming the basis of argument in favor of naval subsidies to commercial lines of steamers.

The example of Britain was not unheeded by the United States. An act of Congress of March 3, 1845, provided for the transportation of mail between the United States and foreign countries, envisaged the making of mail contracts, set ocean postage rates, and made it clear that preference was to be given to American steamers in the award of subsidies.[18] With the encouragement of this act, the Ocean Steam Navigation Company of New York was organized, and placed the steamers *Washington* and *Hermann* in the trade between New York, Cowes, and Bremen in 1847 and 1848. For a subsidy of $200,000 a year, the company undertook to perform the transatlantic mail service twice a month for ten years.[19]

The provisions of the act of 1845 were not sufficient to bring about the founding of all the lines of mail steamers desired, and on June 12, 1846, a bill was reported into the House of Representatives by Thomas Butler King of Georgia, authorizing and requiring the Secretary of the Navy to enter into a series of contracts for the transportation of the United States mail in ocean steamers.[20] The session passed without further action in this direction, but in January, February, and March, 1847, in the crowded days of the second session of the Twenty-Ninth Congress, a bill from the Committee on Naval Affairs providing for the building and equipment of four steam warships was hotly debated in both the House and the Senate.[21] The bill was finally passed in the closing hours of the session, on March 3, 1847. In its final form, it provided not only for the construction of warships, but also for mail contracts between the Secretary of the Navy and private operators. This significant amendment was the work of Thomas Butler King, chairman of the House Naval Affairs Committee and a "big navy" enthusiast. He had previously urged support of such a measure, and now, at the very close of the session, he was able to introduce it into the bill in the ten minutes allowed for debate. The bill as amended was passed without a record vote, and on the same day was concurred in by the Senate and signed by President Polk.[22]

A mail contract between the Navy Department and Edward K. Collins for the New York-and-Liverpool service was written into the act, as well as provision for steamers on the Panama route. Albert G. Sloo was named as the recipient of a contract for semimonthly voyages between New York and New Orleans with calls at Charleston, Savannah, and Havana, as well as a branch service from Havana to Chagres. For this service, the compensation was not to exceed $290,000 a year. On the Pacific side, the name of the contractor was not specified, but the Secretary of the Navy was instructed to provide for a monthly service in either steamers or sailing vessels between Panama and such port in the territory of Oregon as he might select. Ships for all these lines were to be built under the direct supervision of the Navy Department and were subject to being taken over for government service at any time.[23]

In this instance the United States had recognized and acted upon the general principle that mail steamers, complying with the wishes of a government with respect to construction and speed and carrying out regular voyages in accordance with a government plan, cannot be maintained without aid from public funds. The requirements of speed and regularity, and the frequently noncommercial nature of a mail route make profitable operation without assistance virtually impossible. The voyages of mail vessels cannot be reduced in number with the coming of business depression, nor can their routes be altered to suit new economic inducements. Since the purposes of a mail route do not always coincide with the requirements of a profitable line, a government, if it feels that the regularity and speed of mail ships is a necessity, must be ready to compensate owners for the losses which they may suffer in operating them.

The passage by Congress of the warship bill, with its significant rider relating to the subsidy of ocean steamers, was received with enthusiasm by the maritime world of New York. Even before the complete terms of the bill were available the *New York Herald* congratulated Congress on its wisdom in passing such a measure. It was said that, although Edward Collins would receive the New York–Liverpool contract, the contract for the line to New Orleans and Chagres would probably go to Charles H. Marshall, who was then building for the transatlantic service a steamer which could easily be converted for the other route.[24] When Thomas Butler King was in New York later in March, 1847, he was entertained at the Astor House at a great dinner given by the shippers of the city in appreciation for his assistance in passing the "Mail-Steamer Bill."[25]

Thus both the Navy Department and the Post Office Department were empowered to establish lines to Oregon by acts of March 3, 1847. Cave Johnson, the Postmaster General, was anxious to arrive at some agreement for coöperation, perhaps with the Navy carrying out the service on the Atlantic and the Post Office arranging it on the Pacific. The Secretary of the Navy, however, felt bound by the specific nature of the act of March 3 to contract with Albert G. Sloo for the Atlantic line and to open bidding for the service between Panama and Oregon.[26] With the failure of interdepartmental negotiations, both the Navy and the Post Office advertised for bids, with the inevitable result that the contracts were finally made with the former because of the greater funds at its disposal.

By the terms of the Mail-Steamer Bill, the contract for fortnightly service between New York and New Orleans by way of Charleston, Savannah, and Havana, and for a branch line from Havana to Chagres was to be made with Albert G. Sloo. A recurrent figure in the history of the Panama route, Sloo was born in Kentucky and had moved to Indiana and carried on farming near Vincennes before entering the steamship business. He was described as a man of hobbies, the greatest of which was postal economy— shortening mail routes, cheapening postage, and expediting service. Whether this was for Sloo an end in itself or a means to a comfortable income may be questioned. From his Indiana farm, Sloo moved to New Orleans, where he talked Charles Morgan and others into the establishment of a steamship line on Lake Pontchartrain, thus opening a shorter mail route between New Orleans and Mobile. The line obtained a liberal mail contract, and Sloo was able to sell his interest in it at a handsome profit. In 1845, he was a bidder for the transatlantic mail contract, and two years later, as has been seen, he was named to carry out the Atlantic portion of the Panama route. This contract Sloo assigned to others, while he turned to the Tehuantepec route, in the interests of which he finally ruined himself in the next decade. Characterized as a man of fine presence, open-handed and social, he could, it was said, invent more gigantic schemes and get more men to invest in them than any man of his day. A "prince of lobbyists," Sloo's role with relation to the Panama route was that of promoter rather than builder.[27]

On April 20, 1847, Albert G. Sloo "of Cincinnati" bound himself to carry out mail service in steamers from New York to New Orleans and Chagres at fortnightly intervals for $230,000 a year. From the beginning, however, it was clear that he had not the means to carry it out himself. It is not surprising, therefore, to find that four months later he disposed of the contract in profitable fashion. The arrangement which he made was a complex one, bringing into the business a number of men, some of whom were to remain of great importance to the Panama route for years to come. On August 17, 1847, Sloo assigned the contract to a board of trustees made up of George Law, Bowes R. McIlvaine, and Marshall Owen Roberts. In order actually to carry out the terms of the contract, Law and Roberts, together with Edwin Crosswell and Prosper M. Wetmore, agreed to put up the money to build and operate the required steamers, although the immediate management of the ships would be placed in Law's hands. The vessels would be registered, however, in the names of the trustees, who would appoint and pay all officers and agents. It was agreed that the trustees would pay the investors—Crosswell, Law, Roberts, and Wetmore—and also Sloo, $10,000 each annually from the income of the line, and that the remainder of the net earnings should be used to repay the investment of the four men who were to build the ships with legal interest and a commission of 10 per cent on the money which they had advanced. Earnings beyond this were to be divided equally, half going to Sloo, and half to Crosswell, Law, Roberts, and Wetmore. To Sloo was reserved the nomination of the commanders of the steamers, by and with the consent of the trustees.[28] The assignment of the contract was duly approved by the Secretary of the Navy, although he reminded Sloo that the responsibility for the fulfillment of the contract still rested officially upon him. Finally on September 3, 1847, the contract was formally assigned to the trustees, so that preparations for opening service in the next year might go forward.[29]

Of the men who had thus taken over the responsibility for operating steamers from New York to the Isthmus, Law and Roberts were the leaders. "Live Oak George" Law was a self-made man of Irish parentage, who had enjoyed little formal education but possessed boundless adaptability and energy. A hard-faced individual, he was ruthless in his business methods, turning his attention chiefly to projects of a constructive nature. Before entering the steamship business Law had taken contracts to build canals and bridges, had become interested in the Harlem and Hudson and Mohawk railroads, and had become chief owner of the Dry Dock Bank. In the decade of the 'fifties, Law withdrew from active participation in the steamship line to the Isthmus of Panama but took an active part in the construction of the Panama Railroad. Prior to the election of 1856, he was the object of a presidential "boom," based chiefly upon popularity gained by his aggressive handling of a difficulty between one of the officers of his steamer *Northern Light* and the Spanish authorities at Havana.[30]

Marshall Owen Roberts, who entered the Panama business in association with Law, remained concerned with various aspects of it until 1868. He had been interested in railroads and river steamboats before 1847 and therefore brought some experience in transportation to the steamship service. Besides previous business success, Roberts had, as early as 1841, discovered the possibilities of profitable combination of business with politics. His political activity and influence played no small part in his manipulation of contracts and mail services. During the Civil War, Roberts profiteered shamelessly by the sale and charter of his steamers for government service. A product of his age and of the terrible competitive nature of the steamship business, Roberts showed a lack of principle, a ruthless individualism, and a cynical view of political corruption for selfish purposes which were matched by many of his contemporaries and competitors.[31]

When the contracts were made, Prosper M. Wetmore was United States Navy agent at New York, and it was his responsibility to arrange for security on the steamers during their construction. It would seem that trust was misplaced in him for in 1850 he was removed from office because of the discovery of serious defalcations in his accounts. It was reported that he returned a total of $92,092 to the Treasury.[32]

The construction of steamers to fulfill the Atlantic service was undertaken by the associates concerned, but they soon turned to a corporate organization as the best means of carrying out their project. On March 6, 1848, a bill to charter the United States Mail

Steamship Company was introduced into the Senate of the New York Legislature at Albany.[33] After being reported on favorably by the Committee on Commerce and Navigation and considered by the Committee of the Whole, the bill was passed by the Senate on March 23, 1848. The bill of incorporation constituted George Law, Marshall O. Roberts, Bowes R. McIlvaine, the trustees of the mail contract, and their associates as a corporate body named the United States Mail Steamship Company with a capital stock of $1,500,000 divided into shares of $100 each.[34] Provisions were thus completed for carrying out service in steamers between the Atlantic coast and the Isthmus of Panama.

For the line between Panama and Oregon, the act failed to name any individual with whom the contract was to be made, as had been done for the transatlantic and Chagres services, and no limit was set to the amount which might be spent. John Young Mason, Secretary of the Navy, after examining the law carefully and consulting with President Polk, deemed it his duty to advertise for bids. He believed that the specific naming of Collins and Sloo in the other acts, and the option given him of determining whether the Pacific service should be carried out in sailing vessels or in steamers left no doubt that Congress intended the matter to be decided by competitive bidding.[35]

The advertisement for offers for the mail service between Panama and Oregon was issued on May 4, 1847, and at least five bids were received. These were turned over to Commodore Charles Morris on June 17, with the request that he consult with some of the chiefs of bureaus in the Navy Department regarding these proposals and that he make specific recommendations, particularly on the respective merits of steam or sail for the service. Morris, after conferring with Commodore Warrington, decided that, considering the distance involved and the frequency of service required, steamers offered the only practicable means of carrying out the mail service. He therefore gave no consideration to the offers to supply sailing vessels for the line. This left three bidders to be considered: Jabez M. Woodward, C. H. Todd, and Arnold Harris.[36]

Woodward, who had been interested for some time in the opening of a regular line of communication to Oregon, was bidding simultaneously for a similar service for the Post Office Department. It was reported that he had been in communication with President

Polk since 1845 on the subject of transportation to Oregon. In that year, when the Oregon boundary controversy with England was assuming alarming proportions, he had assisted in making plans for the transportation of large numbers of emigrants to Oregon. It was proposed to carry them by way of Panama, and this plan the President approved, though the amicable settlement of the Oregon question in 1846 made the rapid population of the area unnecessary. When Collins and Sloo applied for subsidies to assist their Liverpool and Chagres lines, Woodward was said to have framed a similar bill for the line from Panama to Oregon. However, when the act was passed, Woodward's name was left out of the engrossed bill either by accident or intent, and he was forced to enter open bidding.[37] The offer from Woodward asked a subsidy of $250,000 a year for ten years, but failed to specify the number of ships he intended to employ or their size.[38]

The second and lowest bidder was C. H. Todd of New York, whose offer was acknowledged by the Secretary of the Navy on June 17, 1847. The offer made by Todd did not specify the number of ships which he would employ, but proposed to contract for the service at the rate of $50,000 a year for each vessel. Secretary Mason offered to close the contract with him for $150,000 a year, to be payable quarterly upon full performance. The mail was to be carried once a month in each direction between Panama and Oregon, in steam vessels, either screw or paddle wheelers. In order to carry out the requirements of the contract there were to be at least three ships easily convertible into warships, two of them not less than 1,000 tons, and the third not less than 600 tons, with approved engines. The transportation of a government agent free of charge was required, while payment under the contract was designated to commence with the opening of service, by October 1, 1848, and continue for ten years unless Congress should direct otherwise.[39] By July 7, 1847, it was known that Todd would refuse to contract on these terms. Actually, however, when on July 12th he replied to Secretary Mason's offer, it was with so many objections to the conditions that it amounted virtually to a refusal. He demurred at placing the ships at the disposal of the United States government if it desired to use them and at the requirement that they be approved by naval inspectors before they might begin service under the contract. The right of Congress to put an end to the contract under the period of ten years was also a cause for objection, one which the Secretary did not feel at liberty to remove since no time limit had been specified in the original act. He therefore hesitated to make a contract for so long a time without the approval or disapproval of Congress.[40] It is at least probable that Todd was closely allied to Woodward and that, when his associate found himself unable to enter the contract under the terms which had been set, Woodward turned to the third bidder for an alliance.[41]

Arnold Harris, a citizen of Nashville, Tennessee, a person with influential political connections, had tendered a bid for the service at $199,000 a year. It was this offer whose acceptance Commodore Morris advised.[42] On July 26, 1847, the Secretary of the Navy wrote Harris, offering to make a contract with him at the rate he had named, under the same conditions which had been suggested to Todd, for a period of ten years, subject to the right of Congress to abrogate it at an earlier period "upon such conditions of equity and justice as it may deem just toward the contractor to establish."[43]

Like Sloo of Cincinnati, Harris had no intention of carrying out the contract himself. That he bid for it only to assign it to someone else at a profit was made amply clear by an agreement which he made with Woodward on July 7, 1847. This was even before Secretary Mason had formally decided to accept Harris' offer, but when it was already known that Todd would be unable to carry out the contract which he had received. By the agreement, it was provided that Harris would accept the contract, with Woodward becoming surety for its performance, and that then, for the sum of one dollar and the New Orleans agency for the steamers at a salary of $5,000 a year during the ten-year duration of the contract, Harris would assign the contract to Woodward, or to a person whom the latter might designate, within five days of its execution.[44]

Harris signified his willingness to enter the contract, and on the last day of July, 1847, the form was forwarded to him from the Navy Department, with instructions to return it filled out and with a bond which had met with the satisfaction of the Navy agent at New York.[45] Harris' reply indicated that he too had found difficulties with the contract. He wished an extension of a year in the time for the completion of one of the steamers, and of four months for the other two, while the clause reserving to the Navy Department the right to exercise control over the ships at all times caused him apprehension. Secretary Mason reassured him that this clause could have no other purpose than to secure the faithful performance of the contract. Harris evidently asked that the compensation might begin before the opening of the service, but this also was refused. A hint of Harris' plans for the future was given in his request, which was granted by the Secretary of the Navy, that the words "or his assigns" might be added after his name in the contract.[46]

The subsequent course of Arnold Harris in relation to the mail contract is not clear. The agreement which he had made in July with Woodward remained unfulfilled. Whether a misunderstanding with Woodward arose or whether, now that he had the contract in his grasp, Harris believed that he could sell it for more than the $50,000 which Woodward had promised to pay him as agent, it is impossible with the present evidence to say. In September Secretary Mason wrote to Harris, asking whether or not he expected to execute the contract, for if he did not, the Navy Department would feel at liberty to engage with others.[47] When no reply to the September letter had been received by November 6, 1847, Mason wrote again, informing Harris that unless word was received from him by November 10, it would be considered that he had declined to enter the contract.[48] This brought a prompt response from Harris, with a request for further time to complete his arrangements. Secretary Mason wrote him that, since the price at which he proposed to render the service was so much below any other bid which had not already been declined, an additional week would be granted. He went on to reassure Harris concerning the assent of Congress to the ten-year contract, saying that he had no reason to doubt that it would be approved.[49] The contract was finally completed and signed on the original terms on November 16, 1847.[50]

Three days after Harris signed the contract, he transferred it to William Henry Aspinwall, his surety for its performance. The proposed transfer had been privately known to the Secretary of the Navy at the very time he signed the contract with Harris, for on the same day he wrote Aspinwall, outlining the general terms of the contract and stating that he had no objection to recognizing the assignment which Harris proposed to make "in favor of the sureties" and to making payments accordingly.[51]

Woodward and his ally Todd had no idea of accepting this

decision without a struggle. When Harris had seemed about to
lose the contract in early November, Woodward came from New
York to Washington to call on Secretary Mason in the interest of
this business. He was duly notified of the extension of time granted
to Harris and of the final decision in his favor.[52] After the contract
had been awarded, Todd wrote to the Navy Department, asking
for a copy of it. The Secretary replied in rather an annoyed
manner, saying that, because of the nature and purpose of his
request, it might well be denied, but that the copy would be sent
him in order to leave no room for misapprehension on the subject.
Mason went on to say: "It would have been more satisfactory, had
you stated in what particular concessions were made to Mr. Harris
which were denied to you."[53]

Woodward now proceeded to bring suit against Harris and
Aspinwall in the Court of Chancery, New York, requesting an
injunction to restrain Aspinwall from executing the contract. The
point was made that Harris had bound himself by the agreement
of July 7, 1847, to assign the contract to Woodward, and that
therefore the assignment to Aspinwall was invalid. In the course
of the proceedings, it became clear that the arrangement between
Harris and Aspinwall had been made without the knowledge
reaching Aspinwall that Harris was already committed to an
assignment to Woodward. Judge Edmonds, who heard the case,
ruled on February 7, 1848, that the injunction must be denied, on
the grounds that there had been no mutuality in the agreement.
The terms had bound Harris to sell but had not required Woodward
to buy. It was decided that the assignment to Aspinwall was valid,
since he had known nothing of Woodward's claim, whereas the
latter, by his long inaction, had treated the agreement as terminated. Aspinwall wrote this news to the Secretary of the Navy,
saying that he was not sorry that this effort had been made to secure
the contract, since as a result of such decided opinion Woodward might now cease troubling himself and Aspinwall about the
matter.[54]

Harris' new arrangement was sufficiently more profitable than
the one which he had concluded with Woodward to account for the
change. Under its terms he received one-tenth of the profits derived
from the operation of the service. This ran until the early summer
of 1850, when Aspinwall bought out Harris' interest by agreeing to

pay him his one-tenth up to January 1, 1851, and a lump sum of $80,000 for a quitclaim for his share thereafter. The size of the proportion up to the end of 1850 is indicated by Harris' refusal to accept an offer of $70,000 in place of it.[55]

It was a matter of considerable surprise that a man of the undoubted business ability and sound judgment of William Henry Aspinwall should embark upon such a venture as the operation of steamers on the Pacific coast. As a partner in the great firm of Howland and Aspinwall, which handled the largest trading, exporting, and importing business of any house in New York, he could hardly be expected to enter wild or uncertain speculations. The son of a merchant, John Aspinwall, and the grandson of a sea captain, he was closely related to the Howland family, who were important merchants trading to England, the Mediterranean, and Hispanic America. Having been apprenticed to his uncles, Gardiner Greene Howland and Samuel Shaw Howland, he was admitted to partnership in the firm with a quarter interest in 1832, at the age of twenty-five. Five years later the management of the entire business, which by this time had a capital of $200,000, was turned over to William Henry Aspinwall and his cousin William Edgar Howland. The house, which now took the name of Howland and Aspinwall, continued to prosper, trading not only to Europe and the Far East, but also gaining preëminence among New York firms carrying on commerce with Hispanic America. It was undoubtedly this experience which suggested to Aspinwall the possibilities of opening a more satisfactory route across the Isthmus of Panama and of developing regular communication along the Pacific coast. By 1846, the Aspinwall fortune was estimated at $400,000, and Aspinwall was looked upon as one of the soundest and ablest merchants in New York.[56]

That such a man should enter upon an uncertain venture on a distant and sparsely settled coastline, involving the building and operation of expensive steamships, was shocking to Aspinwall's business associates. Alfred Robinson, who had been active in the commerce of California since 1829 and probably knew conditions on the Pacific coast better than anyone then in New York, wrote in later years regarding the project:

To give an idea of how little I thought of the speculation when these steamers were started, I will mention that Mr. Aspinwall was extremely desirous that I should take an interest in the steamers, and I thought it was out of the question that it should pay, that all the profit that could possibly be derived from the venture was from the few passengers we might pick up, and some little freight, which would not amount to much of anything. We supposed that the compensation from the Government for carrying the mails would just about defray the expense of running the steamers, and all that we got beyond that would be the remuneration from passage and freight custom.[57]

Aspinwall, however, was a man of vision and courage, and, where small men could see only the probability of the moment, he could grasp the possibility of the future. Just as Howland and Aspinwall were pioneers in the building and operation of clipper ships on the ocean routes of the world, so the house envisioned increasing population and trade along the Pacific coast. The line of steamers from Panama to Oregon was only part of the plan in Aspinwall's mind. He saw the need for facilitated travel across the Isthmus of Panama and projected a railroad there in 1848. There is also evidence that the original project included the operation of American steamships along the western coast of South America in competition with the British ships of the Pacific Steam Navigation Company.[58] Among the builders of the Panama route to the Pacific coast Aspinwall stands out, not only as the ablest leader and most commanding personality, but also as a man of admirable character, devoted to the task of providing efficient, rapid, and safe communication between the Atlantic and Pacific coasts of the United States.

Although the outlines of the Pacific line had been sketched, there yet remained many details of performance to be arranged. The contract for mail service from Panama to Oregon had named Astoria as the northern terminus of the line of steamers, but had reserved to the Navy Department the right of changing this point. On December 20, 1847, Aspinwall wrote the Secretary of the Navy, evidently requesting that the steamers be permitted to turn around at San Francisco and that sailing vessels carry out the remainder of the voyage. He also asked for a definite and final statement concerning the northern terminus. Secretary Mason passed this letter on to the Postmaster General for his opinion. In reply, Cave Johnson wrote that lack of proper information made a reasoned answer impossible. He suggested, however, that, since the Columbia Bar was said to be dangerous, the mail might be delivered at the mouth of the Umpqua or the Klamath rivers and be carried thence overland to the settlements on the Willamette and Columbia.[59] At the end of May, 1848, Johnson wrote C. Gilliam, special agent of the Post Office Department at Oregon City, who was then in the capital, informing him that the steamers, which would afford additional facilities for mail and also the best and most convenient route for emigrants to Oregon, would be on the Pacific coast by the spring of 1849. He asked for information on the best port for landing the mails and for possible deposits of coal which might be of use to the steamers.[60] Gilliam's reply unhesitatingly recommended the mouth of the Klamath River as the point for the landing of the mails in Oregon, and this information was immediately transmitted to the Secretary of the Navy.[61]

On June 10, Secretary Mason finally replied to Aspinwall's letter of nearly six months before, excusing his delay with the necessity of consulting with the Post Office Department. On the recommendation of the Postmaster General, he suggested the mouth of the Klamath River as the northern terminus. The steamers would be allowed to terminate their voyages at San Francisco for the present, provided they touched, free of further charge to the Navy Department, at three ports south of San Francisco held by the forces of the United States, and provided that the mail service north of San Francisco be performed regularly in sailing vessels. In American ports, the steamers operated by Aspinwall were to be regarded as government transports and therefore not subject to tonnage dues or port charges, while coal and supplies for them might be landed and deposited free of duty. In closing, Secretary Mason wrote:

I regret the delay which has occurred in answering your communication; but anxious as I am that the enterprise in which you are engaged shall realize all the advantages contemplated by the law, and especially that it shall establish and maintain a speedy, certain, and safe communication with our interestng settlements on the distant Pacific, and give the inhabitants of that region the full facilities intended for them in the most efficient manner, I have not been prepared to answer your letter ... at an earlier day. My first duty is to secure these public objects, I shall not be unwilling, in promoting them, to make the service less onerous to you.[62]

In order to carry out the contract for steamship service on the Pacific coast, a bill to incorporate the Pacific Mail Steamship Company was reported into the New York Senate on April 1, 1848. It was passed by the Senate on April 4, and by the Assembly on the twelfth of the same month.[63] Those associated with Aspinwall as incorporators were his uncle, Gardiner Greene Howland, a retired "special partner" in Howland and Aspinwall, a very wealthy man whose fortune was estimated as $500,000; Henry Chauncey, a "Down Easter" from Maine, who was engaged in the crockery business in New York and was supposedly "worth" $200,000; and Edwin Bartlett.[64] The charter of incorporation bore the date of April 12, 1848, and erected the company for a period of twenty years for

the purpose of building, equipping, furnishing, purchasing, chartering, and owning vessels, to be propelled solely or partially by the power or aid of steam or other expansive fluid or motive power, to be run and propelled in navigating the Pacific Ocean ...

The capital stock of $500,000 was divided into five hundred shares.[65] At the time of organization, William H. Aspinwall was elected president of the company, and the stockholders agreed to pay him or his assignees a commission of 2½ per cent on all receipts from all sources at home and abroad in consideration of his foundation of the company and his transference to it of his interest in the mail contract. Under the terms of the organization, Aspinwall was authorized to select the house of Howland and Aspinwall for the transaction of the commercial business of the company with its commissions restricted to 2½ per cent on amounts advanced or disbursed, to 1½ per cent for effecting insurance, and to the "usual commission" for the sale of merchandise placed in their hands to the account of the company.[66] Thus the individual interest of Aspinwall and the resources and experience of the great mercantile house of which he was a partner were closely united with the new company for the performance of the steamship service north along the Pacific coast from Panama.

The contract for steamship service between New York, New Orleans, and Chagres, which had been entered with Albert G. Sloo and in turn transferred to George Law, Marshall O. Roberts, and Bowes R. McIlvaine, required that the service be performed twice a month in five steamers, four of them being not less than 1,500 tons burden driven by engines of at least 1,000 horsepower, and the fifth being not less than 1,000 tons. The ships were to be suitable for rapid conversion into warships; to ensure this their plans were to be approved by the Navy Department and their building supervised by a naval constructor appointed by the Navy Department. It was provided that the engines and boilers should be placed as far as possible below the water line in order to secure them from enemy fire. Each of the steamers was to have as her commander an officer of the United States Navy, not below the rank of lieutenant, selected by the contractor with the approval and consent of the Secretary of the Navy, while she was also to carry four midshipmen of the Navy to serve as watch officers.[67]

By the end of March, 1847, even before the contract had formally been executed between the Navy Department and Sloo, the latter had forwarded specifications for steamers to the Secretary of the Navy, who in turn sent them on to the Bureau of Construction and Repair. The steamers as proposed would have a length of 250 feet, a beam of 36 feet, and a depth of 28 feet. In his reply to Secretary Mason, Commodore Morris reported that, in the estimation of the board, ships of these dimensions would not be convertible into warships "at the least possible cost," since the height of the upper deck would be too great to allow guns of proper calibre to be mounted on it with safety, while the removal of the deck would weaken the ships materially and would therefore be inadvisable. Morris suggested that it would be most satisfactory if a conference could be arranged between Sloo and his naval architects and the Board of Construction and Repair.[68]

It was some time after this that actual construction of the steamers was commenced. To supervise the work for the Navy, William Skiddy, a New York naval architect, was appointed naval constructor on January 24, 1848, with directions to familiarize himself with the requirements of the Navy Department for the ships and to report frequently on progress in building.[69]

Instead of following the terms of the contract, the ships which were laid down for service on the Atlantic were much larger than had been specified. The *Ohio* was built by Bishop and Simonson, New York, and had a length of keel of 240 feet, a beam of 46 feet, and a depth of hold from the spar deck of 33 feet. Her tonnage, with the spar deck, was about 3,000. The other ship, the *Georgia,* was constructed in the yard of Smith and Dimon in New York and was slightly larger than the *Ohio,* her tonnage with the spar deck measuring about 3,300. Because the ships were so much larger than had been required by the contract, the owners proposed to build only two at that time and to fill in the service with the smaller steamer *Falcon*. Since the *Ohio* was launched August 12, 1848, and the *Georgia* on September 6 of the same year, there was no chance that they would be completed in time to begin the mail service on October 1 according to the agreement; thus the *Falcon* had the honor of pioneering the route. The engines for both steamers were ordered from T. F. Secor and Company of New York, and their construction lagged far behind the building of the hulls. However, when William Skiddy made slighting reports on the slowness in this part of the work, George Law, who was closely supervising the building of the steamers, wrote angrily to the Secretary of the Navy, saying that Skiddy spoke of that which he knew not, since he had been conspicuously absent from the shipyards and the ironworks for a long period of time.[70] The *Ohio* did not sail on her first voyage from New York until September, 1849, and the *Georgia* not until January, 1850. The long delay was in great part due to the difficulty in constructing the engines and boilers, which were on a scale larger than that usually handled by American ironworkers of that period.

Aspinwall and his associates were more successful in carrying out the requirements of their contract. They had been required to build three steamers, two of which were to be not less than 1,000 tons burden, and one not less than 600 tons, but there were no requirements for drawing officers from the United States Navy.[71] The three steamers finally ordered were practically sister ships, the *California* and *Panama* being laid down in the yard of William H. Webb, New York, on January 4 and February 21, 1848, respectively, and the *Oregon* being built at the yard of Smith and Dimon, New York, in the same year. The *California* was launched on May 19, 1848, the *Panama* on July 29, and the *Oregon* on August 5, 1848. The steamers had a length of 200 feet, beam of 33 feet, 10 inches, and a depth of 20 feet. In tonnage they ranged just over 1,000. They were driven by single side-lever engines supplied with steam by two boilers, and, since the service for which they were intended was on rather a remote and sparsely populated coast, their passenger accommodations were small, the *California* carrying about fifty or sixty cabin passengers, with 150 or 200 in the steerage.[72]

On September 19, 1848, Aspinwall reported that the *California* was ready for the mail service and asked the Secretary of the Navy to designate a board to inspect her. He also requested the loan of two guns for the protection of the ship and mails, returnable whenever requested by the commander of the Pacific Squadron. The guns were ordered furnished to the *California*.[73] The board, composed of Captain Isaac McKeever, Commandant of the Navy Yard in New York, Commander W. L. Hudson, and Constructor T. Hartt, was ordered to inspect the *California* and particularly to report whether she was suitable for conversion into a warship.[74] After examination, the board reported that the *California* was suitable for the service intended, and that, with the addition of guns, she might easily be used as a warship.[75] On October 5, Aspinwall was notified that the *California* had been accepted, and on the next day she sailed from New York for her station on the Pacific.

Later in the same year Captain Matthew Calbraith Perry was ordered to supervise the construction of all ships under contracts with the Navy Department, as well as to assume general direction of the naval officers who might serve in these ships. In summing up his duties, Secretary Mason wrote:

The experiment of providing effective steam ships of war, available for Naval purposes on sudden emergencies, by means of contracts with our citizens for the transportation of the mails to different points in foreign countries, promises to be eminently successful. The employment of young officers of the Navy on board the steamers of these lines, add [*sic*] largely to their knowledge of steam and steam machinery, a professional knowledge becoming daily more important; but the relation which they will bear to their commanders who may not be officers of the Navy, will make it very important to them, that an officer of rank and experience should possess the powers and perform the duties now assigned to you.[76]

By early December, both the other steamers of the Pacific Mail Steamship Company had been completed and had been passed upon by Perry. In commenting on them, he wrote that, although they were admirably adapted to the service for which they were built, in order to be effective as naval vessels they should, he believed, have been constructed with two engines and an additional boiler.[77]

Even before the ocean mail services under the act of March 3, 1847, had been placed in operation, Congress began to regret its action and to move in the direction of their abolition. The contractors for the lines found themselves in some financial difficulty in the early summer of 1848, with constant calls for funds to be used in the completion of the steamers and no income to balance them. The payments could not begin until the service was actually under way, and freight and passenger income would not be received until there were ships in operation. Therefore, an amendment was added to the Naval Appropriation Bill, which was under consideration in committee of the House of Representatives in June of 1848. This amendment set aside $874,000 for the transportation of mail on the three lines provided and directed the Secretary of the Navy to advance to the contractors $25,000 a month on each steamer built for these services, between the time of her launching and the date of her completion for sea. However, the total amount advanced to any one contractor was not to exceed one year's mail payment, while the advances were to be secured by mortgages on the ships building.[78] The House concurred in the amendment and passed the bill, which was then sent to the Senate.[79]

In the Senate, the amendment was attacked violently, the leaders of the opposition being John Milton Niles of Connecticut and William Allen of Ohio. The latter made it clear that he intended to move toward the complete discontinuance of ocean steamship companies as carriers of mail under government subsidy at the expiration of the present contracts, and that he meant to bring about the abolition of the system.[80] On July 19, Niles moved that the contracts, instead of running for ten years, be limited to five years and that the provision for advances to aid in completing the steamers be stricken out. He pointed out the poor security for the loans, remarking that, if the government were to provide the capital for carrying out such contracts, the applicants might be expected to be numberless.[81] The *New York Herald* commented editorially on the day's proceedings:

From the strenuous opposition of Mr. Niles to this proposition, and to the ten years' contracts moving to reduce them to five, and urging the wants of the Treasury, and the heavy expense of these steamers, as calculated to lead to their abandonment by the government altogether, we apprehend there is a strong effort to revoke as far as possible, the original design of a systematic ocean steam communication under the patronage of the government; a system which, if pursued with skill, enterprise, and perseverance, is calculated to give us the control of the Pacific trade, and a full share of the Atlantic business, with a complete monopoly of the coastwise transportation of mails and passengers between the Isthmus of Chagres and New York.[82]

The debate was continued on the following day, the amendment being finally upheld by a vote of twenty-five to twenty-four.[83] The vote on the amendment was twice reconsidered, but the provision was each time upheld by an increasing plurality, and it finally became law as part of the Naval Appropriation Act of August 3, 1848.[84] This included the terms of the original amendment regarding the total appropriation of $874,000 for the mail service and the monthly advances of $25,000 on each vessel between launching and completion. The date for the beginning of payment on the Panama-Oregon line was set for October 1, 1848, and the steamers of this service were required to stop for mails at San Diego, Monterey, and San Francisco.[85]

In September, arrangements for the advances on the steamers building went forward, with Prosper Wetmore, Navy agent in New York, placing liens upon the steamers, which were to run for one year from the time of the beginning of the contract service. On October 4, 1848, Wetmore wrote the Secretary of the Navy that he had obtained deeds of trust from the assignees of both Sloo and Harris as security for the advances to be made by the Navy Department.[86]

Thus by the close of 1848 the mail service which was to link the Atlantic and Pacific coasts of the United States, aided by the United States government, was ready to go into operation, with corporate structures reared upon some of the great mercantile fortunes of New York and with steamers built and ready to carry out the duties set for them.

CHAPTER II

PIONEER YEARS, 1849–1851

EVEN BEFORE CONGRESS provided for mail service to the Pacific coast, the United States government had concerned itself with transportation. In January, 1847, the Secretary of the Navy informed one of the members of the House of Representatives that mail for the Pacific would be forwarded by the Navy if it reached the Department before a specified day and hour.[1] Later in the same year, James M. Shively traveled overland from Washington to Astoria, and it was announced that he would leave Independence, Missouri, in April, taking charge of letters directed to him there and destined for settlers in Oregon.[2]

On October 6, 1848, the *California,* pioneer of the Pacific Mail fleet, put to sea from New York to take her place on the line between Panama and the northwest coast. She carried a handful of passengers destined for Rio de Janeiro and Valparaiso, as well as mail for the Brazil and Pacific Squadrons of the United States Navy. Her bunkers were filled with 520 tons of coal, and she also had aboard stores for twelve months and a complete set of spare parts for the engine. In spite of the heavy load, which placed her far down in the water and therefore slowed down her paddles, Constructor Skiddy reported that the *California* made a speed of ten knots outside the bar under steam alone.[3] After calling at Rio for coal and provisions, the ship passed through the Straits of Magellan in the early part of December, 1848, paused briefly at Valparaiso, Callao, and Paita, and came to anchor off the city of Panama on January 17, 1849.[4]

The *Panama,* second Pacific Mail steamer to be completed, followed the *California* out of New York on December 1, 1848, but engine trouble forced her to return to port under sail, and it was February 17, 1849, before she put to sea again, this time commanded for the voyage as far as Panama by Lieutenant David D. Porter, U.S.N.[5] In the meantime, the *Oregon* had been completed and took her departure from Quarantine, New York, on December 9, 1848. She was commanded by Captain Richard H. Pearson, and, proceeding by way of Rio de Janeiro, the Straits of Magellan, Val-

---

[1] For notes to chap. ii, see pp. 264–267.

paraiso, and Paita, arrived at Panama on the twenty-third of February, 1849.[6]

On the Atlantic side, the steamers of the United States Mail Steamship Company were in no such state of readiness to carry out the contract as were the Pacific Mail ships. The *Ohio* and *Georgia* had been launched by the end of September, 1848, but their engines were not completed, and would not be for some time to come, so that the ships could not be ready for sea until nearly a year later.[7] To fill the gap, a new steamer, the *Falcon,* of 891 tons, was purchased and placed on the route between New York and New Orleans by way of Charleston, Savannah, and Havana on September 10, 1848. By a letter of October 21, George Law and Marshall Roberts applied to the Secretary of the Navy for permission to use the *Falcon* temporarily in the service between New York and Chagres until the steamers under construction could be completed. Secretary Mason replied that, in view of the importance of the service, the *Falcon* would be accepted, provided she were passed by a naval examiner. The temporary character of the arrangement was emphasized, while the compensation for the services of the *Falcon* was set at one-fifth of the total for the services of five steamers as provided in the contract.[8] Commodore Perry duly inspected the *Falcon,* and upon his finding her satisfactory she was accepted by the Navy Department for service under contract. She proceeded to sea from New York on December 1, 1848, with ninety-five passengers aboard, bound for Chagres by way of Charleston, Savannah, Havana, and New Orleans.[9] It was expected that the *California* would reach Panama in time to take the passengers and mail of the *Falcon* aboard as soon as they had crossed the Isthmus, and would be ready to carry them to the coast of California.

The route which had thus been set up and placed in operation by the end of 1848 was one which promised small returns for the operators beyond the government subsidy. Aspinwall had grand plans in mind, but it would normally take years to build up a sufficiently large population on the Pacific coast to make really profitable the steamers which were being placed in service. The circumstance which, from the beginning, made the demand for transportation over the Panama route overwhelming and the facilities provided utterly inadequate, thus bringing rich returns to the operators of ships, was the result of a discovery which could not possibly have entered into the reasoned calculations of the most farsighted businessman of the United States. In January, 1848, gold in amazing quantity was discovered on the American River in Alta California. Official notice of this first reached the national capital in September, 1848, and confirmation of the extent and richness of the gold deposits in the Sierra Nevada continued to arrive until the last doubt was removed by the report of Governor Mason of California, which was included in President Polk's annual message of December 5, 1848. A rising tide of excitement overspread the United States, and thousands of men began to emigrate westward to reap the golden harvest of California.[10] The overland route was closed by the storms of winter and would not be practicable until April or May of the next year, when spring was sufficiently advanced to provide food for animals. There remained two water routes to California: one around Cape Horn and the other across the Isthmus of Panama. The former was perhaps the surer, since the traveler could make the entire voyage in one ship, and it appealed particularly to the residents of New England. The Panama route, with departure either from New York or New Orleans for the Isthmus, offered the quickest means of reaching California. With regular lines of steamers already established, this route was attractive to those who could afford the cash outlay which was required for the purchase of tickets and the expenses of the isthmian transit.

The *Falcon* had sailed from New York prior to the presidential message of December 5, but before she reached Chagres, she called at New Orleans, and here excitement regarding the gold of California was abroad. When she left New Orleans on December 18, she had 193 passengers aboard, including General Persifor F. Smith, the new commanding officer of the United States Army in California, who was going out with his family and staff.[11] Even when the bark *John Benson* sailed from New York for Chagres on December 11, she had only sixty passengers, one of whom later wrote that they did not know at the time they sailed how general and intense the gold excitement would become. Aboard the *John Benson* went Alfred Robinson, newly appointed San Francisco agent for the Pacific Mail Steamship Company, and with him were twenty-three who had through tickets for the *California* to San Francisco.[12] President Aspinwall already had an inkling of the

future, however, for he included in a final letter of instructions to
Robinson the following suggestion :

If the Steamer [*California*] is in Panamá, & more passengers offer than can
comfortably be accommodated an appeal from those likely to be left to Genl
Smith, Price Steenbergen and others who are berthed, would produce from the
latter an expression of opinion which would justify Capt Forbes in crowding a
little.[13]

The *Falcon* reached Chagres on December 27, 1848, and the *John
Benson* put in two days later. When the *California* anchored at
Panama on January 17, 1849, five more vessels had landed their
living cargoes at the mouth of the Chagres River, while by the time
she sailed northward from Panama on January 31, ten vessels—of
which four were steamers, two barks, three brigs, and one a
schooner—had arrived on the Atlantic side of the Isthmus. These
brought a total of 726 passengers destined for a steamer which had
been constructed to carry some 250 passengers at the outside.[14]

Matters were not improved by the fact that the *California*
already had aboard seventeen cabin passengers, and fifty-two in
the steerage. These were Peruvians from Callao, of whom the
steamer might have brought a full complement if the captain had
not declined to take more, since the gold excitement had already
reached the west coast of South America and transportation to
California was at a premium.[15] The passengers from New York
and New Orleans who had purchased through tickets were adjudged to have prior rights to space on the steamer, but the other
Americans in Panama, even though they had no reservations, demanded stoutly that the Peruvians be put ashore or transferred
to the sailing ship *Philadelphia,* which was under charter to
Howland and Aspinwall. Public meetings were held, and angry
committees waited upon Zachrisson and Nelson, the Panama agents
of the Pacific Mail, while General Smith issued a proclamation that
none but citizens of the United States might enter upon the public
lands of the republic, thus excluding the Peruvians from the mines.
In spite of all this, the South Americans held firm, not even allowing themselves to be persuaded to go ashore, since they well knew
that the temper of the American mob in Panama might prevent
their return to the ship. The affair was finally settled by placing the
Peruvians in hastily constructed berths, leaving the staterooms
open for travelers from the United States. Berths were built in the

open spaces aboard the *California* while she lay at Panama, and when she sailed, there were on the ship about 365 passengers in addition to the crew of thirty-six.[16]

On the voyage north, she called at Acapulco, San Blas, Mazatlán, San Diego, and Monterey before putting into San Francisco on February 28, 1849. The steamer had been expected earlier, and on the first of February the *Alta California* had written:

Look Out For The Steamer!
The knowing ones say that we may daily look for the first steamer. If this be so, ought not our citizens to take some steps to manifest their joy at an occasion so full of interest to this Port? We most strenuously recommend the holding of a public meeting, the appointment of a committee of arrangements, and the raising of a fund for burning of powder and spermaceti on the occasion. It is an event so fraught with future hopes of advantage, that our memories will almost deserve execration if we do not celebrate the event with proper style and spirit. It is an epoch that deserves to be brought into bold relief, and he who takes an active part in getting up a judicious observance of the occasion, will, ten years hence, think it the proudest event in his life. Come, come, you that have amassed so much gold since the opening of the mines, "down with your dust," and let us show the newcomers that this is a "land 'o cakes," jollity, generosity, and kind-feelings, as well as a land of enterprise and gold.[17]

Enthusiasm continued after the arrival of the steamer, for the same paper reported her arrival on the 28th:

The California is a truly magnificent vessel, and her fine appearance as she came in sight off the Town, called forth cheer upon cheer from our enraptured citizens, who were assembled in masses upon the heights commanding a view of the Bay, and in dense crowds at the principle [*sic*] Wharves and landing places. She passed the vessels of war in the harbor under a salute from each, returned by hearty cheering from the crowded decks, and at eleven was safely moored at the anchorage off the town.[18]

Though it had been expected that the *California* would return immediately to Panama, the attraction of the mines was so great that, within a week of her arrival, the ship had been deserted by all her officers and crew with the exception of Captain Cleveland Forbes and one of the engine-room boys. The ship had exhausted her coal supply on the trip north, and as the collier which was expected from England had not yet put in an appearance, it would have been impossible for her to start southward in any event.[19]

The sailing of the *California* from Panama only temporarily relieved the crowded situation on the Isthmus. Facilities for transportation from the Atlantic and Gulf coasts of the United States were so much more adequate than those on the Pacific side that increasing numbers of travelers waited at Panama for passage to San Francisco. Sailing vessels from New York, Boston, Philadelphia, Baltimore, and New Orleans brought loads of passengers to Chagres, while the trips of the *Falcon* were supplemented by other and larger steamers bringing passengers from New York and New Orleans. When the *Oregon,* second of the Pacific Mail steamers to reach the Pacific coast, put into Panama on February 23, 1849, there were some 1,200 persons between Chagres and Panama destined for California.[20] She sailed for San Francisco on March 13 with 250 passengers aboard, of whom 77 were in the cabin and 173 in the steerage.[21] Omitting Acapulco and Mazatlán, the *Oregon* called at San Blas for coal and proceeded to San Francisco with brief stops at San Diego and Monterey. She entered San Francisco Bay on April 1, 1849, and owing to the supply of coal aboard and to the excellent discipline of Captain Pearson, she sailed on her return voyage to Panama on April 12, 1849.[22]

The *Panama,* after having her engine repaired, left New York for her station on the Pacific on February 17, 1849, well after the beginning of the "gold fever" in New York, carrying eighty-one through passengers for San Francisco.[23] When she reached Panama in May, it was estimated that about two thousand persons were waiting there for passage to California. She added 209 to her passenger list, making a total of 290 when she started northward on May 18, 1849. The expansion was obtained in part by persuading the cabin passengers to take an additional person in each of the staterooms.[24] The *Panama* arrived in San Francisco on June 4, 1849, and sailed south for Panama on the twentieth of the same month. In the meantime, the coal ship had arrived, and the *California,* having obtained fuel and a crew, had sailed for Panama on May 1. With the three steamers in operation on the Pacific, the mail service was carried forward with a surprising degree of promptness and regularity, in spite of the difficulties of the place and the time.

The Pacific Mail steamers were entirely inadequate to carry the travelers who arrived in Panama and demanded passage to San Francisco. The sailing vessels available in Panama and those which called or were sent there by their owners for the purpose, were therefore able to fill what passenger accommodations they had for

Steamer *Oregon*, One of the Pacific Mail Pioneers, 1848

Steamer *Illinois* of the United Mail Steamship Company, 1851

Vanderbilt's *Star of the West*, 1852

Steamer *George Law* of the United States Mail Steamship Company

the voyage to San Francisco. The voyage from Panama to San Francisco could not be made by a sailing vessel on a direct course because of the prevailing winds and currents which came down the coast. Ships therefore were obliged to run into the Pacific to about the longitude of the Hawaiian Islands, and then, having obtained sufficient "westing," shape their courses for San Francisco. This necessarily slow voyage in a sailing vessel accounted for the great desire of travelers, who were anxious to reach California as soon as possible, to secure passage in a steamer, and as soon as adequate steamship accommodations were available on the Pacific, the passenger trade between Panama and San Francisco in sailing vessels disappeared. Even before the first arrival of the *California* in Panama from New York, a ninety-ton schooner had sailed for San Francisco with some sixty passengers aboard. Two of Howland and Aspinwall's ships which were in port when the *California* arrived—the *Philadelphia,* which was unloading coal, and another ship in ballast—advertised that they would take passengers north.[25] As the winter turned to spring, every available keel at Panama was made ready to sail for San Francisco. The whaling bark *Equator* sold her cargo of whale oil at Panama and took 130 passengers for San Francisco, while the whaler *Niantic* sailed in April with 300. A fifty-ton Peruvian-built schooner, worm-eaten and weather-beaten and minus her keel, was sold for $5,000 to a party of fifty-two "Argonauts," who sailed in her on March 21, 1849. Persons even attempted to make the voyage up the coast in canoes.[26]

It was only to be expected that under these conditions the demand for passage would cause the price of tickets to increase. The original fare from Panama to San Francisco in the first cabin of the Pacific Mail steamers had been set at $250, with the lower cabin at $200 and steerage $100.[27] There was considerable resale of tickets, however, and it was reported that on the first voyages of both the *Oregon* and *Panama* to San Francisco, single steerage tickets brought as high as $1,000.[28] In the sailing vessels, the price of passage to San Francisco ranged from $100 to $300, though usually the cabin fare was not over $200.[29]

The resale of tickets made good business, and as early as March, 1849, a traveler at Panama wrote:

An immense business has been done in ticket speculation. A regular "'Change," upon the Wall Street plan, is held daily for the sale of tickets in the various vessels up for California; and many have realized handsome sums by purchasing and selling. Bulletins are kept in the coffee houses, where all are at liberty to post advertisements and notices free of charge; and it is to this spot every anxious ticket-hunter, dealer, or pedler is drawn, as regular as the day dawns, and often before his optics are able to distinguish light from darkness.[30]

A year later the same business was still going forward briskly. Nothing of special importance has transpired at Panamá during the week, if we can except the operations on " 'Change" in tickets of steamships and sailing vessels. A large operation has been realized in this line, and no little ingenuity displayed, and "cutting under" manifested by stockjobbers in tickets and transfers. The *bulls* and *bears* have had a pretty tight time of it ... the bulls keep pushing up and the bears trying to pull down, and in this way the commercial mart is daily enlivened by the keen-sighted wisdom of ticket vendors, and the not-infrequent peculiar *greenness* of purchasers. The advance on steamship tickets is from $50 to $150 from first cost ... The market closes firm for the holders, while those on the "anxious seat" are expecting a decline, considering the brisk competition which is making itself felt on the Pacific side.[31]

In July, 1849, the Pacific Mail advanced its rates between Panama and San Francisco to $300 for the cabin, and $150 in the steerage.[32] Even on the southbound voyages there was opportunity for profit in the resale of tickets, particularly in the winter of 1849–1850 when miners were anxious to return to the East.

Speculation in Steamer Tickets.—A very profitable investment may frequently be made by those who conform their ideas of principle and right to the work, in the tickets of the Panamá monthly steamers from this port. The price of cabin passage in either of the steamers to Panamá is 300 dollars, and the steerage tickets are sold at the Company's office for 150 dollars. Within the past week we have seen four hundred and fifty dollars paid for one of the last mentioned, and cabin tickets have been sold at nearly corresponding rates. The rush for home, the limited number of tickets issued, and the appointment of but one day for securing the same, gives the "speculative turn of mind" a rare opportunity for realizing something handsome from their purchase and sale at greatly enhanced prices.[33]

On the Atlantic, the United States Mail Steamship Company did little toward new construction which would meet the needs of the increase in travel over what had been expected. The *Ohio* was finally finished and placed in the service on September 20, 1849, while the *Georgia* sailed on her maiden voyage on January 28, 1850. Arrangements were made so that the *Ohio* generally plied between New York and New Orleans by way of Havana, whence the *Falcon* took the passengers bound for the Isthmus. The *Georgia* was operated from New York to Chagres direct, with calls at Havana for coal.

Although the contract had required that the United States Mail Steamship Company must build five steamers to carry out the service, the company made no move to construct more than the *Ohio* and *Georgia*. The reason given was that the two ships built were much larger than those required by the contract, and that further construction was delayed to test the success of such revolutionary ships, with their unusually great length and beam and shallow draft.[34]

On the Pacific, where steamers were much harder to obtain than on the Atlantic, the Pacific Mail Steamship Company set about the expansion of its fleet as soon as the extent of the movement to California was known. The ships and organization which had been planned were, of course, wholly inadequate, and adjustments had to be made. Early in 1849, President Aspinwall of the Pacific Mail wrote to a friend:

I fear that I have lost all character with you as a correspondent. I must get Louisa to exculpate me by letting you know what a snarl I am in from this California fever.—I am half ruined by postage and have hired two clerks to answer letters—and these have proved so inadequate that I have had to resort to printed circulars.[35]

During most of 1849, the service between San Francisco and Panama was maintained by the *California, Oregon,* and *Panama,* but plans were under way to augment the size of the fleet. The British steamer *Unicorn,* which had been purchased by Edward Cunard from the line bearing his father's name, was sent to the Pacific with passengers, sailing from New York on April 23, 1849, and arriving at San Francisco on October 31.[36] She was chartered by the Pacific Mail, sailing for Panama on December 1, 1849. Although she was too small and slow to operate very successfully with the other Pacific Mail steamers, she was purchased in 1850 and remained in service as a spare boat until April, 1853. In October, 1849, the *Tennessee,* a large steamer of 1,275 tons, which had been completed earlier in the year for service between New York and Savannah, was purchased by the Pacific Mail for $200,000 and sent to the Pacific.[37] She was late in reaching Panama, and her arrival on March 12, 1850, was enthusiastically described in the *Panama Echo:*

... this great leviathan of the Pacific came careening up in majestic style, towards the anchorage of the bay of Panamá, and as she neared the place of mooring, the batture was lined with smiling countenances and sparkling eyes and stalwart arms, all ready to join in the loud huzza—hail, all hail; the welcome of the glorious ship, old *Tennessee*—and the chorus of that beautiful melody

"Away down in Tennessee,
A li, e li, o li, u li, e, ..."

was instantly on the lips of the gratified concourse who were assembled to witness the ship's swanlike approach to the harbor![38]

When the *Tennessee* started northward from Panama, she had aboard 551 passengers, the largest number thus far carried from Panama to San Francisco by one ship. Close on the heels of the *Tennessee,* the Pacific Mail sent out the *Carolina,* a little twin-screw steamer of 545 tons, which had been built in Philadelphia in 1849 and sold for service in the Pacific before completion. In 1850, another ship was built especially for the Pacific Mail. This was the *Columbia,* a side-wheeler of 777 tons, which was intended for the mail service from San Francisco to Oregon but was placed on the San Francisco–Panama line occasionally in the years between 1851 and 1854. The *Fremont* was bought in 1851 and sent to the Pacific coast to supplement the *Columbia* on the Oregon run, while at the close of that year, the new steamer *Golden Gate,* built to the order of the Pacific Mail at the yard of William H. Webb in New York, reached San Francisco. This steamer was the first to be constructed particularly for the trade in which she was engaged. Her length of 269 feet, 6 inches and beam of 40 feet, with a tonnage of 2,067 made her easily the largest ship in the service, her passenger accommodations were commodious and comfortable, and she was famed for her speed. Always a favorite with Californians, she was often fondly referred to in the press as the "steam clipper." On the occasion of her first arrival in San Francisco, the *Herald* said:

Crowds of interested citizens visited her during the day, and all were filled with admiration at her immense proportions and elegant accommodations. She is the finest specimen of naval architecture on the Pacific, being the largest and swiftest steamer in our waters, and equalled by few anywhere. Her long deck forms a noble promenade, while her beautifully fitted up accommodations, and well ventilated cabins, remind one more of a drawing room than the interior of a ship.[39]

With the *Golden Gate* it may be said that the Pacific Mail had struck its stride in the construction and operation of steamers adequate for the service which they carried on.

The coming of new ships to the line of the Pacific Mail made it possible to perform the mail service entirely in steamers. In June, 1848, the company had been allowed by the Secretary of the Navy to terminate the voyages of its steamers at San Francisco, sending the mails on to Oregon in sailing vessels. From the first voyage of the *California*, the agent of the Pacific Mail at San Francisco had been especially reminded to arrange for the forwarding of the mail in a chartered sailing vessel, and he was repeatedly urged to maintain a vessel exclusively for this service so that no complaint of irregularity might interfere with payment for the mail service.[40]

In January, 1850, William Ballard Preston, now Secretary of the Navy, ordered the Pacific Mail to begin service north from San Francisco in steamers by June 10 of that year. The terminus was now set at Fort Nisqually on Puget Sound, with a call required at Astoria in each direction.[41] When there was a hint that the Pacific Mail had it in mind to call at Astoria southbound only, Preston wrote Aspinwall, sharply reminding him that the order of January 2, 1850, specifying stops in both directions must be considered a requirement.[42] The Pacific Mail did not take kindly to sending steamers north to Puget Sound and, in June, 1850, presented the Navy Department with a plan which had the endorsement of Samuel H. Thurston, Territorial Representative of Oregon in the national capital. The company named Astoria as the northern terminus of the line, with calls at Trinidad Bay in both directions, and agreed to send the steamers on up the Columbia and Willamette to Portland until a river steamer was in regular operation on the Columbia. This service was to be performed by the *Carolina* until the *Columbia*, which was fitting out at that time, could take her place on the route.[43] To this plan, Secretary Preston replied that he would not change the arrangement as required in January, 1850, and also that the voyages on to Puget Sound must be performed by one of the three original steamers, since only they had been accepted by the Navy Department under the contract.[44] Furthermore, when Thurston discovered that service in one of the larger ships would be required, he withdrew his support of Aspinwall's plan, since the promised additional trip each month with calls at the mouths of the Rogue and Umpqua would be impossible in the large steamers, and therefore the benefits which would have come to the residents of Oregon would not be realized.[45]

In spite of the Navy Department, the Pacific Mail began to send steamers to Oregon in June, 1850, placing the *Carolina* on the route and terminating her voyages at the Columbia. With the advent of a new secretary of the navy, William A. Graham, in the summer of 1850, a more favorable policy toward the mail contractors was inaugurated. In reply to a request for advice in the matter, the Postmaster General unhesitatingly recommended Astoria as the terminus of the line. He wrote that an extension north of Astoria was unfavorably regarded and objected to by the people and authorities of Oregon, since it would benefit, to their own disadvantage, interests which they considered hostile to themselves.[46]

Taking these factors into consideration, Secretary Graham wrote Aspinwall on October 1, 1850, that Astoria might be considered the northern terminus of the line and that, after January 1, 1851, the mail must be carried from Panama to Astoria monthly in each direction in steamers, with calls at San Diego, Monterey, and San Francisco. At the same time, he wrote that the Navy Department would accept for service, to the same degree and in the same manner as the *California, Oregon,* and *Panama,* the steamers *Tennessee* and *Columbia* to be held in reserve for service if there were accidents or delays. It was made clear, however, that the acceptance of two additional ships by the Navy was in no way to change the amount of compensation to be paid for the mail service.[47] Thus the Oregon mail service was finally settled to the satisfaction of all concerned. Steamers now came from Panama to San Francisco, where the mail as well as passengers for Oregon were transferred to the *Columbia* or one of her consorts, for the voyage on up the coast to Astoria. For a while the experiment of continuing the voyage of the Panama steamer to Oregon was tried, but the greater suitability of the smaller ships to the Oregon coast led to its abandonment. The southbound steamer from Oregon was scheduled to reach San Francisco in ample time to put her mail aboard the ship for Panama before the sailing of the latter.

With its increased fleet and the constant demand for passage between San Francisco and Panama, the Pacific Mail in the summer of 1850 instituted sailings between the two ports at fortnightly intervals. Beginning with the sailing of the *Tennessee* on July 15, 1850, from San Francisco, a steamer departed on the first and fifteenth of each month. The ship which went on the first was designated the "mail steamer," and carried out the contract, so that the company was careful to see that this ship was always one of those accepted for mail service by the Navy Department. On the fifteenth, the "intermediate steamer" sailed. This ship might or might not have been passed upon by the Navy Department and did not carry the United States mail under contract. California now received mail from the Atlantic coast twice a month, but the additional service was "wholly voluntary on the part of the directors of the company, for which they received no remuneration, so far only as they valued the approbation and good will of the public."[48] Strong feeling was evidenced both in California and in the eastern United States that this informal arrangement should be superseded by a government contract, assuring the transportation of the mail at semimonthly intervals and making proper payment for the service. As early as June of 1850, the Postmaster General strongly recommended the establishment of a fortnightly service on the Pacific.[49]

Aspinwall wrote to the Pacific Mail agents in San Francisco in June, 1850:

I have recently been at Washington to arrange to secure if possible the additional mail service on the Pacific, for I have no doubt Congress will order a semi-monthly mail from Panamá to Oregon—& you may depend upon it, we have the best chance.[50]

On September 27, 1850, an amendment was offered to the Naval Appropriation Bill in the Senate which authorized the Secretary of the Navy to rearrange the running of mail steamers on the Atlantic in order to ensure more speed between New York and Havana, and to increase the service on the Pacific to semimonthly frequency. The added service was to go into effect only if the cost did not exceed the "usual rate of cost at which additional mail service may be ordered." Opponents of the amendment attacked it on the ground that it created a monopoly, pointing out that additional mail could be carried by ships of competing lines already on the Pacific. In defending the bill, Senator Gwin of California said:

I know that there is great objection to extending facilities to contractors; but these contractors are the pioneers of that ocean. They deserve the encouragement and patronage of this Government. They risked a great deal in establishing that line—more than any citizen of the United States ever risked in a similar enterprise. If they have been successful, they deserve their success.

After further discussion, the amendment was laid on the table, and at next day's meeting the Senate defeated it.[51]

In spite of this reverse, an executive order from the Post Office Department on October 10, 1850, provided for a regular semimonthly mail service on the Pacific, with mails to be dispatched on the first and fifteenth of each month in ships of the Pacific Mail Steamship Company. At the same time, postmasters were directed to send no mail in any ships except those under contract to carry them. This service went into official operation in December, 1850, although nearly three months elapsed before Congress made provisions for payments and contracts to cover it.[52]

Not until the closing days of the Thirty-first Congress did the matter reach the point of discussion once more. A Senate amendment to the Naval Appropriation Bill again carried the provision, and, after being discussed in the House of Representatives, it passed the Senate on March 3, 1851. It appropriated $874,600 for the transportation of the United States mails between New York and Liverpool, between New York, New Orleans, and Chagres, and between Panama and Oregon. This was to be sufficient to make the service on the Pacific semimonthly, though not at a cost of more than 75 per cent in addition to what was already paid for the service. Arrangements were to be made for better connections at the Isthmus. The money which had been advanced to contractors in 1848 and 1849 in order to finish their steamers was to be repaid by 10 per cent deductions from mail payment, interest to be paid on the outstanding balance. Whenever a better route from the Atlantic to the Pacific was established, the Postmaster General and the Secretary of the Navy were to arrange with the contractors to have it used; if they were unable to agree on a reduced compensation, the matter might be referred to Congress.[53] The last provision referred to the Nicaragua route, then in the process of opening.

Ten days after the passage of the act described, an agreement was reached between the Secretary of the Navy and the Postmaster General, acting jointly, and William H. Aspinwall, president of the Pacific Mail Steamship Company. By this, the company agreed to operate six steamers between Panama and Astoria, four of which should be of at least 1,000 tons burden and two of at least 600 tons, making the run from one end of the line to the other in not less than twenty-five days, including stops at way ports. Two voyages a month in each direction were required, and for the additional service $149,250 a year would be paid, making a total subsidy of $348,250. The Pacific Mail was also required to carry letter mails free in the steamers which it was then running from New York to Chagres, when requested to do so by the Postmaster General. A mail agent was to be carried on all ships, and the power was given to the Postmaster General to make "reasonable" changes in the service, allowing increased compensation within the limits of the law. A system of forfeitures for failure to make trips, or for loss, injury, or delay of the mails was worked out, and it was provided that terms for carrying the mails by a better route were to be adjusted when such a route was opened.

And it is further expressly stipulated and agreed, that no member of Congress shall be admitted to any share or part in this contract or agreement, or to any benefit to arise therefrom, except as a stockholder in the said company...[54]

The contract was ratified and confirmed by the board of directors of the Pacific Mail on March 16 and received the assent of the Navy Department on the twenty-first, after which it was transmitted to the Post Office Department.[55]

In the meantime, the Pacific Mail was prospering as a business corporation. In the early summer of 1850, the capital stock of the company was increased from the original $500,000 to $2,000,000. The additional amount was subscribed mainly in New York, only about $400,000 of it being available to Californians. The stock was not placed upon the open market but was sold privately to persons believed to be desirable as stockholders.[56]

At the same time, a reorganization of the operation of the Pacific Mail was carried out. This involved a divorce of the affairs of the steamship company from those of the house of Howland and Aspinwall on the Pacific coast. The original plan of Aspinwall had been to give the place of chief agent in charge of the steamers to Captain G. W. P. Bissell, with headquarters at some central point on the route, probably at San Blas. With the greatly increased passenger traffic of 1849, this arrangement was altered to give the general charge of the steamers to Captain William C. Stout, who resided at Panama.[57] Alfred Robinson was appointed San Francisco agent at the end of 1848 and also served the interests of Howland and Aspinwall.[58] The position of superintending engineer was held by John Van Dewater, who remained at Panama. With the reorganization of 1850, Robinson, who by that time had been joined by Captain Bissell in the firm of Robinson and Bissell, was relieved of the agency for the Pacific Mail, though he continued to hold that of Howland and Aspinwall. Complaints of the slowness of the San Francisco agency in forwarding receipts to New York, of incomplete records, and even hints of incapacity were constantly forthcoming from the headquarters of the Pacific Mail in New York in 1849 and 1850, and these perhaps accounted for the removal of Robinson and Bissell. The place was taken by Captain Ebenezer Knight, former commander of the transatlantic packet *New World.*[59]

July, 1850, saw the payment of the first returns to stockholders in the Pacific Mail, a dividend of 50 per cent, which was highly satisfactory considering the resources of the company and the expense involved in the purchase of steamers and in placing them on the Pacific.[60] The companies which held the mail contracts by way of the Panama route were clearly doing well financially at the end of two years of operation. The combination of mail subsidy from the United States government with profits from passengers and express brought satisfactory incomes to the men who had set them in operation.

The demand for passage to California by way of the Isthmus of Panama brought a rush of competitors to the field. There were more passengers than one line could carry, and steamers from other routes were quickly placed in service. Competition, bitter and ruthless—which was to be the chief characteristic of steamship operation on the Panama route—was not welcomed by the mail lines which had pioneered the service. They generally met competitors either by reducing fares, with the idea of making the business unprofitable for the newcomer, or by purchasing the opposing ships and adding them to their own fleets. The pioneer years witnessed not only the intrusion of ships owned by J. Howard and Son, New York merchants, but also a bitter rivalry between the mail lines themselves. Law's group sent steamers to the Pacific, and Howland and Aspinwall operated vessels from New York to Chagres. Eventually the Howard competition was largely bought

out, and the mail lines, after a little more than a year of rate cutting and bad temper, agreed to divide the field between them, thus
enabling themselves to face more successfully severe rivalry coming
from new directions.

The first competitor on the Atlantic was the steamer *Crescent
City,* which had been built in 1847 for the trade between New York
and New Orleans. She was a larger ship than the *Falcon* of the
United States Mail Steamship Company, and proved herself to be
faster as well. The *Crescent City* had as her New York agent the
firm of J. Howard and Son, but after January, 1849, she was
owned chiefly by Charles Morgan, a New York shipowner whose
career was particularly identified with communication between the
Atlantic seaboard and the Gulf of Mexico. She sailed from New
York for Chagres direct on December 23, 1848, arriving at her
destination January 2, 1849, only a week after the *Falcon,* which
had taken longer in coming from New York since she had called
at New Orleans and Havana.[61] The opposition was carried on
by this steamer alone for some six months, until she was joined
in July, 1849, by the *Empire City,* a vessel of 1,751 tons, with
elaborate passenger accommodations.[62] After the advent of the
new steamer, the company operating the two ships was commonly
known as the "Empire City Line." It was discovered that, in
order to compete effectively with the lines already in the field,
it would be necessary to have ships in operation on the Pacific
as well as the Atlantic, and therefore the Empire City Line set
about providing steamers to carry on the service between Panama
and San Francisco. With vessels on both sides, it would be possible
to sell through tickets in ships of the same company and to assure
passengers in New York that they would be accommodated in a
steamer for San Francisco when they reached Panama. The iron
screw steamer *Sarah Sands* was chartered to begin the service,
sailing from New York on December 13, 1849, with forty-one
through passengers for San Francisco.[63] She was a British vessel,
well built and comfortable but exceedingly slow. For nearly three
years prior to her charter for the California trade, the *Sarah Sands*
had plowed back and forth between Liverpool and New York.
It was not until June 5, 1850, over six months after she had
cleared New York, that the steamer put in an appearance at San
Francisco. Even the voyage from Panama, on which she carried

490 passengers, had consumed two months and six days.[64] In the
meantime, two additional steamers had been sent out from New
York to operate with the *Sarah Sands* between San Francisco and
Panama. These were the *New Orleans,* a small side-wheeler of 761
tons, and the *Northerner* of 1,103 tons, also a paddler. The latter,
formerly on the New York–Charleston run, was commanded on
the voyage to California by Captain Robert W. ("Bully") Water-
man, who came from a record-breaking voyage in Howland and
Aspinwall's clipper *Sea Witch* and was to become notorious the
next year for his voyage to California in the clipper *Challenge.*
Although the *New Orleans* left New York first, the *Northerner*
made the better passage of the two, arriving at San Francisco on
August 15, 1850, the *New Orleans* coming in on September 24.

As the line got under way, J. Howard and Son, its agents, proposed to the Postmaster General that it be given a contract to carry
the California mail monthly between New York and Chagres.
There was an act of Congress of March 3, 1845, which empowered
the Postmaster General to contract for ocean mail lines, and under
this the offer was submitted. The Howards proposed to carry out
the service in the *Empire City* and the *Crescent City,* semimonthly,
for $110,000 a year, which was considerably less than the amount
the United States Mail Steamship Company was receiving from
the Navy Department for its service. Postmaster General Collamer
replied that, although the act under which the bid was submitted
had not been repealed, all power of the Postmaster General under
it had been withdrawn by a subsequent act, which declared that
no further money should be spent by the Post Office Department
for mail service outside the United States.[65]

No sooner had the *Northerner* and *New Orleans* reached the
Pacific, than the Pacific Mail entered negotiations for their withdrawal. In October, 1850, the old company was successful in gaining control not only of the *Northerner* and *Sarah Sands* on the
Pacific, but also of the *Crescent City* and *Empire City* on the
Atlantic. The last two ships named continued to operate for the
remainder of the year under the name of the Empire City Line, but
were fitted into the interests of the Pacific Mail in its current campaign against the United States Mail Steamship Company. President Aspinwall believed that the most serious competition had
been removed by this action and that therefore rates of passage
need not be reduced.[66]

The *New Orleans* continued to ply alone on the Pacific for the Empire City Line until she was joined in 1851 by the *Commodore Stockton,* a little side-wheeler of 436 tons, and the *Monumental City,* another snail-like screw steamer, which made two voyages from Panama to San Francisco for these operators.

The *Commodore Stockton* was the cause of some excitement in Panama, when she returned to port on August 2, 1851, having sprung a leak. Her hundred-odd passengers were irritated at this delay, since they had thus missed the mail steamer; but when they were refused the refund of their passage money on the grounds that there was no cash, they became dangerous. Going aft in a body to demand their money, they were told there was none, but that they might stay aboard free of charge until funds arrived. This did not satisfy them, and they proceeded forward, where the crew were discharging coal, compelled them to cease work by threats of violence, cut the tackle to pieces, and took possession of the ship. Calm was not restored until troops were dispatched to Taboga, where the *Commodore Stockton* was lying. These were able to pacify the mutineers, who agreed to return the ship to her owners but still insisted on the return of their passage money.[67]

In the early months of 1852, the competing line on the Atlantic was revived by placing the new steamer *Sierra Nevada* on the New York–Chagres run, connecting with the *New Orleans* on the Pacific.[68] In October of the same year, the *Sierra Nevada* was sold to Cornelius Vanderbilt and sent to the Pacific; and in December, the *New Orleans* was withdrawn and sent to Australia for sale, thus ending the competition offered by the Empire City Line.

In the meantime, a far more lively spectacle was presented by the two original lines, the United States Mail Steamship Company and the Pacific Mail Steamship Company. As far as the mail service was concerned, the spheres of the Panama route were divided between them, the former operating on the Atlantic side and the latter on the Pacific. For purposes of passenger transportation and the carriage of express matter, however, there was nothing to keep one from trespassing on the preserve of the other. Some lack of sympathy between them was indicated in June, 1849, when the editors of the *New York Herald* were requested by the proprietors of the Pacific Mail to announce that the latter were in no way connected with any line of steamers or sailing vessels between New York and Chagres and that their arrangements related only to the Pacific, where all their energies and attentions were directed.[69]

In November of the same year, an announcement was published that the "substantial and elegant steamship *Isthmus,* having been rebuilt and greatly enlarged, with fine accommodations for passengers in cabin and steerage" would sail from New York for San Francisco on the twenty-sixth of the month.[70] The date of departure had to be postponed, but when the *Isthmus* finally sailed on December 17, 1849, it was to operate on the Pacific coast between Panama and San Francisco for George Law, Marshall Roberts, and their associates, connecting at the Isthmus with the mail steamers *Ohio* and *Georgia.*[71] The *Isthmus* steamed into San Francisco Bay on May 4, 1850, and was followed on June 6 by the *Columbus,* a little wooden screw steamer of 460 tons, which had been dispatched from New York early in the year to run with the *Isthmus.*[72] In March, 1850, the *Republic,* a virtually new steamer of 853 tons, was sent to the Pacific, arriving in San Francisco on August 21, while on October 25, the *Antelope,* a side-wheeler of 425 tons, arrived, completing the quartette of steamers designed to compete with the ships of the Pacific Mail. Although the backers of this line were the same as those of the United States Mail Steamship Company and through tickets were issued, the organization was generally known, informally at least, as the "Law Line," a not inappropriate name, considering that George Law was the controlling figure. The steamers of the Law Line were smaller than those of the Pacific Mail and had not the advantage of uniformity in construction and speed, but they were able to carry passengers, and they proceeded to do so at rates lower than those charged by the pioneer company.

If it was possible for George Law and his associates to compete with the Pacific Mail between Panama and San Francisco, it was even more possible for Howland and Aspinwall, the supporting house of the Pacific Mail, to carry on the contest on the New York–Chagres route. The *Cherokee,* a side-wheeler of 1,245 tons, built in 1848 for the New York–Savannah trade, was purchased by Howland and Aspinwall and dispatched for Chagres on December 13, 1849. On January 29, 1850, Howland and Aspinwall bought the *Philadelphia* for $190,000.[73] She was a side-wheel steamer of 898 tons, built in Philadelphia in 1849. Another steamer, the *Caribbean,* of 1,050 tons, was under construction, and was intended to join the steamers in the Howland and Aspinwall line at the time the competition came to an end. As already narrated, in October, 1850, Howland and Aspinwall purchased the *Empire City* and the *Crescent City,* although they continued to operate under the name of the old line until the end of the year.[74] With this acquisition, they extended their field of operations to the New Orleans–Chagres route, placing the *Philadelphia* on this in November, 1850.[75] Howland and Aspinwall steamers were popular on the Atlantic, and Aspinwall was able to write to his San Francisco agent in May of 1850 that the *Cherokee* was becoming a favorite and that no difficulty should be found in filling her. For this reason "it will not be policy to compel passengers to buy them [through tickets], as the oposition Agents will probably resort to reduced prices to fill their steamers."[76]

At the end of less than a year of active competition, the United States Mail Steamship Company and the Pacific Mail Steamship Company came together on January 21, 1851, and signed an agreement, which was to regulate their relations with one another for the duration of the mail contracts which they held. By this agreement, the United States Mail sold to the Pacific Mail its four steamers on the Pacific, the *Isthmus, Antelope, Columbus,* and *Republic* for $511,000, of which $100,000 was to be in Pacific Mail stock at par, the remainder applying on the purchase of the Atlantic ships which Howland and Aspinwall had been operating, the *Cherokee* and *Philadelphia,* together with the *Empire City,* the *Crescent City,* and the unfinished *Caribbean.* For the first four, a total of $800,000 in United States Mail stock was to be paid, while the entire cost of building and finishing the *Caribbean,* with a commission of 2½ per cent, would be paid by her new owners. It was also provided that the two new steamers which the Pacific Mail at that time had under construction would be finished for the United States Mail, which would offer them to the Navy Department as the last of the five ships which they were to build to carry out their contract. In this instance, a change was made in the arrangements; although one of the new steamers was finished for the United States Mail as the *Illinois,* the other became the *Golden Gate* and went to the Pacific. The two companies agreed to co-

operate in business matters, encouraging the sale of through
tickets and carrying through freight. For the freight, the receipts
were to be divided, with 64 per cent going to the Pacific Mail and
36 per cent to the United States Mail. Arnold Harris, the original
recipient of the mail contract for service on the Pacific, was settled
with the position of agent at New Orleans, the post which Jabez
Woodward had originally promised him. Finally, the parties to
the contract agreed that, after it went into effect on April 1, 1851,
neither of them would engage in any competition with the other.
The arrangement thus made was destined to stand until the end of
the mail contracts in 1859, when conditions on the Panama route
were quite different from those of eight years before.[77]

There were other, and less successful, attempts at competition
in the pioneer years. Even before all the Pacific Mail steamers were
on the coast, it was reported that a new line of steamers was to be
established between Panama and San Francisco by Allen and
Paxson of New York. Shortly afterward, news came that the
Hartford, first of the line, had cleared New York for the Pacific,
but the vessel never reached San Francisco.[78]

In January, 1850, the citizens of California began to contem-
plate the organization of a line of steamers in opposition to the
Pacific Mail. Public meetings were held in San Francisco for the
purpose of organization on the evenings of January 9 and 12, 1850,
and at the latter meeting subscriptions for stock were taken at the
rate of $1,000 a share. That the inspiration for these meetings was
not entirely local was made clear by the announcement that
$300,000 worth of stock had already been subscribed in the United
States. At the meeting of January twelfth, $200,000 in stock was
taken by Californians.[79] Later in the month, meetings were held in
Sacramento, and it was announced that the steamers were to
connect at the Isthmus with those of J. Howard and Son.[80] The
formal organization of the company as the California Steam Packet
Company was announced on February 21, and at the same time it
was stated that stock subscriptions in San Francisco and Sacramento in the two weeks in which the books had been open had
reached about $500,000. Thomas O. Larkin had been elected presi-
dent of the company, and he planned to sail for New York within
a few weeks to purchase suitable steamers.[81] Having advanced thus
far, the California Steam Packet Company disappeared from the

Lithograph, courtesy of Robert W. McRoberts

Steamer *Cortes*, 1852

Courtesy of Roger D. Lapham

Steamer *Sonora* of the Pacific Mail Steamship Company, 1853

Poster Advertising "Opposition Line" to California, 1853

public press. It was common talk that Howard and Son were interested in the venture, and it is probable that their service on the Pacific, which opened later in 1850, was expected to answer the need which the California company had planned to fill.[82] This was but the first abortive attempt to found in California a steamship service to the eastern United States which could successfully challenge the power of the great companies already in the field.

From the very beginning, in periods of active competition the speed of rival steamers was an important item, particularly to those who traveled on them. In February, 1849, the *Crescent City* and the *Falcon,* northbound from Chagres for New York were in Havana together, and one of the passengers in the *Crescent City* found, while ashore,

that there was quite a feeling existing between the friends of the two boats regarding their relative speed, and bets in small amounts (hats, boots, &c.) were freely made, though the Crescent City seemed to be the greatest favorite, and we also learned that the Falcon had for some time wished to have an opportunity for trying speed with the Crescent City, and now there was a chance.

The *Falcon* got under way at 1:30 P.M., on February 24, while the *Crescent City* was still taking in coal, the latter ship not passing the Morro until four o'clock that afternoon. Ahead on the horizon was the *Falcon,* hull down under a cloud of smoke, but by midnight the ships were abeam, and in the morning the *Falcon* was astern

and that with only the ordinary head of steam on, while the flames were blazing clean from the funnel of the *Falcon,* she apparently using her blowers, but to no purpose. She was beaten handsomely, and that, too, in smooth water, and she lost the boots, while the *Crescent City* takes the hats.[83]

Racing must have presented a temptation in the Pacific as well, for in May, 1850, Aspinwall wrote to Robinson, his agent in San Francisco:

As the presence of opposition Steamers may create rivalry you will please give particular instructions that there shall be no racing—& the pressure of Steam exceed in no case 13 lbs with the Cut off.[84]

When the Pacific Mail had silenced the opposition of Howard and Son in October, 1850, the San Francisco agents were informed that the steamers should again run under the head of steam originally ordered. Although in order to meet active competition, a pressure of thirteen pounds with the cut off had been allowed if necessary, the *Tennessee* had been run up as high as fourteen and fifteen pounds. "While it is desirable to save time—the wear & tear of machinery & expenditure of fuel are more important considerations."[85]

The Pacific Mail had no idea of being of undue assistance to competitors, and when Howard and Son first announced that they planned to enter the Pacific trade, Robinson was informed of the company's policy as follows:

I reiterate the orders of the Company that you will on no account part with the smallest part of the provisions or Coal placed at so heavy an expenditure & with so much difficulty at San Francisco, except in such cases as we may specially advise.[86]

The cost of passage to California by way of Panama varied in the pioneer years, depending on the demand for accommodations and the amount of competition faced by the lines operating. When the first voyage of the *Falcon* was advertised in November, 1848, the rate from New York to Chagres in the saloon was set at $150 and in the lower cabin at $120, whereas from New Orleans to Chagres the prices were $100 and $80.[87] On a voyage of the *Isthmus,* after the beginning of the gold excitement in New York, the rate for the after-cabin staterooms remained at $150, but the forward cabin was reduced to $100, and it was advertised that the ship had good accommodations for sixteen deck passengers—who would be berthed below and who would mess with the crew—at $65 to Chagres.[88] The competition of the *Crescent City* and *Empire City* failed to reduce fares until August, 1849, when the *Falcon* advertised to carry passengers from New York to Chagres in after staterooms for $100, in forward staterooms for $80, and in steerage for $50. At this time, the *Falcon's* commander was instructed thus by Roberts: "If you come in competition with any other steam Ship the rates of passage to New York can be reduced, and printed handbills have been sent on board the Falcon for circulation giving the reduced prices of passage to New York."[89]

At the same time, sailing vessels were advertising to carry cabin passengers to Chagres for $70 and second cabin for $50.[90] Although fares on the *Falcon* were reduced, the *Ohio,* when she came out in August, 1849, held to the old rates ranging from $150 for after-cabin staterooms to $80 for steerage.[91] By September, however, the *Ohio* also had come down to $100 for cabin and $50 for steerage.[92] When the *Cherokee* and *Philadelphia* of Howland and Aspinwall appeared on the scene in the early part of 1850, their rates ranged from $125 to $90 in the cabin, whereas the steerage was $65.[93] At the same time, cabin fares in the *Georgia,* a newer and larger ship, were $100, and steerage $50.[94] The fares in the *Empire City* and *Crescent City* were placed at the same level as those charged by Howland and Aspinwall.[95] By October, 1850, all the competing lines on the Atlantic had come to the same rates, a first-cabin stateroom berth from New York to Chagres being $100 and the steerage rate $50.[96] During the period of competition, the San Francisco agents of the Pacific Mail were instructed thus:

We authorized by the last Mail the Agents at Panama & Chagres to reduce the homeward rates in our Chagres line to the standard adopted by Howard's and Law's Lines. You will please remind the pursers in the Pacific of this—The prices will necessarily fluctuate somewhat so that they may engage passengers at our advertised rates & difference between these and those at which other passengers are engaged will be refunded by the pursers on this side. It will be well for the pursers on the Pacific to state generally that the passage will be uniform in price—without stating the discretion we have given.[97]

In 1851, with the coming of more determined competition from Cornelius Vanderbilt and Edward Mills, first-cabin staterooms went to $80, though steerage rose to $60.[98] The steamers of August 28 of the same year, at a time of particularly bitter competition, carried cabin passengers for as little as $20, and steerage for $10.[99]

On the Pacific side, the Pacific Mail originally set its cabin rate at $250.[100] in 1849, however, before the advent of competition, the fares were increased to $300 for cabin and $150 for steerage, which were easily obtained in a period of monopoly.[101] When Howard and Son entered the Pacific field with the *Sarah Sands, New Orleans,* and *Northerner,* they advertised for passengers at the same rates which the Pacific Mail charged.[102]

With the entrance of George Law's competition on the Pacific, however, rates were reduced drastically. The *Antelope,* in November, 1850, advertised to carry cabin passengers for $125.[103] The Pacific Mail retaliated by lowering the rates on its slower steamers to $275 for cabin and $125 for steerage, and later to $175 for cabin and $85 in the steerage.[104] Throughout the remainder of 1850 and 1851, rates on the Pacific continued to fluctuate between $300 and $100 for cabin passage and $125 and $60 for steerage. In May of

1851, it was stated that no less than six steamers were at Panama awaiting passengers for San Francisco, and a Panama correspondent of the *New York Herald* wrote as follows:

Competition is, as a matter of course, very great, and passage to San Francisco can be had for a mere song; $100 in the first cabin, $75 in the second, and $50 in the steerage. It is a perfect farce for any one to think of purchasing through tickets from New York to San Francisco. There will never be for the future a time when there will be less than four steamers here, and passengers can always, with every degree of safety, wait to purchase their tickets here for San Francisco. Many a poor man, who cannot afford to pay $400 to California, did he know these facts, would not hesitate a moment in leaving for the new El Dorado of the West. A man can travel from New York to California, under present circumstances, for $100 in the steerage, and $150 or $175 in the cabin; and I hope that this will meet the eye of many who can afford to pay this amount, and of which, I have no doubt, there are hundreds.[105]

In June, 1851, the Pacific Mail advertised rates in the *Isthmus,* a slow boat, from San Francisco to Panama at $100 cabin and $60 steerage.[106] By October, cabin rates on the *Isthmus* had risen to $175 and steerage to $90, while the faster mail steamers like the *Tennessee* were still charging $300 for berths in staterooms in the cabin, though open berths in the cabin could be had for $175 and steerage berths for $100.[107]

When the United States Mail, the Pacific Mail, and Howard and Son were all operating steamers on both Atlantic and Pacific, it was to their advantage to sell through tickets from New York to San Francisco or in the other direction, thus assuring their ships of full passenger lists on both coasts. Sometimes these through fares were merely arrived at by adding together the local fares, but again, they represented a real reduction over the sum of the two single fares. In December, 1849, the United States Mail advertised through first-cabin rates at $380, second-cabin at $280, and steerage at $200.[108] By July, 1850, these had been raised to $400 for first class and $200 for steerage, though in the same month the first class was reduced to $380, the steerage remaining the same.[109] By November, 1850, first cabin on these steamers had fallen to $250, with a $225 rate to New Orleans, while the forward cabin was $175 from San Francisco to New York and $165 to New Orleans.[110] After the agreement between the United States Mail and the Pacific Mail, through rates went higher again; in April, 1851, fares between New York and San Francisco were $330 in the first-cabin staterooms, $290 in the lower cabin, and $105 in steerage. Agents were instructed, however, to sell tickets at $5 less than any competitor until the fare reached $10.[111]

The shifting rates of passage on the Panama route during the pioneer years only illustrate the still uncertain and chaotic nature of its organization. The year 1851 saw the formation of an agreement between the two lines carrying the mail under contract and also what seemed the beginning of a monopoly on the route. This was not to be, however, for the same year witnessed the entrance of Cornelius Vanderbilt and Edward Mills into the business of transportation between the eastern United States and California. Instead of ushering in an era of quiet monopoly, the year 1851 saw the massing of storm clouds of competition of the bitterest sort.

CHAPTER III

BATTLE OF THE TITANS, 1851–1860

THE STORY of the Panama steamers between 1851 and 1860 was one of exciting, if also ruinous, competition. Its chief feature was the opening of a route over the Isthmus of Nicaragua, which rivaled that at Panama and was vigorously promoted by Cornelius Vanderbilt, Charles Morgan, and Cornelius Kingsland Garrison. Vanderbilt, first associated with Morgan and Garrison, only to be later opposed by them, was one of the principal competitors of the mail lines. He sent ships to Panama after the closing of the Nicaragua route, and with the expiration of the original contract he arranged to carry the mails in his ships. The Pacific Mail and the United States Mail companies fought back with rate cuts, subsidies for withdrawal, and offers of compromise. Finally, at the end of the period, Vanderbilt gained for himself an important place in the councils of the Pacific Mail as the price of his coöperation. Although Vanderbilt and his associates dominated the scene, competitors like Edward Mills, Davis, Brooks and Company, and others complicated the situation. The record of these years is a confused one, but above the details of rates and compromises there is to be discerned the dominant struggle between the "vested interests," represented by the pioneer lines holding the mail contracts, and the newcomers, vigorous, unscrupulous, rough, in their purpose to gain for themselves as great a part as possible in the lucrative trade.

Within a year of the opening of the route to the Pacific coast by way of Panama rumors were afloat in both New York and California that there would soon be facilities for the transportation of passengers and treasure by way of the Isthmus of Nicaragua. The most obvious advantage of this route lay in its shorter distance; from New York to San Francisco by way of Panama was 5,245 miles, whereas it was only 4,871 by way of Nicaragua. For New Orleans, the difference in favor of Nicaragua was even greater, amounting to 525 miles, since the Panama route was 4,676 miles and that via Nicaragua was 4,151.[1] It was also pointed out that, although the distance between the oceans was greater over Nica-

---

[1] For notes to chap. iii, see pp. 268–272.

ragua—amounting to some 174 miles, as compared to the journey
of about 55 miles across the Isthmus of Panama—all but about
18 miles of the Nicaragua crossing could be made by water through
the use of the San Juan River and Lake Nicaragua. The land
journey at Panama amounted to considerably more than that.[2]
Furthermore, the higher latitude of Nicaragua was said to make
the climate cooler and the route less subject to tropical fevers.

The man most closely associated with the opening of the Nicaragua route was Cornelius Vanderbilt, a New Yorker who, in 1849
at the age of fifty-five, had already accumulated a fortune as a
result of his ability and ruthless persistence in the operation of
ferries, river steamers, and Sound liners in the waters adjacent to
New York. Prior to 1849 Vanderbilt had not been engaged in
ocean shipping, but in that year an arrangement was made between
the government of Nicaragua and the American Atlantic and
Pacific Ship Canal Company, in which Vanderbilt was a principal
stockholder, giving to that organization a right of way through
the country.[3] In 1849, Vanderbilt visited the Isthmus region once
to make arrangements for the route and in December started for
Chagres on an expedition to take the steamer *Orus* to the mouth
of the San Juan in order to test the possibility of ascending that
river, as well as to investigate the navigation of Lake Nicaragua.
The *Crescent City,* on which Vanderbilt and his party had taken
passage from New York, broke down before reaching her destination, and Vanderbilt returned to New York early in 1850, the
members of his party continuing on the expedition as planned.[4]
In 1850, Vanderbilt attempted to find backing in England for his
enterprise. Failing in this, he procured a charter from the Nica-
raguan government for himself in the name of the Accessory
Transit Company to arrange for transportation facilities over the
route.[5]

That the prospect of a transit at Nicaragua interested others was
shown in the summer of 1850, when it was reported in the press
of both New York and San Francisco that agents of the steamers
of George Law and of the Empire City Line on the Pacific had
made arrangements for the construction of wharves for their
steamers at Realejo, at the Pacific end of the Nicaragua crossing.
The two companies would make that port their principal coal
and provision depot on the Pacific, calling there in both directions

and eventually using it as a terminus to the exclusion of Panama.[6] Before the lines could carry out these threats, which were directed against the Pacific Mail, they had both come to terms with the rival company, and the opening of the Nicaragua route was left to Vanderbilt, its original projector.

For the next twelve months, the subject of the Nicaragua route aroused increasing interest, particularly in California where the importance of the isthmian communication was felt to be vital. The newspapers of San Francisco were filled with discussions of the new route, strong feelings, favorable and unfavorable, being expressed. Some doubt was felt concerning the safety of travel through the region and the adequacy of means of transportation across the Isthmus. It was new country for travelers as compared with the beaten roads of Panama, and most of the discussions of it displayed a great fund of ignorance on the part of the writers.[7]

In the meantime, Cornelius Vanderbilt went ahead with his plans for opening the route. In December, 1850, he presented a memorial to Congress, offering to carry the mails from New York to California in six steamships at the rate of $180,000 per year, as compared to the $389,000 which the government was paying for the service at that time. He further proposed to place his ships at the disposal of the United States government in time of war upon payment of their actual cost to him.[8] Referred to the Secretary of the Navy, he presented his offer to carry the mails twice a month, agreeing to accomplish the whole trip between New York and San Francisco within twenty-five days.[9] To this Secretary Graham replied promptly that the Navy Department was not authorized to receive proposals for mail service and that, although an extension had just been arranged, it was confined to the existing contracts.[10]

Vanderbilt had not waited for government aid to start his service, however. On December 26, 1850, his first ocean steamer, the *Prometheus,* took her departure from New York for Havana, San Juan de Nicaragua, at the mouth of the San Juan River, and Chagres. She continued to sail to Chagres during the winter and spring, for the Pacific portion of the line was not yet in operation, and Vanderbilt was unable to announce a through service to San Francisco until the summer of 1851. The San Francisco newspapers of July 4, 1851, contained the first advertisement of "Vanderbilt's

Independent Line." The steamer *Pacific* had come from New York
and was ready to depart on July 14, connecting with the *Prometheus* at the Isthmus. For the first trip, until the connection over
Nicaragua was sure, the steamers were advertised to continue to
the Isthmus of Panama, where passengers might cross if they did
not care to risk the wilds of Nicaragua. It was announced that
"Commodore Vanderbilt is now at San Juan del Sud, and his well
known reputation guarantees the perfection of the arrangements
for forwarding passengers and treasure direct."[11] On the Atlantic,
the *Prometheus* was joined in October, 1851, by the *Daniel Webster*,
while the *Independence* and *North America* arrived in San Francisco in September and October, respectively, to augment the line
on the Pacific. The route proved to be not much faster than that
by way of Panama, the first passage requiring thirty-one days from
San Francisco to New York, whereas in the fall of 1851 the trip took
as long as thirty-three days. The steamers were built for the trade
in which they were engaged, and probably their accommodations
were more attractive to the traveler than those of some of the
rather ill-assorted fleet of the Pacific Mail. The Nicaragua route
early had its critics, however, as indicated in the following comment by Gilmor Meredith in a letter to his father written in
December, 1851.

As to the success of Vanderbilt's Nicaragua line—I think it doubtful [;]
many persons who have gone home by that route pronounce it a failure and
represent the treatment received from the Agents of the line whilst crossing
the land as being uncourteous harsh and uncivil, the boats on the lake and
river small and without accommodations for even 50 persons—they represent
themselves as having passed through great hardships and wind up by advising
all parties to take the Panama Route . . .[12]

Although Meredith was in the employ of the Pacific Mail, he was
writing a personal letter, and the evidence shows that he was
stating matters frankly.

Nicaragua so caught the imagination of the day that in November, 1851, Howland and Aspinwall felt it necessary to write an
open letter to James Gordon Bennett, editor of the *New York
Herald,* stoutly denying that they had applied to the government
of Nicaragua for the right of transit through that country or that
they had any interest in or knowledge of such an application.[13]

The ships of Cornelius Vanderbilt were not the only competitors met by the mail lines in 1851. Edward Mills, a New Yorker who had previously interested himself in transatlantic steamships but with little success, now came to try his luck in the promising field of Panama competition. To carry on the Atlantic portion of his service, Mills built the steamer *Brother Jonathan* for the New York–Chagres service and placed her on the line at the end of May, 1851. Having no ships of his own on the Pacific, Mills was forced to make arrangements with the owners of other vessels on the Pacific in order to sell through tickets in competition with the mail lines and the Vanderbilt steamers. This led to unfortunate results when some two hundred passengers from the *Brother Jonathan* arrived in Panama in November, 1851, bearing tickets for the steamer *Union,* a vessel owned by the "Independent Line," which had been lost south of San Diego early in the previous July. Since the passengers had paid only $100 each for their through tickets, a sum considerably less than the rate then prevailing on the Pacific Mail steamers, and the mail steamer about to leave Panama already had her full complement of passengers, they were not given places aboard her. Zachrisson and Nelson, the Panama agents for Mills, refused to refund the passage money, since Mills had forwarded no funds on which they could draw to do this. It was stated that most of the passengers were too poor to go on to San Francisco or to return to New York, but before matters became desperate for them, the Panama agents arranged to forward them to their destination.[14] The affair was badly handled, however, and Mills's attitude, as revealed in a letter published in the *New York Herald,* was hardly one which would make matters better.

The California passengers must admit that I have reduced the passage one half, since I commenced running the steamer Brother Jonathan; and if they meet with some little detention on the Pacific side, which is rather beyond my control, they will, upon reflection, give me credit for some advantage to themselves, the scurrilous and abusive stories of the agents and runners of the monopoly notwithstanding.[15]

Mills's next cargo of passengers by the *Brother Jonathan* fared little better. When they arrived in Panama, the *Monumental City,* for which they had tickets, was not in the harbor to receive them. This time money had been sent out to the agents from which refunds could be made, but the amount was only large enough to make payments in the ratio of $70 for each $110 ticket. A meeting of the passengers was held to call upon Amos B. Corwine, the American consul at Panama, but little could be done. Corwine issued a warning to prospective passengers from the United States, however, cautioning them to buy through tickets only from "responsible houses," which indicated rather clearly his opinion of the activities of Edward Mills.[16]

The *Brother Jonathan* was purchased from Mills by Vanderbilt in March, 1852, and sent to the Pacific by her new owner, but the field was by no means cleared of steamers offering competition to the mail ships. The whole period of importance of the Panama route was characterized by recurrent "rashes" of rather impermanent lines of steamers. These appeared upon the scene to divert traffic from the old lines with offers of low rates, only to fade away after a voyage or two, having been forced out of the business because of insufficient financial backing to stand a long period of ruinous rates or having sold their ships to one of the old lines at a good profit. The years 1852 and 1853 saw an unusually large crop of such short-lived steamship companies in the field. At the end of January, 1852, just as Mills was selling out to Vanderbilt, the steamer *City of New York* was advertised to sail from New York for San Juan and Chagres, as the first of an Independent Line for which Palmer, Haight and Company were agents.[17] Early the next month, two steamers, the *Benjamin Franklin* and the *William Penn,* which had until this time been in the Philadelphia–Boston trade, were advertised to sail from Philadelphia for Chagres, connecting at the Isthmus with "other steamers now in the Pacific" for San Francisco. The "other steamers" were not specified, but the *Benjamin Franklin* did sail from Philadelphia about the middle of February with one hundred eighty-seven passengers for Chagres.[18] By the next month, Palmer and Haight were advertising the *City of New York* and also the *William Penn* as sailing from New York, while the *Benjamin Franklin* had dropped from the picture.[19] Each of these ships made one voyage before being withdrawn. Spofford, Tileston and Company, who were particularly interested in the New York–Havana business, sent out the *Pioneer* for a single voyage to the Isthmus in January, 1852, and over a year later placed their steamer *Union* on the same run for one voyage.

The revival of J. Howard and Son on the Atlantic in 1852 with the *Sierra Nevada* has already been mentioned. The same year saw the entrance of a somewhat more determined rival on each coast in the companies of Jones and Johnson on the Atlantic and Davis, Brooks and Company on the Pacific in a combination which was known as the New York and San Francisco Steamship Line. The ships originally announced for the route were the *Union* for the Atlantic run and the *Winfield Scott* for the Pacific, but it was actually the *United States,* a steamer of 1,216 tons, built in 1851 as the *Bienville,* which sailed from New York for Chagres on January 21, 1852. Since the withdrawal of Mills rates had risen, and the new competitors charged for the through voyage from New York to San Francisco $315 in staterooms in first cabin, $255 second cabin and $200 steerage.[20] These fares were exactly the same as those charged in steamers of the mail lines, except that the latter asked $270 for second-cabin passage instead of $255.[21] Again arrangements were unsatisfactory at the Isthmus, and the passengers by the *United States* arrived at Panama over two months before the *Winfield Scott* was ready to carry them north. Many of these had expended all their money on through tickets and, with no prospect of the arrival of the promised steamer to carry them on to San Francisco, they were in a difficult position, being unable to raise funds with which to purchase tickets by the mail line. New York papers advised strongly against the purchase of through tickets by the "independent" lines.[22] After April, 1852, the *Winfield Scott* was in operation on the Pacific and proved herself to be a fast and dependable steamer. In October of the same year, she was joined by the *Cortes.* On the Atlantic, the *United States* kept up the line until February, 1853, by which time Edward Mills had appeared with a new steamer, the *Uncle Sam,* which he operated from New York to Chagres between December, 1852, and May, 1853.

The mail lines were not prepared to take the competition offered by Vanderbilt and the independent lines by way of Panama without a fight. A letter which appeared in the *New York Herald* of September 15, 1852, evidently emanating from the camp of the Empire City Line, read in part as follows:

The public of the United States, and particularly the travelling community, should feel under great obligations—which they undoubtedly do—to Geo. Law, Esq., whose public spirit is only equalled by his ability, in consummating any project he may have in view for the public weal.

We are informed that Mr. Law, with that true philanthropic feeling which has ever been evinced through his eventful career, has ordered the captains of his splendid ships, forming, as they do, the connecting link with our far off States, to bring up passengers from Aspinwall to New York, for the hardly remunerating price of five dollars. . . . The evil minded persons who state that Mr. Law is attempting to drive off all opposition to his splendid line of sea steamers, and then to establish a tariff of prices to suit himself, must not be listened to; for a charge so preposterous carries its own conviction with it.[23]

Rates like those referred to above may have been offered informally just before sailing, but in October, 1852, the United States Mail Steamship Company was advertising steerage fares from New York to Aspinwall (which had now replaced Chagres as the port of debarkation on the Atlantic side of the Isthmus of Panama) at $35, with second cabin $10 higher and first cabin at $55 and $65.[24] In January, 1853, the mail lines were charging $305 for through passage from New York to San Francisco in the first cabin, with second cabin $200 and steerage $85. From Panama to San Francisco only, second cabin was $145 and steerage $50.[25] At the Isthmus, when this $50 steerage rate to San Francisco was announced, there was great speculation and excitement, for the "independent" steamer held up her price to $75, and enough passengers were arriving to fill her accommodations at that figure.[26]

In the spring of 1853, it became clear to the Pacific Mail that Davis, Brooks and Company, already operating the *Winfield Scott* and *Cortes,* had plans under way to place more steamers on the Pacific. In order to forestall this move, the steamers of Davis, Brooks and Company were purchased by the Pacific Mail in May, 1853, and although this entailed a heavy investment—and one which brought to the Pacific Mail steamers which were not needed —it was felt by the directors of the company to be a lesser evil than facing increased competition and consequently divided business and decreased receipts.[27] The investment was somewhat reduced, though perhaps with doubtful wisdom, when the *Cortes* was almost immediately sold for $120,000 to the Nicaragua Steamship Company, the chief competitor remaining in the Pacific.[28]

In the meantime, the Nicaragua route was continuing to operate with a degree of success, though its course could hardly be said to have been tranquil. In 1852, two new steamers, the *Northern Light* and the *Star of the West,* were completed for Vanderbilt and placed on the New York–San Juan run. This made it possible to place the *Daniel Webster* on the line between New Orleans and San Juan. The same year saw the Pacific line augmented by the screw steamers, *Monumental City* and *S. S. Lewis,* and the paddler, *Brother Jonathan,* which had been purchased from Mills. The addition of these vessels made possible the maintenance of a fortnightly service, thus challenging the mail lines in frequency of sailings as well as in speed.

At the beginning of 1853, Vanderbilt transferred the steamers, which he had thus far owned himself, to the nominal ownership of the Accessory Transit Company, a corporation previously concerned only with the actual transit of the Isthmus. For the seven steamers thus "purchased," the Transit Company paid Vanderbilt $1,200,000 cash, an additional $1,500,000 to be payable within twelve months. This cash was to be raised by the issue of 45,000 new shares of stock at $30 a share. It was announced that, since there was a market for the stock at 39¼, a number of leading Wall Street capitalists had already taken 40,000 of the new shares at 30.²⁹ Having thus arranged the affairs of his California line, Vanderbilt departed from New York in May, 1853, for a five months' cruise to northern Europe and the Mediterranean in his new steamer *North Star*. Before sailing, he resigned the presidency of the company and committed its management to Charles Morgan, as New York agent, and Cornelius Kingsland Garrison. The latter had been highly successful with his commercial and banking partnership of Garrison and Fritts at Panama since 1849 and as San Francisco agent for Vanderbilt's steamers at a salary of $60,000 a year.³⁰ During Vanderbilt's absence on the *North Star,* Morgan and Garrison were able so to manipulate the stock of the Accessory Transit Company (often referred to as the Nicaragua Transit Company or the Nicaragua Steamship Company) that its control passed from the hands of Vanderbilt into their own, and he returned to New York in September, 1853, to find the company in the possession of the men whom he had left as representatives. In order to make their position more secure, Garrison arranged with Captain Knight, the San Francisco agent of the Pacific Mail, in May, 1853, for a working agreement between the two companies. By this arrangement, first-class rates were set at $244, second-class at $188, and steerage at $113, exclusive of Isthmus transit. Knight's action was repudiated by the New York headquarters of the Pacific

Mail, thereby gaining for the pioneer line an enhanced standing in the eyes of Californians. The *Alta* wrote:

It is evident that the company do not intend and will not take an undue advantage of the public. In every other matter the acts of Capt. Knight, who is very greatly esteemed, are acknowledged and respected by the officers and directors. In this, however, they were forced to dissent from him.[31]

The attempt at coöperation was succeeded by a period of exceedingly bitter rivalry between the routes. Through rates in the first cabin on the mail steamers were reduced from \$300 to \$100, second cabin went down to \$75, and steerage, which had been \$150, was placed at \$50. The *New York Herald* for September 10, 1853, prophesied:

With this foretaste of the benefit of low prices, and the signs of the controversy, exhibiting evidences of a deeper depression, we have no doubt that passengers will be paid for their patronage until the weaker party shall be compelled to knock under and draw off.[32]

In the same month, the stock of the Pacific Mail was reported to be declining owing to the competition with the Nicaragua Transit, in which, it was then predicted, the Pacific Mail would come off second best. The time made by way of Nicaragua was said to be consistently less than that by Panama, and it seemed within the realm of possibility that the mail contract would be annulled by Congress and given to the Transit Company. It was also reported that a route across Mexico from Vera Cruz to Acapulco was being opened by the Mexican Ocean Mail and Inland Company, which would make the time between New York and San Francisco even shorter than by Nicaragua.[33]

Feeling between the two companies was not improved by such occurrences as that reported by the *Sierra Nevada,* a steamer which had been added to the Nicaragua Transit fleet in the Pacific in the spring of 1853. When the *Sierra Nevada* put into San Francisco from San Juan in May, 1853, J. H. Foster, her purser, reported that about 1:00 A.M. on May 3, when she was northbound off Cerros Island, a steamer's lights were sighted on the starboard bow. The ship proved to be the *Golden Gate* of the Pacific Mail.

... it blowing fresh and considerable sea running, put our helm to starboard in order to give her a berth, and from some unaccountable motive she crossed our bows, and had not our engines been instantly stopped on seeing her design, would have struck us by the forward rigging; but fortunately our bowsprit only was carried away, by coming in contact with her larboard quarter as she passed.[34]

The *Alta* came promptly to the defense of Captain Patterson of the *Golden Gate,* drawing upon seemingly inexhaustible reserves of sarcasm for the benefit of Purser Foster, upon whose "remarkable fondness for such innocent amusement as the misstatement of facts in his official reports we have on one or two occasions remarked. . . ." However, when the *Golden Gate* returned to San Francisco and an opportunity was presented to have the incident explained, the press had forgotten it.[35]

The same spirit of bitter rivalry was shown the next year when the *Yankee Blade* of the Independent Line ran out of coal at Coiba Island, near Panama. The Pacific Mail steamer *Sonora* passed, and in response to the guns and distress rockets of the *Yankee Blade,* the *Sonora* fired rockets of acknowledgment but made no move to change her course, continuing into Panama where some of her passengers reported the occurrence. Aid was provided, but the *Yankee Blade* appeared just as the rescue steamer was about to sail, having cut enough wood on Coiba Island to bring her into port.[36]

Competition was reflected in the popular ballads of the day. One, entitled "Humbug Steamship Companies" opened with the lines:

> The greatest imposition that the public ever saw,
> Are the California steamships that run to Panama.

and continued:

> They have opposition on the route, with cabins very nice,
> And advertise to take you for half the usual price;
> They get thousands from the mountains, and then deny their bills,
> So you have to pay their prices, or go back into the hills.
> . . . .
> You are driven round the steerage like a drove of hungry swine,
> And kicked ashore at Panama by the Independent Line;
> Your baggage is thrown overboard, the like you never saw,
> A trip or two will sicken you of going to Panama.

The chorus of this ballad ran thus:

> Then come along, come along, you that want to go,
> The best accommodations, and the passage very low;
> Our boats they are large enough, don't be afraid,
> The *Golden Gate* is going down to beat the *Yankee Blade.*[37]

The rate war between the mail lines and the Nicaragua Transit, which opened in September, 1853, was destined to be short-lived; by the middle of the next month, the fares had mounted to their former places, with the Nicaragua Transit charging even more than the mail companies. Cabin fares on the *Panama* were $220 and $250, and the *Pacific* set hers at $300, while the $150 second-cabin rate and $100 steerage of the former steamer were each increased by twenty-five dollars by the rival vessel.[38]

However, the Panama and Nicaragua companies were not to be left long to quarrel with one another alone. Cornelius Vanderbilt was no man to be jockeyed out of the control of a line of steamers without a fight, and the early months of 1854 saw hostilities begin in earnest. Vanderbilt had lost the Nicaragua steamers, but he had one ship at hand and he proceeded to place her in service. This was the *North Star,* in which he had made his European cruise in 1853. Although the *North Star* might be called a "private yacht," she was rather a fast passenger steamer, which Vanderbilt chose to use temporarily as a yacht. With a tonnage of 1,867 and a length of 262 feet, 6 inches, she was about as large as the best of the steamers on the route, and her double-beam engines made her an exceptionally fast ship.[39] The *North Star* took her first sailing from New York for Aspinwall on February 20, 1854, on the same day on which the *George Law* of the United States Mail Steamship Company sailed for Aspinwall and the *Star of the West* of the Nicaragua Transit started for San Juan. For the Pacific side of the route, Vanderbilt entered an agreement with the ubiquitous Edward Mills, who had sent his steamer *Uncle Sam* there in 1853 to run in connection with the *Yankee Blade,* a new steamer which he was building for the Atlantic. By this arrangement, the *Yankee Blade* was sent around South America to join the *Uncle Sam,* the *North Star* holding up the Atlantic end of the line alone. The combination was announced in New York on January 20, 1854, and by February 2 the *Yankee Blade* had departed to take up her station on the Pacific.[40]

The new Independent Line, as Vanderbilt and Mills called their combination, proceeded to cut rates alarmingly. In February, 1854, through cabin fares in their steamers were $150, with steerage $75.[41] Less than three months later, cabin had been reduced to $100 and steerage to $60, and although cabin remained at $100, second cabin was $80, and steerage $35 in June, 1854.[42] The mail lines and the Nicaragua Transit followed to some extent the lead set by the Independent Line. For the sailing from San Francisco to New York of March 16, 1854, upper-deck staterooms by the *Golden Gate* and *George Law* were $200, but in the main cabin rooms were $150, while the second cabin was $125 and the steerage $45. The ships of the Nicaragua Transit held to higher fares, with their first-cabin berths ranging from $200 to $225, the second-cabin $175, and the steerage $60.[43] In June, the mail lines raised their rates, and charged $225 for first cabin, $130 for second and $75 in the steerage.[44]

By the end of the summer of 1854, both the mail lines and the Nicaragua Transit had suffered considerably from the competition of the Independent Line of Vanderbilt and Mills, which was increasingly recognized as being entirely the creation of Vanderbilt. Again it seemed wiser to buy out the opposing steamers rather than to operate at ruinous rates. Thus on September 1, 1854, it was announced that the *North Star,* the *Yankee Blade,* and the *Uncle Sam* had been purchased jointly by the United States Mail Steamship Company, the Pacific Mail Steamship Company, and the Nicaragua Transit Company and would be withdrawn from opposition. The sum paid for the three ships was $800,000, and Vanderbilt received an additional bonus of $100,000 for his promise never again to interest himself in the passenger trade between New York and California. Of the amount paid, the Nicaragua Transit contributed $500,000, receiving the steamers *Uncle Sam* and *Yankee Blade,* and the mail lines gave $400,000 for the remaining ship and Vanderbilt's promise. The *North Star* was taken over by the United States Mail Steamship Company and placed on its New York–Aspinwall run. The bonus paid Vanderbilt for staying out of the Nicaragua route was finally arranged on the basis of a monthly subsidy of $40,000.[45] In commenting on the settlement, the *Alta* wrote:

Vanderbilt is slippery, very much like an Irishman's flea, and we should not be at all surprised if a line of opposition steamers were puffing away in the course of six months, established, at least indirectly, through his means.[46]

Once Vanderbilt was again shelved, the mail lines and the Nicaragua Transit increased their rates to $206.25 for first cabin, $168 for second, and $112.25 for steerage. They also arranged to sail from their termini in alternate weeks, thus giving a weekly service between New York and California.[47]

Although the Panama and Nicaragua lines might unite to put down a third competitor, peace between them was highly impermanent, once their joint objective had been achieved. The very nature of their position made them rivals, and efforts to secure complete coöperation between them were not long-lived. The system of sailing in alternate weeks was unsatisfactory to the Nicaragua line, since, particularly in San Francisco, businessmen and travelers were accustomed to the sailing of steamers for the East at the first and middle of each month, and therefore arranged their affairs to suit the fortnightly "steamer day," which was an integral part of San Francisco life. This meant that the Pacific Mail steamers, which retained the old sailing dates, had a distinct advantage over the Nicaragua vessels, which shifted their days of departure. In January, 1855, it was announced that the combination between the lines had been terminated, that in the future, steamers of both lines would sail on the same days, and that passage rates would resume a competitive character.[48] By March, however, another agreement had been entered, providing again for the staggered sailings and for increased rates. The contract was made for twelve months, and as a bonus to the Nicaragua Company the Pacific Mail agreed to divide the gross receipts for the first three months of the period. This arrangement would, of course, be greatly to the disadvantage of the Pacific Mail, since it carried the larger number of passengers and, having a longer route, was placed at greater expense to operate its steamers. No sooner had the Pacific Mail paid over the money under this agreement, than the Nicaragua line set about annulling the contract, cutting its rates below those agreed upon and claiming release upon grounds which seemed unjustifiable to the directors of the Pacific Mail.[49] In May and June, the lines continued to lower rates and allude to one another ill-temperedly in their newspaper advertisements. The mail lines had a new talking point with the opening of the Panama Railroad in January of 1855. Now passengers could be carried across the Isthmus in less than a day, which not only made a much easier journey than that across Nicaragua, but also increased the speed of service between New York and San Francisco by way of Panama. Facilities for landing and embarkation at Panama were not yet perfected, however, and the Nicaragua Line could urge passengers to take its route, avoiding the "deadly Panama fever" and two miles of dangerous boating in Panama Bay, to which the United States Mail and the Pacific Mail retorted that with the Panama Railroad from ocean to ocean there was no exposure to "deadly miasmas" and dangerous navigation in open river and lake boats.[50]

By June, 1855, there was more talk of agreement between the mail lines and the Nicaragua line, which even went as far as an offer from the Nicaragua Transit Company to the Pacific Mail to transport the passengers of the latter company across the Isthmus of Nicaragua for $15 each if the Pacific Mail would run its steamers between San Francisco and San Juan. Since the Panama Railroad placed its rate at $25 per passenger for the journey from Panama to Aspinwall, it was suggested in the press that the offer, amounting to a virtual amalgamation of the companies, be adopted.[51] Rates were still being cut at the first of July, but in September an agreement was reached which provided for the pooling and equal division of the gross receipts of the two concerns, retroactively from the first of July, 1854. This was of course a distinct victory for the Nicaragua line, since it had lighter expenses of operation and carried fewer passengers than did the steamers going by Panama.[52] The extent of this triumph was indicated by the report in November, 1855, that the amount due the Nicaragua Transit Company from the United States Mail and the Pacific Mail on account of their excess of freight and passengers was $101,949.62 for the period from July 1, 1854, to October 6, 1855, with an additional $12,313.70 due from the Pacific Mail alone.[53]

Changes were taking place within the Nicaragua Transit Company, however, and it was about to face difficulties in operation which were to halt its proceedings altogether. Almost from the beginning of its operation there had been sharp criticisms of the management of its steamers and transit facilities. In January, 1853, the *Alta* reported:

The steamer S.S. Lewis is said by most reliable authority to have arrived here in the most filthy condition; so much so indeed as to create nausea to those who visited her. She is in a very leaky condition, and has several feet of water in her hold. The lives and property of the public should not be trifled with by speculators in passengers to this country, and a proper investigation should be made in the case, as it is evident that the present condition of the ship, and such as it has been represented to have been during the voyage, is calculated to induce sickness and death, especially when human beings are packed together in dense masses, and coming from a notoriously unhealthy part.[54]

Far more serious was the series of marine disasters which the Nicaragua Transit Company suffered on the Pacific. Beginning with the *North America* in 1852 and continuing with the *Independence* and *S.S. Lewis* in close succession in 1853 and the *Yankee Blade* in 1854, at least 155 lives were lost, as well as large amounts of treasure and freight. The conditions under which the ships were wrecked aroused seemingly justified criticism of the conduct of the officers and crews and of the lack of measures taken by the owners properly to provide for the safety of the passengers. This was particularly striking since in the same period the Pacific Mail had had but two ships wrecked, and these without the loss of any lives, mail, or treasure. In the years from 1853 to 1855 also, the steamers operating to Nicaragua had suffered particularly heavily from the ravages of cholera aboard, whereas the mail steamers by way of Panama were comparatively free from epidemics at sea.[55] Travel by way of Nicaragua began to drop off, partly owing to the better facilities offered by the Panama route after the opening of the railroad and partly because of the increasingly unsettled political condition of Nicaragua. The record of the peak year for eastbound traffic via Nicaragua—the season of 1853, with 10,396 travelers— overtopped that of the Panama route for the same year by 164 persons; but in 1855 there were only 7,750 passengers who went east by Nicaragua, whereas 10,397 went by Panama. In 1856, 3,530 went east by Nicaragua, and 12,245 by Panama. The westbound figures told much the same story, except that the peak of westbound travel via Nicaragua was not reached until 1854 with 13,063, though Panama had 16,445 in the same year. In 1855, 11,237 went by Nicaragua, 15,412 by Panama; and in 1856 the Nicaragua figures dropped to 4,523, with those of Panama ascending to 18,090.[56]

In November, 1855, it was reported that the agreement so recently entered between the Panama and Nicaragua lines was again to cease. This time the end of the agreement was said to be the result of the refusal of the Pacific Mail to lend $100,000 to the Nicaragua Transit for meeting obligations due on December 1.[57]

Rumors filled the air in the early days of 1856 of possible arrangements between the two companies, and in the meantime they continued to cut rates below one another as of old. There was even a hint that the outcome would be the complete merger of the two lines.[58] It was becoming increasingly clear that important changes had taken place within the structure of the Nicaragua Transit Company. Vanderbilt had been able to gain control of a sufficient amount of stock to remove Charles Morgan from his position as agent for the line, and when Morgan pressed large claims against the company, Vanderbilt came forward with funds to meet them, assuming the agency for the concern in January, 1856.[59]

In Nicaragua, William Walker, the American filibuster who had been in the area since June of 1855 and had been virtual master of the country since November, allied himself with Morgan and Garrison, who had been ousted from the Nicaragua Transit Company by Vanderbilt. On February 18, 1856, at Walker's behest, President Rivas of Nicaragua annulled the charter of the Accessory Transit Company by virtue of which the Nicaragua Transit Company operated through the region.[60] The *Star of the West* of March 8, 1856, was the last vessel to sail from New York to Nicaragua for Vanderbilt, and on the Pacific the *Brother Jonathan* was the final ship. Passengers who had booked from New York on the *Northern Light* for March 24 were informed on the eighteenth that operations had been suspended and that their passage money would be refunded.[61]

It was rumored that the Nicaragua Transit Company would place its steamers on the Panama route, but this was denied. It was pointed out that, under existing agreements with the Pacific Mail, that company paid the Nicaragua Transit Company a monthly subsidy of $40,000 whether it operated steamers or not; thus it could lay up its ships and still receive an annual sum equal to 6 per cent of its capital stock at $30 per share, which was the price at which the stock was issued to Vanderbilt in January, 1853, when he sold his steamers to the company.[62]

With the end of competition, steerage rates on the mail lines went up from $100 to $125, and second cabin from $175 to $200, but first cabin remained at $250, the price when the Vanderbilt steamers were running.[63]

Morgan and Garrison had not aided Walker and procured the

termination of the charter of the Accessory Transit Company merely for the pleasure of having a thrust at Vanderbilt. They had definite plans to resume the Nicaragua service, and now that the old charter was annulled, they arranged to have a new one issued to themselves. Morgan and Garrison obtained the services of the *Orizaba,* and later the *Cahawba, Texas,* and *Tennessee,* on the Atlantic. The *Sierra Nevada* was used in the Pacific and was joined there by the *Orizaba,* sent around in the summer of 1856. Thus they carried on the Nicaragua route from early April, 1856, until the last of March, 1857.[64] By June, 1856, rates via Nicaragua had been reduced to $175 in the first cabin, $125 in second cabin, and $90 steerage.[65] As the year went on, fares declined still further. In November the Nicaragua steamers were carrying first-class passengers for $125 and $150, second-cabin for $120, and steerage for $50, while the mail lines were meeting the steerage fare, but charging $125 for second cabin and $250 for first cabin.[66] Since the mail lines were paying $25 of the $50 steerage fare to the Panama Railroad for the isthmian transit, it left little return for the sea voyage on both oceans. Morgan and Garrison had elaborate plans in mind for the improvement of their steamers and went so far as to order a new vessel from the yard of Jacob Westervelt, but other events interposed to close the line.[67] While Morgan and Garrison were backing Walker, Vanderbilt was lending his support to the Costa Rican invasion of Nicaragua, which aimed at the end of Walker's authority. Another element entered the picture of New York shipping men interesting themselves in the affairs of a Spanish-American republic when George Law, of United States Mail fame, sent a consignment of four hundred rifles with bayonets to Charles Frederick Henningsen, a lieutenant of Walker's, in the late fall of 1856. The rifles had been in Law's hands since Louis Kossuth's visit to New York in 1851, when he had purchased them from the United States government presumably for revolutionary purposes in Europe. They had been the cause of occasional newspaper comment in New York, as possible uses for them arose. Now it was rumored that Law might have it in mind to override Walker with Henningsen and obtain a new Nicaragua contract for himself.[68] The extent of Law's interest in Nicaragua is not clear, but some indication was given in May, 1857, when, in reporting the winning of a lawsuit which would give Law $10,000, the *Herald* remarked that "he will need all that and more too to square up his accounts in the Nicaragua speculation."[69] In any event, Vanderbilt's choice of the Costa Ricans proved to be a shrewd one. In the spring of 1857 they were victorious over the forces of Walker, who capitulated and departed from Nicaragua on May 1, 1857. Even before this the operation of the transit route had become impossible, and the steamers of Morgan and Garrison were withdrawn in March, 1857.[70] Seven years were to elapse before another really effective service could be placed in operation by way of the Isthmus of Nicaragua, and the mail lines were left temporarily in virtual command of the route to California.

If competition was ended for the moment, there was no cessation of planning and discussion concerning the possibility of providing some. Since the beginnings of the route the idea of steamers owned and controlled in California, which might place the convenience and service of the people of the state ahead of dividends, had been discussed. Now in April and May, 1857, came the announcement of the formation of the California and New York Steamship Company, which would be "a people's line" charging rates of only $150 for first cabin, and $50 for second cabin for the through voyage, and constructing two enormous steamers—475 feet long and of 7,000 tons, driven by two sets of paddle wheels—to carry out the service. Meetings were held in San Francisco at which officers and directors for the company were elected, and some $250,000 or $300,000 of the $1,000,000 stock taken by individuals.[71] The president of the company was Marshall O. Roberts, who was still interested in the United States Mail Steamship Company, the line with which the "People's Line" proposed to compete on the Atlantic, and among the members of the board of directors was Leland Stanford.[72] It was evidently to this organization that the Sacramento correspondent of the *San Francisco Bulletin* referred when, in March, 1858, he questioned the wisdom of the Senate Commerce and Navigation Committee in urging California's congressmen to block the renewal of the Pacific Mail's contract in 1858 in favor of the "California Steamship Company." He went on to say that, though this company had existed on paper for a year and a half, it had done nothing. Since its officers were lawyers and politicians, his guess was that it was mainly a scheme to make it possible for San Francisco interests to borrow money in New York on the faith of the company by first obtaining the endorsement of the California legislature for it.[73] The rates by the mail lines had gone up to $300 first cabin, $250 second, and $150 steerage by the summer of 1857, and strong feeling against them was being aroused in California. It was pointed out that the emigration of laborers and mechanics to California was being much reduced by the cost of transportation, and that numbers of desirable citizens were going from Atlantic states into the Middle West rather than coming to the Pacific coast, merely because of the high cost of getting to California.[74]

In September, 1857, the joyful news was announced in San Francisco that Morgan and Garrison had made arrangements with the government of Costa Rica for the reopening of the Nicaragua route in the near future.[75] December saw orders received by the San Francisco agents of the Nicaragua Steamship Company to get the *Sierra Nevada* and *Orizaba* ready for service in January, 1858, but January passed and no steamers sailed.[76] The condition of Nicaragua was still uncertain, and the ships were to go by way of Panama.

Still another organization was announced in New York late in 1857, and in San Francisco at the beginning of 1858. This was to be called the Atlantic and Pacific Ship Canal Company and, having no connection with the old Nicaragua company, it proposed to ignore Morgan and Garrison's new arrangements with Nicaragua and Costa Rica and to build a railroad across Nicaragua. At the head of the company was H. S. Stebbins, the directors being H. H. Wolf, R. Varick, I. P. Yelverton, and David White. The company ambitiously proposed to begin service in February, 1858, but it was not until November of that year that the old *Washington*, a transatlantic liner built a decade before, sailed from New York with passengers for San Juan. Her sister ship, the *Hermann,* which had been sent to the Pacific to carry out that part of the route, became entangled in legal difficulties at Panama and was sent directly to San Francisco, leaving four hundred passengers presumably waiting at San Juan del Sur. Actually, the *Washington,* on the two voyages which she did make, continued to Panama and sent her passengers forward by mail steamers on the Pacific. By the end of 1858, the American Atlantic and Pacific Ship Canal Company had ceased to operate.[77]

Even though Morgan and Garrison had not sent their ships in January, 1858, as originally announced, the plan did not seem dead. In February, sailings for the next month were posted, with the *Orizaba* on the Pacific and the *Northern Light* on the Atlantic. Since Vanderbilt owned the latter ship and Morgan and Garrison held the former, this looked much as though the old rivals had come to terms and were pledged to operate together.[78] The *San Francisco Bulletin* wrote happily:

> We congratulate the public that we again have an opposition line of steamers ... While there is a powerful opposition, there will not be the slightest doubt but that the safety and comfort of the travelling community will be amply cared for, and the rates of passage kept within the reach of all.[79]

On March 5, the *Orizaba* took her sailing from San Francisco for Panama, while from the other end of the line the *Northern Light* sailed from New York on the tenth. The *Sierra Nevada* was to sail on April 5 from San Francisco, but on the last day of March the following announcement appeared on the newspapers:

> *To the Public.*—The public are respectfully informed that, by orders received by the steamer "John L. Stephens," the "Sierra Nevada" is withdrawn, and will Not sail for Panama on 5th April. Parties holding Tickets will have their Money Refunded by application to the undersigned; or their Tickets will be good for the "John L. Stephens," without additional expense.
>
> C. K. Garrison & Co., Agents.[80]

The press of San Francisco was furious. The whole matter of an opposition by Morgan, Garrison, and Vanderbilt was denounced as a ruse on their part, in collusion with the mail companies, to discourage subscriptions to the stock of the Atlantic and Pacific Ship Canal Company and to head off anyone who might have it in mind to run opposition steamers by way of Panama. Vanderbilt's monthly bonus from the mail lines was increased at this time from $40,000 to $56,000 as long as there was no opposition by way of Nicaragua or any other route. Therefore this move on his part had all the characteristics of being merely a clever way of extracting more money from the mail lines and keeping others out of the field.[81] Another explanation for the action was that, by announcing an opposition line and lowering the rates, immigration might be stimulated, and that once immigrants had made their plans to come to California, they would pay monopoly fares rather than retrace their steps. The *Bulletin* said:

There is nothing that has occurred in a long time, which has cast such a gloom and created so much disappointment among citizens, as the announcement of the discontinuance of the Opposition Line of Steamers to the East. Many and deep are the anathemas hurled at the Mail Company for their monopoly on the route, and bitter the curses at the treachery and base avarice of Vanderbilt and Garrison, in colluding to break down a healthy competition, and in the deception practised by them upon the public.[82]

The matter went beyond newspaper editorials. On April 1 an indignation meeting was held in Portsmouth Plaza, San Francisco, attended by some fifteen hundred persons, chiefly miners who had come to San Francisco to go east by the *Sierra Nevada*. Rather than go by the Pacific Mail steamer, they voted to charter a vessel or to proceed to San Pedro in the coastwise steamer *Senator* and go thence overland to Texas. A number of them did sail on the *Senator* on April 3, and even though many may have eventually gone by the Pacific Mail Steamer, the temper of the hour was shown by the meeting.[83]

Almost as soon as the sailing of the *Sierra Nevada* was canceled, the suggestion was made that the state of California might have to back a competing company if private capital could not be found to do it. On April 14, a bill was introduced into the state Senate which would direct the governor, the comptroller, and the treasurer of the state to issue bonds of the state to the amount of $500,000 at 7 per cent interest. These bonds were to be redeemable after twenty years for a loan to be given to any corporation on condition that it give security for the redemption of the bonds and agree to place first-class steamers on the run between San Francisco and New York. These steamers would make monthly trips, carrying one thousand passengers at rates not to exceed $150 for first cabin and $75 for second cabin. The contractors would pay the interest on the bonds, and the governor, the treasurer, and the comptroller would appoint an agent for the state to see that the requirements were complied with. The proposal never materialized into the steamship line envisaged.[84]

In 1858 another route, across the Isthmus of Tehuantepec, came to brief maturity. Although the distance from ocean to ocean at Tehuantepec was three times that at Panama this route was the closest of the isthmian transits to ports in the United States. Also, it offered a low and comparatively easy crossing. It had been a significant route of trade in colonial times, and as early as 1842 steps were taken to open an improved road from the mouth of the Coatzacoalcos River on the Gulf of Mexico to Ventosa (later Salina Cruz) on the Pacific. In 1853, the ubiquitous Albert G. Sloo obtained from the Mexican government a concession to open a road across the Isthmus. The Tehuantepec Company, organized in Louisiana, proposed to construct a railroad from ocean to ocean, but Sloo's financial resources failed, and he transferred the grant to Peter A. Hargous in 1855.[85]

In the meantime, the Gadsden Treaty of 1853 between Mexico and the United States had officially opened the Isthmus to the use of citizens of the United States and permitted the sending of mails by that route.[86] Two years later, the Post Office Department established a mail route between New Orleans and San Francisco by way of Tehuantepec, but no bids were received that year, and when the route was advertised again in 1857, the only offer tendered was unsatisfactory.[87]

In 1858, Postmaster General Aaron V. Brown took active steps to enlist interest in Tehuantepec. He pointed out to members of Congress its strategic significance, since in time of war it would be much more feasible to protect a route using only the Gulf of Mexico than those routes which involved the Caribbean as well.[88] By May, 1858, the Post Office had received several bids for the service, and Brown determined to accept that of the Louisiana Tehuantepec Company. The first contract was made to run for one year only, terminating on September 31, 1859, when the Panama contracts also ran out. Thus the Post Office would be free to keep both routes, or to dispense with one.[89] Signed in June, 1858, the contract with the Louisiana Tehuantepec Company called for semimonthly service from New Orleans to San Francisco, for which the payment would be $250,000 annually. The new line placed its own steamers on the run from New Orleans to the mouth of the Coatzacoalcos, and arranged with the Pacific Mail to call at Ventosa to pick up its mail and passengers for San Francisco. The results of this experiment were very disappointing, both in the character of the mail service performed and in the income of the company from passengers, and the route was abandoned in 1859.[90]

July, 1858, saw the organization of yet another company to oppose the "monopoly." This was known as the People's California Steamship Company and was backed chiefly by William T. Coleman and Darius Ogden Mills. The company, which had a capital stock of $1,500,000, proposed to build eight screw steamers to carry on a fortnightly service between San Francisco and New York by way of Panama. With a prospectus issued and plans made, the People's California Steamship Company went no further toward placing steamers on the Panama route.[91]

The year 1858 continued to its end with nothing more than rumors of new lines, if the feeble effort of the *Washington* be excepted. From June on, Vanderbilt's name was often mentioned in connection with the opening of a competing line through Nicaragua or with the sale of all his ships, which were being held in port, to the Pacific Mail.[92] In October it was reported that the *Adriatic, Atlantic,* and *Baltic* of the Collins Line, now that they had been withdrawn from the Liverpool service, would be placed on a line by way of Nicaragua or Panama, but nothing of the sort materialized before the close of the year.[93]

The year 1859 saw boisterous action on the Panama route. With the expiration of the original mail contract and the withdrawal of the United States Mail Steamship Company from the isthmian trade, the whole scene was thrown into confusion. Both the Pacific Mail and Vanderbilt grasped for a new mail contract, and the "Commodore" was finally successful. In order to fill the gap left in the Atlantic service by the retirement of the United States Mail, the Panama Railroad joined forces with the Pacific Mail to place on the New York–Aspinwall route steamers which in size and speed outclassed anything Vanderbilt could offer in competition. The intense rivalry which followed was one of the most exciting periods in the history of the Panama route, but it was immensely expensive owing to high operating costs and reduced income resulting from slashed rates. Early in 1860 a truce was finally called, and the Pacific Mail capitulated, agreeing to confine its activities to the Pacific, with Vanderbilt running the Atlantic portion of the route. The negotiation of a close operating agreement and the acquisition by Vanderbilt of a large interest in the Pacific Mail closed the years of competition with what appeared to be a monopoly on the Panama service.

If 1858 had been a year of disappointments for those who looked upon keen rivalry between the Panama steamship lines as desirable, the year that followed went a long way toward making up for it. Before the end of January, 1859, the San Francisco newspapers had announced a line of steamers between New York and San Francisco by way of Panama, a line composed of the *Northern Light,* the *North Star,* and the *Ariel* on the Atlantic, and the *Cortes, Orizaba, Sierra Nevada,* and *Uncle Sam* on the Pacific. This meant that Vanderbilt was really entering the field once more, having come to final agreements with Morgan and Garrison, the latter becoming San Francisco agent for the steamers. It was reported that Vanderbilt was not satisfied with the monthly payment of $56,000 which the Pacific Mail had been making since 1858, and that he had demanded $100,000 a month, which the Pacific Mail had refused to pay. Others said that the mail lines had attempted to evade payment of the subsidy to Vanderbilt, thereby provoking his anger, but all agreed that competition of the hottest character could be expected.[94] Rates for the opposition steamers were set at $250 first cabin, $175 to $200 second cabin, and $85 steerage.[95] The new service went into effect with the sailing of the *Northern Light* from New York on March 10, 1859, and of the *Orizaba* from San Francisco on the fifth of the same month, continuing with fortnightly sailings from each end of the line. In the spring there was some talk of arrangements being made between Vanderbilt and the mail lines, but no tangible results were achieved.[96]

The subject of more pressing interest to all concerned with the Panama route was the award of the mail contract for service after October 1, 1859. Although the original contracts had been for the term of ten years and had therefore expired September 30, 1858, the Postmaster General and the Secretary of the Navy had signed an agreement on June 16, 1858, by which the mail service was to be extended for another year, ending September 30, 1859.[97] Since the Postmaster General believed that the contracts with the United States Mail Steamship Company and the Pacific Mail Steamship Company gave exorbitant compensation, he determined to invite bids for the nine months' service from October 1, 1859, until July 1, 1860, thereby giving Congress an opportunity to place the service on the basis which it felt wisest before making any long-term contract.[98] As early as February, 1859, it was reported that the president and vice-president of the Pacific Mail were in Washington "looking after" the mail contract.[99]

Both Vanderbilt and the Pacific Mail bid on the contract, but it was awarded to one Daniel H. Johnson, who was described as a "galvanized runner" and totally unable to carry it out upon his own resources. Because of this report it was generally believed that Johnson was merely a representative of other persons, and he was referred to in the press as the "broker" of Joseph L. White and Company. Under the contract, signed on May 30, 1859, Johnson agreed to transport the mail twice a month between New York and New Orleans and San Francisco by way of Nicaragua at $216,000 a year or, specifically, $162,000 for the nine-month period which the contract was to run. Since the previous contracts by way of Panama had cost $741,187 per year, this constituted a marked saving.[100] With a good deal of doubt of Johnson's ability to fulfill his contract, and with the rumor afloat that he might be willing to sell it at a modest profit, speculation ran riot concerning the form which the mail service to California would assume after the end of September. Johnson himself stoutly affirmed that he was solidly backed and that he would charter ships to carry through the contract.[101] A settlement between Vanderbilt and the Pacific Mail was proposed, by which the latter would take over Vanderbilt's ships on the Pacific, while the Atlantic side would be operated by a combination of which Vanderbilt, Aspinwall, Moses Taylor, Daniel Drew, and the Panama Railroad would be leaders.[102] Another guess was that a new company—in which Aspinwall, Taylor, Drew, and perhaps Vanderbilt would be interested—might purchase all Vanderbilt's ships for some $2,600,000 and operate them.[103] As late as June 21, 1859, there were still predictions that an agreement would be reached between Vanderbilt and the Pacific Mail, but the day of its consummation was not expected immediately.[104]

July brought a solution of the puzzle, at least for the time being. It was clear that the United States Mail Steamship Company—of which it had been said that it was in the hands of a "number of heartless banking speculators, knowing little about maritime affairs, and less anxious about the multitudes who entrust their lives to their keeping, than of the semi-annual dividends"—would not remain in the New York–Aspinwall business after the termina-

tion of the contract.[105] Therefore if the Pacific Mail expected to
maintain itself, it would have to come to terms with Vanderbilt,
thus obtaining transportation for its passengers on the Atlantic,
place steamers under its own house flag in service from New
York to Aspinwall, or make arrangements with a new concern to
carry out the line for it. The way out which it chose was a combination of the last two policies. The Collins Line had suspended service
between New York and Liverpool in 1858, and its three splendid
steamers *Adriatic, Atlantic,* and *Baltic* had lain in New York since
that time, although, as has been mentioned, there had been talk of
placing them on the Panama or Nicaragua service in the fall of
1858. Now, on July 9, 1859, the three steamers were purchased
from Brown Brothers and Company, New York bankers who had
been deeply interested in the Collins Line, by the Pacific Mail
Steamship Company and the Panama Railroad acting jointly.
Some doubted the wisdom of this move for the Panama Railroad
since it already had an excellent business and paid good dividends,
whereas the Collins steamers, although well-built and fast, were
more expensive to run than Vanderbilt's ships.[106] For the operation
of the new steamers the North Atlantic Steamship Company was
formed, in which the Panama Railroad was a stockholder to the
extent of $500,000, represented by the steamers *Atlantic* and
Baltic, and the Pacific Mail was a stockholder for $400,000, repre-
sented by the *Adriatic.* Directors in the company were Aspinwall,
W. Whitewright, Jr., Charles H. Russell, Henry Chauncey, J. T.
Soutter, Edward Bartlett, and J. W. Raymond. Since payment
for the three ships had been half in Pacific Mail stock, which had
been bought below par, the actual cost of the ships was said to be
not far from $780,000. The *Atlantic* and *Baltic* were prepared for
service from New York to Aspinwall, and the *Adriatic* was held in
reserve to be sent to the Pacific if Vanderbilt's competition there
made it necessary.[107] The ships were scheduled to begin transportation of the mails in October, 1859, in order to leave no break in
the mail service after the withdrawal of the United States Mail
Steamship Company.

    To give his line a corporate organization, Vanderbilt organized
the Atlantic and Pacific Steamship Company, chartered by the
New York legislature in April, 1859, which took final form on
October 3 just before service began. The list of its backers showed

that most of the old United States Mail organization had gone over to Vanderbilt. The names of Marshall O. Roberts and Moses Taylor appeared on the list of directors with those of Vanderbilt and Charles Morgan, while the secretary and New York agent was Vanderbilt's son-in-law, Daniel B. Allen.[108]

The nature of the new "mail line" remained a mystery almost to the time at which operations were to commence. A month before it was to send out its first ship, it was variously styled—in the same newspaper and on the same day—the "Merchants and Miners Line to California" and the "Nicaragua Mail Line." It was announced that the *Keystone State* had been chartered for the Atlantic side of the service, and that the old *Hermann,* which had made her way around to San Francisco, would take the passengers and mail north from Nicaragua.[109] On October 4 it was stated that the Pacific Mail had chartered to Johnson their steamer *St. Louis* for the Atlantic service, and that the run from San Juan del Sur to San Francisco would be made by the *Pacific,* which belonged to Vanderbilt. The Pacific Mail, it was reported, had chartered the *California* to Johnson to be at San Juan to take the passengers and mail if the *Pacific* did not arrive. Then, at the last moment, the Pacific Mail withdrew the *St. Louis* from her berth for Central America, stating that the amount required for her charter had not been paid.[110] Up to the last, the matter of the contract was in doubt. Postmaster General Holt and Assistant Postmaster General King had come to New York on October 4 to confer on the subject, but could reach no decision. It was generally understood that Vanderbilt would receive a provisional contract if Johnson were deemed unready to carry out his, but the Pacific Mail claimed that it had obtained this for itself already. Finally, about noon on the fifth of October, the sailing day, Johnson notified the Postmaster General that he would be unable to carry out his contract, and the provisional contract was given to Vanderbilt. The Post Office was doubtful about Johnson's arrangements for carrying the mail across Nicaragua, and the news that filibusters had just departed for Nicaragua made it timid about sending the mails by that route. Furthermore, it was found that the *St. Louis* had no coal or supplies aboard, and it looked very much as though she had never been intended to sail. The provisional contract which Vanderbilt had ready when Johnson withdrew provided that Vanderbilt carry a semimonthly mail from New York and New Orleans to San Francisco by way of Panama for the nine months' period at a yearly rate of $37,500 for the New York service and $150,000 for the New Orleans service. This did not include the isthmian transit, which was in the hands of the Panama Railroad at $100,000 a year, but it was provided that, if the line could be transferred to Nicaragua, Vanderbilt would receive $37,500 more for carrying the mail across the Isthmus.[111]

Thus the Vanderbilt steamers became the "mail steamers," and the ships which had carried the mails for more than a decade passed into the position of "opposition." The *San Francisco Alta California* took occasion to remark on the departure of the *John L. Stephens* from San Francisco on September 20, 1859, with the last mail to be carried under the old contract:

The Pacific Mail Steamship Company is deserving of all praise for the prompt and safe manner in which the mails have been transported during the past ten years. Since the going into effect of the original contract, they have not lost a single mail.... The prompt and efficient manner in which the service has been performed by the Mail Company, is certainly deserving of high commendation ...[112]

An era in the history of the Panama route was closed when this contract expired. In the character of their ships and service, as well as in the qualities of their leaders and their financial histories, the Pacific Mail and the United States Mail present frequent contrasts. A comparison of their careers during this decade and more of service is therefore of interest.

The United States Mail Steamship Company had not achieved the degree of public favor of the Pacific Mail, and there were few regrets at its passing in 1859. Throughout the career of the company its directors were more interested in bringing in immediate financial returns than in building a lasting reputation for good service. It had been notoriously slow in completing the steamers required under the mail contract, and only in February, 1854, was the *George Law,* last of the five ships required, accepted by the Navy Department, though they should all have been in service five years earlier.[113] Later in the same year, the *Illinois* being expensive to run, the company asked that the *North Star* be accepted for service in her place. Upon examination, however, it was reported that she did not come up to the requirements of the act of March

3, 1847, and therefore could not be accepted.[114] The next year, the Secretary of the Navy felt it necessary to write sharply to Marshall O. Roberts, president of the United States Mail, pointing out that, although the company might be allowed to withdraw for necessary repairs vessels accepted for the mail service, it would certainly conflict with the law to withdraw such vessels permanently and substitute others which had not been accepted. Yet the *Ohio, Georgia,* and *Illinois* had all been out of service since the first half of 1854, and there appeared to be no intention to repair them or return them to the line. He therefore required that the ships built for the service be placed on it.[115] In spite of this demand, the *Georgia* was not returned to the line, and the *Ohio* served only briefly, though the *Illinois* did go back into service until 1859. Aside from the vessels which had been acquired and placed on the line up to the end of 1851, the following ships were used in the United States Mail Steamship Company's service between New York and the Isthmus: *George Law, North Star, Ariel, Star of the West, St. Louis, Northern Light, Granada,* and *Moses Taylor.* Of these, only the *George Law* was actually built for the company, the others being purchased or chartered to carry out the service. After the summer of 1852, the United States Mail Steamship Company rearranged its services, sending the New York–Aspinwall ship directly through by way of the Windward Passage, and making of the New York–New Orleans and the New Orleans–Aspinwall lines separate services. This of course had the effect of a marked acceleration of the through California line.

In the eleven years of operation of the United States Mail it suffered only one serious disaster, that of the loss of the *Central America,* formerly the *George Law,* in a hurricane on September 12, 1857. Some 423 lives were lost, and the company was severely blamed by the general public, though this censure seems to have been rather unjust. At that time, the *Alta* wrote as follows regarding the company:

The vast income of the Company, instead of being applied to the building of new and seaworthy steamers, is appropriated to bolstering up spavined and shaky banks, and inflated stock jobbing schemes, or furnishing Fifth Avenue palaces; and when at last some one of the old and overtaxed vessels becomes tabooed in public opinion, she is taken upon the ways, "examined," painted, re-christened, and palmed off upon deluded travellers as a new boat. But for the catastrophe of the Central America, doubtless, we should have had the present line of rattle traps introduced to us under fictitious names, after a course of tar and oakum, to give a semblance of repairs.[116]

Little information on the financial condition of the United States Mail was recorded in the contemporary press, but what there was did not indicate spectacular success. For the period from September, 1853, until May, 1857, when reports of sales of stock of the company were published, the prices paid ranged from $64 to $20, with the average a little over $35 per share. For stock whose par value was set at $100 this was not remarkably good.[117] Dividends were evidently paid, but their frequency and amount is uncertain. The one recorded was declared on June 24, 1853, being 10 per cent of the capital stock of the company for the year ending March 31, 1853.[118]

The most important change within the company took place in March, 1853, when George Law, who held 7,182 of the 15,000 shares of the company's stock, sold them to Marshall O. Roberts for $80,000, and divorced himself from the affairs of the company. Roberts, in turn, sold these shares to the United States Mail Steamship Company itself within less than a month.[119]

In marked contrast to the United States Mail, the Pacific Mail Steamship Company had given an excellent report of itself in the first decade of the Panama service. Its contracts with the government had generally been fulfilled in a most satisfactory manner. After the coming of the *Golden Gate* in November, 1851, the following ships were placed on the run between San Francisco and Panama: *John L. Stephens, Winfield Scott, Sonora,* and *Golden Age*. Two other steamers, the *San Francisco* and *St. Louis,* were built for the service but were not placed on it before 1860, the *San Francisco* being lost at sea en route to California and the *St. Louis* remaining on the Atlantic, not coming to the San Francisco–Panama run until 1861. Of these, the *John L. Stephens* and *San Francisco* were inspected by naval officers before leaving New York and were accepted for service under the contract, in spite of the fact that the six steamers required were already in service.[120] The *Golden Age, Sonora,* and *John L. Stephens* were splendid steamers, superior in size, accommodations, and speed to anything else on the Pacific coast, and together with the *Golden Gate,* which was older but the fastest of all, they carried on excellent service, having

records for the voyage between Panama and San Francisco ranging from eleven days, four and a half hours for the *Golden Gate* to
eleven days, twenty-one hours for the *Sonora*.[121] In addition to
these vessels, the large number of older or smaller steamers with
which the line had been opened or which had been purchased to
quell competition made it possible to hold at least one vessel in
reserve at each end of the line, thus obviating the chance of
detention in the event of breakdown.

In the period of great demand for passage, the semimonthly
sailings instituted in the summer of 1850 were found to be insufficient. Therefore, in 1851, slow steamers like the *Sarah Sands* were
placed in operation on their own schedules, giving an extra sailing
at reduced prices every two or three months. By the end of the
summer of 1851 there was a regular policy of sending four, and
even five, ships a month from San Francisco to Panama. Under
this schedule the steamers sailing on the first and fifteenth were
the larger and faster ships, which had been accepted for mail
service; the other ships made slower time and met the rates of
opposition lines. The decline of trade led to the abandonment of
this policy at the end of 1852, after which only the two mail
steamers sailed monthly. Again in April, May, and June, 1853, the
Pacific Mail sent its ships from San Francisco to Panama at weekly
intervals, but the innovation was not popular in San Francisco,
breaking up the old business habit of "steamer day." It was therefore abandoned in favor of the semimonthly sailings. A simpli-
fication of the mail service was allowed in 1854, when the San
Francisco–Panama steamers were given permission to omit the
calls at Monterey and San Diego which had been required by the
contract, on condition that mail service for the coast of California
south of San Francisco be arranged by local coastwise vessels.[122]
Shortly after the opening of the Panama Railroad, the old steamers
Panama and *Oregon* were placed on a freight service along the
coast from San Francisco to Panama. After sailings in January
and February, 1856, the service was abandoned.[123]

In its business affairs the Pacific Mail was comparatively pros-
perous. The charter of the company was amended on April 5,
1853, to allow an increase in the capital stock from $2,000,000 to
$4,000,000, and an act of the New York legislature of February
14, 1856, provided for reducing the shares of the company from a

par value of $1,000 to $100 each, at the same time increasing the number of directors to nine.[124]

The terms of organization of the Pacific Mail have already been outlined. By these the stockholders agreed to pay Aspinwall a 2½ per cent commission on all receipts of the company, in consideration of his services in originating the company and transferring the mail contract to it. The report of a committee appointed to investigate the affairs of the company in 1854 stated that the amount of his commission, actual and estimated, from May 1, 1853, to October 1, 1854, was $84,328.85, of which $35,000 remained undrawn because of the financial state of the company. Also, he had never claimed this commission on anything besides passage money and mail pay, while his services as president had been without salary and he had charged no interest on his advances to the company.

The house of Howland and Aspinwall had been selected at the time of organization to transact the commercial business of the company, with its commissions restricted to 2½ per cent on amounts advanced or disbursed, and 1½ per cent on insurance arranged. From May 1, 1853, until October 1, 1854, it had been paid $64,322.20 in general commissions and $15,000 additional commissions for collecting marine losses. The advances of the house had sometimes been as much as $1,100,000 and never under $465,000; on October 1, 1854, they amounted to $671,000.[125] The close connection between the Pacific Mail and Howland and Aspinwall came to an end at the beginning of 1856, the commercial agency being resigned on January 1 of that year. At the meeting of the board of directors of the Pacific Mail on March 3, 1856, Aspinwall tendered his resignation of the presidency of the company, stating that he would have resigned earlier had it not been for the financial difficulties of that period. That a more prosperous era had arrived was evinced by the fact that, since the first of the year, the balance due to Howland and Aspinwall had been paid off, all disbursements had been made in cash, and the company had a balance of $200,000 in the Life and Trust Company besides a $95,000 current-expense fund in the Bank of America. In place of Aspinwall, William H. Davidge was elected to the presidency, Aspinwall remaining on the board of directors.[126]

The financial difficulties which Aspinwall mentioned were those arising out of the period of competition of 1852 and 1853, culminating with the buying out of Davis, Brooks and Company in 1853, a step which had entailed heavy expenditure and had saddled the company with more steamers than it needed. At that time dividends had been suspended until 1856, and the report of October, 1854, indicated a deficit of $428,094, or about 11½ per cent on the capital of the company.[127]

On May 1, 1857, the company was able to report a surplus of $1,128,422.51, which in the next year was reduced to only $423,246, but rose for 1859 to $3,302,902.46.[128] Again, in the year 1859–1860, which saw the bitter competition with Vanderbilt and the Pacific Mail's backing of the expensive North Atlantic Steamship Company, the surplus was reduced to $911,188.[129]

The stock of the Pacific Mail, first reported in the financial list of the *New York Herald* in February, 1853, underwent violent changes in the course of the next seven years. Standing at 110½ on February 4, 1853, it had fallen to 80 by September of that year, after the purchase of the Davis-Brooks ships. It continued to drop, however, selling in August, 1855, for 33. Rising past 70 with the resumption of dividends in 1856, it continued to fluctuate through the 'sixties and 'seventies until the late spring and early summer of 1858, when it began to rise, passing 100 in October. The "Financial and Commercial" column of the *New York Herald* commented in June, 1858:

The stock of the Pacific Mail Steamship Company flies about strangely. It is one of the most sensitive securities on the market. The slightest breath of a favorable or unfavorable character will inflate or depress prices two or three per cent in as many hours.[130]

The stock did not remain firm during the rest of 1858 or in 1859, going as low as 71 and as high as 106¾.[131] In September the *Herald* remarked:

It is the opinion of many that the speculative mania of the old Wall Street operators—who now dread western railways as a plague—will find employment in bulling Panama and Pacific Mail, which have the combined merits of intrinsic worth and comparative freshness as speculative stocks.[132]

The dividends paid by the Pacific Mail did not long remain at the 50-per cent peak of 1850. At the beginning of 1853 the company was paying semiannual dividends of 10 per cent, which were, of course, suspended after the Davis-Brooks purchase of May of that year.[133] Beginning in May, 1856, however, 25 per cent was paid in the year 1856, 30 per cent in 1857, and 26 per cent in 1858, while the competition of 1859 reduced dividends to 10 per cent.[134] Between the May dividend of 1856 and that of August, 1858, some $2,500,000 was paid out by the company to its stockholders.[135] The Pacific Mail had truly been built on sounder foundations than had its sister company on the Atlantic, and the termination of the mail contract in 1859 saw it ready to support a through line from New York to San Francisco rather than close up its affairs and sell its ships at auction as did the United States Mail Steamship Company.

The contest between the North Atlantic Steamship Company and its parent, the Pacific Mail, and Vanderbilt's Atlantic and Pacific Steamship Company had started with a will on October 5, 1859, when the *Baltic* and the *Northern Light* left New York together for Aspinwall direct. Although the *Atlantic* and *Baltic* had seen nine and ten years' hard service in the transatlantic trade, they were still fast ships, and larger than anything Vanderbilt could oppose to them. Voyage in and voyage out, they beat Vanderbilt's ships by one to three days, carrying more passengers and cutting rates as low as the "Commodore" would. In the summer of 1859, Vanderbilt had reduced the through first-class passage from $150 to $125, and then to $100, while second cabin went to $75, and steerage to $50. But when the *Atlantic* and *Baltic* went into service, steerage went to $45, of which $25 of course went to the Panama Railroad.[136] The holders of the new mail contract were sensitive about their hard-won position of importance and resented it when the North Atlantic Steamship Company and the Pacific Mail continued to advertise as "the old mail line." The vexation of Vanderbilt's Atlantic and Pacific Steamship Company at this sort of thing was shown in the following advertisement, which appeared in the *New York Herald* on December 12, 1859:

Caution to the public.

Beware of ticket swindlers, bogus passage offices, and concerns falsely styling themselves "mail" companies. Unless you be on your guard you will be deceived and defrauded.

This is the only line carrying the United States mails on this route, under contract with the Government.[137]

Such competition was encouraging for travelers and must have been stimulating to the officers and crews of the ships, but it was an expensive matter for the owners. Vanderbilt confessed that he was losing a great deal of money, and though the Pacific Mail claimed to be making a profit, an examination of its books and the passing of its November dividend revealed that it was feeling the strain. The Pacific Mail was adjudged to be better able to hold out under the competition because of its large reserves and its association with the Panama Railroad, which was doing excellently with the increased traffic brought by the low rates on the steamers.[138]

Conversations between the rival lines began within a month of the opening of competition, and by late November, 1859, it seemed likely that an agreement would be reached. On the twenty-sixth Vanderbilt offered to buy out the Pacific Mail, paying it $2,000,000 cash for its seven ships; the company would then wind up its affairs, since it would be able to pay its stockholders $110 per share. A snag in the negotiations was struck when Vanderbilt required that the directors of the Pacific Mail give individual guarantees that there would be no renewal of competition. They were willing to give it for the company, but as that would be liquidated, Vanderbilt wished more assurance, and this Aspinwall in particular refused to give. On this point, the whole arrangement broke up on November 30, and competition continued as usual.[139] There were loud denunciations of Aspinwall and Davidge, who had managed the negotiations for the Pacific Mail, as stockjobbers. As rumors of the liquidation of that company went abroad, its stock rose from 71 on November 1 to 93½ on the twenty-sixth, while after negotiations were broken off, it declined to 79. It was said that an inner circle had bought and sold at the right times and had done handsomely for themselves on the transaction.[140]

The middle of February, 1860, saw fresh rumors of peace negotiations, and by the seventeenth of the month it was generally understood that these had been completed. The terms, as they were announced, provided for a division of the service, with Vanderbilt taking over complete control on the Atlantic and the Pacific Mail on the other coast, under an operating agreement which was to run for five years from February 17, 1860. Vanderbilt's ships on the Pacific, the *Cortes, Orizaba, Sierra Nevada,* and *Uncle Sam,* were purchased by the Pacific Mail. To pay for them, the capital stock of the latter company was increased to $4,000,000. Permission to do this had been received in 1853. Five thousand shares of this stock were transferred to Vanderbilt at par in payment for the steamers, in addition to which he received $250,000, paid from receipts of the Pacific Mail after February, 1860, in monthly installments of 10 per cent. For carrying on the mail service on the Pacific, Vanderbilt paid the Pacific Mail $173,800 out of his $250,000 annual contract, though this was not yet a binding contract beyond July 1, 1860, and was therefore not extended finally beyond that date. The gross revenues of the service were to be divided, 70 per cent going to the Pacific Mail, and 30 per cent to Vanderbilt for his service on the Atlantic. This arrangement made Vanderbilt an important stockholder in the Pacific Mail and therefore guaranteed that company some degree of freedom from competition.[141]

It was reported after the arrangement that a majority of the board of the Panama Railroad, which also held the balance of power in the Pacific Mail, was opposed to the coalition with Vanderbilt. Aspinwall, who favored the agreement, proposed to the objecting members a business trip to the Isthmus, and made it plain that he would accompany them. The men took the bait, and when Aspinwall's personal baggage was sent aboard the steamer, they were confident that nothing untoward would happen in their absence. At the last moment, Aspinwall said that unfortunately business would keep him in New York, and left the ship. Those opposed to the combination remained aboard, finding upon their return that arrangements had been completed for the coalition.[142]

With the completion of the peace, the effect on the service was not long in manifesting itself. The rates for the steamers of February 21, 1860, were raised to a paying level. From New York to San Francisco the fares were fixed at $200 first cabin, $150 second cabin, and $100 steerage, while in the opposite direction they were $25 higher.[143] The *Baltic* took her last sailing from New York on March 5, 1860, ending the period of nearly a decade during which the name of "Commodore" Vanderbilt was almost a synonym for competition on the isthmian route to California.

CHAPTER IV

THE CLOSING YEARS, 1860–1869

IN CONTRAST to the previous period, with its struggles for domination of isthmian communication, the last decade of the Panama route's primary importance was not characterized by outstanding competition among steamship companies. Rivalry was not absent certainly and from 1864 to 1868 it was bitter enough, but even then less violent than before. The agreement between Vanderbilt and the Pacific Mail lasted until 1865, when the latter arranged to take over the entire route from New York to San Francisco. Although this combination brought a temporary peace in the competition between the rival steamship lines, within the Pacific Mail itself there was a great fight for control of the company between groups whose personnel and aims were very divergent. The rivalry for the isthmian route between companies was replaced by a struggle for leadership in the pioneer concern. The history of the Panama lines—their operation complicated by problems incident to the Civil War and dogged by competition almost to the end—was, in these last years, chiefly the problem of rule within the Pacific Mail.

The joint service of Vanderbilt and the Pacific Mail Steamship Company, which went into effect in March, 1860, was carried out until November of 1865. During these years, the *Ariel, Champion, Costa Rica, New York, Northern Light, North Star,* and *Ocean Queen* kept up the line between New York and Aspinwall. Of these steamers, only the *Costa Rica* and *New York* were new vessels, built in this period. The Pacific Mail carried on between San Francisco and Panama with the *California, Cortes, Golden Age, Golden Gate, Hermann, John L. Stephens, Orizaba, Sonora, St. Louis, Uncle Sam,* and *Washington.* Four new steamers were added to the line—the *Colorado, Constitution, Golden City,* and *Sacramento* —enormous ships for the day, all but one being over 3,000 tons and more than 300 feet long. An employee of the company wrote of the last of these in 1863, "The 'Sacramento' is a perfect 'beauty'—a duck—*much* prettier model than either of the others & nautical men & engineers say, will be the swiftest ship in the world. . . ."[1] The splendid reputation already enjoyed by the Pacific Mail was

[1] For notes to chap. iv, see pp. 272–275.

perhaps even enhanced in these years. In 1862, the historian of the Panama Railroad wrote:

> The Pacific Mail Steam-ship Company has always been characterized by the great and judicious liberality of its management.
>
> No expense has been spared since the first formation of the Company to carry on their business with the greatest possible safety and despatch, both for the passengers and freight; and the comforts and general requirements of passengers have been so effectively secured by able and courteous officers that it may be truthfully referred to as one of the most universally popular steamship lines in the world.[2]

Charles Toll Bidwell, British consul at Panama, wrote that the Pacific Mail had the largest and probably the best-paying steamers in the world, and that finer ships and better accommodations for passengers would not often be met with.

> I have seen seven hundred or eight hundred, and even a thousand passengers on one of these ships comfortably "stowed away" and provided for a twelve days' voyage, with as little to-do as if they were merely to cross the Channel, while for newly-married ladies there are four-post bedsteads in cabins as large as ordinary bedrooms on shore.[3]

Vanderbilt's ships, on the other hand, maintained a reputation which was hardly enviable. They were described in the press of both coasts as "floating pig stys," not half manned and badly provisioned, and their owner was characterized as the "Nero of the sea."[4] The *Panama Star and Herald* in 1864 surmised that, in spite of certain improvements in the operation of his ships, nothing permanent in this direction would be achieved so long as Vanderbilt had anything to do with them.

> We sincerely trust that when the P.M.S.S. Company get their fine new steamers, now in course of construction for the Atlantic line, they will throw Vanderbilt forever overboard and let the public have at last safe and decent ships to travel on between New York and Aspinwall.[5]

In March, 1860, the peace terms went into effect. Vanderbilt's ships alone plied from New York to Aspinwall, and those of the Pacific Mail had the San Francisco–Panama run to themselves. Sailings were stepped up from two to three each month, steamers clearing both New York and San Francisco on approximately the first, eleventh, and twentieth. Vanderbilt's steamers during this period were managed by Daniel B. Allen, and in 1864 the Atlantic Mail Steamship Company was organized to operate them. Allen was president of this company, and among its directors was Cornelius K. Garrison, who had earlier been active in affairs relating to the isthmian routes to California.[6] Near the close of the same year it was reported that important changes were to be made in the operation of the steamers between New York and Aspinwall, that the sole management of the line on the Isthmus was to be given to D. M. Corwine, already agent for the Pacific Mail, and that the steamers were being refitted with particular attention paid to the steward's and culinary departments.[7] The next year, however, the Panama correspondent of the *New York Herald* remarked that, though the Vanderbilt line might alter its name to the Atlantic Mail Steamship Company and turn the "V" in the signal flag worn by the steamers upside down to resemble an "A," "they are the same ships, and the management is the same as when they bore the old name of Vanderbilt, and they still remain a libel upon American enterprise and liberality."[8]

At the same time, the Pacific Mail was going through rather an interesting period of development. In spite of the fact that serious competition had been removed, the financial condition of the company did not show signs of immediate prosperity. Dividends for 1860 amounted to 20 per cent, for 1861 and 1862 to 15 per cent, and in 1863 they were restored to 20 per cent, made in quarterly payments.[9] After the coalition with Vanderbilt in the spring of 1860, the stock of the company had risen to 105¾, but a year later it had gone as low at 64½, and showed little sign of stability, fluctuating violently with reports of changes in management, or threatened competition.[10] The disappearance of Frederick Hoffman, secretary of the company in May, 1860, immediately after being asked to turn over the stock ledger for the payment of dividends, and the subsequent discovery that the books of the company were in some disorder did not tend to have a stabilizing effect.[11] In October, 1860, the financial column of the *Herald* contained the following remarks:

It is earnestly hoped that an effort will be made by the stockholders in this company [the Pacific Mail] to choose at the coming election a board of directors which shall command the confidence of the public. It cannot be disguised that the suspicion of stock speculating attaches to several members of the present board, and that in consequence the stock does not command the position to which its merit really entitles it. Many brokers will not deal in it at any price; very few bankers will lend upon it.[12]

At the meeting referred to, the clique of Vanderbilt was defeated. Allan McLane, who opposed it, was elected president of the company, and the majority of the board was made up of his followers. Thus a more conservative group gained the ascendancy; McLane represented the Panama Railroad, the banking house of Brown Brothers spoke through Howard Potter, and Aspinwall, Comstock, Francis Skiddy, Charles A. Davis, Frederick H. Wolcott, and James T. Soutter, together with Vanderbilt's Daniel B. Allen, were elected to the board.[13]

The future looked bright for the Pacific Mail at the end of 1860. With growing political unrest in the eastern United States, emigration to California was on the increase, and the steamers were sailing full on every voyage. It was reported that the expenses of operation were entirely met by the receipts at San Francisco and that the income from the westbound traffic was clear profit. It was said that this amounted to as much as $60,000 per voyage, and, at three trips each month, to $2,160,000 a year in addition to mail pay and the Oregon service. There was talk of a 30-per cent dividend, but it has been seen that the dividends for that year amounted to only 20 per cent.[14]

The next spring the contract for the Oregon mail service was taken from the Pacific Mail in favor of land service, and the six steamers which had been on that run were sold to Flint and Holladay for $250,000, although they had been held on the books of the company at $561,512. In the last year, also, the *John L. Stephens* had been condemned, and her valuation marked down from $191,000 to $35,000. All this left the balance of the company for May 1, 1861, at $201,283.14, a comparatively low figure which was responsible for the fall of the stock to 64½ at that time.[15] By November the company's balance had gone up only to $230,431, but stock had reached 97¾ by this time and continued generally upward, passing 100 in February, 1862.[16] Pacific Mail stock rose rather consistently for the remainder of 1862, going as high as 130 in October; in the next year it passed 200 in July, remaining above that mark for the rest of the year.[17] In April, 1863, it was reported that the Pacific Mail had it in mind to institute a weekly service between Panama and San Francisco and that, if Vanderbilt were unable or unwilling to follow suit on the Atlantic, the contract between them would be abrogated, and the Pacific Mail would place its ships on both oceans.[18]

At the same time, it was said that Aspinwall, who was still a member of the board of directors of the Pacific Mail, had gone to London to aid in the establishment of a line of foreign steamers, presumably British, from England to Panama by way of New York. These would connect with others on the Pacific, for which the house of Howland and Aspinwall would have the agency.[19] Although this plan did not materialize, Aspinwall, the founder of the company, did resign from the board of directors in September, 1863, and his name was soon to be found in the list of its opponents.[20]

Already there were strong forces at work to bring about a change in the financial policy of the Pacific Mail, and these bore fruit in the year 1864. As early as 1859 it was clear that the house of Brown Brothers was interested in the stock of the Pacific Mail Steamship Company.[21] This banking firm's parent headquarters were in Baltimore, but it had large and virtually independent branches in New York and London. In 1864 a group of the important shareholders in the Pacific Mail, under the leadership of Brown Brothers, determined to buy and hold a large block of Pacific Mail stock with the purpose of establishing a shareholding body with permanent interests, not influenced by fluctuations of the market and by stock operators. Thus it was hoped that a farsighted financial policy for the company could be adopted. At the request of this group, Brown Brothers purchased ten thousand shares of Pacific Mail stock, one quarter of the capital stock of the company, and these shares were distributed in varying amounts among Francis Skiddy, Charles A. Davis, Allan McLane, Howard Potter, William Dennistoun, M. H. Grinnell, L. W. Jerome, and Elisha Riggs. This stock, in addition to what was already held by these shareholders and by Brown Brothers, gave them a controlling interest in the company. An agreement was entered October 11, 1864, by which Brown Brothers were given irrevocable power of attorney to vote this stock deposited with them until December 1, 1868.[22]

Since this group felt that the arrangement with Vanderbilt's steamers on the Atlantic was not to the advantage of the Pacific Mail, steps were taken in 1865 to sever the connection and to set up service from New York to Aspinwall in Pacific Mail ships. It was believed that the arrangement by which the Pacific Mail received 70 per cent of the through fares and freight money and Vanderbilt's Atlantic Mail Steamship Company received 30 per cent was detrimental to the former company, which suffered from the general unpopularity of the route caused by the inferior ships and poor service rendered on the Atlantic. It was not only that the Pacific Mail did not receive due advantage from its superior ships and service, but also that the unpopularity of the Atlantic line tended to stimulate opposition. An amendment to the charter was obtained by an act of the New York legislature of May 15, 1865, which increased the capital of the company from $4,000,000 to $10,000,000, giving it the wherewithal to treat with the Atlantic Mail Steamship Company.[23] Of this increase, $4,000,000 in new stock was issued to the existing stockholders in August, 1865, of which 25 per cent was declared as a dividend, payment for the other 75 per cent to be called for at the pleasure of the company.[24]

In the meantime, negotiations had been under way with the Atlantic Mail Steamship Company. In September, 1865, an agreement was reached by which the Vanderbilt company would sell its ships on the New York–Aspinwall line, together with its good will, and would withdraw from that field of operation. For this, the Pacific Mail turned over twenty thousand of the new shares of stock with a par value of $2,000,000; of these shares ten thousand were paid up, and the other ten thousand half paid. The Atlantic Mail was to remain in business, operating steamers from New York to New Orleans and from New Orleans to Aspinwall. It was agreed that the stock turned over should be held and voted by Brown Brothers until December 1, 1868. This was in order to ensure that the Atlantic Mail would not use the stock received to establish a competing line with the Pacific Mail or by winding up its business enable its principal stockholders so to compete.[25] The stock which the Brown Brothers pool had purchased at about $70 per share rose in price with increasing public confidence in the Pacific Mail and, with the paper-money inflation of the Civil War, remained above 275 on the market from the time of the formation of the pool until the issue of new stock, sometimes going as high as 317. It was reported that the pool realized not less than $12,000,000 on this increase in price. With the issue of the new stock in 1865 the price dropped to 165, but recovered rapidly and remained above 200 for the remainder of the year.[26]

The Pacific Mail now operated ships on the through line from New York to San Francisco by way of Panama, and, effective

The *Constitution*, Built for the Pacific Mail Steamship Company in 1860–1861

Steamer *Golden City* of the Pacific Mail Steamship Company, 1863

Steamer *Dakota* of the North American Steamship Company, 1865, at Victoria, B. C.

Steamer *Montana* of the Pacific Mail Steamship Company in
Hunter's Point Dry Dock, 1865

November 1, 1865, its steamers went on the New York–Aspinwall run. To begin the service, the *Atlantic* and *Baltic* of North Atlantic Steamship Company fame were placed on the route with the new Pacific Mail Steamer *Henry Chauncey,* while the former Vanderbilt ships *Champion, Costa Rica, New York,* and *Ocean Queen* were also employed. Before 1869, however, the Pacific Mail had placed three new steamers, the *Alaska, Arizona,* and *Rising Star,* on the line. Satisfaction was expressed at the improved ships and service which the Pacific Mail gave on the Atlantic, and a lowering of the rate from New York to Aspinwall was also popular.[27]

These years were characterized by great expansion of the Pacific Mail, for it was realized that the completion of the transcontinental railroad would greatly curtail the traffic by way of Panama. It was therefore determined to open a steamship service to Japan and China. A mail contract for this line was obtained in 1865, and the construction of steamers was begun in order to have them ready to enter the service when it opened on January 1, 1867. In 1866, a line from Aspinwall to New Orleans by way of Havana was opened, and there were even persistent rumors that the Pacific Mail intended to inaugurate a transatlantic service from New York to Southampton and Le Havre.[28] Beginning in April, 1868, the frequency of sailings on the Panama line was increased from ten-day to weekly intervals, although this schedule was discontinued at the end of January, 1869, and sailings were again trimonthly.[29]

Passenger travel, particularly westbound, was large, while after the Civil War an increasing amount of freight was sent by way of the Panama route, the amount coming from New York to San Francisco by steamer exceeding that sent in sailing vessels. After 1865, it was usual for westbound steamers to report cargoes of merchandise ranging from 1,000 to 2,000 tons, and generally over 1,500 tons, whereas in the five preceding years cargoes were very seldom over 1,000, and usually about 500 or 600, tons.[30]

During this time the internal history of the Pacific Mail's management presented a lively picture. In order to finance the new China line, and because of the public support which the stock increase of 1865 had received, it was proposed that the capital of the Pacific Mail be further expanded to $20,000,000. This proposal was made by Leonard W. Jerome, a stock operator of no mean ability who was one of the directors of the company as well as a member of the Brown Brothers pool. The action was sanctioned by the New York legislature on May 1, 1866, and it was announced to the stockholders in November of that year that 50,000 of the new shares would be issued to them, full paid, as a stock dividend, one share of new stock going for every three shares of old.[31] On the next day, a cash dividend of 5 per cent, payable December 1, 1866, was reported, in addition to the stock dividend which would be payable January 2, 1867.[32] The other 50,000 new shares, Jerome agreed to take from the company at $200 a share. This time, however, the sale of the increased stock was not successful, since the stock, which had stood at 242 on November 15, 1866, had fallen to 172 by the first of December and thereafter failed to go higher. Though Jerome took only 30,000 of the 50,000 shares which he had contracted to take, this was enough to ruin him, leading to his resignation from the board of directors of the company by February, 1867.[33] In 1867, dividends of 12 per cent were paid, but in 1868 dividends were suspended, to be resumed in 1869. During 1868 and 1869 the stock of the company remained in the region of 100, falling as low as 80 at some times, but also going up as far as 126. At the end of June, 1869, it stood at 87⅛.[34]

In the election of directors in November, 1867, there took place a bitter fight for control of the company. The division was over the Brown Brothers pool, with a group of "outsiders" determined to reduce its influence. The Brown group had assumed great power through its policy of gaining voting privileges on stock even though it might not own it, as it had done with the stock turned over to the Atlantic Mail Steamship Company in 1865. It was claimed by its opponents that this group was operating the company for its own rather than for the company's benefit. The charge was brought forward that, since the same group controlled the Novelty Iron Works, which was equipped to build vertical-beam engines, it had kept the company building expensive side-wheel steamers long after these had been outmoded for ocean service. It was admitted by the Brown faction that the Novelty Iron Works had built engines for eleven Pacific Mail steamers in the period 1860–1867, at a contract price of $2,909,851.75, but it was denied that the company had not received full value in these and that they were not the most satisfactory marine engines in the world. Also, the statement was brought forward that Louis McLane, president of

Wells Fargo Express Company, was also a director and president *pro tempore* of the Pacific Mail, and that through this connection Wells Fargo acted as agent for all the freight business of the steamship company, receiving "several hundred thousand dollars'" commission a year. McLane replied to this in a sworn statement to the effect that the commission of Wells Fargo for the year ended September 1, 1867, amounted to less than $80,000, and that the work of Wells Fargo in securing shipment, advancing money, collecting freight money, handling goods, looking after advertising, and so forth, was well worth the price. It would seem that the increased freight shipments by way of Panama might bear out this contention.

On the side of the Brown Brothers group, the argument was brought forward that the opposition—including such names as William H. Seward, Jr., Spencer K. Green, A. W. Dimock, Charles F. Davenport, George B. Hartson, Charles A. Meigs, O. W. Joslyn, Oliver Charlick, Thomas F. Mason, H. S. Camblos, Frederick W. Lockwood, and Frederick Butterfield—held a controlling interest in the stock of the Atlantic Mail Steamship Company, and that they wished to have the restrictions removed from the voting of the Pacific Mail stock held for that company. Then, it was asserted, they would enter into competition with the Pacific Mail again and, holding control of both companies, would arrange affairs unfavorably for the Pacific Mail.

As the time for electing directors for the Pacific Mail approached, the campaign rose in intensity. Proxies were purchased, ill-natured pamphlets published, and injunctions to prevent the voting of various blocks of stock were issued and overruled in bewildering succession. The election, which had been set for November 20, 1867, was postponed by court order to December 16, but before that date satisfactory arrangements had been made which left the Brown Brothers group in control of the company.[35] Command of the Pacific Mail remained in the hands of the banking interests, who seem to have been more concerned with the purely financial aspects of the organization—with the position of its stock and its prospects—than with the operation of ships or the details of service. It should be remembered also that in 1867 the rapidly advancing transcontinental railroad pointed to the early decline of the importance of the Panama route, and that the Pacific Mail's line to the Orient, opened in that year, became increasingly its chief interest.

At the same time that controversy was going on within the Pacific Mail, the whole problem of the mail contract and of the carriage of mail by way of Panama was pressing. It has already been seen that, when the mail service for which Johnson contracted in 1859 failed to materializè, Cornelius Vanderbilt obtained a temporary contract to carry the mail by way of Panama from October 1, 1859, until July 1 of the next year for $187,500. Before July 1, 1860, it was expected that some permanent arrangement could be made for mail service by way of the Isthmus. However, no settlement was reached, though the Postmaster General recommended in February, 1860, that $350,000 be set aside for transportation of mail from New York and New Orleans to San Francisco by way of Panama.[36] In the Post Office Appropriation Act for the year ending June 30, 1861, provision was made for contracting for mail transportation between the Atlantic and Pacific, but compensation was restricted to the postages received. This had been as high as $300,000 for 1859, but, with the institution of the overland mail service the year before and the sending of most of the letter mails by that route, the class of mail paying a high tariff was removed from the sea route. The steamers were thus left to carry some 90 per cent of the bulk of the mail, in the way of printed matter, postage on which would amount to only about 10 per cent of the total. When asked to contract on this basis, Vanderbilt refused.[37]

In response to a recommendation made by the Postmaster General, the Senate in 1860 passed a bill which authorized him to contract for a trimonthly service to California by way of Panama for a sum not to exceed $400,000 a year; but the House of Representatives failed to concur in this, and the session closed with no provision made except for the payment of postages, which Vanderbilt refused to accept. The companies operating, Vanderbilt's and the Pacific Mail, had offered to carry the mails for $300,000 a year, or for twenty-five cents a pound on printed matter. Either of these offers would have been acceptable to the Post Office Department, but neither of them could be accepted, because of Congressional inaction. Finally, on July 2, 1860, the *Ariel* sailed from New York for Aspinwall without the United States mails aboard.[38]

Since the overland mail service was totally inadequate to carry other than letters, some arrangement had to be made for transporting mail by water. A telegram from the Postmaster General to Vanderbilt, sent June 30, 1860, promised special presidential pressure on Congress to obtain payment of $300,000 a year for the mail service (at least up to March 4, 1861), and this promise was accepted as satisfactory. Since the "Commodore" was at Saratoga taking the waters at the time the telegram was sent, it was delayed in reaching him. This delay accounted for the noncarriage of the mail by the *Ariel* on July 2, but the *Northern Light* on the eleventh again flew the mail flag.[39] The *New York Herald*, familiar with the ways of Congress, remarked on this occasion:

> It is apparently a piece of liberality on his [Vanderbilt's] part; for he is old enough to know that Congress will have little scruple in cheating him out of the $300,000 to which the President and the Postmaster deem him entitled. By the time the bill is before the House to pay him, it will probably be discovered once more that he is a corsair and a pirate, and the overland mail company will, perhaps, get the money as a reward for their virtue.[40]

For the service from July 1, 1860, to March 4, 1861, the sum of $236,249.99 was finally paid.[41] In his recommendations for the year ending June 30, 1862, Postmaster General Holt put down $350,000 for the mail service by way of the Isthmus, and this was authorized by an act of February 19, 1861. To make up this sum, the postages received were to be paid over to the contractor, and the sum necessary above that to make the $350,000 was to be paid from the Treasury.[42]

This contract was not renewed, and after 1861 there was an increasing tendency to send the mail across the continent. It was announced in California that, beginning July 1, 1861, mail would be dispatched daily overland from Placerville, and that there would be no further service by way of Panama.[43] In spite of such announcements, the overland stages were unable to carry the more bulky printed matter, while severe storms in the early summer of 1862 and Indian hostilities in September, 1864, and from January to March, 1865, forced the Postmaster General to close the overland route and order all the mails sent by way of Panama.[44]

The temporary agreement of February, 1861, by which $350,000 a year was paid for mail service by the Panama route, expired on June 30 of the same year in spite of the fact that the Postmaster General had recommended that it continue for the next fiscal year.[45]

The amount paid for transportation of mail from New York to San Francisco via Panama, exclusive of the railroad transit of the Isthmus, ran from $11,343.77 to $31,098.58 annually in the period 1861 to 1869, with a considerable increase in the amount toward the end of the period.[46] It is clear that some funds aside from those just cited went for the transportation of mail by water, for in 1866, when the sum set down for the service was $24,888.58, the Postmaster General stated that the compensation then paid for the steamship service from New York to Aspinwall and from Panama to San Francisco was $112,500 per year.[47] The additional amount may have been included in the item for "overland and marine" mail service which the reports of the Postmaster General contained but which they did not break down into itemized accounts.

A good deal of complaint was voiced of the overland mail service, which was slower than that by steamer, its schedule providing for twenty-five-day trips. It was stated in San Francisco in 1865 that the average time for letters by the overland route was actually thirty-five to forty days, whereas the steamers made the journey in eighteen to twenty-two days.[48] As late as March, 1869, on the very eve of the completion of the transcontinental railroad, the mails were ordered diverted to the steamers, and when the *Constitution* came into San Francisco without the mails which should have come in her, it was surmised that "a large portion of these are temporarily located in the mud awaiting the completion of the railroad."[49]

Along with the internal battles of the Pacific Mail and the problems of mail service, the operation of the Panama route was still characterized by competition. Although this rivalry was no longer the center of interest, the route did present a lively picture during a part of the decade ending in 1869. The withdrawal of Cornelius Vanderbilt from the field of "opposition" failed to put an end to that institution. Before the year 1860 was out, there were rumors that Marshall Owen Roberts, of United States Mail Steamship Company renown, was preparing to place vessels on the Panama route in competition with the ships of Vanderbilt and the Pacific Mail. Roberts controlled the ships which had been operated by the United States Mail, and certainly the summer of 1860 saw the *Granada* and the *Moses Taylor* clear New York for San Francisco heavily laden with coal.[50] The *Granada* was lost entering San

Francisco Bay on October 13, 1860, and when the *Moses Taylor* arrived eight days later, it was stated that she had been intended for a new line from San Francisco to New York by way of Tehuantepec, but that since her departure from New York arrangements had been made between her owners and the Pacific Mail by which she would not be placed on the route.[51]

Two years elapsed before there was further rumor of opposition, but in the early summer of 1862 the chartering of the Central American Transit Company under the laws of New Jersey was announced. At first, this was believed in some quarters to be another effort to "blackmail" the Pacific Mail into buying up old steamers at outrageous prices, but by the late summer it was clear that the line really intended to begin operations that fall.[52] In August, 1862, the *America* was advertised to sail from New York on October 25 for San Juan de Nicaragua; there her passengers would go ashore to make the transit of Nicaragua to San Juan del Sur, whence they would sail in the *Moses Taylor* for San Francisco.[53] The Central American Transit Company, under the leadership of M. O. Roberts, began operations in October as scheduled, with sailings from both ends of the line at rather irregular intervals.

At the beginning the Pacific Mail did not lower its rates of passage, and the "People's Opposition Line," as the Central American Transit Company styled itself in San Francisco, took first-class passengers at $200, second-class at $150, and steerage for $90.[54] By December of that year the Pacific Mail ships were taking first-class for $163 and $137, second-class for $83, and steerage for $60, whereas the opposition asked $125 for first-class, $80 for second and $40 for steerage.[55] On the Atlantic, Roberts placed the *Illinois* on the New York–San Juan run in October of 1863, while the *America* was sent to the Pacific to join the *Moses Taylor*. In the summer of 1864, the *Illinois* was superseded by the new steamer *Golden Rule,* which was assisted for one voyage at the beginning of 1865 by the *Western Metropolis*. In 1863, steerage rates by the Central American Transit steamers had gone as low as $35, to which point the Pacific Mail did not follow, but by the end of that year, steerage was $75 in the *Moses Taylor* and first cabin was $175, whereas on the *St. Louis* of the Pacific Mail it was $185.[56] Passenger fares were no better stabilized in 1864 or 1865, steerage varying from $45 to $125, second cabin from $65 to $184.25, and first cabin from $150 to $325.[57] In August, 1864, there was an attempt to fix the first-class rate of both lines at $400, the sum being in greenbacks, an equivalent of about $160 gold.[58]

In May, 1865, the *Golden Rule* was lost on Roncador Reef in the Caribbean, and her place on the Atlantic line of the Central American Transit was taken by the *Ericsson* and then permanently by the *Santiago de Cuba.*

It was said that travel between the coasts had never been so cheap as in the early part of 1865, when cabin passengers were taken for $50 including isthmian transit, and one group of eleven steerage passengers went by the Nicaragua route for $11 apiece.[59] In the latter part of the year, however, the steerage rate went up to $100 and more, and first cabin was $250 to $350.[60]

With January, 1866, there came reports of a new group which planned to place steamers on the Panama route in competition with those of the Pacific Mail Steamship Company. This project took the form of increased backing and different control for the Central American Transit Company rather than the establishment of a competing company. In its leadership, the group numbered some of those active in the founding and operation of the Pacific Mail who had become disaffected by the events of the last few years and by the growing hold of the Brown Brothers pool on the affairs of the old company. William H. Webb, the shipbuilder, became the president of the Central American Transit, with William H. Aspinwall, Moses Taylor, Gustavus Vasa Fox, David Dows, William H. Guion, Charles Dana, and Pickering Clark as important associates.[61] At first, it was said that the steamers *Morning Star, Evening Star, Guiding Star,* and *Rising Star* would be employed on the Atlantic, and that the screw steamers *Merrimac, Mississippi, Mariposa,* and *Monterey* would go to the Pacific. The capital for the organization was stated to be $4,000,000, or very much less than that of the Pacific Mail.[62]

At the beginning of 1866 the rates by the Central American Transit Company steamers were $150 first class, $100 second class, and $50 steerage, those of the Pacific Mail being exactly double.[63] In the spring, however, the Pacific Mail lowered its steerage to $44.25, though on the *America* and *Moses Taylor* it was $30.[64]

With the September sailings of the *Santiago de Cuba* from New York and the *Moses Taylor* from San Francisco, the opposition announced a change in its name to the North American Steamship Company. In October, 1866, another ex-transport, the *San Francisco*, joined the *Santiago de Cuba*, thus giving service at approximately semiweekly intervals. The fleet was augmented in 1867 by the new steamers *Nebraska, Nevada,* and *Oregonian,* and the chartered former transatlantic liners *Arago* and *Fulton* were placed on the Atlantic run in the early months of 1868. In November, 1867, the increased fleet had made it possible, not only to make sailings to Nicaragua, but also to meet the Pacific Mail on its own ground and send ships to Panama and Aspinwall. The challenge thus thrown down was accepted squarely by the Pacific Mail, which announced that it was prepared to reduce its passenger and freight rates to such a point that it would be impossible for an opposition to make a profit, even though the company might be obliged to pass its dividends.[65]

Although the competition by the North American Steamship Company on the Panama route lasted only about a year, it was the most damaging which the Pacific Mail had met. Equipped with splendid steamers and well managed, the new company asserted that it found the business not unprofitable, and its directors declared they had no idea of entering any sort of compromise short of an acknowledged share in the traffic between New York and San Francisco.[66] In February, 1868, the North American Steamship Company withdrew its steamers from the Nicaragua route and thenceforward concentrated on the Panama line. It reduced its rates to $100 first cabin, $80 second cabin, and $40 steerage, whereupon the Pacific Mail retaliated by offering first-cabin rooms at rates ranging from $126 to $76, second-cabin at $45.50, and steerage for $35.50.[67] There were constant rumors in the early fall of 1868 that the North American Steamship Company was about to withdraw its ships, to which I. W. Raymond, the San Francisco agent, replied with a flat denial and the accusation that the reports were circulated by the agents of the Pacific Mail.[68] At that very time, however, the ships of the North American Steamship Company were making their last voyages, and by the end of November, 1868, the opposition was at an end.[69] The superior financial background of the Pacific Mail had won out, and for the remaining months of the period before the transcontinental railroad was opened the Panama route was held as a monopoly by the pioneer company. With the end of competition, passenger rates were increased, though steerage passengers could still go from New York to San Francisco for $75, second-class for $150, and first-class for $200 to $275.[70]

During the period of the Civil War, the Panama route assumed a position of particular significance in relation to the struggle. Not only did the steamers offer the fastest practicable route by which troops could be sent from the Pacific coast to join the Union armies, but, more important still, the supply of gold bullion, so needed by the North and so coveted by the South, came from the mines of California by way of the Panama route. When the Confederate navy first began to fit out commerce destroyers and to commission privateers, it was only to be expected that the steamers bringing treasure from Aspinwall to New York should be looked upon as highly desirable prey. It might be very well to strike at the Union through the destruction of seaborne commerce, but it was much more to the point to capture supplies of specie so desperately needed by the Confederacy to bolster up its foreign credit.

When the commerce destroyers were first sent out, it was suggested that the treasure steamers be provided with naval convoy, a steam warship being stationed at Aspinwall which could accompany the homeward-bound ships at least through the Windward Passage. Instead of this, even the usual ordinary-sized warship was withdrawn from Aspinwall and replaced by the little 8-gun brig *Perry,* "so small and so old [launched 1843] as to be unfit for service in any other part of the world."[71] The only move which was taken to protect the steamers was to place a 6-pounder on each of them.

On December 7, 1862, the *Ariel,* mail steamer, was southbound from New York to Aspinwall when she was overhauled off Cape Maysi, the eastern extremity of Cuba, by the C.S.S. *Alabama,* commanded by Captain Raphael Semmes. The *Alabama* had been lying in wait for the *Champion,* which was due northbound and was expected to have aboard $1,353,536.77 in treasure. Since the *Ariel* was going in the other direction, she had only about $9,500 in treasure, for the use of the ship. Semmes detained the *Ariel* for two and a half days, going with her as far as the coast of Jamaica and then releasing her to proceed on her voyage. The number of her passengers and crew was too great to be accommodated on the

Alabama, so the vessel was spared, though what treasure she had was of course confiscated. The one hundred and twenty United States Marines aboard had their arms and ammunition taken from them and were paroled, and Captain Jones was required to give a release bond on the ship and cargo for $228,000, payable thirty days after the acknowledgment of the Confederacy.[72]

News of the *Ariel's* capture brought consternation in both the eastern United States and California. On the return voyage, she had left all the treasure for her, some $500,000, at Aspinwall, since Captain Jones feared that the *Alabama* might be waiting to capture him again northbound.[73] It was feared that one of the other steamers on the Atlantic, the *America, Champion,* or *Ocean Queen,* might have been captured, and on the application of Senator Latham of California the Secretary of the Navy sent the U.S.S. *Connecticut* to Aspinwall to bring the treasure waiting there to New York. At the same time, Secretary of the Navy Welles telegraphed Vanderbilt that naval vessels would hereafter be provided to convoy all eastbound California steamers.[74] In spite of these precautions an immediate change in the treasure routing took place. From the beginning of 1862 until January, 1865, the California shipments of specie were divided at the Isthmus, the larger portion being sent in steamers of the Royal Mail Steam Packet Company from Aspinwall to Liverpool, where it could be transshipped to Cunarders for the voyage to New York, thus making the Atlantic section of the trip by a more roundabout but much safer route, being under the British flag the entire time. For example, when the *Solent* steamed away from Aspinwall on the evening of February 7, 1863, she carried about $5,000,000 in treasure, which was said to be the largest amount ever carried in a single vessel. Of the specie which reached Panama by the *Sonora* on February 14, 1863, $1,188,000 went by way of England to New York, and only about $275,000 was sent direct in the American mail steamer.[75]

Already there had been at least one instance of the use of naval convoys on the Panama route when the *Champion* was accompanied by the gunboat *Keystone State* from Aspinwall through the Windward Passage and the Bahamas on her northbound voyage of October 5, 1861. The first ship to sail with convoy after the *Ariel's* capture was the *Champion* again, and for her the gunboat *Augusta* was sent to Aspinwall. The departure of the two ships from Aspinwall was delayed several days because of a strike among the dock laborers, which prevented the *Augusta* from taking in coal.[76] The *Connecticut* took the place of the *Augusta* later in January, 1863, and accompanied the mail steamers from Aspinwall through the danger zone of the Caribbean and the Windward Passage to the open Atlantic. After the sailing of April 9, 1863, the protection was seemingly withdrawn. There was sometimes danger north of the point at which the warship left her convoy. In March, 1863, the *Northern Light* was chased by an unknown ship off the Florida coast; the stranger desisted only when one of the Union blockading squadron hove in sight.[77] In the spring of 1864 warships were again detailed to accompany the mail steamers on the Atlantic, and this time they remained with them for the entire voyage from New York to Aspinwall and return.[78] This practice must not have been continued, for in October of the same year the policy was announced again as one just going into effect, when the *North Star* was accompanied out of New York by the *Glaucus* for Aspinwall.[79] The story was told in San Francisco in January, 1865, that Vanderbilt had discharged Captain Jones, commander of the *North Star,* because he had towed his convoy gunboat into Port Royal, Jamaica, when she became disabled in a storm and thereby used too much coal. The dismissal seemed particularly unjust because Captain Jones had been under orders not to leave Aspinwall without the *Augusta* and not to lose sight of her during the voyage. Vanderbilt's decision must have been altered, for Captain Jones commanded the *Ariel* on two voyages to Aspinwall later in 1865.[80] With the tightening of the Union blockade and the collapse of the Confederacy in the early months of 1865 the convoy system was abandoned, and the mail steamers again carried their accustomed cargoes of specie.

On the Pacific there was also fear that the treasure steamers might be captured, though until the cruise of the *Shenandoah* in 1864 and 1865 this had little actual basis. The first "scare," however, was not of Confederates but of pirates. When the *Uncle Sam* put into Acapulco southbound in January, 1861, it was reported that a mysterious vessel had been seen cruising off the port for three or four days. It was hinted that she was the United States sloop-of-war *Levant,* which had been some time missing on her voyage from the Hawaiian Islands to Panama, and that, having been taken over by her crew, she was lying in wait to capture the

Uncle Sam and her treasure. The mail steamer's armament consisted of a brass 9-pounder and the private arms of the passengers, but

nolens volens, we went to sea, all lights extinguished save a blaze of red fire some fifteen feet above the smoke stack; and notwithstanding a keen look-out was maintained, we saw nothing of any such craft . . .[81]

With the beginning of hostilities, steamers on the Panama route on the Pacific were armed, the *St. Louis* sailing from San Francisco on July 1, 1861, armed with two brass cannon besides a Dahlgren, small arms, and sabres. She was ordered to proceed directly to Panama without calling at Acapulco, having taken enough coal at Benicia to carry her through the voyage. Had she remained longer in San Francisco, she would have received iron-plate armor, "but there is not the slightest danger of any of the 'Pirates of the Gulf' running her down this trip."[82] When the new steamer *Sacramento* sailed from New York in June, 1864, to take her place on the Pacific Mail's San Francisco–Panama line, she was armed with one 100-pounder, and four 20-pound Parrott rifles.[83]

Instead of convoys on the Pacific, the ships at the disposal of Flag Officer J. B. Montgomery at San Francisco were stationed off points along the coast which were believed to offer favorable bases for Confederate ships. Thus, the *Wyoming* was ordered to cruise off the coast of Lower California from Margarita Island to Bonita Island, watching particularly Magdalena Bay, and the *Saranac* was sent to the vicinity of Cape San Lucas to "afford all necessary protection to our mail steamers in their transit to and from San Francisco . . ."[84]

Although the Confederate plans to make a privateer of the ship *J. M. Chapman* in 1863 and to capture the Panama Railroad steamer *Salvador* in 1864 were both foiled by the United States authorities, they constituted the most serious threats to the mail steamers in the course of the Civil War.[85]

After the close of hostilities, the *Shenandoah* was still in operation on the Pacific, because news had not reached her of the collapse of the Confederacy. Even when she had left the Pacific, there were rumors in San Francisco that she was at large, and when the *Colorado* sailed from San Francisco on August 3, 1865, she was convoyed by the U.S.S. *Saginaw*, though it was said that, since the *Colorado* was reputedly the fastest steamer afloat, there was little fear that the *Shenandoah* would get near her. The *Saginaw* evidently did not accompany the *Colorado* far down the coast, for she returned to port on August 10, a week after sailing.[88]

It spoke well for the speed and efficiency of the mail steamers, as well as for the watchfulness of the Union warships, that none of their vital cargoes of men and gold from California should have fallen into the hands of the Confederates. Since the Panama route was comparatively lacking in excitement during the Civil War, it received little attention, but the importance of the service which it rendered during that period was of the first magnitude, forming as it did the chief means of communication between the eastern and western areas of the embattled Union.

With the continued growth of American population on the Pacific coast after 1848 it became clear that the Panama route would sooner or later be superseded by overland communication. Increasing demands in Congress for overland mail service marked this growth, and the stagecoach line which was finally established in 1858, though less efficient than the steamers, was nevertheless a beginning. The brief interlude of the Pony Express in 1860 and 1861 carried business and political news between the coasts faster than the steamers, and the completion of a transcontinental telegraph in 1861 made of the mail ships carriers of confirmatory details rather than of first tidings of great events. When the rails of the Central Pacific began to stretch eastward from Sacramento into the foothills of the Sierra in 1863, and when the Union Pacific commenced to lay track westward over Nebraska two years later, the end of the paramount importance of the Panama route was in sight. The railroad would carry express and passengers, as well as all the mail, and the role of the steamers in the building of California would be over. On May 10, 1869, President Stanford of the Central Pacific drove home the last spike of the transcontinental railroad. The great work of the Panama steamers was past, and though generations of usefulness lay ahead of them, they had ceased to be the chief link between the Pacific coast and the rest of the nation.

In 1874, a traveler from Panama to San Francisco reported that the Pacific Mail steamers were carrying crowds of passengers on every trip. The fare from New York to California was about half as much by Panama as it was by rail, which made this route a favorite with the impecunious. Service was slower than in the old days, however, for the steamers now made frequent calls on the Central American and Mexican coast. The company was putting its best efforts into the transpacific line by this time, and the Panama steamers suffered as a result. They were described as "cheap and nasty," their awnings full of holes, the furniture shabby, and the food bad.[87] This state of affairs, better than any generalization, showed the secondary place to which the Panama route declined after the railroad had spanned the continent.

CHAPTER V

THE PANAMA STEAMERS

IN THE COURSE of the twenty years in which the Panama route
to California was a vital artery of communication, the ships
employed on it and the mechanics of their operation changed
but little. There were increases in the sizes of the steamers, the
facilities for overhauling and provisioning them at the ends of
the line were improved, and their business management underwent
some alteration, but in the main the operation of the sea part of
the route remained the same. The same types of ship, the same
materials for hull construction, the same methods of propulsion,
similar passenger accommodations, nearly the same problems of
supply and the same dangers were to be met by the captain of the
Alaska or the *Constitution* in 1869 as had confronted the commanders of the *Falcon* and *California* in 1848 and 1849.

With the exception of the sailing ships pressed into service at
the time of the opening of the route, before the steamers required
for the unexpected demands of travelers in 1848 and 1849 could
be obtained, vessels propelled by steam were used exclusively on
the through line by way of the Isthmus. These steamers may be
conveniently divided into three general classes. First, the three
original steamers built by the Pacific Mail Steamship Company,
which stand alone among the ships built particularly for the route,
since they were planned before its demands were known and were
therefore not entirely suited to the service in which they were
engaged. Although they were not small for their day, the original
trio of the Pacific Mail were bluff-bowed, wall-sided ships, designed
for hard service on a distant coast line, and with small space for
passengers. In line with accepted standards of the naval architecture of the day, most of their accommodations for passengers
and crew were below, and there were few cabins built on the decks
of these steamers. The needs of the trade caused these ships to be
altered, with the addition of deckhouses and increased passenger
accommodations.

Then there were the many steamers which were not built for the
Panama route but were purchased or chartered to fill the demand
for transportation to California. Many of these were similar to

Two Views of Chagres

former were expensive to operate. The chief distinguishing feature of the Panama steamers lay in an innovation, claimed by George Law as an idea of his own, which consisted in building a deckhouse extending from one end of the ship to the other, in which public rooms for passengers, officers' quarters, and staterooms might be placed, and then in building over that a hurricane deck the entire length and breadth of the ship, which formed a canopy for the promenade below and itself gave greatly increased deck space for passengers. This was introduced in the *Empire City,* which was completed in July, 1849, and appeared also in Law's own steamers *Ohio* and *Georgia* later that year.[2] For ships operating in tropical waters, this increase in cabins on deck and in open space was particularly welcome, and it was adopted by the Pacific Mail for almost all its steamers after 1851. The general freedom of the Pacific coast from violent storms made it possible, in ships designed for that run, to extend the upper two decks beyond the hull of the ship, building them out amidships as far as the sides of the paddle boxes. This gave a ship like the *Golden City,* for instance, which had a breadth of hull of 45 feet, a beam "over the guards" of 75 feet, providing much greater space for staterooms and open decks. The clipper bows, traditional in sailing vessels and adopted in the early steamers, were discarded for most steamers built for the Panama route, though some of the earlier ships like the *Ohio, Georgia,* and *Golden Gate* had overhanging bows, decorated by figureheads and extended by bowsprits. There was also a rather unsightly combination of a straight stem with a bowsprit which continued to find favor with builders until the middle of the eighteen-fifties. A further development took place when first a pilothouse, then officers' quarters, and later deckhouses containing staterooms appeared on what had been the wide expanse of the hurricane deck, unbroken except for smokestacks, masts, and life-boats. The open deck below was then generally enclosed forward of the paddle boxes, thus raising the freeboard of the ship and giving more space for passenger accommodations.

The shipbuilders of New York produced most of the Panama steamers, just as its financiers backed the lines on which they ran. Along lower Manhattan Island on the East River stretched the shipyards, world famous for the excellence of the vessels built there and preëminent in the United States for steamship construction.

Such builders as William Henry Webb, Jacob Aaron Westervelt, Brown and Bell, Smith and Dimon, and William H. Brown carried the art of constructing ocean-going wooden side-wheelers to its highest point, although in addition they turned out splendid Sound liners and river steamboats as well as famous packet ships and clippers. Of 108 steamers which served on the Panama and Nicaragua routes, 87 were built in New York and its vicinity. Webb's yards accounted for 18 of these, with other builders not far behind. Philadelphia was the only other port at which any number of Panama steamers were built, although they came singly from as far north as Portland and as far south as Baltimore. Two of the steamers were built on the Great Lakes and three vessels in the British Isles.

Although under different ownership, the "iron works" which constructed engines for the steamers were located near the shipyards. Here there was less diversity than for hull construction, since 22 out of 64 engines built at New York came from the Novelty Iron Works of Stillman, Allen and Company. Theopholus Secor, whose establishment was later purchased by Charles Morgan and called the Morgan Iron Works, and James P. Allaire were the other principal builders of engines.[4]

In size the Panama steamers were large for their period, even though they might seem dwarfed by the liners of the next century. George Law's *Ohio* of 1849 was 246 feet long on her spar deck, and had a tonnage of 2,432, as compared with the Collins liner *Atlantic* of the same year, which had a length of 284 feet on her main deck and a tonnage of 2,849. The Cunarder *America*, built in 1848, was 270 feet long, with a tonnage of 1,825. Though the first Pacific Mail trio was composed of steamers about 200 feet in length, the *Golden Gate,* which was finished in 1851, was 269 feet, 6 inches long, with a tonnage of 2,067. A decade and more later, the Pacific Mail was bringing out such ships as the *Golden City,* which had a length on deck of 343 feet, and a tonnage of 3,374, which did not compare badly with the Cunard steamer *Scotia,* built the year before, which was 3,871 tons burden and 400 feet long. Ships like the *Golden City* were reaching the extreme size to which wooden ships could be built with safety, though the *Great Republic* and her sisters for the Pacific Mail's China line were 360 feet in length, which was rather a record for wooden, ocean-going ship construction.[5]

The ships of the Panama route burned coal, the *Georgia* consuming some fifty-five to sixty tons per day at ordinary speed.[6] As more engines were built, they became increasingly efficient; in 1865, fifteen years after the *Georgia,* the *Golden City,* built by William H. Webb for the Pacific Mail Steamship Company, used an average of thirty-six and a half tons per day on a voyage from Panama to San Francisco, making a total of four hundred eighty-five tons for the voyage.[7] A large amount of space aboard these ships was occupied by the coal carried, and since wooden ships, unlike steel vessels, had no ballast tanks which could be filled with sea water as the coal was burned, they rode higher and higher out of the water as the voyage progressed. The chief engineer of the *Oregon* reported that, as the supply of coal decreased, the "vessel [was] very light and rolling much. Wheels out of the water half the time . . ." and again, "Burning wood and small coal mixed. Ship rolling paddles 6 feet out of water."[8]

The coal was running low when the engineer wrote the last sentence quoted, but sometimes, particularly in the first years of the route, it ran out altogether. On her first voyage from Panama to San Francisco the *California* used the last coal in the bunkers when she was near Point Conception, and only after spars, bunks, transoms, and cabin ornaments had been hacked to pieces and found to be entirely inadequate to keep up the fires until the ship reached Monterey, were about a hundred sacks of coal discovered stowed away along the keel as ballast. This carried the steamer into Monterey, and there she lay for five days while crew, and such passengers as would work for five dollars a day, cut wood ashore to take her to San Francisco.[9] When she did reach San Francisco, there was no coal for her, and she was unable to start south until May 1, 1849, because of lack of fuel. On the voyage back to Panama she again ran out of coal, and was obliged to burn spars, bulkheads, berths, and boats to a value of about $4,000 in order to make Taboga Island.[10] The *Oregon,* being at San Francisco with only seventy tons of coal aboard, put to sea nevertheless and, when she ran out, continued under sail to San Blas, where the Pacific Mail had a supply ready.[11]

On the Panama steamers the boilers were of the flue type, and the first ships used salt water in them, not having condensers or sufficient capacity in their fresh-water tanks to carry water for the boilers. Thus Dr. Arthur B. Stout, surgeon of the *California,* commented as follows:

We are constantly discovering badly finished work in the ship. It is now the pipes for blowing out the salt from the boilers which are defective, and occasioned us a loss of twenty-five minutes yesterday, during which the steamer stopped for repairing them.[12]

On the *Ohio,* finished the next year, however, there were tanks large enough to carry ten thousand gallons of fresh water besides a condenser which could be used if necessary.[13]

The *Oregon*'s engineer reported that the temperature in her fireroom and bunkers went as high as 132 degrees, and that sometimes so many of his firemen and stokers were overcome by the heat that those who remained well had to stand double watches.[14] In an effort to overcome this the *San Francisco,* built in 1853, had her fireroom made airtight, with forced ventilation, instead of depending on hatchways with wind sails set above them to bring the air below.[15]

Ships of the middle-nineteenth century were fitted with sails as a matter of course, and sometimes these were useful in augmenting the engines, as well as in providing a means of getting into port, should the engines or coal supply fail. When the *Panama* broke down after leaving New York for the Pacific, she was able to return under sail, and when the *California* remained in San Francisco because of lack of coal, President Aspinwall of the Pacific Mail wrote to Alfred Robinson, the San Francisco agent of the company, that it would

have been better to put to sea under canvas ... or else all the spars & rigging carried by these vessels had better be removed for if not to be counted on in an emergency like this, it is useless to be encumbered with them when under steam.[16]

The passenger accommodations on the Panama steamers varied in detail with the different ships, but in the main were the same throughout the period under consideration. In the deckhouse, the officers' quarters were usually located, together with a companionway to the saloon below, which might be expanded into a social hall. The galley was also sometimes located in the deckhouse, and in some ships there was a smoking room for the exclusive use of male passengers. Forward, on deck and below, was the fore-

castle containing the quarters of the crew. The decks below were
sometimes arranged with first- and second-class accommodations
along the entire deck from bow to stern, with the steerage quarters
below these, or with the steerage forward and the cabin space aft
on the same decks. In the first class there were staterooms along
either side, opening into the dining saloon and other public rooms,
which extended down the middle of the ship. Staterooms usually
contained three berths, one above another, together with a
cushioned locker which could accommodate another passenger;
each room had a mirror, toilet stand, washbowl, water bottles and
glasses. There were two-berth staterooms, and also rooms with four
berths. The floors were covered with carpet, and the berths were
screened with outer damask curtains, extending from top to bottom,
and inner cambric curtains. Outside the staterooms, the saloons
were furnished with long tables, at which passengers sat for meals
and which could be used for reading or writing between meals.
Long "railroad seats," with reversible backs, were fixed along either
side of the tables, with racks for glasses above them. In the *Northern
Light*, built in 1851, the dining saloon extended the entire width of
the ship, with no staterooms on the sides to interfere with light and
ventilation. This, however, was a distinct innovation and did not
become common in ocean steamers until after 1870.[17] The *Ohio,* built
in 1849, had a barber's shop, and, adjoining it, "a hot and cold water
shower bath."[18] In this vessel also great attention was paid to the
ventilation of the staterooms, each of them being connected with
an air trunk which ran the length of the ship, the speed of the
vessel forcing air through it.[19] The ships on the Pacific were increasingly built with large windows instead of portholes for the
comfort of passengers in the tropics.[20]

Second-cabin accommodations were not separated from the first-
class, their difference consisting merely in less commodious sleeping quarters. These were open berths, curtained from one another,
but with a large number in one room. Sometimes there were also
staterooms available for second-cabin passengers. They dined at
the same table and used the same decks as the first class, but slept
forward or below.

For the steerage, there were no private rooms, and often no
segregation of the sexes. When separate dormitories were provided
for men and women in the steerage, the fact was deemed worthy

of special notice in the contemporary press.[21] On the *Champion*, the steerage deck was 50 feet long and 29 feet, 6 inches wide, with a height of 7 feet, 2 inches. The entire space was filled with berths, the passages between them ranging from a foot and a half to 6 feet, 4 inches in width. The berths were arranged in tiers of three, one above another, with 2 feet, 6 inches between the upper berth and the deck above, and 2 feet between each of the other berths. The berths themselves were made by stretching canvas over wooden bars and fastening it with wooden pins in the tops of the bars. Thus between four bars there would be formed a sort of canvas bag in which the passenger would sleep. The majority of the berths contained three such bags, and three passengers were expected to occupy them. Since there were high boards at the ends, the occupants entered from the side, the holder of the inner berth climbing through the two outer ones to reach his own. The space allotted to one person in these berths measured 6 feet in length and 1 foot, 1½ inches in width.[22] Since the steerage berths were of rather a temporary character, it was possible to increase the capacity of the steamers when demand for transportation was great. In the first steamers, food for the steerage was served from the galley direct to the passengers and eaten wherever a place could be found. As early as 1850, however, the Pacific Mail directed that alterations be made in the steerage of the company's steamers in order to afford the steerage passengers a table from which to eat and in other respects to make them more comfortable. The point was made, however, that this must be done without diminishing the number of berths. At the same time, cutlery was provided for steerage passengers, who had hitherto been under the necessity of providing their own.[23]

Aside from the steerage quarters, the Panama steamers were generally well and even elaborately furnished, the quality of fittings being often superior to those found in much larger steamers of later times. Nevertheless, the newspaper writer must be set down as an enthusiast who described the *Crescent City* as follows:

There can be nothing we have ever read of, either in the courtly magnificence of Louis Quatorze, or in the fabled history of Aladin [*sic*], or the Arabian nights, that can excel, much less surpass, the luxury and splendor of the saloons of this ship.[24]

Life-saving apparatus on the Panama steamers was not very adequate, the *New York,* for instance, being built to carry about seven hundred passengers, for whom six lifeboats were provided. The *Colorado,* which could carry 1,500 in her steerage alone, had twelve boats. In 1858 the Pacific Mail did begin the practice of placing on board their steamers iron lifeboats with air chambers built into their sides.[25]

The cost of operating steamers, particularly on the Pacific coast, was comparatively high. The scarcity of labor in San Francisco in the "boom" years and the remoteness of the coast from supplies of coal and sources of supply for manufactured articles largely accounted for this. When the little 460-ton screw steamer *Columbus* operated from Panama to San Francisco for George Law in 1850 and 1851, the cost of her round voyages ranged between $20,540.08 and $27,410.91. On her third voyage, in September and October, 1850, the disbursements of the *Columbus* amounted to $20,540.08, of which $6,636.46 went toward wages for the crew and for labor while the ship was in port, $4,796 covered the cost of the coal for the voyage, while the ship's provisions cost $2,538.32.[26] Very generous estimates made in October, 1851, placed the total expense of a round voyage of the *Panama* from San Francisco to Panama— including coal, wages, stores, provisions, replacement and wear and tear—at about $70,000. At the same time, it was predicted that the cost of operating the *Golden Gate* for the round voyage would be $137,000.[27] The *Golden Gate* was an expensive ship to run; Gilmor Meredith, writing in December, 1851, said that she could not make money because she cost so much to operate, but even then the estimate given above is too high.[28] In May, 1855, the total cost of outfitting the *Golden Gate* at San Francisco was $19,497.37. If we add as much again for outfitting at Panama and $34,560 for 1,440 tons of coal at $24 per ton, a total of about $73,555 is reached.[29] The cost of outfitting the steamers at San Francisco, for which accurate figures exist, tended to decrease over the years. In 1859 the cost to the *Golden Gate* was $15,703.58; in 1862 it was $11,834.72 for the *Constitution;* and in 1868, $11,850.55 for the *Sacramento.*[30] A committee of stockholders of the Pacific Mail found that in 1855 the total expense of a round voyage to Panama amounted to $76,000, and since the company was running twenty-four voyages a year, the outlay for the Panama line reached about $1,824,000.[31]

On the United States Mail, the management tried to keep down expenses by constantly urging agents and officers to buy supplies with care and at the lowest prices. Marshall O. Roberts directed his commanders on the Atlantic to buy only fresh meat and vegetables at ports on the voyage since all stores which could be kept were bought in New York under his own supervision.[31a]

In spite of these heavy costs of operation the steamers on the Pacific were run at a profit except in times of bitter competition when rates were cut to losing figures in order to attract passengers away from rival lines. To take a few examples, the through-passenger receipts from San Francisco to Panama by the *California,* sailing April 1, 1851, amounted to $3,410, in June of the next year the *Golden Gate's* passenger waybill was $25,637.50, and later that year the *Golden Gate* took in $36,297.50.[32] In a report made to a general meeting of stockholders of the Pacific Mail in October, 1854, the average passenger receipts of the first-class steamers like the *Golden Gate, John L. Stephens,* and *Sonora* were placed at $38,679 for each one-way voyage in 1853, and at $34,542 in 1854. The smaller steamers like the *Oregon, California,* and *Panama* averaged receipts of $18,762 in 1853 and $17,442 in 1854. A few voyages were made by very small, or third-class steamers in 1853, on which they carried an average of forty-nine passengers, bringing in an average of $4,632 per trip.[33] In May, 1855, the total gross receipts for the *Golden Gate* on one round voyage amounted to $81,776, though in the same month the *Sonora* reported gross receipts of only $38,432, which meant a considerable loss on the voyage.[34]

Passage receipts tended to decrease in the latter part of the eighteen-fifties, particularly during the strong competition of 1859. Moreover, after the beginning of the Civil War the east-bound passenger lists were comparatively small, and the westbound ships, for which no figures are available, carried large numbers. The *Sonora's* waybill to Panama was $13,796.88 on March 7, 1859, as compared with that of $27,435.31 of the *Golden Gate* in the summer before. In October, 1862, and January, 1863, waybills had fallen as low as $7,519.75 and $5,623.62.[35] The effect of the opening of the transcontinental railroad on traffic via Panama is reflected in the figures for April, May, and June of 1869. On her voyage of April 6, 1869, the waybill of the *Constitution* was $19,790.99, and on May 12 the *Colorado's* was $19,470.94. By June 22, the *Colorado's* waybill amounted to only $6,512.82, and on June 30, the receipts of the *Constitution* were $8,770.63.[36]

Unfortunately, accounts of the operating expenses for steamers on the Atlantic part of the route are not available, and the reports of receipts are too fragmentary to be of significance. The generalization may safely be made, however, that the cost of operation was appreciably less on the Atlantic, because of the greater labor supply and the proximity of coal mines. In periods when the through receipts for the route were divided, the proportion going to the Atlantic steamers was a third to a quarter of the total, which indicates roughly the proportionally smaller expense which that part of the route bore.

When the first Pacific Mail steamers were sent to the west coast, it was reported that doubts of their ability to make the voyage were so strong that insurance on them was difficult to arrange, and what little they were able to effect was at high rates.[37] The policy of the company in 1854 was to insure vessels at or near their full value on the voyage from New York to San Francisco, keeping the insurance up to only half the value of the ships while they were on the Pacific station. Stores in transit to the Pacific were also fully insured. It was found that by taking policies with English rather than American companies, premiums were returned while the ships lay idle in port, and recoveries were more certain in case of partial damage. In the period from May 1, 1853, to October, 1854, some $600,000 had been collected by the Pacific Mail from underwriters, and $40,000 remained due from companies in liquidation.[38]

By 1857 the company had completely abandoned the practice of insuring its ships on the route between Panama and San Francisco. It was found to be impossible to insure against fire on reasonable terms, and therefore a sinking fund was established by the company to care for its own losses.[39] This policy was followed with a good deal of success by the Pacific Mail, at least as late as 1859, the reserve fund for insurance—invested in bank stocks, treasury notes, and state and city securities—having reached $300,887.87 in the latter year.[40]

For the officers and crews of the Panama steamers, men were drawn chiefly from ordinary American seafaring types, New York being the center from which most of them were shipped for the

Atlantic steamers, and San Francisco for the Pacific vessels. Negroes were frequently, but not always, used in the galley and as waiters. Almost at the beginning of the Panama lines, President Aspinwall of the Pacific Mail wrote that the best arrangement for cooks and stewards would probably be to import them from China, but this was not done until the Pacific Mail opened its Oriental line in 1867.[41]

By the terms of the contract with the Navy Department, the United States Mail Steamship Company was required to use naval officers as commanders and watch officers for its ships. These men were nominated by the operators of the steamers and granted leaves of absence by the Secretary of the Navy for the period of their service. It was general practice to place an officer with the grade of lieutenant in the Navy in command of a steamer, giving to passed midshipmen the places as watch officers.[42] Since many officers recognized the increasingly important place which steamers would play in naval warfare, they were anxious to obtain places in command of mail steamships. In the Navy as it was in 1849 there were comparatively few opportunities to become familiar with steamers, and service with the mail lines offered to young officers a splendid chance to gain experience and also to exercise command at an earlier age than would be possible in the regular service.[43] The customary period of absence from the Navy was three years, after which the officer returned to active duty.[44] Some officers resigned their commissions and remained in the service of the mail lines rather than return to naval duty at the end of the leave.

Although the requirement of naval officers in mail steamers did not extend to the ships of the Pacific Mail, a number of the ships of that company were commanded by them. During their terms in merchant ships, the junior officers were on a level with those of the merchant service, and relations between men of naval and mercantile backgrounds seem to have been harmonious. The system was followed as long as the mail contracts with the Navy Department continued in force, and was terminated in the fall of 1859.

The naval officers who commanded the United States Mail steamers saw to it that their ships were run in smart fashion. Their logs abound with references to the constant round of holystoning, painting, tarring, and cleaning. The crews were strictly disciplined, and confinement under single or double was a not infrequent punishment for insolence to officers or passengers or for drunkenness. Crews were not hard to obtain for these ships, and in 1852, George Law directed that all officers and men be engaged for only a month at a time.[44a]

The unusual attraction of the gold regions of California to all able-bodied men made it necessary for the Pacific Mail to face the rather serious problem of keeping their crews aboard the steamers after reaching San Francisco in order to be able to carry out the mail contract. Even before the *California* had reached the Pacific coast, the administration of the company had realized the necessity of taking steps to keep the men on the ship. Alfred Robinson, the agent, was provided with a strong letter from the Secretary of the Navy to Commodore Thomas ap Catesby Jones, commander of the Pacific Squadron, which would secure a row guard from the warships for the *California* and make it unnecessary for her to lower her boats while in San Francisco. Aspinwall wrote also that, if Robinson failed in his efforts to keep the men aboard, "you must hire men for the run on the best terms you can."[45]

Even before she reached San Francisco the *California* had trouble with her crew, a mutiny breaking out among the stokers between San Blas and Mazatlán. Acting Captain John T. Marshall acceded to the men's demands at the time, but while the ship lay at Mazatlán, he obtained the aid of Mexican authorities to have the mutineers put ashore, and shipped Mexicans in their places.[46] When the ship reached San Francisco, several of the officers and crew deserted on the very day of arrival, and before a week was out, almost all had left her. Since there was no coal with which to make a return voyage, the incentive to keep a crew aboard was less than it would otherwise have been. Commodore Jones was called on for a detachment of men to take charge of the ship to keep her from drifting ashore, and one of the engine-room boys who returned to the ship was able to keep the machinery oiled and in good condition. When Captain Pearson arrived in the *Oregon*, he was able to hold his crew aboard with the assistance of Commodore Jones and sailed on schedule for Panama.[47]

On receiving news of the plight of the *California*, Aspinwall wrote the Secretary of the Navy, asking him for a letter to Jones which the latter would treat as an order, requesting the commodore to aid captains of mail steamers in carrying out the contract. He suggested that this assistance take the form not only of helping them to retain their crews, but also of supplying the ships with men from the warships if absolutely necessary.

The public interest & credit, as well as the reputation of the boats & the convenience of the mercantile community, call for the greatest regularity obtainable in the present state of things—& by landing and embarking passengers in the boats of the Squadron—by furnishing a row guard in port & by loaning men for the trip to Panama & back when not obtainable other- wise, I should hope that a creditable degree of regularity might be obtainable, as there will be no expense or effort spared on board the steamers to induce the crews to remain . . .[48]

In acknowledging this rather sweeping request, Secretary Preston said that, although Jones would be urged to afford such facilities to the mail steamers as he could, consistent with the public interest, he could not be ordered to do more.[49] At a later date, it is clear that mail steamers were manned and operated by naval officers and crews. In 1862, after the burning of the *Golden Gate,* southbound to Panama, it was suggested that the spare steamer *California* might be brought up to San Francisco with the mails and passengers by officers and crew from the U.S.S. *Saranac,* as had been done once before by seamen from the *St. Mary's.*[50]

When the Pacific Mail ships set out from New York, their crews were signed on for a period of three years at the rate of $12 per month, the commanders receiving $1,800 a year. On the arrival of the steamer *Oregon* at San Francisco, Captain Pearson realized that he could not keep a crew at $12 a month, when Commodore Jones told him that new men could not be had for $300 a month. He therefore raised the monthly pay of the men to $112, paying his chief officer $250 per month and his cook $200 per month.[51] In the course of the next year, the Pacific Mail not only raised the pay of its men, but arranged that the officers should receive a bonus at the end of each year of service, as a reward for their faithfulness to the company. Thus the pay of first officers and pursers was set at $1,800 per year, with a bonus of $600 at the end of the year in addition.[52]

In 1850 reports reached the Pacific Mail headquarters in New York that officers on the company's ships were carrying freight on their own account. Since this was forbidden, Vice-President Comstock asked that officers doing this be reported to the company in order that they might be replaced by others. He asked also how many times Captain Porter's family had traveled with him on the *Unicorn*. It had come to his attention that this commander had been carrying vegetables up the coast on speculation. Concerning this activity Comstock remarked,

It seems strange that there should be constant complaints of fare & scarcity of the very articles which according to our information he is in the habit of taking to San Francisco for sale.[53]

One of the engineers of the Pacific Mail Steamship Company wrote that in the latter part of 1849 the rush eastward was as great as the movement of passengers in the opposite direction had been earlier in the year. Most of the crews were made up of men who worked their passage, not always because they could not afford to go otherwise, but often because there were not enough passenger accommodations.

All sorts of men were shipped as the crew in my engine department; I had beach combers, merchants, mechanics, laborers, doctors, ministers of the gospel, and men of all trades and religions; and so eager were these men to ship as crews that we were compelled to keep guard on shipboard, to prevent overloading the ship with stowaways.[54]

Such arrangements might be justified in the emergency conditions which existed on the Pacific coast in the "gold rush" period, but they could not be synonymous with a well-managed line of steamers. The home office of the Pacific Mail wrote to Robinson at the beginning of 1850, ordering particularly that the system of allowing persons to work for their passage must be discontinued. The complaints of the passengers who had come south on the *Panama* had been endless regarding the incapacity of stewards, cooks, and waiters, and the want of cleanliness in all the arrangements of the ship. "If good waiters cannot be obtained, they must be sent out . . . when we send stewards and cooks."[55]

In 1852 the standard wage for seamen on the San Francisco–Panama run was $40 to $45 per month. Captains generally received $125 to $150 a month, first officers $60, second officers $40 and stewards and cooks $50 to $55.[56] Pacific Mail captains received $250 per month and 5 per cent "primage" on freight receipts in 1854; mates were paid $50 to $150 depending on their grade, pursers $150, and surgeons $100 per month. In the engineer's department, the chief was paid $208.33 per month, and his assistants $80 to $110 depending on grade. The monthly wages for the rest of the crew were: carpenter $100, storekeeper $50 to $80, steward and stewardess $70 to $125, cooks $60 to $120, firemen $70, water tenders $70, coal heavers $45, oilers $50, baker $90, butcher $70, porter $40 to $50, pantryman $45 to $65, waiters $35 to $45, seamen $35 to $40, and boys $12 to $15.[57] The crews were supplied to the Pacific Mail steamers in San Francisco by James Murray, who took charge of getting men together and shipping them, and his payment, ranging from $190 to $331 for each crew, was a regular item in the expense accounts of the ships at San Francisco.[58]

The only period in which the condition or treatment of the crews on the Panama steamers engaged public attention was from 1860 to 1865 on the Vanderbilt steamers between New York and Aspinwall. Sympathy began at the top, and it was pointed out that, in spite of the dangerous nature of the run and the able men needed to command ships on it, Vanderbilt was notorious for the poor pay and hard conditions of his captains.[59] The duties of baggage master, physician, purser, and chaplain were combined in one officer on the *Ariel* in 1860, and this overworked officer was reported to receive $50 per month.[60] On one voyage of the *North Star* in 1860 a passenger reported that there were only eight stokers and firemen carried on the ship, each of whom worked two out of the four watches daily, giving a man twelve hours of work in the twenty-four. Two of these men died on the voyage. To care for the 350 passengers aboard, there were but eight stewards, who had not only to wait daily on eleven sittings at meals in the cabin, but also to care for the staterooms.[61] In 1862 an investigation was carried on at Aspinwall in the case of a member of the crew of the *Ariel*, who claimed that he had been kidnaped on the wharf in New York and made to serve unwillingly in the crew. The second officer of the steamer was found guilty of throwing down, striking, and kicking members of the crew, and striking a passenger who remonstrated with him. It should be remembered in this connection, however, that such treatment was not uncommon at sea in the nineteenth century and was often the only means by which the officers could hold a crew of "hard cases" under their control. According to testimony given in the investigation, when men deserted at Aspinwall, the petty officers went out along the line of the Panama Railroad, where they were likely to find the fugitives, and catching them, manacled them and confined them aboard the ship until after she had put to sea. It was learned that men were sent aboard at New York as waiters, without legal shipping papers, at $12 per month, and were then forced to work in the firerooms in the places of men who should have been employed at $30 a month.[62] Such conditions were undoubtedly bad, but the fact that they received so much attention in the press would indicate that they were not common and that life in the forecastle of most of the Panama steamers was not entirely a hell afloat.

The problem of providing facilities for the overhaul and repair of the steamers was much more difficult on the Pacific than on the Atlantic. For ships operating between New York or New Orleans and the Isthmus, there were ample machine shops and dry-dock facilities at the northern termini of their routes. By 1850, the United States Mail Company had established a coal supply at Porto Bello, where the steamers could lie close to shore while native laborers filled their bunkers, and fresh water was taken aboard. As late as 1856, the line's ships still went to Porto Bello to clean ship and water.[62a] It was customary to keep supplies of coal at Aspinwall, after the establishment of that port, but there were no facilities for repair. When the *North Star* broke her shaft near Aspinwall southbound, she managed to make port, and then waited until the next steamer, the *Costa Rica,* arrived, to be towed back to New York by her.

Conditions on the Pacific were very different, and from the beginning the operators of ships on the run between Panama and San Francisco planned carefully to provide repair bases there. The first three steamers of the Pacific Mail carried with them complete sets of spare parts for their machinery for use in an emergency. The original plan of the directors of the Pacific Mail was to place the headquarters of the line at some point intermediate between Panama and Oregon, probably at San Blas. Altered conditions, due to the press of passengers for California, resulted in the establishment of the center of operations at Panama and in the appointment of Captain William C. Stout as general agent for the line with headquarters there.[63] Not only was Panama closer to New York in communicating time, but it was also the nearest port on the route to Callao, Peru, where it was possible to have repairs made to the machinery of the ships.[64] In accordance with this policy, the San Francisco agent of the company was ordered to keep the steamers at the northern terminus for as short a time as possible, since every spare day should be spent at Panama where they could be overhauled and caulked.[65] Skilled mechanics were difficult to obtain, and the home organization sent them out from New York whenever possible. When one of the foremen of the Novelty Iron Works traveled to California, he was given cabin passage free in return for not more than five weeks' work at Panama for the Pacific Mail.[66]

The base for the ships at Panama was on the island of Taboga, situated about twelve miles out in the Bay of Panama. Not only was the air cooler and more refreshing here than on the mainland, but there were also excellent springs from which the fresh-water tanks of the ships could be filled. The very heavy tides of the Bay of Panama made it possible to run a ship close inshore at high tide and have her lying completely out of water on the sand when the tide was low. Thus bottoms could be cleaned and repaired without the necessity of constructing a dry dock. Coal and supplies for the Pacific Mail ships were kept at Taboga, and as soon as a steamer had landed her passengers at Panama, she proceeded to Taboga, where she lay until time to return to Panama for the embarkation of travelers and freight from the Atlantic. A strike of the laborers at Taboga for wages of $3 per day in 1855 was settled by sending down about seventy men from Panama to coal the *John L. Stephens*. Although a disturbance was at first feared, the Panameños were allowed to proceed with their work unmolested. The *Panama Star and Herald* remarked in this connection, "In the present dull times we should suppose four to six dimes good daily wages for these lazy fellows."[67]

As the number of ships in operation increased and the relative importance of Panama as a base declined in relation to San Francisco, plans were made to abandon Taboga and transfer headquarters to a point more convenient to the city of Panama. On March 1, 1853, the island of Flamenco, the outer one of a group of three rocky islands off the city, was purchased by the Pacific Mail as a base.[68] Two years later the works of the Pacific Mail were removed from Taboga, and thereafter the ships lay at Flamenco, where storehouses, carpenter and blacksmith shops, and coal yards were constructed.[69] The wide band of tidal flats surrounding the city of Panama made it impossible to construct wharves there at which the ships could lie during their stay in port. A small steamer was maintained on the bay to bring out passengers and baggage to the ships, and the Panama Railroad constructed great iron lighters, in which provisions and coal could be brought alongside the ships as they lay at anchor in the bay.[70] The construction of a gridiron for the use of the steamers was commenced in 1862. It was placed on Flamenco and afforded a better place for the ships to lie at low tide while they were being cleaned than the sand beach which had been used hitherto.[71] After 1855 it was the invariable practice of the Pacific Mail to keep an extra steamer at Panama, so that in the event of accident to the regular ship there would be a vessel ready to carry passengers and mail north upon their arrival on the Pacific side.

At the beginning it was the plan to establish way stations at which coal, water, and provisions could be obtained between Panama and San Francisco. Coal for the first ships was deposited at San Blas, but the excellent harbor of Acapulco led to its adoption for the purpose. A coal yard was placed there, and the steamers called regularly in both directions to take on coal if it were needed, as well as fresh provisions.[72]

When it was realized that the flow of population to California in 1848 and 1849 would make of that region a well-settled area, the original plan of making Panama the chief depot of the route was modified to include more extensive works at or near San Francisco. Although in February, 1850, orders had been issued to keep the steamers as short a time as possible at San Francisco, in June of the same year instructions were sent out to give the ships a layover of a month in that port between trips.[73] Even in the previous year Aspinwall had instructed Alfred Robinson to buy land in the neighborhood of Carquinez Strait, and before the year was out a tract on the north side of the strait, at Benicia, had been purchased from General Vallejo.[74] The splendid location of Benicia, with deep water coming directly up to the shore line, and the low price of the land there as compared with San Francisco, explain its choice as a base of operations for the steamers. In February, 1850, the *Unicorn* made a trip from San Francisco to Benicia with "a numerous party of ladies and gentlemen ... in whose honor Commodore Jones gave a grand ball aboard the Savannah."[75] The construction of docks and machine shops at Benicia was undertaken, and by the end of June, 1850, steamers of the Pacific Mail were receiving their supplies of coal from the depot which had been established there.[76] Thus, as at the other end of the route, the base of the Pacific Mail was located away from the center of population, and once the steamers had discharged their passengers and cargo at San Francisco, they proceeded to Benicia for cleaning, refitting, and provisioning, to return to the city usually the day before they were scheduled to sail. The ironworks and machine shops of the Pacific Mail at Benicia became the first large industrial enterprise of California. Two-story brick buildings were constructed at a cost of approximately $100,000, and the machinery and furnishings cost as much again. Inside the buildings were offices, storerooms, drafting rooms, pattern and boiler shops, machine shops, a finishing room, a blacksmith shop, a foundry, cove ovens, and a crane. Machinery and boilers of the largest size then in use could be constructed or repaired here. With such a large establishment, it was expected that not only ships of the Pacific Mail but also other vessels needing repairs could be cared for here.[77] For the first six months of 1854 the pay roll of the Benicia works amounted to $107,248.02, the profits for the period being placed at $32,438.94. This last figure was reached by crediting the repairs of steamers at cost only, whereas if they had been entered at the rate at which the work could be done elsewhere, it might have been placed at $72,000.[78] A visitor to the establishment in 1857 described it as follows:

The scene presented at the wharf seemed to be one of unusual activity, and the sounds of the various instruments wielded by the sturdy arms of the hundred workmen, together with the noise of the massive machinery of the foundry were absolutely deafening. The decks and the hold of the Golden Gate were alive with laborers, repairing and burnishing machinery, cleaning cabins, scouring furniture, and coaling the vessel ... She is apparently in perfect order, and ready to take her departure from San Francisco. ...[79]

To the administration of the Pacific Mail, the investment in the Benicia works did not seem to be entirely wise or justified, and in 1855 President Aspinwall recommended that the establishment be sold.[80] In spite of this recommendation, and rumors in San Francisco in 1856 that operations at the Benicia foundry and machine shop would be abandoned, it was held by the company.[81] According to the annual report for 1858, the investment in machinery, stock, and tools at Benicia amounted to $121,700, and the real estate there was held at $290,900.69, by far the largest single holding of the company ashore.[82]

The efficiency of the Benicia works was demonstrated in May, 1858, when the *Golden Gate* put back into San Francisco with a broken shaft. A telegram was sent by the agents of the company in the city to the superintendent and resident engineer at Benicia to prepare the *Sonora* for sea immediately. The ship was dismantled at the time, a great part of her machinery had been taken to pieces for examination, and her condenser was in the shop undergoing repairs. Within twenty-six hours of the receipt of the telegram the engine had been put together and was in working order, 400 tons of coal were aboard, the specie, mails, freight, and baggage had been transferred from the *Golden Gate,* and the *Sonora,* repainted outside and provisioned and equipped for sea, was on her way to take passengers aboard at San Francisco.[83]

It was not until 1868 that the Pacific Mail announced that it would have the repairs made on its ships by contract in the future, giving up the Benicia plant. The sale of the property in 1869 ended the connection of the Pacific Mail with Benicia, though instead of having all its work done by outside contract, a machine shop was erected in San Francisco in which some necessary repairs could be made.[84] The day had passed when the company needed to provide all the equipment necessary for the operation of its ships.

No dry dock was ever constructed at Benicia, and, for underwater repairs and cleaning, the ships were constrained to depend upon the tides of Panama until the building of the dock at Mare Island Navy Yard. The Bureau of Yards and Docks of the Navy Department adopted a regular scale of prices at which merchant ships might use the Mare Island dock, and for all the steamers operating on the Pacific coast until the completion of the dry dock at Hunter's Point, the Navy Yard was the center for repairs to hulls.[85]

When steamers first began to come to San Francisco, there were no wharves; passengers, baggage, and cargo were landed in small boats and lighters. With the construction of wharves, the operators of steamships deemed it important to gain rights to use them, thereby facilitating landing and embarkation. In 1850 the San Francisco agents of the Pacific Mail invested $10,000 in Central Wharf in order to secure privileges of use.[86] Cunningham's Wharf was leased by the Pacific Mail for its exclusive use in May, 1854, at the rate of $1,500 per month. Barriers and gates were built to "facilitate the business of the ships, and to protect their passengers from the annoyance of loafers and the confusion of the multitude that congregate on the wharves upon the arrival or departure of a vessel."[87] Three years later, in 1857, the wharf at the foot of Folsom Street was leased by the Pacific Mail because of the deeper water there, and steamers of the company began to use that exclusively for their arrival and departure.[88] With the opening of the China line in 1867, the Pacific Mail undertook the construction of new wharves, warehouses, and coal yards just south of Rincon Point in San Francisco, and after the completion of this rather extensive establishment the ships of the company used it as long as its house flag continued to fly in San Francisco Bay.[89]

One absolute requisite to the operation of steamers is an adequate supply of fuel, and the provision of coal for the Panama steamers, particularly in the Pacific, caused much concern to their operators. The Atlantic ports were near the centers of production, and steamers could take on coal at New York or have it shipped to Porto Bello and Aspinwall to be loaded there, but on the Pacific matters were more complex. Since the natural resources of the area were not yet entirely known, there was the possibility of using a supply of coal which might be developed there. The alternative lay in shipping the coal around Cape Horn from the eastern United States or England. Even before the steamers had been built for the Pacific run, the Postmaster General wrote the Secretary of the Navy that a fine coal mine had been discovered in Oregon, which might be of use to the steamers which were to operate on the Pacific.[90] A more attractive source seemed to be the mines which the Hudson's Bay Company reported to have discovered on Vancouver Island, from which Sir George Simpson, governor of the Hudson's Bay Company, agreed to supply the steamers. The company agreed to send out miners from England to place the mine in efficient operation, and until they could arrive, it arranged to have Indians prepare five hundred or a thousand tons of coal at the mine for the use of the steamers.[91] In December, 1848, Captain Stout, general agent for the

Pacific Mail on the coast, returned to San Francisco from a trip to Oregon, reporting that he had been able to obtain an abundance of coal in the British possessions to the north.[92] A great deal of correspondence took place about the coal to be brought from Vancouver Island. It took longer to mine it than had been anticipated, and news did not reach New York that it was actually ready for use until January, 1850.[93] When there was an opportunity to test it, this coal proved to be rather unsatisfactory, having only about two-thirds the strength of Welsh coal.[94] In a letter of October 12, 1850, Aspinwall wrote that what Vancouver coal had been tried had been so disappointing that no measures should be taken to obtain any more; the supply already on hand might be sold.[95]

From the beginning, entire dependence had not been placed on the coal supply of the Pacific area, and ships had been chartered to bring fuel from England and the eastern United States. These cargoes were landed at Panama, San Blas, and San Francisco. As has already been noted, the ship bound for San Francisco was late in reaching her destination, and the first southbound voyage of the *California* was delayed thereby. The home office knew that this might be so, and the following order was intended to take effect in such an emergency:

If at any time you have to send a steamer off short of coal, do not let it be known that we are short at San Diego & San Blas, leaving the coast under steam they will find their sails will secure them a fair passage in case of need—& the less said about any disappointment the better.[96]

As the line was in operation for a longer period, the supplies of coal were built up, and shortages became fewer. In line with its original policy of keeping the ships in San Francisco for short periods only, the Pacific Mail planned to place its principal coal depot at Acapulco, sending two or three thousand tons there as a beginning.[97]

Coal was very expensive even for the pioneer company with its careful arrangements; for the lines which placed competing steamers on the route it cost even more. When the *Isthmus* of Law's Line arrived on her first trip, the coal supply which had been intended for her was not ready, and she was finally forced to pay $100 per ton for some coal which accidentally became available at Realejo.[98] In a ship which the same owners chartered in 1851, the cost of coal was figured at $24.50 per ton, of which $20 went for freight.[99] Sometimes coal could be had for as little as $15 a ton; again it would rise to $45. To balance these fluctuations as much as possible, the companies which did not invest in coal depots ashore purchased or chartered hulks, into which coal could be unloaded as it was purchased and from which it could be placed directly in the bunkers of the steamers when they were ready for it.[100]

In 1851 it was reported that the Pacific Mail had purchased a tract of coal land along the Kanawha River in Virginia, so that it could produce coal for itself and thereby reduce the expense.[101] A little more than two years later, in July, 1853, the statement was made that 3,000 acres of coal land in George's Creek Valley, in the Cumberland district of Maryland, had been purchased by the Pacific Mail, and that the steamers on the Pacific could be supplied with it for $9 per ton less than they were paying at the time by shipping it over the Panama Railroad.[102] These sources of coal in the United States did not stop importation of English coal altogether, although the foreign purchases of San Francisco, Acapulco, and Panama, which had been 92,611 tons in 1852, dropped to 34,177 in 1853.[103]

In October, 1854, the Pacific Mail had on hand at Benicia, Acapulco, and Panama 21,252 tons of coal, which had cost the company an average of $24 per ton.[104] When President Aspinwall reported to the stockholders in June, 1855, he pointed out that the supply of coal kept on hand by the company must always be large. Prudence dictated a supply of about 16,000 tons, making enough for six months at each of the three coal depots. On his business trip to California earlier in 1855 Aspinwall had been able to purchase 5,000 tons at a little over half cost owing to the business depression, but the policy of trusting to purchases on the spot was one to be condemned.[105] Increasing facilities for transportation tended to reduce the price, and in 1858 the Pacific Mail held its coal at $19 per ton; a year later, the 24,086 tons which were on the Pacific coast were counted in at $18 per ton.[106]

On neither the Atlantic nor the Pacific were the steamers of the Panama lines free from marine disasters. However, considering the wooden hulls and cabins of the steamers, the inadequate lifesaving facilities, the sometimes overly small crews, and the frequently uncertain engines, the ships came off remarkably well.

On the Pacific, too, the absence of proper lights and buoys and the undependable nature of some of the charts available made the matter of navigation a difficult one.

The safety record of the Pacific Mail was particularly enviable. With the exception of the *Golden Gate,* which burned at sea in 1862, there was no loss of life in its ships because of fire or wreck in the twenty-year period considered. In contrast, the great Royal Mail Steam Packet Company lost no less than six ships in the decade from 1842 to 1852, and the famous Collins Line was crippled by the loss of the *Arctic* and *Pacific* within two years of one another, with staggering lists of drowned and missing.

The most frequent and the least serious of difficulties at sea resulted from trouble with the engines. It has already been seen how the *Panama* was forced to turn back to New York on her trip to the Pacific coast because of mechanical breakdown. In December, 1849, the *Crescent City* had a somewhat similar experience. She was four days out of New York, bound for Chagres with a small passenger list of fifty-five, when the crosshead of the engine broke, also breaking the connecting rod between it and the crank and bending the piston rod. All sail was immediately made, and the buckets were taken off the ends of the arms of the paddle wheels so that her progress would be impeded as little as possible, but the wind was light, and she made slight headway. Guns and rockets were fired during the night to attract attention, and the next morning, December 17, the schooner *Sarah A. Smith,* bound from Belfast, Maine, to Key West with a cargo of lumber, came alongside. Charles Morgan and Captain Stoddard, owners of the *Crescent City,* went aboard the schooner and arranged to charter her to carry passengers to Chagres, buying the cargo of lumber and jettisoning it. On the morning of the eighteenth a committee of passengers went aboard the *Sarah A. Smith* to decide how many she could carry. They estimated that she would accommodate thirty comfortably. Provisions were sent aboard, and with her passengers she made sail for Chagres about 1:00 P.M. that day. The same day, the brig *Roscoe* of Boston passed, bound for Havana, and took off a few passengers, and the brig *Marcia* of Bath took six or eight more, leaving some fifteen on the *Crescent City.* On the morning of December 27, she fell in with the steamer *Governor Dudley,* which gave her a tow to Charleston, where repairs could be made.[107]

Sometimes engine trouble had more serious consequences. When the *Golden Gate,* having broken her center shaft off the Mexican coast, made the voyage in to San Diego on one engine and one wheel, she could not be maneuvered sufficiently quickly in leaving the harbor and went aground off Point Loma. The tide fell before the steamer *Goliah,* which was in the harbor, could pull her off, and, a gale arising in the night, she pounded on the bank, sustaining serious damage. It took a good deal of trouble to get the *Golden Gate* off and repair her hull, and three months elapsed before she was ready to enter service again.[108]

There were only two steamers on the Panama route which were pounded to pieces by the sheer force of the elements, and these were both on the Atlantic. The first was the *San Francisco,* a steamer built for the Pacific Mail Steamship Company by William H. Webb in 1853, which was chartered to carry about five hundred troops with their officers and provisions to California as she went to take her station on the Pacific.[109] Sailing from New York on the morning of December 22, 1853, with 750 persons aboard, she encountered very heavy weather on the evening of the second day out. An hour after the storm reached her, she broached to, and though the ship was placed on her course again and kept before the wind by giving her all the steam which the boilers would bear, the engine gave out altogether before the night was over, and she fell into the trough of the sea. Her guards were carried away, and the waves swept the deck at every roll. One passenger attempted to describe the main deck of the *San Francisco* that night.

Here a scene of confusion indescribable and confounding presented itself. The live stock, of which there was considerable, had escaped from their pens on the same deck, and soldiers, bullocks, calves, pigs, sheep and poultry were all mingled together amid the broken standees [berths].[110]

By keeping the steam pumps at work and forming bucket lines of soldiers the steamer was kept fairly free of water, but the storm continued to increase in violence, and there seemed to be no prospect of repairing the engine. On December 24 a sea swept away the whole promenade deck abaft the paddles, the staterooms of which contained about 150 persons. The starboard paddle box was crushed, and both smokestacks went overboard. On Christmas the sea moderated somewhat, and on the twenty-seventh the engine was repaired sufficiently to be put in motion for a few minutes, only to expire again, leaving less hope than ever that it could be placed in working order. The next day cholera broke out among the soldiers and crew, owing to exposure and lack of proper food, and men began to die by dozens. A ship was finally sighted that day and, coming alongside, took off some of those aboard the *San Francisco*. On the last day of 1853 more of the persons aboard were taken by a passing ship, and the last of the officers, with Captain Watkins, left the shattered hulk on January 5, 1854.[111] The survivors of the disaster, of whom there were about 550, had nothing but praise for the conduct of the officers and crew, and there was no charge that the ship had been badly built If any culprit was to be found, it was the engine, which failed so soon after its testing began.[112] The *San Francisco* had been sighted on December 26 by the *Maria Freeman*, which was unable to render assistance because of the high seas, and she brought the first news of the disaster into Halifax on January 4. When the intelligence reached Washington, Senator Gwin applied to the Secretary of the Navy for a ship to go to the aid of the *San Francisco*. The senator was informed that there was no government vessel in port fit for immediate service, and therefore a merchant vessel was chartered to go in search of the wreck.[113]

The other serious loss on the Atlantic was that of the *Central America,* formerly the *George Law,* belonging to the United States Mail Steamship Company. She was northbound from Havana to New York when she encountered a severe gale off the Florida coast and foundered on September 12, 1857, with a loss of about 423 lives and $8,000,000 in treasure. As far as could be ascertained, the ship was perfectly sound when she left Havana on September 8, and she made no water until the head of steam was unaccountably allowed to go down on the eleventh, and she fell into the trough of the sea. Efforts to get up steam again were not successful, and after the ship lost headway, water entered through the ports, paddle-wheel shaft, and parts of the upper works until the fires were extinguished, after which the seas literally beat the ship to pieces.[114]

In this instance also the loss of the ship was due rather to the failure of the engines than to any structural defect. The disaster, however, aroused public feeling against the United States Mail

Steamship Company. The following popular ballad gives the tone of the comment:

> The "Central America," painted so fine,
>   Went down like a thousand of brick,
> And all the old tubs that are now on the line
>   Will follow her, two at a lick.
> 'Twould be very fine were the owners aboard,
>   And sink where they never would rise;
> 'Twould any amount of amusement afford,
>   And cancel a million of lies.[115]

On the Pacific, most of the disasters were the result of the ships running ashore at night or in a fog. The years from 1851 to 1854 saw no less than eight such wrecks, some of them taking place under conditions highly uncomplimentary to the officers and crews of the steamers. The *Union,* of the Independent Line, southbound from San Francisco to Panama, went aground and was lost at San Quentin, about two hundred miles below San Diego on July 5, 1851. It was reported by the passengers that the crew became drunk on July 4 and remained so all day, and that when the ship struck at three o'clock the next morning, there was no watch on deck and the helmsman was too drunk to handle the wheel. The passengers, baggage, treasure, and provisions were all landed, and a party was immediately dispatched to San Diego, the rest camping at San Quentin Bay until the *Northerner* arrived on July 19 and took them aboard.[116]

On February 27, 1852, Vanderbilt's steamer *North America* was wrecked near Acapulco, and on August 17 of the same year the *Pioneer,* also belonging to Vanderbilt, went ashore at San Simeon Bay.[117] Vanderbilt lost two more steamers the next year, the *Independence,* wrecked on Margarita Island on February 16, 1853, with a loss of 125 lives, and the *S.S. Lewis,* a screw steamer, which mistook her bearings in entering San Francisco Bay and struck eleven miles north of the Heads, near Bolinas Bay. Her passengers and baggage were landed safely, but the ship broke up within a day.[118] The Pacific Mail did not escape entirely in 1853. Its steamer *Tennessee* went ashore in Bolinas Bay on March sixth, having missed the entrance of San Francisco Bay in a dense fog. The passengers, mail, and baggage were taken off, and for some time there was hope of saving the vessel, but she finally broke up.

Near the end of the same year, on December 2, the *Winfield Scott,* then owned by the Pacific Mail, struck on Anacapa Island in a dense fog. The vessel was a total loss, though in this wreck also no blame was attached to officers or crew, and all the passengers and mails, together with the specie aboard, were safely landed.[119]

On October 1, 1854, the steamer *Yankee Blade* of the Independent Opposition Line attempted to "cut the corner" too closely at Point Arguello, and, while running at full speed, struck a reef three-quarters of a mile offshore. Here the conduct of neither officers nor crew was exemplary. Captain Randall left the ship in the first boat, to examine the shore line, and after his return the sending of women and children ashore began. There was a good deal of confusion in launching the boats, and one of them, containing twenty-one passengers and the first officer of the steamer, was swamped, with a loss of seventeen lives. About two hundred of the nine hundred-odd persons aboard had been landed by dark, and the rest were compelled to remain aboard all night. The wind rose after dark and the ship began to break up. All discipline over the crew was lost, and some of them, together with a number of steerage passengers, broke into the spirit room and proceeded to get drunk. They then took complete possession of the ship, opening bags and trunks, robbing, beating, and threatening to murder passengers. Only at dawn was a semblance of order restored, and the landing of passengers continued, with the aid of the steamer *Goliah,* which came past in the morning. Some thirty lives were lost in the *Yankee Blade,* and Captain Randall was blamed severely for running so close inshore, and then for leaving the ship at once and losing control of the crew.[120]

On the Atlantic the only steamer to be wrecked was the *Golden Rule* of the Central American Transit Company, which struck on Roncador Reef, in the Caribbean, early in the morning of May 30, 1865. Within thirty minutes the ship had bilged, but all the passengers, and about half the baggage and stores, were transferred to a small island near by, whence officers were sent out in the ship's boats to Old Providence and Aspinwall for aid. Two gunboats arrived from Aspinwall on June 9, taking off all the passengers, after a not unhappy sojourn of ten days on the island.[121]

Although several of the Panama steamers were burned while in dock, only one, the *Golden Gate* of the Pacific Mail Steamship

Company, was burned at sea. When she was southbound from San Francisco to Panama on July 27, 1862, about fifteen miles west of Manzanillo, the *Golden Gate* was reported to be afire amidships. What efforts were made to extinguish the fire were unavailing, and the steamer was turned toward the beach at full speed. The wisdom of this action may be questioned, since the speed of the ship spread the fire aft. It also made it impossible to launch the boats, and persons jumping overboard forward of the wheels were in danger of being struck by the turning paddles. When the *Golden Gate* was beached, she was a mass of flames, and the surf all around her offered an uninviting alternative to the blazing ship. The loss of life in this disaster amounted to about 223, together with $1,400,000 in treasure. Fortunately for the survivors, the town of Manzanillo was near, and they were hospitably cared for until they were taken off by the *St. Louis* of the Pacific Mail.[122] With a commendable spirit of generosity the directors of the company voted half pay to the widows and orphans of members of the crew lost in the *Golden Gate* from July, 1862, until January 1, 1864.[123] This disaster cast no undue reflection upon the Pacific Mail, since in a day of wooden ships fire at sea was well-nigh impossible to fight successfully. It is rather remarkable that in the twenty-year period there were no more disasters of this nature.

In general, it may be said that the steamers carrying on the Panama lines were as fast, safe, and comfortable as most others of the day. The operation of some was a scandal, but more often they were excellently administered, carrying out their appointed tasks faithfully and well.

CHAPTER VI

THE VOYAGE

THE CHARACTER of the ocean part of the journey from New York or New Orleans to San Francisco by way of Panama was much the same in 1869 as in 1849. Although the size and speed of the ships increased and facilities for the accommodation of large numbers of travelers were improved, the broad aspects of the voyage remained similar from year to year. After 1850, the number of passengers carried in each direction was generally between ten and twenty thousand a year, but the trend was not constant, and there were periods in 1863 when the ships were as badly crowded as in 1849. The passing of the pioneer years resulted in some variation in the character of the passengers, but the cabins in which they were accommodated, the food they ate, the games they played, and even the complaints they made remained the same over the years. From the reports of these travelers it is possible to gain some impression of life on board the Panama steamers in the years when the route flourished. In evaluating this testimony, it must be remembered that travelers, and particularly travelers in hot climates, are often more forcibly impressed by the unpleasant than by the pleasant. For this reason, the hardships and discomforts of the voyage may sometimes have been unduly magnified. In many instances there was valid cause for dissatisfaction, but in the record this may have received more attention than it deserved.

Steamers bound for the Isthmus almost invariably departed from either New York or New Orleans. According to the original mail contract, vessels were required to go from New York to New Orleans by way of Charleston, Savannah, and Havana, and then to call at Havana again before proceeding to Chagres. This required fully two or three weeks to negotiate.

The United States Mail steamers hove to only briefly off the bar at Charleston and Tybee Light below Savannah, where chartered steamers met them with mail and passengers. This saved time, and also money, for if the ships docked, state laws required that their colored crew members be bonded. In order to meet the terms of the contract, and also accelerate service, the United States Mail Company operated interlocking schedules with Havana as the focal point. Thus, for example, the *Georgia* came into Havana Harbor early on the morning of April 19, 1850. Both the *Ohio* and *Falcon* were already at anchor there. The *Ohio* had just come in from New Orleans, and having sent her Isthmus-bound passengers aboard the *Georgia*, she sailed for New York that same evening. Early on the following morning, the *Falcon* left for New Orleans with the *Georgia*'s passengers who were destined for that port, and the *Georgia* herself, having completed coaling, stood out for Chagres about the middle of the afternoon. Competition and increased emphasis on speedy passages, together with the enlargement of the fleet, led to the abandonment of this system by the United States Mail steamers in favor of the direct, nonstop passage for most voyages after 1852.[1] The shortest course from New York is one almost due south, past the low-lying Bahamas, through the Windward Passage between Cuba and Hispaniola, and thence directly across the Caribbean to the Isthmus. If this course were followed, a call at Kingston for coal and provisions might be made. The chief alternative was to follow the coast south from New York, round the tip of Florida and, after a call at Havana, continue to Chagres around the western end of Cuba. When the voyage was made on one of these courses, the usual time required was between nine and eleven days. In times of keen competition, however, when fast passages meant favor with the traveling public, there were occasional trips of seven and a half or eight days.

On the Pacific, the steamers followed the coast to the northwestward after rounding Cape Mala and leaving the Gulf of Panama. The first ships called at Acapulco, San Blas, Mazatlán, San Diego, and Monterey before reaching San Francisco, but here also, with the advent of competition and consequent demands for greater speed, the intermediate ports were dropped. After 1851, the voyage was generally broken only once by a call at either Acapulco or Manzanillo, where supplies of coal and provisions could be replenished. The export of large quantities of silver bullion from Manzanillo made calls there profitable, and the superb landlocked bay of Acapulco was admirably suited to its use as a supply depot.[1a] In the pioneer years, the voyage from Panama to San Francisco required between eighteen and twenty-one days, though there were occasional passages of as low as sixteen. With the advent of larger

[1] For notes to chap. vi, see pp. 279–281.

and faster steamers like the *Golden Gate* and the *John L. Stephens*, this time was greatly reduced, the run being made in eleven days, twenty-two hours on one occasion. The schedule time was held at about fourteen days, however, even for ships which could make the voyage in less. A company regulation of the Pacific Mail in 1865 forbade commanders to bring their ships into San Francisco in less than thirteen and a half days from Panama, and this time remained usual until 1869.[2]

The through journey from New York to California in the early years could hardly take less than thirty-three or thirty-five days, given the most favorable traveling conditions and connections on the Isthmus. With the completion of the Panama Railroad, however, which reduced the time for crossing the Isthmus to one day, the through trip could be made quite regularly in twenty-three to twenty-six days, depending on the speed of the steamers used. The standard passage was set between twenty-one and twenty-one and a half days when the Pacific Mail came into control of the whole route in 1865. Although faster time could be made, this standard allowed the steamers to proceed at more economical speeds and yet gave better service than could dependably be had overland until the completion of the transcontinental railroad.

To characterize the passengers traveling on the Panama steamers would be impossible. A traveler in 1849 was particularly impressed by the quiet demeanor of those on the *Crescent City*, in spite of the fact that the stewardess was the only woman aboard.[3] The same year a steerage passenger on the *California* wrote, "Ned and others kept us awake nearly all night kicking up Bob, singing, swearing, smoking, etc."[4] In February, 1850, John B. Peirce wrote to his wife from the *Cherokee* as follows:

We have no noise or boisterous mirth, each passing the time as best suits his taste & some coiled up over the wheel taking the breeze, some leaning over the rails, others in chairs, or on seats under a large awning spread over the quarter deck, some reading, others smoking, others in little knots conversing, other little parties enjoying a little bit of a sing, some studying maps of Gold regions and all apparently good natured and happy. These are all cabin passengers. There are the steerage passengers & crew forward. Hard sun brown men with Hoosier rig or a tan colored short frock with trows[ers], heavy soled boots or barefoot as the case may be, with the round top slouch hat California cut—all colors, white, red, green, brown, black & dun—some hitched up in the rigging, some seated on the rail, others coiled up on the hurricane deck among their trunks and baggage, others stretched out on casks, barrells [*sic*] or boxes or in whatever position they happen to hit.[5]

The chief change noticeable in the passengers was that, with the settlement of California, a greater proportion of the company aboard a ship was made up of women and children. In 1851, Gilmor Meredith, a bachelor, wrote while aboard the *California,* "The greatest annoyance on board is the number of babies and children, the noise they keep up is frightful and I sometimes fancy I am in Pandemonium."[6] In 1863, in a detailed account of the voyage from New York to Aspinwall, the passengers were described as follows:

The only difference that I could perceive between the majority of the first and of the second and steerage passengers was that the two former had more money than the latter, consequently were able to pay for more comforts and conveniences. So far as the people themselves were concerned they were about the same. In fact, many of those in the steerage appeared to be the superiors in every respect of the greater part who were entitled to be considered a better class. I do not think that there were over thirty-five passengers on board who would have been considered first class on board a European steamer. I should say that half the passengers were women and children. Of the latter there one hundred and four, not counting babies. These, I should think, were too numerous to mention. There were many cases in which respectable families had purchased steerage tickets, not knowing what the steerage was.... We had many families on board going to California for the first time, and some returning after a short absence. There were male and female adventurers, farmers, merchants, officers, laborers, mechanics, loafers, thieves and pickpockets on board, and some of the latter did not wait until their arrival in California to ply their avocation...[7]

The men who traveled to California in the pioneer years went without their families, entering an unsettled area to wrest from it mineral wealth, to use in establishing themselves there or to take back with them to their eastern homes. In later years the human tide was composed of the families of these men, coming to join them in California, and of other men attracted by the business or industrial possibilities of the newly settled state. There were also many who looked upon the West as a place where life was easy and where the foundations laid by others could be used to advantage. During the years of the Civil War, the emigration to California included many who were anxious to escape the drafts for service in the Union armies, and in the same period the unsettled conditions in the East caused the number going in that direction to become smaller than usual.

Arrival and departure of the steamers were events which held interest for those aboard and ashore as well. The sailing of the

Falcon on her first voyage from New York to Chagres was described thus by a passenger:

The gong sounded through the saloon and along the decks, warning ashore those who were not going.

Then the good bye's were hurried, warm-hearted and very hard to say.

But they were all soon said, Captain Thompson appeared on deck, in his glazed cap, as manly, fine looking an officer as ever did service in our merchant marine,—he spoke a few quiet words, and made a few signals, and the steamer left her birth [*sic*]. Down the river we passed swiftly threading our way among the Jersey ferry-boats, and all the other moving craft,—down the bay, while we watched the city receding from our view.[8]

In November, 1849, Philip Hone wrote to a friend,

. . . it was amusing to see the carts on their way to the vessels [bound for Chagres] loaded with loafer-looking men, and their multifarious luggage of old trunks, dirty bedding, awkward culinary utensils, spades and pick-axes for digging gold, and bags to put it in . . .[9]

A traveler in 1863 found the press on the dock so great that it took his cab half an hour to move from the end of the pier to a place opposite the gangway of the *North Star,* on which he was sailing. Once aboard, the crowd was no less.

Moving about could not be attempted; it was an impossibility; for, besides the crowds of men, women and children, the decks were piled up with baggage. Big trunks, little trunks, chests, valises, carpet bags, bedding and bundles were strewn in every direction, completely blocking up every gangway. When the second gong sounded "All ashore" the rush for the pier commenced. This conflicted with the passengers still coming on board, which caused more oaths and torn clothing. Soon after the captain made his appearance, and he was obliged to take his chance with the others. Not being a small man, he got on board with difficulty. As soon as he reached the deck he was obliged, after going to his room for a few minutes, to seek safety in the pilothouse; for when it became known who he was a crowd at once made for him, asking every imaginable question about matters that he had nothing whatever to do with. The last gong sounded, the light lines were cast off, the last man jumped on a wharf post as we moved out of the dock, and we were on our way to Aspinwall.[10]

After leaving the dock, passengers were herded below to have their tickets examined, so that those without them could be sent ashore with the pilot. In April, 1854, it was reported that the *Northern Light* and *North Star* discharged nineteen persons with the pilots, these having stowed away among the freight and baggage.[11] On the *North Star's* sailing on October 3, 1863, one woman was found who had no ticket, and two others, who had boarded the wrong vessel, were sent back with the pilot.[12]

In going aboard the ship at Panama for the voyage up the Pacific coast, there was much confusion, particularly in the early years when passage was at a premium and facilities for going to the ships were not systematized. Until the arrival of the tender *Taboga* in 1850, passengers went aboard in native boats, and even afterward some chose to save money by making their own arrangements. Levi Stowell laconically described his embarkation on the *California* thus:

Jan. 30, 1849 ... Packing to go on the ship. Great bustle. Equipments to buy, cups, spoons etc. etc. Hired a canoe, all embarked for the ship at 5 o'clock.[13]

A passenger by the *Oregon* wrote of going aboard as follows:

... we tumbled in among the stone ballast of a large bungo [dugout] provided to convey us to the United States Mail Steamer, "Oregon," which lay at anchor some three miles out in the bay. After receiving our complement of fifteen or twenty passengers, with a considerable supply of cigars and claret, which landed safely on our shins or "stove in the hold," we succeeded in prevailing upon our swarthy navigators to shove off.... Hoisting a bull's hide and leg-of-mutton sail on the rude bean poles used for masts, and tugging at the clumsy oars, *el patron* ... in due time laid us alongside: preliminary to which he displayed his bungling seamanship by hauling down his bull hide too late, and treating us to a stern chase with oars only, against a strong tide, approved by the cachinatory applause of our friends on board.

Recovering from this, however, we reached the gangway, and amidst the howling, confusion, and fright of the crews of the various *canoas*, we clambered up the side and trod the deck, rejoicing once more at the prospect of proceeding to our destination.[14]

At Panama also, the passengers going aboard the steamers were carefully scrutinized, and each one was required to show his ticket before embarking. In November, 1863, it was reported that a number who had gone out on the tender *Taboga* to the *Golden City* were compelled to return to Panama, since they had no tickets. They had succeeded in getting from New York to Panama with the payment of little or no money, but they were turned back here. Some of these held receipts from persons on board the ship on the Atlantic side for amounts ranging from $5 to $15, having been told that these would enable them to get aboard the Pacific steamer with no more trouble. These persons had of course been swindled, sometimes of all they had.[15]

The arrival and departure of the steamers at San Francisco were events of great interest to the townspeople as well as to the passengers in the ship. If the ship did not arrive on time, considerable excitement and speculation concerning her whereabouts and probable time of arrival resulted. Thus the *Alta* remarked on June 19, 1850:

Every one is on the *qui vive* now for the arrival of the "Tennessee." Small bets involving sundry calls for intoxicating beverages are freely made that she will be in to-day. The knowin' uns who made bets upon her arrival yesterday, endeavored to hedge last evening and get on the other side of the fence. All the bets are on the fancy order, and no very great amount is expected to change hands. The *brick* market, it is thought, will be very materially affected by her arrival, however, of which the down-y ones will doubtless avail themselves. The "Chickaninny Club" are to hold a meeting on the occasion.[16]

Signal stations were established in San Francisco, and as soon as an incoming vessel was sighted from the Heads, this information was relayed by semaphore telegraph to the station atop Telegraph Hill, where it was repeated so that the whole town could see it. Not only were the arms of the signal extended horizontally when a side-wheel steamer appeared, but a large flag marked "U.S.M." indicated when a mail steamer was off the harbor. Crowds of citizens repaired to the landing when a steamer was signaled, and her gun was fired as she entered the harbor. They were eager for the newspapers and intelligence which she carried and curious to inspect her human cargo as it came ashore. The all-important mail was transferred from the ship to the post office, there to be sorted and delivered on the next and succeeding days to long lines of hopeful Argonauts.

The day of the departure of the mail steamer from San Francisco, or "steamer day," was a time of settling accounts, making remittances to eastern creditors, and taking stock of mercantile affairs. It was a time of feverish activity, Gilmor Meredith writing his father that "for the last 72 hours previous to the departure of the steamer I had only 5 hours sleep...."[17] At first, this event took place only once a month, then fortnightly, when the Pacific Mail instituted regular sailings at that frequency in 1851, then every ten days. But when the steamers went weekly, the merchants balked, signing an agreement to attempt collection of city bills only twice a month.[18] The sailing of a steamer was a colorful event, with crowds aboard and ashore calling to one another as the ship backed out of her wharf and headed for sea. When Senator Eugene Casserly departed for the East in the *Colorado* on November 20, 1868, a party of his friends chartered the bay-and-river steamer *Washoe*, obtained the services of Kidd's band, and followed on the quarter of the *Colorado* down the bay, the band playing "Auld Lang Syne." At the Golden Gate, the *Washoe* turned back, the crowd on her deck giving the *Colorado* three cheers and a "tiger," and the steamer joined in the salute with her whistle, while the mail steamer responded by dipping her colors and firing a parting gun.[19]

The principal discomforts of the voyage by way of Panama, aside from those arising from seasickness and the heat of the tropics, were the aggravation of these by the overcrowding of the steamers at some periods and by the inability or unwillingness of some of the operators, especially those on the Atlantic part of the route, to keep the ships clean and well staffed. It appears that these offenses grew more flagrant, or were at least noticed more in the public press, as the years went on, and that the worst period was on the Atlantic between 1860 and 1865, when the ships of Cornelius Vanderbilt were practically unrivaled in these respects.

The ships between Panama and San Francisco were heavily crowded in 1849, but this could be forgiven by all, since a state of emergency existed. Demand for passage arose to an extent which the operators could not possibly have foreseen. The consequent crowding of the available ships was due to the wishes of the travelers rather than to any systematic policy of placing inadequate ships on the run. Levi Stowell, who had steerage passage on the *California*, wrote that he found the berths "holes" and therefore slept on deck on a post and bar of iron. "Got up, neck, back and arms nearly broke rubbing on the bars, ropes, etc., etc." On another night, he reported sleeping on a chair in the cabin.[20] Another passenger on the *California* wrote as follows:

Every-where the ship is crowded; the passengers on each side of the machinery, the upper and lower forward decks, the long steerage extending from the bows far aft on both sides of the engine—all are full, and many of the berths are occupied by two passengers each ... The state rooms and cabins are all crowded to their utmost capacity, and of course the passengers are deprived of many of the conveniences to which they are accustomed. The writer of this article obtained his ticket very early in New York, and yet has had no berth on this ship, and neither sheet nor pillow since he left Panama, and had he not fortunately kept his camp blanket within reach, would have been under the necessity of sleeping in his clothes during the whole voyage. Yet while this is the case, and while selfishness and even personal comfort would object to crowding the ship in such a manner, another consideration leads to the acquittal of the officers from blame. Humanity to the Americans at Panama demanded that not an individual should be refused passage, who could consistently be taken.[21]

Elisha Oscar Crosby, sailing in the *California,* provided himself with a hammock and, hanging it in the rigging, slept there most of the way from Panama to San Francisco.[22] When Albert Williams traveled north on the first voyage of the *Oregon,* he wrote that the fear of being overcrowded proved to be groundless and that no inconvenience was experienced from numbers.[23]

On the Atlantic in the early years there were few complaints. John B. Peirce, traveling on the *Cherokee* in February, 1850, wrote to his wife:

We have a good ship, a good master, and good waiters, who give us good food and plenty of it. . . . We had three in our state room and each one had a trunk and a valise. They started adrift in the night & the way they danced and sashayed back and forth upside down in the middle was a caution to everything in their way.[24]

Two days later, he wrote again, saying that in going on deck that morning he had to step over the prostrate forms of a number of men sleeping on the floor of the saloon, doing so not because the ship was crowded, but because it was cooler there than in the staterooms.[25]

Reports of overcrowded ships on the Atlantic began in the next decade. George Gordon wrote in a pamphlet in 1860 that four years before the *Illinois* of the United States Mail Steamship Company had sailed from New York with 1,150 passengers aboard whereas her certificate permitted her to carry only 763. This large number meant that meals were being served continually in the dining saloon, while the lower cabin, into which the second-class staterooms opened, was completely filled with standee berths three tiers in height, leaving only gangways at the sides.[26] The Vanderbilt ships between New York and Aspinwall were the recipients of most bitter criticism on this score. It was reported that in May, 1860, the *Northern Light* had sailed from New York with a nominal passenger list of 890, but with really more than a thousand aboard. A large number of the passengers could not even get benches on which to lie at night, and one person had obtained a berth by paying a steward $25 in addition to the regular passage money.

This is on a par with all the rest of the Vanderbilt coterie's grasping conduct. Not one of the whole Company from the Commodore down, have the slightest regard for even the most ordinary comfort of the unfortunate passengers who are forced to travel on their ships.

With them the "almighty dollar" is not only the primary, but the only consideration, and the "dear public" once within their clutches, have literally got to "sweat it out" until the end of the voyage; and we really believe if one of their vessels were to sink with a full living cargo on board, the Company would only lament the loss of their ship, and never give a second thought to the sacrifice of life.[27]

In 1863 the *North Star* left New York for Aspinwall with a passenger list of 925, although, including those not listed and the officers and crew, there was an estimated 1,200 on board. The decks were encumbered with lines of trunks piled around them for the entire voyage, and only two of the seven lifeboats were ready to be launched, the remainder being secured on deck and filled with baggage. Sanitary facilities were meager, since, according to the reporter, "there were four water closets for the use of about three hundred people of the first and second cabins." At night, the benches and decks, as well as the cabin floors, were appropriated by sleeping passengers. In his description of a night on board, the writer said:

Although it is very dark, you will observe that the benches around the ship's rail are filled with human beings. Some are stretched full length, others half reclining. You will see as you inspect these benches females in the close embrace of the sterner sex, their heads reclining in the most loving manner on the shoulders of their male protectors. You will naturally enough suppose them to be husband and wife or sister and brother. They are in some cases, but more frequently are not, but only a couple whose acquaintance dates back to the ship's sailing, or probably a shorter time ... Amidships, and alongside of a boat that should not be there, we discover a number of human beings stretched at full length on deck with their feet towards the rail, leaving but a narrow space to walk. Around the mainmast is a dark mass composed of forty or fifty persons, of all ages and both sexes, heaped together en masse, and all apparently are sound asleep ... We ... go down into the second cabin ... Directly at the foot of the steps, lying on her back, is an Irish woman weighing not less than two hundred and fifty pounds. She is almost without clothing, so great is the heat. Around her, like a litter of pigs, are five children, the eldest being

about five years of age. Every berth is filled. Women can be seen in this second
cabin who have apparently lost all sense of decency, who at home would cover
the legs of a piano, so particular were they in regard to anything appearing
naked.[28]

On a northbound trip of the *Northern Light* in 1864, the passengers were not allowed on the ship at Aspinwall until just before
sailing time and then were crowded aboard with great confusion
and haste, upon which the ship immediately put to sea. When the
first-cabin passengers went to the purser's office to be assigned to
their rooms, they were informed that there were not enough cabins
for all, and many were unable to obtain even pillows or blankets.
Those who were not assigned cabins were informed by the steward
that, although none were to be had, they could be "obtained"
through the payment of a fee of $10. The ship's supply of pro-
visions was low, and she therefore made good speed to New York
in order to arrive before running out.[29]

A determined attack upon conditions aboard the Vanderbilt
steamers was carried on, particularly under the leadership of
F. W. Rice, United States consul at Aspinwall, who from 1862
on deluged the Department of State with letters detailing abuses
of passengers and crew on the ships. Newspapers took up the
matter, printing scathing articles, some of which were said to
have come from the pen of Rice himself.[30] In the summer of 1864
a bill passed the House of Representatives, requiring that copies of
inspection certificates be posted on the steamers, that copies of
the passenger list be always open to inspection, and that one such
list be filed with the collector of customs before sailing, giving the
number on board and to be received. Permits to go to sea were to
be issued only upon this statement under oath, and a pilot who
took a ship to sea without this would be fined $100 and have his
license revoked. On arrival, similar lists were to be prepared and
presented to the consul as well as to the collector of the port. In the
Senate, Vanderbilt was able to bring pressure to bear against this
bill, but it was finally passed in August, 1864, though, from reports,
conditions aboard the ships remained much the same as long as
they were operated by Vanderbilt.[31]

As has been said, the first- and second-cabin passengers on the
Panama steamers ate at table in assigned seats, with the first cabin
enjoying priority of sitting, followed by the second cabin. In 1849

steerage passengers were reminded that they would fare the same as the crew as far as provisions were concerned, and that they must provide themselves with knife, fork, spoon, and plate, in addition to bedding.[32] With the beginning of competition, more consideration was shown the steerage, and cutlery was provided for their use.[33] Steerage food and meals on the pioneer steamers on the Pacific presented something of the picturesque. Stowell wrote that the steerage passengers on the *California* were served with coffee, jerked beef, and hard bread for breakfast on the first morning out from Panama. Later in the voyage, he commented,

Still hard living. *Most miserable stuff* for coffee and tea, black bread, thin mush and no salt, dirty molasses, etc. Grabbing for fresh meat. [Two days later.] Fried bread for breakfast, hem! Fat living.

At Monterey, he said that he got the first bread and butter since leaving the *Falcon.*[34]

Captain Pearson, who commanded the *Oregon,* said that he had only provisions and utensils to care for about sixty cabin passengers and his crew when his ship reached Panama from the Atlantic, and that the taking of great numbers of steerage presented serious problems. Since there were no utensils for the steerage passengers, and not even a galley in which to cook for them, makeshifts had to be arranged.

Salt beef, jerked beef, hard bread, beans and rice, were about all the provisions that could be gathered up in Panama.

I was in a sad dilemma how to cook for so many. I heard, however, that an old colored man had a ship's stove at Gorgona, and was doing a good business cooking for passengers as they passed through that place. I sent two men over that horrible road to buy that old stove, gave $300 for it with its tins and coppers, and had it packed across in pieces on the heads of natives, and gave the two men a free passage to California for their trouble. The old stove (which the natives had broken by numerous ugly falls) was placed on the forward deck, tied together with wires, and a shed built over it; and it took the place of a steerage galley for two voyages until I could get a better one.[35]

Tables were not served in the steerage, the passengers being divided into messes of four to twenty-four members, who chose one of their number to go to the galley where the food was served out, and bring it to them.

Nothing is more disgusting than to see this greedy crowd thrusting and elbowing each other at the door of the filthy cooking-place. Contending who shall be first they shout and swear, and often proceed to blows. The Americans of a certain class have no idea of civility; and yet there is not one of these Yankees who cannot read, write, and calculate, and who does not possess a certain ease of manner. However, they triumphantly bear away their provender in a bucket worthy to figure at the repast of a kennel of hounds, and squat upon the deck round their scanty pittance—for, in these steamers, people dine without tables or chairs.[36]

Food in the steerage on the early steamers on the Pacific consisted mainly of salt beef, pork, yams, rice, and sea biscuit, with soup occasionally, fresh meat on Sundays and Thursdays, coffee for breakfast, and tea for supper.[37]

Complaints of such fare and accommodations were not long in reaching the New York headquarters of the Pacific Mail, and they brought sharp orders from the executives to the San Francisco agents.

At whatever expense the fare in the Steamers must be improved for both Cabin and Steerage passengers—all are loud in their condemnation of it. The stoppage at way ports must be availed of to obtain fresh provisions & vegetables & whatever delicacies they may afford. You will give special instructions to these ends. If the stories of the emigrants be true, a false spirit of economy denies them the comforts ... they have every right to expect. The steamers are abundantly supplied with linen and yet I hear a clean napkin or towel is a rarity. If you can procure game or other fare likely to stop the complaints— you will do so even at additional cost. Is there any reason why the water on board should be bad?[38]

Later in the same year more instructions were sent out, which seem worthy of quotation.

I regret to say that with scarcely an exception the Panama's passengers complain of bad fare—much of the food being altogether unfit for use—I have seen some of them and think there must have been some good cause for their dissatisfaction. I believe the highest prices are paid by you for stores & there is no good reason why they should not be of the best quality. I think some change should at once be made in the parties from whom you procure them. Besides the unpopularity we gain & the injustice we show passengers by not giving them proper fare ... their complaints deprive us of all passengers in the Chagres steamers homeward.[39]

The cabin passengers fared much better than the steerage. A passenger on the Atlantic side in 1849 told of "four full luxurious meals" a day for both the first- and second-class passengers, served at the same tables and precisely alike.[40] A passenger by the *Tennessee* from Panama to San Francisco in the spring of 1850 stated that everything was clean and eatable at the table, with good butter and potatoes, which they had not seen since leaving New York. Fruits and fresh vegetables were served in quantity on board.[41] John B. Peirce went north in the same ship, and wrote to his wife of the food as follows:

Is not a monopoly worth having? Well can they afford to give us chickens, Turkey, Goose, Duck, Beef, Pork, Lamb & Kid all fresh, Beef, Ham, Pork & Fish salted, Rasins [*sic*], Prunes, Almonds, Filberts, Preserves, Tea, Coffee, Loaf Sugar, Pies, Puddings, Cakes, Cheese, Butter, Sardines, Green Peas, Green Corn, Green Beans, Pickles, Oranges, Bananas, Hot Cakes, Honey, Jams, Buckwheats, Eggs, Omelets, &c, &c. Well can they afford us the luxuries of the table, they are well paid, and I dont complain of our living, it is good enough and too good.[42]

Experience on the Pacific steamers differed, however. In October, 1849, George Schenck complained that in the *Panama* a cow which had died a natural death in the morning was served at the cabin table on the afternoon of the same day, that the biscuits were full of worms, some being as much as an inch long, and that musty flour was used for making bread, the good flour being saved for sale in San Francisco.[43]

The routine of meals on the ships on the Pacific coast began with coffee served in the cabin at six o'clock in the morning, though for a favored few it was brought to the staterooms.[44] Breakfast hours were from 8:00 to 10:00 A.M., in two sittings, dinner came from 1:00 to 3:00 P.M., and supper from 6:00 to 8:00. At eleven o'clock the lights were extinguished in the cabin.[45] Bayard Taylor was shocked by the actions of his fellow countrymen at table on the steamer, writing:

At the first tingle of the bell, all hands started off as if a shot had exploded among them; conversation was broken off in the middle of a word; the deck was instantly cleared, and the passengers, tumbling pell-mell down the cabin-stairs, found every seat taken by others who had probably been sitting in them for half an hour. The bell, however, had an equally convulsive effect upon these. There was a confused grabbing motion for a few seconds, and lo! the plates were cleared. A chicken parted in twain as if by magic, each half leaping into an opposite plate; a dish of sweet potatoes vanished before a single hand; beef-steak flew in all directions; and while about half the passengers had all their breakfast piled at once upon their plates, the other half were regaled by a "plentiful lack."[46]

In 1852, the Pacific Mail advertised that the tables of its steamers were supplied with the best stores to be procured in New York and

San Francisco, that a provision depot had been established at Panama, and that a special agent was maintained at Acapulco for the purpose of obtaining fresh food for the steamers.[47] An excellent reputation for good food was built up by the Pacific Mail, while the ships on the Atlantic suffered in comparison. Occasionally there was complaint, as when a passenger by the *Sacramento* in 1865 wrote that in ten trips made by way of Panama, he had never been served with food as meager in quantity, as deficient in quality, or as badly cooked and served as on the voyage which he was then making.[48] This was nothing, however, compared to the maledictions called down upon the head of Cornelius Vanderbilt for the quality of food provided on his Aspinwall steamers between 1860 and 1865. A letter signed by all but three of the cabin passengers of the *Champion* in 1861 stated that the meat served was so tainted as to be offensive to the smell, that in the voyage of ten days there were no clean tablecloths, sheets, or pillowcases, and that the ship was provided with neither bathrooms nor spittoons.[49] The British consul at Panama wrote of Vanderbilt's ships, "It is beyond me to describe the nasty food, filthy table cloths, and dirty knives and forks." Provisions were all brought from New York packed in ice, and as all the ice was melted or consumed several days before reaching New York again, the quality, flavor, and odor of the meat was not improved.[50] One traveler in 1861 composed an acrostic on the Vanderbilt steamers, to be read "after one had partaken of what cannot be obtained on board this wretched line—a clean, wholesome meal."

ACROSTIC
To be read after dinner.

Vexed as we are with our accommodation,
And keen to punish, could we do it well,
No man we feel can curb your speculation,
Deserts like yours are meted out in hell.
Each sinful soul who treads this crowded deck,
Retains his blessings and gives you his curse;
But should these lines be sacrificed by wreck,
In hell, old fellow, you may look for worse.
Leave earth to others, then seek heaven's goal,
Think less of wealth, and save your worthless soul.
—VICTIM[51]

Stores for the steamers on the Pacific were often expensive to purchase, the agent for Law's steamers reporting in 1851 that beef and pork sold for $60 a barrel at Panama, beans and peas were ten cents a pound, and chickens $1 each. He considered the purchase of chickens and preserved meats necessary for the small steamers, however, since they were unable to carry beef cattle or hogs on board and could not do entirely without fresh meat. In accounting for heavy expenditures for provisions, he wrote to the owners:

The cabin table of Howland & Aspinwall's boats is well served, and unless yours is equally good, you will lose the good name which it is necessary to have to get return passengers from San Francisco.[52]

Most of the Pacific Mail ships were large enough to carry livestock, and—as was the practice of ships on long voyages in the nineteenth century—cattle, sheep, hogs, and poultry were carried on board, to be slaughtered as fresh meat was needed for the table.[53] A northbound traveler by the *Cortes* in 1852 described how cattle were towed alongside at Acapulco and hoisted aboard by the horns.[54] In 1853, a stir was created in the streets of San Francisco when Burnham and Marnn, butchers, decorated the cattle which had been purchased for the *Tennessee* and marched them to the ship through the streets to the lively music of fife and drum. The Pacific Mail was accused of doing this as an advertisement, but the butchers claimed the idea and execution as their own.[55]

The steamers of the United States Mail Steamship Company were criticized for the deficient quantity and quality of their food, as well as for poor service. On a voyage of the *George Law* in the winter of 1855, a passenger said not only that no fruit was served, but that the storekeeper was even prohibited from keeping fruit and condiments for sale. He wrote as follows of the beginning of the voyage:

Bang, jam, blow, freeze, cold and comfortless embarkation on the George Law on the 5th of February, 1855; thermometer at 24 deg.; vessel under way at 2 P.M.; passengers freezing, huddled in the cabins looking for stoves but finding none. A slight pipe containing steam ejected from the boilers, runs underneath the tables, and half warms the feet of a few. Two o'clock passes, three, four, and cold and hungry scores of repentant humanity, innocent of food since an early breakfast, long for the dinner that is to warm and sustain their sinking frames.

Starving and Freezing Passenger.—Waiter, what is the dinner hour?

Rough Jacketed and Hurrying Waiter (scornfully).—We don't give no dinner, sir; only gives tea at 6 o'clock today.

Starving and Freezing Passenger.—Bring me a bottle of porter or ale, and some crackers and cheese—anything eatable and warming.

Waiter.—Store room ain't open, sir. Not allowed to get any stores until regular meal, sir.[56]

The officers of the United States Mail steamers were highly praised, but since the management of the line, which was neither farsighted nor generous, appointed the crews, the commanders were deprived of a degree of control over the stewards and crew generally which they would have had if the appointment and dismissal had been in their hands.[57]

Service on the Pacific Mail was sometimes criticized, and the *Golden Gate* was frequently a target in 1857 and 1858. The complaint was made that Captain Whitney sacrificed the comfort of most of his passengers for the convenience of a few favorites who catered to his vanity and provided him with wine. Such a criticism has some of the earmarks of coming from an individual who was disappointed in not being placed at the captain's table. Others criticized the conduct of the officers generally, the food, and, particularly, the insolence of the colored waiters.[58]

The service of the Vanderbilt ships was damned along with the ships themselves, the crowded conditions on board, and the food. The *Panama Star and Herald* wrote of the *Ariel* in 1860:

We are assured that a more filthy, nasty, pigstie could not be found any where than the whole ship is from one end to the other. The dirty, greasy table cloths were rendered still more disgusting by being used at night as pillows by the niggirs [sic] round the cabin; the food is represented as abomnible [sic]; the staterooms uncleaned; in fact everything a perfect disgrace to both captain and owners.[59]

Passengers stated that on the voyage described above all the deck space usually allotted to steerage was filled with sheep and cattle, that the second-cabin passengers were placed with the first cabin, their deck room being filled with baggage and freight. All the glasses from the staterooms had to be used on the tables at meals, and it was necessary to wash the soup spoons before the next course could be served. The first-cabin passengers signed a resolution to contribute $1 each to Vanderbilt for the purchase of tablecloths, knives, and forks. Future passengers were advised to provide themselves before sailing with six dozen eggs, cooked; ten pounds of crackers; one pitcher; two tumblers; one chair or camp stool;

one dozen towels; one or more cakes of soap ; and one life preserver.[60] It was stated that stewards charged ill passengers outrageous prices for ice or gruel, and that both the Negro stewards and stewardesses were insolent, dishonest, and overbearing. One passenger found proof that his mattress had not been turned over for four months, and bed linen was not changed during an entire trip. Towels were provided every two or three days, but some were mere rags.[61]

Ice, which was an important commodity, was usually shipped to the Isthmus from the Atlantic states, where it was carried across for the ships on the other side. Passengers were charged for what they required, except at meals, the price being twenty-five cents per pound on the Vanderbilt ships in 1864, and seven cents per pound on the Pacific Mail vessels at the same time.[62] The Vanderbilt ships sometimes ran out of ice altogether, or, like the *Ocean Queen* in October, 1865, stinted the passengers so successfully on the voyage that two tons could be sold at Aspinwall.[63]

Illness was not uncommon on the Panama steamers, particularly on the Pacific side when passengers had been forced to remain for some time in the tropics. Americans seemingly refused to accustom themselves to the manner of life of the part of the world in which they were temporarily situated, and by too violent exercise and unwise eating and drinking did more than the climate to make themselves ill. Some voyages would be entirely free from illness or deaths, whereas others would come to an end with decimated passenger lists. "Panama fever" and cholera were the two most prevalent diseases; the former often disappeared as the ships left the tropics, but the latter was more frequently fatal. The Nicaragua steamers suffered heavily from cholera on the Pacific, though perhaps the most disastrous epidemic was aboard the *Philadelphia* between Aspinwall and New York in the summer of 1852. The plague-stricken ship put into Key West but was not allowed to land those who were ill, and before the end of the voyage over one-third of the 155 passengers had died. On the Pacific, it was said that statistics showed fewer deaths among the passengers aboard the Pacific Mail ships than on other lines.[64] Of the surgeons on the ships, President Aspinwall wrote to the Pacific Mail agents in San Francisco:

I regret also to hear that charges for Medical attendance have been made. Please report to me all reports reaching you on this subject—as well as any affecting the professional ability of the Surgeons. Positive orders have been given long since that the pay of the Surgeon should be in lieu of all perquisites. You will feel at liberty to return money charged by them deducting the same from their pay.[65]

Passengers in the Panama steamers in the middle-nineteenth century were not entertained by the elaborate program of deck sports and concerts which travelers of a later day knew, but they often enjoyed themselves, nevertheless. Stowell, on the first voyage of the *California*, wrote:

A plenty of fun on deck, all kinds of games going on, singing, stories, etc.... Moonlight and plenty of singing till 11 o'clock etc. [A few days later.] Lovely moonlight nights, pleasant talks of the girls, and matters and things at home, their enjoyments, and ours, the contrast etc., etc., sitting out on the guards.[66]

Gilmor Meredith wrote to his sister from the *California* on July 22, 1851, that "the ladies talk of having a dance tonight—and our band consists of an Accordian, [a gui]tar with three strings and an old fiddle—we will have a gay time."[67]

Of course, there were gamblers aboard the ships, and it was said that, as soon as breakfast was cleared away from the long tables, gamblers were seated along the whole length of them.[68] One passenger reported that a faro bank was open in the cabin of the *Tennessee* every night.[69] Another less ordinary game was played when the *Golden Age* towed the disabled steamer *Uncle Sam* from Acapulco to San Francisco in March, 1861. During the trip, a game of chess was carried on between Captain Lapidge of the *Uncle Sam* and Mr. M. Elias, a passenger on the *Golden Age,* through the medium of the blackboards of the steamers, the moves being made with chalk. Said to be the first recorded game played by two accompanying vessels at sea, it was won by Elias, who defeated Captain Lapidge in forty-one moves.[70]

On the *Panama*'s first voyage north, M. Hall McAllister, who was a passenger, thus described an amateur dramatic entertainment:

In the evening we had a theatrical performance on the upper deck ... Much amusement was afforded. The chef d'oeuvre of the evening was "The Rescued Maiden." Maiden, Dr. Colton; Ravisher, Derby; Rescuer, Hoope. The performance continued until half past ten.[71]

Another traveler told of the holding of an election for state officials for California, with dances and stump speeches in the evenings.[72]

The *Northerner*'s southbound passengers in March, 1852, amused themselves by editing and publishing a humorous newspaper, detailing events actual and imaginary which took place on board ship and in California.[73]

A California ballad, popular in the 'fifties, ran in part as follows:

> On board the steamer, homeward bound,
> With joyful hearts and noiseful glee;
> Good-by! Good-by! Shake hands all round
> Then travel o'er the sea.
>
> . . . .
>
> 'Tis mirth and jollity on board
> The mind runs wild as home draws nigh—
> No cheerless look, no angry word,
> As homeward bound you fly.[74]

Judged by the standards of sea travel of the day, the Panama route was no worse than most others, and the ships of the Pacific Mail, which eventually came to serve the whole route, were world famous for the excellence of their accommodations and table. In a period when most people who traveled did so from necessity and not for pleasure, those who took the Panama route were as comfortable and happy as were travelers anywhere.

CHAPTER VII

THE ISTHMIAN LINK

TRANSPORTATION across the Isthmus of Panama was a major problem for the traveler by that route. From the mouth of the Chagres River on the Caribbean, where steamers anchored in the early years, to the city of Panama on the Pacific was a journey of about sixty miles. Approximately two-thirds of it could be made in boats on the river; the remaining part had to be negotiated on foot or muleback over wretched trails. In the first years of the route's importance, it was a journey full of hardship and discomfort, not unattended by danger. Health conditions were bad on the Isthmus in the absence of much knowledge of tropical hygiene, and though the terrors of the journey have certainly been exaggerated, they were nonetheless real. At Panama, it was sometimes necessary to wait months for a ship to California. Most travelers were bored there, some fell ill or ran out of funds, and a few got into serious trouble with the inhabitants. The opening of the new port of Aspinwall on the Carribean, and the completion of the Panama Railroad in 1855 removed most of the difficulties of the crossing, and the transit from ocean to ocean became a matter of only a few hours' train ride.

The maintenance of an open highway across the Isthmus was, of course, essential to the operation of the route as a whole. No matter how well the steamers on either side carried out their part of the service, they would mean nothing if the land transit between the oceans were closed. It was at this point that the traveler on a route essentially internal—since it served chiefly to connect parts of the United States—crossed foreign soil and came under at least the nominal jurisdiction of the Republic of New Granada or Colombia. The disastrous effects of internal warfare on the development and maintenance of the Nicaragua route have been noted, and the success of that by way of Panama was to a great degree due to the comparative peace which was maintained on the Isthmus and to the fact that internal dissension and local feeling were never allowed to close the transit.

By the treaty of 1846, right of way across the Isthmus had been guaranteed to the United States, and in the same year British interests pioneered a commercial route from ocean to ocean.[1] When, however, the first Americans came to cross in December, 1848, they found little in the way of organization for the journey. What arrangements the British had made were not available to the travelers from the United States, and they found it necessary to fend for themselves.

Until 1852 all the steamers and sailing vessels coming to the Atlantic side of the Isthmus landed their passengers and cargoes at Chagres, a village composed of unprepossessing huts located on the left bank at the mouth of the river of the same name. With the growth of the traffic, an American town of Chagres grew up across the river, consisting mainly of hotels and saloons, catering to the wants of travelers during their enforced stay between the time of landing from the steamer and starting up the river on the journey across the Isthmus. The mouth of the Chagres was somewhat sheltered by a headland, on which is situated Fort San Lorenzo, but the depth of the water there was not great enough for ocean steamers, which were forced to lie in the open roadstead, disembarking their passengers either in their own boats or in native craft coming out from the shore. In 1851 the cost per person for the landing from the steamer at Chagres was $2.[2] When the seas were heavy, it was impossible to land, and at times steamers lay pitching and rolling off the mouth of the Chagres for days before the passengers could be put ashore.

The climate at Chagres was reputed to be the most uncomfortable and unhealthful on the Isthmus, and since accommodations for travelers were poor and the food available proverbially bad, they tried to avoid spending a night there, by arranging transportation up the river as soon as possible. For the journey on the river, native canoes or "bungos," hollowed out of a single log, some twenty-five feet in length and two and a half to three feet in width, were the chief means of conveyance. These boats were poled up the river by three or four natives, carried two to four passengers, and were equipped with canopies for the protection of the travelers and their baggage. It was common for passengers on the steamers to make arrangements among themselves before landing, organizing into parties for the journey to Panama and choosing one of their number to make the bargain with the boatmen. Arrangements were

---

[1] For notes to chap. vii, see pp. 281–286.

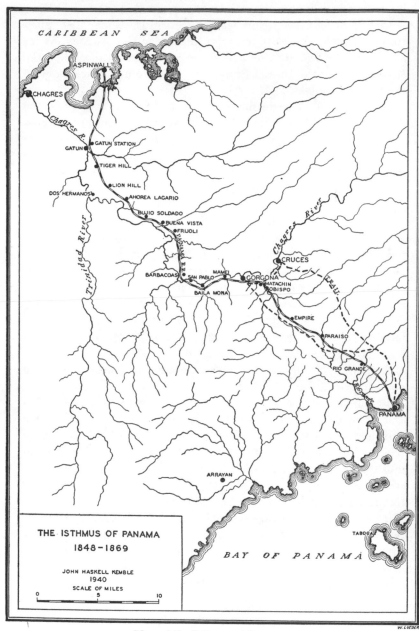

Map of the Isthmus of Panama

at first made with the men of a particular boat, but by 1852 most of the boats on the river were owned by a few men, and it was with these that the agreement had to be made.[3] The first travelers found an unsophisticated lot of boatmen, whose usual rate from Chagres to the head of navigation of the river was $10 per passenger. They were very quick, however, in learning what was the demand for their services, and within a few weeks the price had risen to $40 and $50.[4] In 1851 persons were advised to pay no more than $50 for the hire of a boat, which meant that the cost per person was still about $10, and by 1852 the fare up the river was $4 to $5, indicating an increase of facilities and a decrease of travel.[5] The natives early learned that many Americans were not above cheating them when the occasion offered, and they retaliated in kind. Persons making the journey in 1851 were advised to pay only half the agreed price of the river trip at Chagres, holding the remainder as security for the performance of the journey and paying it only on arrival. Otherwise, boatmen often refused to continue above a certain point on the river without additional payment, and the travelers were helpless to do aught but accede to their demands.[6]

During the dry season, from December until April, the head of navigation of the Chagres was at Gorgona, a village situated thirty-nine and a half miles up the river from its mouth and some twenty miles from Panama. The rains of the remainder of the year made it possible for boats to continue to Cruces, four and a half miles above Gorgona and eighteen miles from Panama. The boat trip up the river to Gorgona required three to three and a half days, depending somewhat on the skill of the boatmen in avoiding eddies and swift currents and in keeping the boat close to the bank where their poles would be effective. Layovers were made at night at villages along the riverbanks, where the travelers, if they arrived early, could often find a cot or hammock in which to sleep, and where meals, of a varying quality, were served.[7] One traveler, George Schenck, who crossed the Isthmus in the fall of 1849, wrote vividly of a meal taken along the Chagres.

The next morning we started on our journey, and about seven o'clock we stopped at a little hut at Gatun to get coffee and something to eat, three of us, Mr. Swain, Mr. Dow and myself. I noticed that we used up all the sugar that they had in the cabin. Some other passengers came along after us, and I thought I would watch and see how they managed about their sweetening, and see if they got any. I presently saw one of the natives, a girl of about sixteen or seventeen years of age go out and get a piece of sugar-cane, and commence chewing it, and occasionally she would eject the juice from her mouth into the coffee while it was being prepared outside the hut. Swain asked me if I was going to have some coffee. I declined to take any under the circumstances.[8]

People were advised not to depend entirely upon the provisions which might be purchased along the river but to carry with them a small stock of such eatables as dried beef, boiled ham, sea biscuits, sardines, and a dozen or so bottles of claret.[9] According to some accounts, many Americans took more than claret, and the journey up the river frequently assumed rather a hilarious character. The wide, tropical river, hemmed in by the vivid green jungle in which strange birds and animals were constantly to be seen, formed a sharp contrast with the previous experience of most of the travelers. Many of them carried firearms, and these received plenty of use in shooting at alligators and monkeys, which frequently presented themselves as unwitting targets.

Almost as soon as the route to California via Panama was opened, the improvement of the isthmian transit was undertaken. The second steamer to sail from New York for Chagres was the *Orus,* a wooden side-wheeler of 247 tons and a length of 158 feet, 7 inches, which had been in service in sheltered waters around New York since 1842. She had been purchased by Howland and Aspinwall, and was sent to the Isthmus to carry passengers up the Chagres. She reached her destination on January 14, 1849, and immediately entered service. It was apparent, however, that the *Orus* was not entirely satisfactory for the river journey. Her draft was too great to allow her to go more than eighteen or twenty miles up the river, where her passengers were transferred to native boats for the remainder of the journey. The captain of the *Orus* was expected to guarantee passage from Chagres to Gorgona for $10, including transit in the canoes above the point at which the steamboat turned back, but he failed to do this, and passengers made their own arrangements for the last part of the trip.[10] The *Orus* could carry only about 150 passengers at a time, and all available room aboard was used for them, the baggage being piled into bungos at Chagres and towed behind her as far as she went up the river.[11] Since the *Orus* was never able to make the whole river voyage to Gorgona and in dry season was useful only as a towboat at the mouth of the Chagres, it was clear that, if the river were to be navigated by steamboats, it would be necessary to have some more adapted to existing conditions. In the summer of 1849 the stern-wheeler *General Herran* was built at Chagres. Entering service in September, she was able to make the run to Gorgona, but this was a performance not always successfully accomplished by even this smaller boat. The additional competition did serve to bring down canoe rates to $4 to $6 per person, and travelers praised the efforts aboard the steamboats to make them comfortable.[12] In June, 1850, the steamer *Raphael Rivas,* built for George Law and the Panama Railroad, appeared on the river. She had an iron hull 110 feet long and 23 feet in beam, and it was expected that she would not draw more than a foot of water.[13] It was found that the *Raphael Rivas,* or the *Ralph Rivas,* as she was called by un-Hispanicised Americans, drew between twenty and thirty inches of water and could not ascend the river above Palenquilla, eleven and a half miles below Gorgona. She made a speed of about three miles an hour against the current, however, and her passengers were often able to reach Gorgona in one day from Chagres.[14] In the summer of 1850, also, Adamson and Company of New Orleans bought a little forty-six-foot, twelve-horsepower steamboat, named her the *Harry Gleason,* and placed her on the Chagres.[15] Later in the year, the Panama Railroad built another iron steamboat, the *Gorgona,* sending her to Chagres to tow barges of materials up the river to be used in the construction of the railroad.[16] Before the close of 1850 still another small steamer, the *Swan,* appeared on the river.[17] The steamer *William H. Aspinwall,* seemingly built on the Isthmus at Navy Bay, made her first trip up the river on February 6, 1851, going every other day from Chagres to Gorgona. It was said that the trip in her was very pleasant. There was room to walk about; and her rain-tight covering and sides might be opened or closed at will.[18] Although in the rainy season the *William H. Aspinwall's* passengers had to go from Gorgona to Cruces in canoes, the trip from Chagres to Gorgona was made in seven and a half hours.[19]

American enterprise was not devoted entirely to steamers. Captain Abraham Bancker, onetime shipping-news collector for the *New York Herald,* organized a line, under the name of the Isthmus Transportation Company, of some forty new ship's boats said to be well covered and well manned, and in them carried on a successful freight and passenger service up the river.[20]

From the head of navigation at Gorgona or Cruces, depending on the season, travelers went overland to Panama. The roads of either route were not wider than trails, and only persons afoot and mules passed over them. Although the Gorgona road was longer than that by Cruces, it was generally considered the easier and pleasanter of the two. However, since it had no paving, it became an impassable morass in rainy season, and travelers were then obliged to go by way of Cruces. This trail was a part of the paved road between Panama and Porto Bello which had been built in the colonial period. Though it had not been well maintained and in parts was in shocking condition, the rains did not put it completely out of use. Gorgona and Cruces were supplied with hotels and saloons, generally operated by Americans, which catered to the wants of travelers on their overnight stays in transferring from river to road. The accommodations were reported to be fairly good, and the climate at this higher altitude was often quite pleasant.[21] When the city of Panama was known to be crowded with Americans and no prospect of a ship for California was in view for some time, travelers sometimes remained at Gorgona, camping on the shore of the river or staying in a hotel, until the arrival of news that transportation to San Francisco was available.[22]

Persons were advised not to attempt to complete the journey on foot after leaving the boats, although some did so. Most travelers hired mules to carry themselves and their baggage and proceeded from Gorgona or Cruces early in the morning, since thus the journey could be made in one day. A great deal of baggage was also carried on the backs of natives. Even persons were transported thus, riding in chairs strapped to the heads of the surprisingly strong Negroes and Indians. For women the journey presented problems, which some met by wearing trousers and riding astride the mules, whereas others clung tenaciously to the long skirts, "preferring to die rather than to outrage modesty, shame their sex, and exhibit their large ankles even to the barbarians, among whom he who wore the least clothing was most in fashion."[23]

At the beginning of 1849 the cost of a mule or horse for the day's ride from Cruces to Panama was $12 to $15; for the transportation of three packages of baggage, weighing in all about 180 pounds, one person paid $44, which by exchange became $56.[24] At the same time travelers were being advised to bring with them only a single trunk and enough to make only one mule load, which was about 250 pounds.[25] The cost of transportation overland fluctuated. In February, 1849, a man paid three natives $15 to carry his baggage from Gorgona to Panama; the next month it was said that a mule to carry two trunks from Gorgona to Panama should not cost more than $10.[26] At that time there were some two hundred pack mules engaged in freighting goods across the Isthmus, the charges for their use varying with the demand. For one person with one trunk and one bag, the rate ranged between $15 and $30; for each additional 100 pounds $5 to $10 was charged.[27] In 1851 the usual charge was $16 for the hire of a mule and $10 per 100 pounds for baggage.[28] The rate for passenger mules in 1853 was $18, and the cost of transporting baggage had gone up to 17 cents a pound.[29] Travelers were strongly advised to be sure of the reliability of the person to whom they entrusted their baggage for the transit from the river to Panama. A recognized local express carrier like Zachrissen, Nelson and Company, Ran Runnels, Henriquez, or Perez was recommended. Even then a written contract was advised, with the stipulation that the baggage be delivered at Panama by a stated time, and persons were warned to pay no more than half the charges until the transit was completed. It was suggested that, if an individual carrier was engaged, he should be taken to the alcalde of Gorgona or Cruces and an assurance of his good character obtained before he was entrusted with baggage.[30]

The transit of the Isthmus, which had been characterized by lack of any sort of uniform management during the pioneer years, began to assume regularity by 1853. In that year the Pacific Mail concluded a contract with Hurtado y Hermanos, the largest mule owners on the Isthmus, to convey passengers and baggage through from one ocean to the other at a fixed rate. This made it possible for passengers to purchase tickets covering all expenses of the transit and to be freed from many of the cares formerly attendant on the journey. The contractors took charge of the baggage on board the steamers and delivered it aboard ship at the other side.[31] At the same time, the independent mule-owners met at the Pacific Mail office in Panama to establish a fixed tariff for passengers and baggage across the Isthmus.[32] It was stated at the beginning of 1854 that the transit was entirely in the hands of James S. Hermann and Company and Messrs. Hinkley and Company and that, in view of stiff competition between those firms, it was possible for passengers to purchase through tickets across the Isthmus—including a ticket to the end of the incomplete railroad plus river and mule transportation—for $25 to $30.[33]

In traveling from the Pacific to the Atlantic, it was possible from the beginning to make a much quicker trip. Counting a day from Panama to Cruces or Gorgona, the boat trip down the river took only another day, making the entire transit about two days as compared to the four or five days usually consumed in going from Chagres to Panama. In 1854 it was reported in the *Panama Weekly Star* that the journey across the Isthmus had been made in the short time of seven hours.[34]

An important part of the isthmian transit in the period before the completion of the Panama Railroad was the safe conduct of specie exported from California. It was generally sent through in charge of an express or steamship company, being packed on mules from Panama to the Chagres and then sent down the river in boats. The primitive facilities for transportation, the poor roads, and the lack of adequate policing made the trip at times a dangerous one, and the attacks on the treasure trains and robbery of specie were not few. In August, 1850, the conductor of Howland and Aspinwall's specie train was robbed of $30,000, and on December 23 of the same year Zachrissen, Nelson and Company's treasure train was attacked a few miles out of Panama, and $120,000 in gold dust seized. Parties were sent out immediately, however, and most of the gold was recovered.[35]

In August, 1850, Henry Tracy, who acted as isthmian agent for the United States Mail Steamship Company and the Law Line, wrote to Marshall O. Roberts in New York, saying that in the future it would be necessary to have the treasure trains well guarded in order to get them safely across the Isthmus. To do this, he requested twelve Colt revolving rifles, twelve pairs of dragoon-size revolvers, twelve pairs of smaller revolvers, twenty-four Bowie knives, one case of powder and ball and two buckshot guns. A cargo of specie would require forty mules, and for each five mules, Tracy said, there should be a mounted rifleman, and each mule should be led by a *peone*. He went on to say:

That robberies have but just commenced, and that there are from 50 to 100 as precious villains on the Isthmus as ever went unhung ... That there will have to be bloodshed before matters become regulated. As I have no doubt within six months there will be an attempt to seize one of the large, but half-guarded trains.[36]

In a letter written the next month, Tracy reverted to the subject of the treasure trains and their guarding:

I am determined that there shall be none [treasure] stole [*sic*] from your trains except there be several funerals, and think you can rely upon good care being taken of it. But I do need the arms I wrote for, and hope they will come on by the "Georgia." I never wear pistols or knives, except I am conducting specie, or am expecting a fight; and therefore hope you will not think what I wrote about arms, the effect of fear so much as of caution. I risk my life, and wish, if it is to be sold, to have it go at a fair price; yet I have less fear of robberies than thefts; and as most thieves are cowards, like to have it distinctly understood that the train I conduct is ready for a fight, as I believe the rogues will always attack the poorest guarded train.[37]

In September, 1851, there was great excitement in the city of Panama when news arrived that the Pacific Mail Steamship Company's treasure train, consisting of between seventy and eighty mules and carrying about $2,000,000 in specie and gold dust, had been robbed some seven miles from Panama. In the fight two men, probably native muleteers, had been killed, and seven mules returned to Panama without their packs. The sum supposed to have been taken amounted to $250,000. A large armed force of Americans, together with fifty or sixty of the National Guard of New Granada, started in pursuit of the robbers, whose escape was held to be an impossibility. The Pacific Mail's treasure was transported across the Isthmus under contract by the house of Mosquera, Hurtado y Cia., and as the contract included insurance, there was no possibility of loss to the company or the shippers.[38] Since the government seemed unable to control affairs on the Isthmus, an extralegal organization was set up under the leadership of Ran Runnels, an American merchant and shipper resident in Panama. An armed guard was organized, with the tacit consent of the governor, which had authority to punish all those guilty of crimes, even to the death penalty. Working with great effectiveness but little publicity, the Runnels Isthmus Guard, which was financed by the Panama Railroad, existed until March 1, 1855, when, with the railroad in operation and treasure carried by that means, the need for it decreased, and it was discontinued.[39]

There were some attempts made before the completion of the railroad to improve the land transit of the Isthmus. In 1850 the Panama Railroad made plans for a plank road from Navy Bay to Panama, with the construction of the railroad itself postponed until later. But after some two miles had been graded, the project was abandoned, and the whole of the energy of the company was turned toward the building of the railroad.[40] In the summer and fall of 1853 the United States Mail Steamship Company and the Pacific Mail Steamship Company, together with the Panama Railroad, agreed to assist with repairs to the Cruces-Panama road, which was in particularly bad shape. The work was first carried on under Edward Allen, a contract being later awarded to Ran Runnels to complete repairs. What had been hitherto bottomless mud holes were filled with stones, after the mud had been cleared away to a solid bottom; holes were macadamized, and sewers built along the side of the road to carry off the water. With the completion, on October 27, 1853, of work on this necessary link in the isthmian transit it was asserted that one of the forcible arguments of those competing with the Panama route had been answered.[41]

Arriving at Panama, the traveler found himself in a city nearly two centuries old, with great stone buildings, paved streets, and an established society. During the years in which the Panama route flourished, the population of the city was between eight and ten thousand inhabitants, but it gave the impression of being larger.[42] Of these, in 1868, about 2,000 were whites, including 300 resident foreigners, 100 of whom were from the United States, 100 French, and the remainder English, Italians, and Spaniards.[43] A few of the Americans who remained at Panama for sojourns ranging from a day to three or four months waiting for a steamer to carry them to California interested themselves in the city and people, making excursions to the ruins of the old city of Panama and beginning the study of Spanish. By far the majority, however, were entirely intolerant of the civilization in which they found themselves; they made every effort to live as they did in the United States and became almost frantic with impatience if the ship which they expected was delayed. For much of the time down to 1852 there were enough emigrants in Panama to give them a feeling of independence and to make them bold in disregarding local custom and law when it interfered with their wishes or desires. As early as the spring of 1849 a traveler could write:

Panama is thoroughly Americanized; has stores for the sale of meats, groceries, bread &c.; the auctioneer's voice may be heard at all hours of the day, in the disposal of assorted lots, placed in his hands by those who must raise funds to get to San Francisco. Brokers' officers are established for buying and selling passage tickets. One announcement I enclose literally:

STEAMER and other TICKETS
BOT and SOLD ON COMMISSION
MONEY LOONED on Steamer Tickets
Enquire Room No. —
AMERICAN HOTEL.[44]

A good deal of drinking, gambling, and shooting went on among the Americans. But when the bishop died in the spring of 1850, the tolling of the church bells of the city annoyed them and caused much grumbling.[45]

There were near-riots when drunken Americans entered the cathedral wearing their hats and showing the utmost disrespect for the character of the building and the feelings of the worshippers there. The reaction of many Americans to Panama was reflected in the following characterization of the city:

Here I find myself again, for the third time, in this far famed city of New Granada—the same dirty, noisy, and unpleasant place to stay in. There is no comfort, no pleasure—nothing which in the least degree tends to make the time pass lightly, but everything is dull, heavy and monotonous. If it could be Yankeeized, there might be some hopes of it; but as it is, it is deplorable.[46]

While they waited in Panama, travelers either stayed in hotels or *pensions,* where board and room cost in the neighborhood of $8 per week, or camped outside the city walls.[47] The number of Americans in the city fluctuated greatly, since a succession of ships might carry northward all who wished to go, whereas a series of delayed sailings would again crowd the town with emigrants. Thus in April, 1850, it was estimated that there were three thousand Americans in Panama, while in February of 1852 the number was said to be nearly four thousand.[48] After 1852, however, there was seldom any large number of travelers waiting in the city, since with the improved coördination of the lines on the Atlantic and Pacific the facilities for travel on both oceans tended to become equal, and the number crossing the Isthmus could be cared for as they came.

The reputation of the Isthmus for its unhealthful climate and high death rate was seemingly not borne out in the period under consideration except in time of epidemics. When the first emigrants crossed in 1848 and 1849, cholera broke out among them, and in both 1849 and 1850 the city of Panama had epidemics of this disease. In general, it was true that illness among the travelers was more often due to their unwise exertion and mental excitement during the crossing and to intemperance in eating and drinking than to the climate.[49] For the year from November 25, 1851, to November 25, 1852, the report of the American Hospital at Panama showed 540 patients admitted, of whom 459 were dismissed, 69 died, and 12 remained at the time of the report. From this, it is estimated that of the thirty thousand who crossed the Isthmus that year, not more than a hundred had died in the transit.[50] Yellow fever was not seen at Panama until it was introduced by emigrants; it appeared as an epidemic in January, 1853, and again in 1855–1856. In 1865, it was reported there had been no smallpox epidemic since 1840, that typhoid fever and dysentery were comparatively rare, and that malaria was the only endemic and common disease of the Isthmus.[51]

The idea of constructing a railroad across the Isthmus of Panama was discussed as early as 1835. In 1841 a Frenchman, Sablá, from Guadalupe, was permitted by the government of New Granada to make a survey of the Isthmus for practicable routes, from the results of which he was able to interest a group of French capitalists sufficiently to form the Compagnie de Panama in 1845. One of the leaders in the group, Matthew Klein, journeyed to Bogotá, and in 1845 completed negotiations for the right to construct a railway across the Isthmus, holding it for ninety-nine years. The work thus begun was brought to an abrupt halt by the establishment of the Second Republic in France and the resultant economic panic in Europe. When the company was unable to make the deposit required to guarantee completion of the railroad, the agreement with Klein was declared canceled on July 2, 1849, and the government of New Granada was at liberty to make arrangements with other persons for the construction of the railway.[52]

It had been clear before the formal abrogation of the French agreement that it could not be consummated, and other groups had set about the task of carrying out the work. From the time in 1847 when William H. Aspinwall had assumed the contract to carry mail from Panama to Oregon, he had in mind the construction of a railroad across the Isthmus to serve as a feeder for the ships on the Pacific and to strengthen the chain of communication binding this area to the rest of the United States. Of the men associated with Aspinwall in this enterprise, Henry Chauncey and John L. Stephens were particularly prominent. The former was a New York capitalist, who had the same large-minded and public-spirited outlook as Aspinwall.[53] Stephens, trained in law at Columbia College, was a notable traveler, who had served as United States chargé d'affaires in Central America, besides traveling independently in that region. His books of travel had been "best sellers" in the field, and his intimate knowledge of the isthmian area made him a valuable acquisition to the American group planning to construct the railroad.[54]

In the early part of 1848 Stephens, with J. L. Baldwin, an engineer, arrived on the Isthmus of Panama for the purpose of making a preliminary survey for the railroad. They expected to be able to run a line from sea to sea without crossing any ridge over 600 feet high, and they were happily surprised in the discovery of a pass not more than 300 feet above sea level.[55]

With this encouragement, Aspinwall, Chauncey, and Stephens presented a memorial to Congress on December 11, 1848, pointing out the importance to the United States of a railroad across the Isthmus, for military and naval purposes as well as for the assistance of commerce and travel to California. They stated, however, that it would be impossible to carry this out with much rapidity without the aid of government funds. Instead of outright grants to assist in the enterprise the Aspinwall group requested that the Secretary of the Navy be empowered to enter a contract with the projectors of the railroad for a period of twenty years after its completion. The contract would call for the transportation of all troops, munitions, naval, and army supplies, as well as the United States mails and its public agents, for a sum not exceeding that paid the Collins Line for carrying the mail from New York to Liverpool.[56] The memorial was referred to the Committee on Military Affairs in the Senate, and on December 14 Thomas Hart Benton, chairman of the committee, introduced a bill which embodied the points made in the memorial, though it limited the compensation to two-thirds of the sum then paid to the Collins Line and provided that no money be paid until the entire transit of the Isthmus could be made by steam power. The railroad was to be commenced within one year of the date of the contract and to be completed within three years of June 1, 1849.[57] The bill met a good deal of opposition in the Senate, not because of disapproval of the idea, but rather because other capitalists, particularly George Law and Adams and Company, were anxious to receive such a contract and therefore offered rival proposals.[58] Since Aspinwall had already secured from New Granada a grant to build, it looked as though the other petitioners were anxious to obtain the contract and then force themselves upon the holder of the grant.[59] In the House of Representatives, Thomas Butler King, of the Committee on Naval Affairs, presented the memorial of Aspinwall, Chauncey, and Stephens on January 16, 1849, but in this bill the compensation recommended had been reduced from $500,000 a year to $250,000.[60] On January 29, Stephen A. Douglas, in the Senate, offered as a substitute for Benton's bill a measure which provided that the sum to be paid the contractors should not exceed $250,000 a year and established passenger and freight rates running from $18 per person and $8 per ton during the first five years of operation to $3 per person and $3 per ton for the fourth five-year period of operation. This contract might be rescinded after ten years, in which event the rates set up would cease to be mandatory. This substitute was agreed to by the Senate.[61] Debate on the bill continued on January 30 and 31, and was resumed on February 6, 1849, with most of the objection coming from men representing the South and West. Some of these feared that such action would delay governmental aid to a transcontinental railroad, whereas others were anxious to assure the opening of the Tehuantepec route, which would place New Orleans in a position of particular advantage with regard to the transit. Atlantic-seaboard and New England senators, including Daniel Webster, supported the bill loyally, but on February 6, 1849, the subject was passed by, and the Senate proceeded to the consideration of other business.[62] On March 14, 1849, Aspinwall commented as follows on his efforts to obtain aid for the Panama Railroad:

I have to thank you for your interesting private letter from Panama which reached me in Washington where I have lost much time this winter in trying to induce favorable action on the part of the Government towards a rail road across Panama; but President making & slavery were too engrossing to admit of attention being bestowed on this or any other matter of interest to California —& we shall therefore limit ourselves to improving the transit in a more economical way—so that by next year at this time, it may be accomplished in 10 or 12 hours from sea to sea.[63]

The grant from New Granada to the American projectors of the trans-isthmian railroad had evidently been made informally prior to December, 1848. When the French company forfeited its right to build, the president of the republic authorized its minister in Washington to transfer the right to such association in the United States as might be able to offer a sufficient guarantee of fulfillment.[64] The contract was entered at Washington on December 28, 1848, just as the proposal of government aid was being discussed in Congress. On June 12, 1849, by a legislative decree of New Granada, the amplification and amendment of the contract was authorized, and this was arranged and signed at Bogotá on April 15, 1850, by Victoriano de Diego Parédes, secretary of state for foreign affairs of New Granada, and John L. Stephens for the Panama Railroad. It was ratified by the Congress of New Granada on May 29, 1850. The contract gave to the Panama Railroad the exclusive right to build and operate a railroad across the Isthmus for forty-nine years, with the reservation that New Granada might purchase the railroad at the end of twenty years for $5,000,000, after thirty years for $4,000,000, or after forty years for $2,000,000. The railroad was to be completed from ocean to ocean within six years of the ratification of the contract, and until that time the Panama Railroad was to enjoy the exclusive privilege of operating steamers on the Chagres. The railroad was given the sole right to use the ports at its termini for loading and unloading goods, and might collect what compensation it wished for the use of its landing facilities. For the building of the line the company was allowed to use whatever means of construction it wished, provided the transit over it could be made within twelve hours. It was given wide land grants, including right of way, land for a terminal on the beach at Panama, the whole of Manzanilla Island in Navy Bay on the Atlantic side, and also 250,000 acres of land to be selected by the grantees from any public lands on the Isthmus. The railroad agreed to carry free the mails of New Granada, and to pay to the republic 5 per cent of all the money which it might receive from mail contracts, an amount which was not to be less than $10,000 per year, in addition to 3 per cent of the net profits of the railroad. Since its supplies were to be duty free and tax free, the Panama Railroad agreed to carry without charge all New Granadan troops and supplies, while passengers and merchandise transported over the road were to be exempt from all national, provincial, and municipal taxes, and foreigners on railroad property were to be tax free for twenty years. Any controversies arising between the railroad and New Granada were to be settled in the courts of New Granada.[65]

As the railroad proved to be a success, the company became anxious to secure it for a longer time than that set by the contract of 1850. In 1859 there was a rumor that an extension of perhaps one hundred years had been arranged with New Granada, but this proved to be baseless.[66] In 1867, however, a contract was entered between Santos Acosta, secretary of finance and public improvements of the United States of Colombia (formerly New Granada), and George M. Totten, engineer-in-chief and general agent of the Panama Railroad. This conceded the use and possession of the railroad to the company for a period of ninety-nine years from January 30, 1875, for which the railroad should pay $1,000,000 in gold to Colombia at the time of the approval of the contract and $250,000 per year during the term of the existing privilege. In consequence of these payments, the claims of the government to the 5 per cent of mail pay and 3 per cent of net profits were renounced. The company bound itself to extend the railroad into the Bay of Panama to such a point that deep-water vessels might come alongside its piers. The right to direct the use of the ports, as well as the collection of such fares, wharfage, lighterage, and storage as it might desire, remained with the company, and passengers and merchandise in interoceanic transit were to be exempt from all dues and taxes. Colombian mails, troops, and officials would be carried free, and products of Colombia were to be carried at half rates for the first twenty-five years of the contract and for two-thirds rates after that time. Any questions between the government and the railroad concerning the understanding or execution of the contract were to be decided at Bogotá by a board of arbitration composed of the president of the Federal Supreme Court, a person chosen by the Panama Railroad, and a third chosen by agreement between the two. The contract was approved July 5, 1867.[67]

At the same time that the projectors of the railroad were attempting to obtain aid from the United States government and were making arrangements with the government of New Granada for the building of the railroad, they were moving toward the organization of a company to implement their plans. It was announced on December 13, 1848, that subscription books for the capital stock of a company to construct a railroad across the Isthmus of Panama would be open for a few days at the Bank of the State of New York. The trustees listed were General Winfield Scott, Cornelius W. Lawrence, Matthew Morgan, Samuel Jandon, C. A. Davis, and William Kent.[68] On April 7, 1849, "An Act to incorporate the Panama Rail-Road Co." passed the New York legislature, which empowered William H. Aspinwall, John L. Stephens, Henry Chauncey, Cornelius W. Lawrence, Gouverneur Kemble, Thomas W. Ludlow, David Thompson, Joseph B. Varnum, Samuel S. Howland, Prosper M. Wetmore, Edwin Bartlett, Horatio Allen, and associates to build a railroad across the Isthmus of Panama and to operate ships. The capital stock was to be not less than $1,000,000 nor more than $5,000,000, with shares at $100 each, and the corporation might commence operations when $500,000 had been subscribed.[69] At the beginning the plan was to issue only $1,000,000 of stock, and for this the books were opened on June 28, 1849. By three o'clock of the afternoon of the opening day, the entire amount had been subscribed, chiefly by New York capitalists.[70] Of the price of the stock, 10 per cent was required at the time of taking it, the balance of the installments being called for in August, 1849, March and April, 1850, and January, February, March, April, May, and June, 1851.[71] At the meeting of organization on July 2, 1849, Thomas W. Ludlow was elected president of the company, John L. Stephens vice-president, and Francis Spies secretary.[72] Ludlow was soon succeeded in the presidency by John L. Stephens, who held office until his death in 1852.

During the first part of 1849 a large surveying party had been on the Isthmus, engaged in making final examinations preparatory to the beginning of construction. Colonel G. W. Hughes, of the United States Topographical Corps, was appointed chief engineer, taking with him to the Isthmus a number of assistants to carry out the work at various sections of the route. A party of thirty-eight left New York on January 22, 1849, others coming by the *Crescent City* in February.[73] These surveys resulted in the location of a summit even lower than that discovered by Baldwin in the previous year, and when Edward Sidell returned to New York in June, 1849, with the results of the work, the future of the Panama Railroad seemed most promising. The plan was to operate steamers on the river at first from Chagres to Gorgona, and to build the railroad from Gorgona to Panama. Thus the Isthmus could be crossed by a passenger in a day, and the Panama Railroad would have an income from fares to aid in the construction of the line from the Atlantic to Gorgona.[74]

The company determined to contract for the construction of the line from Gorgona to Panama, and to this end it was advertised on July 14, 1849, that proposals for the work would be received from contractors up to September 1, and that a decision would be made as soon as possible after that date. The early notice was intended to allow prospective contractors to visit the Isthmus and examine the line as staked out by the engineers before making their bids.[75] A contract for this construction was entered by the Panama Railroad with George M. Totten and John C. Trautwine, though the terms of the agreement are not available. The company had solicited the services of these men, since they had recently been engaged in the construction of the Canal del Dique, connecting the Magdalena River with the Caribbean at Cartagena, and were therefore familiar with climatic and labor conditions in the tropics. Serious difficulties soon faced the contractors, however. The great number of travelers crossing the Isthmus on their way to California caused such a drain on the labor supply that it was almost impossible to engage workmen at a reasonable price, while the cost of freighting on the Chagres was so high as to make the transportation of materials to Gorgona almost out of the question. Furthermore, the flat-bottomed steamer which had been sent out to operate on the Chagres proved to have too deep draft to be able to navigate the river.[76] In February, 1850, the contractors wrote to the headquarters of the company in New York, stating their inability to carry out the contract under the changed conditions and recommending that the plan of construction be changed to begin at Navy Bay on the Atlantic, where supplies and materials could be landed directly from ocean-going vessels. At a meeting of the executive committee of the Panama Railroad on March 12, 1850, these questions were discussed at length. It was decided to relieve Totten and Trautwine of their contract, to suspend construction from Gorgona to Panama, and to begin the line at Navy Bay. At the same time orders were given to sell the iron steamer intended for the navigation of the Chagres, since it had been shown that her operation on the Chagres would be impracticable.[77] She had already been loaded aboard the brig *N. C. Ely,* preparatory to shipping her to the Isthmus.

Although they were no longer the contractors, Totten and Trautwine were retained by the Panama Railroad as engineers in charge of construction, and with the abandonment of work at Gorgona steps were taken to begin work from the Atlantic. The terminus had been placed on Manzanilla Island in Navy Bay, some four miles northeast of the mouth of the Chagres. The bay offered much better protection than did the roadstead at Chagres, and the depth of water off the island made possible the construction of docks alongside which ships could lie for discharging and embarking passengers and freight. The climate at Manzanilla was, if anything, worse than at Chagres, for the island was hemmed in on three sides by swamps and received little ocean breeze. While Totten went to Cartagena to arrange for laborers, Trautwine and Baldwin, chief assistant engineer, proceeded to Navy Bay in May, 1850, and began clearing Manzanilla Island, living aboard an old brig anchored in the bay. About June first Totten arrived from Cartagena with forty laborers, and in July he brought fifty more.[78] In order to speed the construction in the swamps surrounding Manzanilla Island, it was decided to build the road on piles through this region. Pile drivers were sent out from the United States, and actual construction of the road began about December 1, 1850.[79] The first rails were laid on February 24, 1851, and a locomotive and tender were landed on February 22.[80] It was expected that the railroad would reach Gatun, on the Chagres, seven miles from the terminus, by July 1, 1851, and piles and rails were being deposited there by the middle of May.[81] On June 24, 1851, the first locomotive got up steam, and began operation on the railroad at Navy Bay.[82] The swamp between Navy Bay and Gatun, said to be one of the worst on the continent, obstructed the completion of the line between those points until about the first of November, 1851, but by the middle of that month trains were running from the Atlantic terminus to Miller's Station, more than two miles above Gatun.[83]

It was the intention of the railroad to open the line for passenger service when it had reached Bohio Soldado, but when heavy weather made it impossible for the *Georgia* to land her passengers at Chagres in December, 1851, President Stephens was prevailed upon to allow them to be placed ashore at Navy Bay and carried by the railroad to Gatun, whence they took river boats for Gorgona. Even at this time the railroad was equipped with good passenger and baggage cars.[84] In February, 1852, five hundred troops bound for California were carried over the Panama Railroad as far as Gatun, and on March 15 the railroad from Navy Bay to Bohio Soldado was opened for passenger and freight traffic, trains leaving Navy Bay at 6:00 A.M. daily, as well as immediately after the arrival of the mail steamers. Thus Gorgona could be reached in one day from the Atlantic, and the fare which had been $10 to $15 was now $5 for the railroad journey, plus $1.50 to $3 for the river trip from Bohio Soldado to Gorgona.[85] Work was pushed with some rapidity during the remainder of the dry season of 1852 and into the wet season, until by July 7 the line reached Barbacoas, near Gorgona, where the Chagres River was to be crossed by a bridge.[86] In the meantime, the section between Navy Bay and Gatun, which had been laid on piles, was rapidly being cribbed with earth and stone, hundreds of workmen with engines and box cars laboring to fill in the roadbed and make it solid and permanent.[87]

With the opening of the railroad to passenger traffic, the settlement on Navy Bay became the terminus of the steamers coming from New York and New Orleans, as well as of the English vessels which operated to the Isthmus. On February 29, 1852, the cornerstone of the first brick building on the island was laid, intended as an office for the Panama Railroad. Victoriano de Diego Parédes, with whom the original New Granada contract had been made, was at that time on his way to Washington as minister to the United States and requested permission to lay the cornerstone. In his speech, Parédes proposed that the town be called Aspinwall, in honor of the projector of the railroad and of the route as a whole. The suggestion of Parédes was repudiated by his government, which named the town Colon, but American residents and travelers continued to use the name Aspinwall, to some extent at least, until 1890. The town was an active place in 1852, with locomotives and dirt trains constantly in motion and barrow men trundling wheelbarrows loaded with coral rock for the streets which were being constructed. Already there were several large warehouses, three or four hotels, numerous residences built or building, and a large dock for vessels drawing up to twenty feet of water, while the United States Mail Steamship Company had under construction a dock for the sole use of its steamers.[88] By May of 1852 a traveler reported that the growth of Aspinwall was astonishing, "giving evidence of its having been thoroughly Yankeeized." The Panama Railroad office, a two-story frame-and-stucco building with a thirty-foot front, was the most conspicuous structure, but in addition there were not less than five hotels.[89] In July of the same year, the Panama Railroad completed a lighthouse at the mouth of the harbor, which was visible ten miles at sea.[90] The City Hotel at Aspinwall was particularly impressive to a visitor from the other side of the Isthmus in the fall of 1853. He wrote that it was two hundred feet long by sixty feet wide, and was surrounded on both floors by galleries, enclosed by Venetian blinds. The barroom and dining room on the first floor would seat two hundred persons, and by placing cots on the galleries for those who might be unable to get private rooms, the hotel could comfortably accommodate five hundred.[91] At this time, Aspinwall had a population of about three thousand, with at least three hundred houses of substantial character, large machine, carpenter, and blacksmith shops, two hospitals, and three wharves. Another wharf, this one of iron, was under construction, as well as a freight depot for the railroad eighty feet wide by six hundred feet in length. A large train with locomotive was employed exclusively in filling in swamps and leveling and grading land in and around the town. The land, all of which was owned by the Panama Railroad, was rented to its occupants, the income to the railroad ranging from $12,000 to $18,000 per year.[92] The ships at the wharves were unloaded, loaded, and coaled by mule power and by gangs of laborers. Even with this system, the *George Law* in 1853 discharged her mails, eight hundred passengers, baggage, express, and freight in less than ten hours.[93]

The great problem facing the Panama Railroad in the summer

of 1852 was the construction of a bridge across the Chagres River. At Barbacoas, the point selected for the structure, the river was some three hundred feet in width and, though shallow for much of the year, it rose rapidly in the rainy season, sometimes rising as much as forty feet in a single night.[94] To construct this bridge, as well as to complete the railroad, the company determined to resort again to contract, this time making it with M. C. Story of Poughkeepsie, New York, who was one of the largest public works contractors in the United States, having at that time some six thousand men in his employ on the Portland and Montreal Railroad. This contract was announced May 22, 1852, the agreement being that the railroad would be finished within one year. The price for the twenty-one miles from Barbacoas to Panama was rumored to be $3,500,000. George Law became Story's security for the completion of the contract.[95] Law was already a very large backer of the Panama Railroad, having invested some $300,000 in the stock and bonds of the company in July, 1851. In the spring of 1852, it was said that he owned $500,000 worth of stock, as well as more land in New Granada than any other American.[96] The bridge proved to be very difficult to build. With labor troubles to hinder them, the contractors accomplished little during their year of work, and the construction was taken over again by the Panama Railroad in September, 1853.[97]

The city of Panama looked forward to the coming of the railroad with a good deal of anticipation. In October, 1851, the *Panama Star* commented as follows:

The future of Panama centres in the union of the Atlantic and the Pacific, by the completion of the Rail Road from ocean to ocean; thus causing the Isthmus to become part of the great pathway of nations, and Panama the enterposit for the commerce of one half the globe. When that great work is completed, and the iron horse courses along our streets, and the shrill sound of the steam whistle is heard in our vallies [*sic*] and among the mountain fastnesses, then will Panama begin to brush the mildew of ages from her midst, and her pristine days will come again.[98]

With this feeling abroad, there were expressions of satisfaction when, in June, 1853, it was announced that work would soon be commenced in the city of Panama moving toward the Atlantic to meet the rails coming from that direction.[99] Work was actually begun near Panama on June twentieth, and by the middle of

August, 1853, a good part of the right of way had been cleared, and grading was going forward rapidly.[100]

After the Panama Railroad had taken construction into its own hands again in the early fall of 1853, work was carried on with great vigor. The Chagres bridge at Barbacoas was finally completed, and the first engine crossed it on November 26, 1853.[101] By the end of January, 1854, the railroad had placed a locomotive at Panama, and was ready to push northward with a large force of laborers.[102] As the rainy season of 1854 advanced, the railroad progressed into the rough country south of the Chagres. In spite of slides, desertions, and illness, the summit was reached by the beginning of October. In November nearly the whole line had been graded, and working parties on both sides were within half a mile of one another.[103] Finally, on the evening of January 27, 1855, the last rail of the Panama Railroad was laid, and the next day, January twenty-eighth, the first train passed over it from the Atlantic to the Pacific. Passengers by the mail steamer reaching Panama from San Francisco on January twenty-ninth and those arriving at Aspinwall on January thirtieth crossed the Isthmus by rail, though these trips were made with considerable delay owing to damage to the line by unseasonable rains. The passengers who reached Panama on February fifteenth, however, made the crossing in four and one-half hours.[104]

The actual completion of the railroad had been very much in the line of duty, the celebrations coming nearly a month later. On February 2, 1855, there was a meeting of the chief citizens of the city of Panama to adopt measures in connection with the ceremonies of formally opening the railroad. Great enthusiasm was shown, and committees were appointed to plan a grand ball and to ask permission of the provincial government for three days of public rejoicing with bullfighting and horse racing.[105] When the *George Law* left New York on February fifth, she carried a party of sixteen invited guests of the Panama Railroad to participate in the celebration of the opening, who brought with them banners and fireworks.[106] The steamer entered the harbor of Aspinwall on the morning of February 15, 1855, with the flag of New Granada at her fore and the Stars and Stripes at the mizzen.

The white houses, with small windows and green blinds, lent an American aspect to the town, while the shipping lying at anchor in the bay, showed signs of commercial life. The palm trees on shore gracefully waved their tall foliage in the breeze of the trade wind, and the green hills that, on two sides, encircled the bay, rejoiced in the glow of the tropical sun.

The invited guests, together with the 457 regular passengers of the *George Law,* left Aspinwall at 9:00 A.M. on the sixteenth, in a train composed of nine passenger cars and one baggage car. The engine was gaily decorated with flags, and the express car exhibited a profusion of streamers. Passing under an arch of flowers and leaves at Gatun, crowned with the motto, "The problem is solved, success ever attends an enterprising people," the train stopped at Monument Hill near the confluence of the Chagres and the Obispo rivers, where an address in honor of the completion of the railroad was presented by Judge Bowlin, United States minister to New Granada.[107] After a round of dinners and dances in Panama and a trip to Taboga for the guests of the railroad, most of them sailed for New York on February 19, 1855, and the line settled down to everyday operation.[108]

Just before the completion of the railroad, Chief Engineer George M. Totten wrote to Gouverneur Kemble, one of the directors of the company:

Many exclamations are made at the difficulties overcome, which do not strike me. I am ashamed that so much has been expended in overcoming so little, and take no credit for any engineering science displayed in the work. The difficulties have been of another nature, and do not show themselves on the line.[109]

The difficulties to which Totten had reference were undoubtedly those of maintaining an adequate labor supply and of caring for the health of those men who worked on the railroad. At the time of the second survey in the spring of 1849, the greatest trouble was experienced in finding native laborers who would serve faithfully. Although the construction engineers had the assistance of the governor of the province and the alcalde of Gorgona, the workmen persisted in making all sorts of excuses and in running away at every opportunity to obtain the easier service and higher pay which the California-bound emigrants would give them. It was finally found to be more satisfactory to hire Americans stranded in Panama, paying them $1 a day and their board for the period of the survey and providing them with tickets to California upon its termination.[110]

With the beginning of construction of the railroad, Colonel Totten recruited laborers at Cartagena, and also arranged to have them brought from Jamaica. Men from the United States were employed also, particularly mechanics, who were brought to the Isthmus under contract to work for a specified period in return for passage on to California.[111] The natives of the Isthmus, although able-bodied enough, were not dependable, and therefore men from outside were used as far as possible. By the middle of October, 1850, there were between three and four hundred men working at Navy Bay, some being from Cartagena but most of them Irish from New Orleans, and five hundred additional laborers were expected from New York by the beginning of November.[112] In December there were some six hundred men at work, with three hundred more expected shortly. They were stationed at three points, Manzanilla Island, Gatun, and Mount Arrow Root.[113] Frenchmen were imported for work also. In May, 1851, the deputy superintendent at Bohio Soldado by his intemperance and bad conduct got the station into a mutiny, and, Frenchmen being in the majority, the French flag was raised and the Marseillaise sung on the day of the strike. At this point President Stephens of the Panama Railroad appeared and, filled with indignation, refused to have any conference whatever with the strikers until the flag was taken down. To his firmness and his refusal to yield any point whatever was attributed the rapid restoration of quiet and harmony.[114]

During the period in which work was carried on under contract by Story and Law, there was great difficulty in retaining laborers. The large number of desertions was attributed to the badly constructed quarters and the poor food furnished by the contractors and the inadequacy of the medical care provided. It was said upon good authority that the lash was applied by the overseers and that wages were held back until the end of the four months' working period rather than being paid weekly. The natives from the Cartagena region, who formed the majority of the laborers at this time, were not accustomed to such treatment and deserted in large numbers, and the white workmen also complained bitterly.[115] In August, 1853, just at the end of the term of work under the contract, white laborers were hired on the basis of four-month contracts, forfeiting their pay and return passage if they did not fulfill the time required. They worked at such points as the engineers might direct and in competition with native laborers. It was said that the effect of the climate, hard work, and poor living conditions resulted in a mortality of 50 per cent at the end of three months and of 80 per cent at the end of four months. However, considering reports on the construction of the railroad, it should be pointed out that these estimates were greatly exaggerated, albeit the period of the Story-Law contract marked a high point in the death rate.[116]

With the resumption of work by the Panama Railroad itself in the early fall of 1853, vigorous efforts were made to increase the labor supply. An agent was sent to Ireland to get workmen to be sent directly to Aspinwall, and thence he proceeded to Canton to arrange for a shipload of coolies for work on the line. Mechanics were recruited in New York and Pennsylvania and native laborers were solicited from Cartagena. It was planned to have a force of 9,000 men at work on the railroad by January of 1854;[117] at the beginning of October, 1853, there were 1,400 men working, and a month later 300 more had arrived.[118] In Colonel Totten's report to the board of directors of the company in November, 1853, he wrote that the force then employed on the road consisted of 1,200 native laborers, Negroes from Jamaica, and coolies, together with 300 whites, making a total of 1,590. By the beginning of 1854, he expected to have 2,000 natives from the Cartagena region and 500 more from other parts of New Granada. The order of the company for men from Ireland and China was expected to bring 1,000 from the former, and 1,700 from China, making a total of 6,790 who might be expected to be at work early in 1854. In addition, some 150 laborers and mechanics were sent out monthly from the United States. The Irishmen were not as efficient on the Isthmus as in cooler climates, but in the periods of four to six months, for which they were engaged, they did a fair amount of work. It was expected that the Chinese would be feeble and inefficient at first but that, being steady and temperate and little affected by the climate, they might become useful workmen with time. Since the natives from the Cartagena region were as accustomed to work with pick and shovel as Irishmen and were elastic and hardy, Totten considered them the most efficient common laborers which could be employed.[119] A shipload of Irishmen arrived at Aspinwall on January 8, 1854, and the clipper ship *Sea Witch* brought 705 coolies from China on March 30.[120] The latter proved to be a sad disappointment. Although rice, tea, and opium were imported for their use, not only did many of them fall ill, but they were also attacked by chronic melancholy, which led large numbers of them to commit suicide. They deserted from work on the railroad at every opportunity and, coming into Panama, had to be rounded up by the police and sent back to work. There seemed little to be done with the comparatively few who remained by the fall of 1854, though the suggestion was then made that they be sent to Jamaica in exchange for Negroes, the latter being good workers on the railroad, while the Chinese were successful as agricultural laborers in the Jamaican climate.[121]

By April, 1854, the Panama Railroad had some five thousand men at work and expected to increase this number by another thousand, a figure which would be maintained until the completion of the road.[122] This was not carried out, however, for at the time of opening the line to traffic from the Atlantic to the Pacific it was reported that about three thousand men were employed, their wages being eighty cents per day, with lodging and board.[123] After the completion of the railroad, a considerable force was maintained. The number in the spring of 1858 was between seven and eight hundred men—the laborers by this time being mostly natives, and only the mechanics and officials Americans. These laborers were paid $1 a day, and the mechanics $3 to $4 a day.[124]

The material available does not make possible a satisfactory survey of health conditions during the construction of the Panama Railroad, but it is sufficient to show that the illness and mortality among the laborers has been grossly exaggerated. At the time of the survey for the railroad, the health of the party was good, except for cases of cholera introduced by emigrants. William Sidell, one of the engineers, wrote that the fevers of the Isthmus were no more than a substitute for the colds of the north, and that he believed them to be less frequent and less likely to be permanently injurious. With the ordinary comforts and nursing which were available in the United States they would be even more uncommon. He reported, a month after arrival, that he had not seen a mosquito since coming to the Isthmus.[125] With the actual construction of the railroad, most of the men were down with fever occasionally, but by January, 1851, only three had died.[126] In the United States, it was said that the chills and fever of the Isthmus were not different from those experienced in "Michigan and other western states," and that therefore men from that region should be able to stand the climate well.[127]

Large numbers of men had to be constantly imported, however, for in spite of optimistic reports many were taken ill soon after arrival and became entirely useless to the company.[128] An epidemic of cholera in the interior of the Isthmus in the summer of 1852 caused work to be stopped at Tabernilla for a day and made inroads on the white laborers, about fifty in all dying, together with some twenty-five native laborers.[129]

The comparatively heavy mortality during the period of the Story-Law contract, which produced the rather fantastic estimates of 50-per cent and 80-per cent mortality already referred to, was also responsible for the beginning of a legend which is still alive— that the death rate on the Panama Railroad was so high that approximately one life was sacrificed for every tie laid. At the time, this was ridiculed, but the story has persisted, nevertheless.[130] Since the ties of the railroad were two feet, six inches apart, and the length of the railroad, completed, was forty-seven miles, the number of deaths by this calculation would have been 99,264. The total number of men employed by the railroad during construction is not available, but it was not over 15,000, requiring that each man should have died over six times to make "a life for every tie." Among the white laborers, of whom there were about 6,000 all told, there were 293 deaths from the beginning of construction until the completion of the railroad, which was not a bad record for Panama in the middle of the nineteenth century.[131]

The Panama Railroad, as it was "completed" in 1855, was a single-track line, forty-seven miles in length, with a maximum grade of sixty feet per mile. It had been laid on pine ties originally, but in the climate of the Isthmus these rotted rapidly, and in 1855 they were being replaced with expensive but durable lignum vitae ties. There were sidings at Gatun, Barbacoas, Matachin, and the Summit, four tracks at Aspinwall and three at Panama. At Aspinwall the railroad was provided with roundhouse, machine shop, car repair shop, and blacksmith shop. It had six heavy and four light locomotives, as well as twenty-two passenger cars carrying sixty passengers each, fifty-one house freight cars, and seventy-two platform cars. Wood, which the engines burned, was supplied along the line at $3 per cord. Down to the time of opening the railroad, its cost, including rolling stock, land, and all other expenditures, had been $6,564,552.95.[132]

As the facilities of the railroad were improved, running time between the oceans decreased. In December, 1855, the trip from Panama to Aspinwall was made in three hours and ten minutes, with running time of two hours and twenty-five minutes.[133] The regular schedule for the two daily trains in each direction was four hours from terminus to terminus, and passengers by the steamers could count upon arriving at one side of the Isthmus in the morning and being aboard ship and at sea on another ocean by night.[134]

The passenger rate by the Panama Railroad was set at $25, with half fare for children under twelve, and quarter fare for those under six. Freight rates varied; for passenger's baggage it was at first fifteen cents a pound, then ten cents a pound, express freight by the steamer trains being $1.80 per cubic foot. From the beginning there were loud complaints at the high rates charged, and the New York legislature in the spring of 1855 even made an unsuccessful attempt to regulate them.[135] The company was very liberal in giving passes to naval officers, scientific men, authorities and residents of the Isthmus, and travelers who were unable to pay for themselves.[136]

During construction, the Panama Railroad chartered 158 vessels in which supplies and materials were carried to Aspinwall, and in the summer of 1855 the purchase of sailing vessels for a regular line between New York and Aspinwall was begun. By the end of 1855, the brigs *E. Drummond, Caroline, Abbey Taylor,* and *Arabella* had been purchased, and a half interest had been acquired in the barks *Amonoosuck* and *Magdalena.* It was thus possible to bring supplies and men to the Isthmus without dependence on the rates charged by the steamers in operation.[137]

From its inception, the Panama Railroad was definitely a "good thing" financially. When Aspinwall gave his kinsman, Jonathan Meredith, advice concerning the stock and bonds of the company, he wrote:

My own private opinion is that no speculative investment I have ever known— not even the Pacific [Mail] Steamship Co—offers such returns as the railroad Stock for a permanency—the monopoly is complete on the part of the New Granadian Govt. & our own has sanctioned & guaranteed it by the treaty of

neutrality. I have increased my original investment considerably & so has **Mr**
Chauncey & we each hold over $100,000 for which good money has been paid—
and we both take a good lot of bonds in addition—if we can do so fairly.[138]

The original stock issue had been for $1,000,000 of the $5,000,000
allowed by the charter of the company. In May, 1852, a second
stock issue of $1,500,000 was placed on the market. Two issues of
convertible bonds, in May, 1851, and January, 1854, brought the
total capital to $5,000,000, and in 1855 the company requested an
amendment to its charter, allowing the capital to be increased to
$7,000,000.[139] This amendment passed the New York legislature on
April 12, 1855, and the additional stock and bonds were placed
on the market.[140] The first dividend of the Panama Railroad,
amounting to 10 per cent, was declared on December 3, 1852,
payable in stock on January 15, 1853.[141] An additional 5-per cent
dividend was voted in July, 1853, and 7 per cent was paid in 1854,
with 3½ per cent in January, 1855.[142] The dividends were 12 per
cent annually from 1856 through 1860, and in 1868 they were 24
per cent, with an additional 20 per cent, making a total of 44 per
cent.[143] Stock of the company generally remained above par after
April, 1852, with infrequent drops below par during and after
construction days. Not until 1864 did it go above 200, but thereafter it rose rapidly, passing 300 in September, 1867, and reaching
348 in January, 1869. At the middle of June, 1869, it was the
highest stock listed on the New York Exchange, standing at 295,
the next highest being New York Central Railroad at 188¾.[144] With
the beginning of service in 1852 the Panama Railroad began to
bring in money, the gross receipts for the six months ending December 31, 1852, being $250,161.81. Although the statement which has
been made that the Panama Railroad paid for itself before completion is highly untrue—the gross receipts up to December 31,
1854, being but $1,037,556.92—this was rather a good record for a
railway which was still under construction.[145] Between 1856 and
1866 net receipts never fell below $656,517.60, whereas in five of
the eleven years they were over $1,000,000, reaching their highest
point in 1864 with $1,459,453. In this period, 396,032 passengers
were transported over the railroad, $501,218,748 in gold, $147,-
377,113 in silver, $5,130,010 in jewelry, $19,062,567 in paper
money, and 614,535 tons of mail, baggage, merchandise, and coal.
The largest number of passengers to cross in these years was

46,976 in 1859; the smallest number was 20,420 in 1862.[146] The rates charged and the profits which the company made for its stockholders were said by many to be unreasonably high. This may have been so, but the traveler across the Isthmus might well remember that, before the construction of the iron road from ocean to ocean, he had paid more for his transportation and had traveled with much less comfort and speed. Though the rewards of the railroad might be great, its service was great also.

When service by way of Panama was about to be opened in 1848, there was no provision for the transportation of the mails across the Isthmus. Although there were steamship lines on both oceans, and mail agents to accompany the letter bags, there was no one to carry them from Chagres to Panama. To remedy this, the Postmaster General, on October 25, 1848, ordered the extension of the Panama-Astoria mail route to include the isthmian transit, accepting an offer from the Pacific Mail Steamship Company to carry this out for $2,900 per year.[147] In spite of this arrangement, the mail service across the Isthmus was very bad, particularly for the California-bound, since the contractors had no establishment at Chagres. In March, 1849, the mails from one trip of the *Falcon* took six days to cross to Panama, while those in the opposite direction reached their destination too late to catch the steamer.[148] Later that spring, when there was no one at Chagres to receive the mails, Captain Tucker of the *Orus* gave them to a muleteer, telling him that when he reached Panama, he would be paid for his service. On arrival, the man could find no one to pay him and therefore offered the mails for sale to the highest bidder.[149]

Late in 1849 the transportation of mail across the Isthmus was assumed by the government of New Granada under the postal convention of March 6, 1844. By this, the payment for service was by weight, $30 for the first 100 pounds and $12 for each succeeding 100 pounds on a trip. Amos B. Corwine, United States consul at Panama, was appointed mail agent at $500 per year.[150] This system proved to be little more satisfactory than the previous one. The government of New Granada farmed out the mail service to Panamanian business firms, with results which were not conducive to good service.[151] Not only was poor service rendered, but the arrangement also proved unprofitable to the government of New Granada, which was therefore willing to release the United States from its contract at the end of 1851. From March 13, 1850, until December 13, 1851, the United States had paid $70,585.31 for the transportation of the mail across the Isthmus.[152]

To take the place of the New Granadan service the Post Office Department contracted with the Panama Railroad to carry the mail from Aspinwall to Panama, this service beginning January 1, 1852. The rate paid was twenty-two cents a pound for first-class matter, with printed material considerably lower. As the railroad drew toward completion, the Postmaster General felt that the cost of transportation must be less, and therefore attempted to reduce compensation to eighteen cents a pound. The Panama Railroad objected violently to this, and the final outcome was a contract for service at the annual lump sum of $100,000 per year.[153] This held until the expiration of the ocean mail contracts at the end of June, 1860, after which there was no regular contract. For the year ending June 30, 1861, the sum of $25,000 was paid for the isthmian transit of the mails, in 1866 it was $37,500 or $781.23 per mile, and in 1867 it remained the same.[154] The mail service on the Isthmus underwent much the same experience as the ocean lines in the years between 1860 and 1869, being slighted in favor of the overland route and yet kept up because it was indispensable. With the completion of the overland railroad in 1869, mail between parts of the United States ceased to be sent by way of Panama.

The attitude of American travelers on the Isthmus toward the residents and their civilization could hardly result otherwise than in friction. After 1850 there were frequent outbursts of violence between Americans and Panamanians at Chagres and Panama, for which the Americans were probably a good deal to blame. In May, 1850, a riot occurred in Panama in which two Americans and several natives were killed, the trouble arising from the accusation of a Panamanian boy of a theft of which others believed him to be innocent.[155] The United States consuls at Chagres, Aspinwall, and Panama were unremitting in their application for men-of-war to be stationed at each side of the Isthmus for the protection of the lives of travelers, emphasizing the chronic bad feeling existent.[156] In 1854, a Vigilance Committee of twenty-three members was organized at Aspinwall to protect the lives and property of Americans, and Panama was urged to follow suit.[157]

Although it might have been expected that the completion of

the railroad would relieve this tension by removing the travelers from contact with the natives, its effect was quite different. The Isthmus, which had enjoyed an income estimated at $125,000 to $150,000 a month spent by those who passed over the route and paid for the transportation of passengers, baggage, freight, and specie, now found most of this revenue cut off. Travelers no longer lingered at Panama waiting for a steamer but were transported across the Isthmus and from one ship to another within a day. A deep business depression settled over the region almost immediately after the opening of the railroad and caused bitter feelings among the natives toward the railroad and those who traveled over it.[158] The bad feeling engendered resulted in a serious riot at the Panama terminus of the railroad on the evening of April 15, 1856. It was said to have started when a drunken American quarreled with a fruit vendor over a watermelon and drew a pistol, whereupon the native drew a knife, and a fight resulted. There were some 1,950 Americans on the Isthmus at the time, travelers from both coasts, and those at the Panama station were attacked by a mob of the lower element from the city. The police were called out, but sided with the mob, and the affair ended with the killing of fourteen Americans and the injury of twenty-eight more, besides the looting of the station and baggage room and two hotels. About three natives were killed and twelve injured.[159] There were no further serious disturbances after the "watermelon riot," and, as the Isthmus became accustomed to the changed condition resultant from the railroad, relations between natives and Americans tended to improve.

Thus, after half a dozen years of development and change, the transit of the Isthmus of Panama settled down after 1855 and 1856 to a seldom broken succession of short crossings of passengers and freight from ocean to ocean, a passage which formed a satisfactory and dependable link in the chain of communication between the coasts of the United States by way of Panama.

CHAPTER VIII

SIGNIFICANCE OF THE PANAMA ROUTE

THE PRIME CONSIDERATION in bringing government assistance to the opening of the Panama route was that of the development of a more adequate steam navy for the United States through the construction of merchant steamers suitable for conversion for war service. A secondary reason for governmental interest was the opportunity offered for training naval officers in the handling of steamships in a period when the regular Navy had few such ships on its list. Under the contracts let by the Secretary of the Navy in 1847, steamers were built for service on both Atlantic and Pacific coasts. These were carefully supervised in their construction and thoroughly examined when completed by Commodore Matthew Calbraith Perry, officer in charge of their building, and William Skiddy, naval constructor. In the opinion of both these men the steamships so constructed were suitable for war purposes. It was true that their draft was shallower and their beam narrower than in vessels of the regular navy, and also that they were built of unseasoned timber and could not be expected to last indefinitely, but in many ways they were satisfactory. Their cheaper and quicker construction counted in their favor, and it was possible to strengthen their decks sufficiently to carry a few heavy-calibre guns. For scouting service, convoy duty, troop transportation, and the carrying of dispatches they were reported to be entirely useful. Commodore Perry wrote, however, that it would be very expensive to fit them as regular warships "... nor should they in my opinion interfere in the least with the organization and gradual increase of a permanent steam navy." As for the merits of the paddle wheel as compared with the screw propeller, opinions were divergent. Commodore Perry favored the paddle wheel for the propulsion of all ocean-going vessels, but Skiddy, although admitting that the paddle wheel was best for speed, argued that in a line-of-battle ship or frigate the screw was superior, since a vessel so driven could mount a greater number of guns.[1]

In spite of the approval of naval officers, the system of mail contracts with the Navy Department was attacked in Congress

---

[1] For notes to chap. viii, see pp. 286–287.

as early as January, 1849. The chief objections were that the expense involved and the monopolies fostered thereby were undesirable.[2] It was pointed out that the aid given by the British government to the Cunard Line had only kept out competitors and slowed down the transatlantic service. Since the United States Mail Steamship Company had been singularly lax in the fulfillment of its obligations, it was moved in the Senate in 1850 to abrogate its contract.[3] The real strength of much of the attack seemed to lie in the southern states, where it was felt that New York interests had gathered all the "plums" connected with the mail contracts and that the cities of the south Atlantic seaboard and the Gulf coast were being slighted by the government in the distribution of ships and money.[4]

Furthermore, the administration of the Navy Department expressed itself as dissatisfied with the arrangement. Secretary Preston wrote in his report of December 1, 1849:

I cannot withhold the expression of an opinion adverse to embarking any further in the proposed union of public and private means, in this system of Ocean Steamers, as calculated to promote the interest of the navy.[5]

In June, 1850, he wrote to the Chairman of the Senate Committee on Post Office and Post Roads, Thomas J. Rusk, expressing his belief that the program of mail contracts was not only expensive but positively detrimental to the Navy and recommending that in the future the transportation of mails at sea be left to the competition of private enterprise. It was Preston's contention that these contracts had in no way improved the efficiency or effectiveness of the naval forces of the United States.[6]

This position on the part of the Secretary of the Navy was bitterly criticized by the *New York Herald,* which pointed out that British experience in the operation of mail steamers without the assistance of the government had been unsuccessful, and upheld strongly the wisdom of maintaining the system as organized.[7] Preston's successor in the Navy Department, William A. Graham, was more favorable toward the mail contracts, and they were permitted to continue to their conclusion in 1858 and 1859 without further controversy. For the Panama lines, however, there was little effort to renew them at the time of their expiration, and the fight in Congress on behalf of the Collins Line was waged on the grounds of its service to the American merchant marine rather than because of its use in supporting and supplementing the Navy.

However, it should be noted that, when the Civil War brought the need for every available ship, those vessels built under the mail contracts, though more than ten years old, served well as transports and auxiliary cruisers. Had the system begun in 1847 been continued vigorously through 1861, a much better supply of really suitable vessels would have been available at much more reasonable cost than the War and Navy departments were compelled to pay for the ships which they purchased and chartered.

The mail contracts did valuable service in the training which the ships operating under them offered to naval officers. Young men, of the grades of lieutenant and passed midshipman, were given opportunities to serve in and command steamers much earlier than they could have done in the regular Navy. Thus they familiarized themselves with the operation of steamships and fitted themselves for service in the steam navy of the future. Gustavus Vasa Fox, assistant secretary of the navy during the Civil War, commanded a mail steamer, while David D. Porter, one of the greatest of Union naval commanders, took the *Panama* from New York to the Pacific on her maiden voyage and then served for three years as captain of the *Georgia*.

Only once was a steamer on the Panama route pressed into service for naval purposes. This was the little screw steamer *Columbus* of the Pacific Mail Steamship Company, which had never been offered or accepted for operation on the mail line under the contract. She was chartered in 1854 by Commander Thomas A. Dornin to operate with the sloop-of-war *Portsmouth* in the suppression of filibusters. The *Columbus* served but briefly, and much more time was spent in reaching an agreement for satisfactory payment for her use than in actual operation under charter.[8]

The ships of the Panama route provided for both Army and Navy the means for sending men and supplies to the Pacific coast in a short time. In emergency, transportation by Panama was far more satisfactory than the long voyage around Cape Horn. Officers traveling to and from stations on the Pacific coast almost invariably went by way of the Isthmus. Along the Pacific coast itself, the mail steamers were useful in the movement of men, particularly in connection with Indian difficulties in the Oregon and Puget

Sound regions. Such a line of communication was indispensable for the maintenance of effective military and naval establishments on the Pacific until the completion of the transcontinental railroad.

The second purpose which the government considered in aiding in the establishment of regular communication over this route was the transportation of the mail between the Atlantic and Pacific seaboards of the United States. Until the opening of the overland mail line in 1858, there was no other practicable route than that by the Isthmus, and even until 1869 it was the most dependable and, on the average, the fastest. The questions which arose over the transportation of the mail in the first decade of the Panama route were concerned with the details of conveyance rather than with the immediate possibility of a change to another route. At the same time that Secretary of the Navy Preston was reporting unfavorably on the naval side of the contracts, questions about their success were addressed to the Postmaster General. He replied on February 4, 1850, that, with the rush of persons and goods to California and the rise of competing lines of steamers, the owners of the latter were anxious to obtain government contracts for their ships, and therefore took advantage of every delay and unavoidable irregularity in the mail service to complain of the existing system and to demand that the contracts be taken from the lines holding them and given to their competitors. In considering the service as a whole, Postmaster General Collamer outlined three ways in which it might be performed. The mails might be transported in ships of the regular Navy, though this would be very expensive. Any ship which happened to be sailing might be asked to carry mail, but this would result in irregular service and would render connections at the Isthmus highly difficult. The third alternative was to continue the plan then in force, contracting for service for a specified number of years with a responsible company, at a price agreed upon and under government supervision. It was the last method that the Postmaster General unhesitatingly recommended. He went on to state that most of the delays in the mail service had been occasioned by the isthmian transit and that, when this was placed in the hands of a United States agency, improvement could be expected.⁹ A similar answer was given to questions in the early summer of 1850, and when sailings on the Atlantic and Pacific were adjusted to connect properly at Panama, no further change was made in the mail arrangements until the expiration of the contract.[10]

The through mails from coast to coast were placed in charge of mail agents appointed by the Post Office Department. Under the contracts, the agents were carried free of charge in the steamers, and it was their duty to care for the mail on board ship, accompany it across the Isthmus, and deliver it to the postmaster at the destination of the journey. The key to the mail room was in their keeping during the voyage, and they were expected to sort the letters en route.[11] At the end of 1849 the pay of a mail agent was $800 a year, in addition to which he received living aboard the steamers.[12] These positions were often given to political favorites, and the conduct of some of the agents aroused a great deal of criticism. It was not unknown for them to bring merchandise on personal speculation, taking better care of it on the isthmian transit than of the mail bags. One of them, hearing on arrival at Chagres in September, 1850, that cholera was raging in Panama, became so alarmed that he placed the mail bags, together with trunks containing cigars and other items which he had bought at Havana, in charge of an utterly inexperienced traveler and himself returned to New York. The slowness of the mails across the Isthmus was attributed as much to the mail agents as to the New Granadan contractors who were responsible for its transportation until the end of 1851.[13] Criticism was so loud, and the mail agents seemingly so needless, that in 1853 the system was altered. Resident agents were stationed at Aspinwall and Panama to arrange for transshipment, with the ship's purser in charge of the mails at sea.[14]

With the development of competing lines and because of the slowness of the regular mails in crossing the Isthmus, express companies came to carry a good many of the letters being sent between the coasts. These companies were often able to make good their advertisement, "Through ahead of the mails," by the efficiency of the agents and special messengers whom they employed. Letters thus destined were taken to the express office, where the carrying charge was paid; they then were sent through in closed boxes, to be opened and deposited in a post box for delivery upon arrival. This drained revenue from the Post Office Department, and repeated efforts were made to stop it. In 1849, Marshall O. Roberts reported to the Assistant Postmaster General that his company consistently refused to sell tickets to agents of express companies, but that competing lines carried them, and even advertised the fact their steamers took special messengers with mail. The steps taken in 1849 to discourage this practice were unsuccessful, as was another determined attempt made by Postmaster General Hall in 1851. Although the law was squarely behind the Post Office Department and the mail lines, the task of opening and inspecting all express packages was great, and no effective check was ever placed on the practice.[15] When the regular mail service by Panama was good, letters were sent in the usual fashion, but when a competing line of steamers offered faster service or when the regular mails were badly cared for, the express companies enjoyed an increased business in carrying letters outside the mail. Thus, when the overland mail service, even for letters, proved slow and uncertain, resort was had to the Panama route for transporting the mail. The statement was even made, and not denied, that the Overland Mail Company sent its letters by way of Panama in closed boxes and, gaining the speed which only the steamers could give, collected the governmental subsidy for overland mail service. Thus $3 or $4 was paid to the steamship company for service which brought the overland contractors $100. In order to stop this, Cornelius Vanderbilt announced that all express matter would be held over at the Isthmus for ten days, at which a great outcry was raised. Matters were arranged so that the steamers carried the mail when the stages were unable to do so, but until the opening of the railroad the dependable means of sending letters from coast to coast was by the Panama route.[16]

Aside from carrying the mails, the Panama steamers constituted the chief source of news from the rest of the world to California and the north Pacific coast until the advent of the Pony Express and the overland telegraph. Political events in the eastern United States, happenings in Europe, news of intellectual and social importance, all were transported by the Panama route and appeared in the newspapers of California after the arrival of the steamer. When California was admitted to the Union, it was the mail steamer *Oregon* which brought the word to San Francisco. President Aspinwall of the Pacific Mail gave specific orders for the voyage.

We direct the steamer Oregon on her present trip not to touch at the Mexican ports to avoid the Cholera as well as to save time in reaching San Francisco.

About the latter object I am the more anxious as the Bill admitting California as a State has passed the Congress & received the signature of the President— A flag "California a State" went out in the Philadelphia on her last trip—to be displayed by the steamer taking the news to San Francisco & I have also instructed Capt[ai]n Patterson to give a salute on his arrival.[17]

When the *Oregon* reached San Francisco, these instructions were obeyed, as recounted in the *Courier* of October 19, 1850.

... at about half past ten A.M. [October 18, 1850], the booming of cannon was heard in the bay, and in a few minutes the beautiful steamship Oregon hove in sight, completely covered with flags of all nations, the starry flag of our country waving over all. She came up in fine style, in front of the city, firing her heavy guns in quick succession, which were answered by the ships in the harbor, and from cannon on shore, also by the vessels of war at Saucelito. ... the orders of Messrs. Howland and Aspinwall to announce to the people of California, by a national salute, the news of the admission was [*sic*] most gallantly performed ... the guns of the Oregon never fired a more joyous salute.[18]

On the day on which a steamer from the Isthmus was due at San Francisco, her arrival was eagerly awaited. The papers and dispatches on board brought new contact with the rest of the world, and the life and civilization of California seemed to receive renewed momentum with the coming of the mail steamship from Panama.

As a carrier of population to and from the Pacific coast, the Panama route performed a service of the greatest significance. In the period between 1848 and the end of June, 1869, the total arrivals at San Francisco by Panama amounted to at least 400,000 persons, while in the same years, some 295,000 traveled eastbound over the same route.[19] Prior to 1850, the numbers traveling in this way were relatively small owing to the difficulties of the isthmian crossing and the uncertainty of getting passage from Panama to San Francisco. Between 1851 and 1867 the number of passengers westbound fluctuated between 15,000 and 20,000 annually, and competition and low rates in 1868 brought the figure to nearly 40,000. After the completion of the transcontinental railroad in 1869 the number of passengers traveling by way of Panama dwindled rapidly. It would appear that, between 1849 and 1859, approximately one-fifth of the emigrants to California came over the Isthmus of Panama, and in the next decade the lower rates and better accommodations were so attractive that nearly half the emigrants came by this way.[20] The eastbound passage figures, though smaller than the westbound, averaged at least 14,000 a year for the whole period.

An important part of the population of California traveled west by the Isthmus, important not only in numbers but also in the character of the passengers. It is probably true that the comings and goings over Panama were more significant in the development of the region than the overland immigration. The fact that the steamers offered the quickest and easiest means of travel to and from California meant that persons of substance—officials and distinguished travelers—as well as many others went over this route. This was increasingly true after the pioneer years, when the ships and isthmian connections were improved to give satisfactory service. Of the members of the third session of the California state legislature, forty-six had come to the Pacific coast overland, thirty-five by way of Panama, and twenty-one around Cape Horn.[21] Judges and financiers, generals and naval officers, gamblers and women of bad character traveled by way of the Isthmus because it was the obvious way to go for the person who could afford it. Even the overland stages, although holding out possibilities of speed, particularly to those traveling to the Middle West, were uncomfortable and often dangerous. In spite of this competition, the figures of Panama transits rose year by year and reached their highest point just before the advent of the railroad. This indicates something of the continued popularity and acceptance of the side-wheeler steamers and the trains of the Panama Railroad as the best way of travel between the coasts.

Finally, as a carrier of freight, and particularly of specie freight, the Panama route was significant. Gold was California's most important commodity for export in the period under consideration, and almost all the gold of California was shipped out by the steamers until the completion of the railroad across the continent. Charges for carrying treasure were based on a proportion of its value, ranging from 2½ per cent in 1850 to ¼ of 1 per cent ten years later. This included the transportation of the specie across the Isthmus.[22] A total of at least $710,753,857.62 in specie was shipped from San Francisco by way of Panama in the period from 1849 to 1869, with the highest point in the year 1864, when $45,760,900 was sent.[23] The effect of the inflow of precious metal upon the development of the United States was great indeed, and its primary importance in supporting the credit of the Union during the Civil War has not often been questioned.

Mention has been made of the Confederate plans to capture the treasure ships in the course of the war, and also of the attacks on treasure trains crossing the Isthmus of Panama, but there were also occasional attempts made on board the ships to get possession of the gold carried. At the very beginning of the service of the Pacific Mail, President Aspinwall suggested to the San Francisco agent that it would be well not to take gold on board the steamers until just before sailing. He pointed out that it would be safer kept ashore or on board a man-of-war until it was necessary to take it on the mail ship.

In case of a theft or accident under circumstances so unusual some ugly questions might arise as to responsibility—besides parties committing the theft have also an incentive to set fire to the vessel hoping to conceal the crime. Our risks must unavoidably be great without taking any that we can possibly shun.[24]

There was a robbery on the *Oregon* on her trip from San Francisco to Panama in 1849, about $11,000 being removed from the strong box through a hole bored near the seal, later concealed by wax.[25] Later in the period there were occasional robberies aboard ship, though none of them was of a spectacular nature. The strong room of the *Sonora* was entered on one occasion, and two boxes of specie, valued at $18,000, were stolen on the *North Star* between Aspinwall and New York in 1861. But in general the treasure was carried safely over the Panama route until 1869.[26]

Merchandise freight carried by the Panama steamers was limited in its extent to comparatively light commodities which would sell for high prices, thereby justifying the heavy freight charges. The amount was small at first, increasing after 1865, though it never assumed the importance of the other factors mentioned in connection with the significance of the route. Heavy freight for California went out from New York and other Atlantic ports by sailing vessel around Cape Horn. The epic clipper voyages of the early 'fifties form a part of the story of western communication but alongside the great ships plied dozens of others, slower in speed and unknown to fame, which carried bulky merchandise to and from the Pacific coast until long after the completion of the railroad across the continent.

The primary importance of the Panama route in the period from 1848 to 1869 lay in the fact that it provided the best means of communication between the Atlantic seaboard and the Pacific coast of the United States. Passengers, mail, express, and specie traveled over it with greater safety and speed than by any other route. For half that time it was the principal means of communicating intelligence between these areas. As a unit of the naval program of the United States it was at least partially successful, though this phase must be considered as secondary to that of transportation and communication.

For twenty years the steamers with their red paddle wheels and black-plumed smokestacks, the dug-out canoes, and later the screaming locomotives of the Panama Railroad connected California and the Pacific coast with the eastern United States. The transcontinental railroad eclipsed the Panama route in all its functions in 1869, but it is noteworthy that, throughout its formative years, the Pacific seaboard's communication with the nation and with the world was chiefly by the Panama route.

APPENDIX

STEAMERS OPERATING ON THE PANAMA AND NICARAGUA ROUTES, 1848–1869

THE TONNAGES and hull dimensions (length, beam, depth) given in this list, except as otherwise noted, were drawn from the registers and enrollments in the papers of the Bureau of Navigation, Department of Commerce, in the National Archives, Washington, D.C. The tonnages given for ships built prior to 1865 are Old Custom House Measurement, which was derived by the formula:

$$\frac{(\text{length} - \tfrac{3}{5}\,\text{beam}) \times \text{beam} \times \text{depth of hold}}{95}$$

For vessels built during and after 1865 New Custom House Measurement was used, which was designed to give a more accurate measurement of the cubic contents of a ship, basing its "ton" on 100 cubic feet of enclosed space below decks. See Albion, *Square Riggers on Schedule* (Princeton, 1938), p. 298.

For ships built before 1865, but in service then, a program of readmeasurement was carried out, and both tonnages are given. It should be noted that for some the dimensions are given in feet and inches, and for others in feet and tenths of feet. Other dimensions, for instance, draft, are given when available, but are not based on official registry or enrollment. "Tuck" refers to the afterpart of the ship, immediately below the stern or counter, where the ends of the bottom planks are collected and terminated by the tuck-rail. The descriptions like "billethead" and "figurehead" describe an overhanging bow terminated by a bowsprit, whereas "no head," "scroll head," and so forth refer to a straight stem. The dimensions listed without nomination are, in order: length, beam, and depth of hold. Names of builders and building dates were taken chiefly from registers and enrollments. Data on engine details, appearance, and careers of steamers came mainly from contemporary New York, Panama, and San Francisco newspapers and unofficial sources.

Alaska

Wooden side-wheel steamer; 3 decks, 2 masts, round stern, plain head; 4,011 64/100 tons; 346 ft. × 47.6 ft. × 23.5 ft.; vertical-beam engine built by the Novelty Iron Works; diameter of cylinder 8 ft. 9 in., length of stroke 12 ft.

Built by Henry Steers at Greenpoint, Long Island, for the Pacific Mail Steamship Company in 1867 and 1868. Launched November 27, 1867. Entered the Pacific Mail service between New York and Aspinwall August 2, 1868. Continued in this service through June, 1869. Later engaged in the Pacific Mail's San Francisco—Panama and San Francisco—Hong Kong services. Rebuilt in 1882 and served as a coal hulk and store ship at Acapulco until after 1885.

America (1st)

Wooden side-wheel steamer; 2 decks, 3 masts, round stern, no head; 922 $^{53}/_{95}$ tons; 201 ft. × 31 ft. × 18 ft. 8 in.; diameter of cylinder 4 ft. 2 in., length of stroke 10 ft.

Built and owned by William H. Brown, New York. Launched in April, 1853. Sailed from New York for Aspinwall with passengers on October 20, 1853. Continued to San Francisco, where she entered the coastwise service northward to Humboldt Bay, Crescent City, Port Orford, and the Umpqua River. Burned at Crescent City, June, 1855.

America (2d)

Wooden side-wheel steamer; 2 decks, 3 masts, round stern, no head; 2,030 $^{14}/_{95}$ tons; 285 ft. 6 in. × 38 ft. 4 in. × 14 ft. (dimensions as of 1859); readmeasured in 1865, 1,683 $^{24}/_{100}$ tons; vertical-beam engine built by West Point Foundry; diameter of cylinder 5 ft. 10 in., length of stroke 12 ft.

Built at Niagara-on-the-Lake, Ontario, 1854–1855 for Great Western R. R. Co. for service on Lake Ontario as the *America*. Rebuilt at New York in 1858 by Samuel Sneeden, Greenpoint, and changed to United States registry in 1859 under ownership of Peter A. Hargous. Name changed to *Coatzacoalcos* in 1859. Laid up at New York in 1859, valued at $250,000. Sold to Marshall O. Roberts in 1860. Chartered to the Quartermaster's Department, War Department, in 1861 and 1862 at from $1,200 to $1,400 per day. Name changed to *America* in 1862. Operated from New York to San Juan de Nicaragua for Roberts in 1862 and 1863. Sent to the Pacific and sailed between San Francisco and Panama for the People's Line from January 22, 1864, until October 23 of the same year, when she began operating between San Francisco and San Juan del Sur for the Central American Transit Company. Her last sailing from San Francisco on this service was on February 15, 1868. The *America* burned at San Juan del Sur on April 11, 1869.

Antelope

Wooden side-wheel steamer; 2 decks, 2 masts, round stern, round tuck, no head; 424 $^{75}/_{95}$ tons (1847); 650 $^{21}/_{95}$ tons; 178 ft. 8 in. × 27 ft. 8 in. × 17 ft. 4 in. (1850); 581 $^{5}/_{100}$ tons (1865).

Built by Bishop and Simonson, New York; engine built by T. F. Secor. Launched June 17, 1847. Sailed from New York for San Juan del Sur on May 18, 1850. Operated between Panama and San Francisco for George Law between October, 1850, and March, 1851. Sold to the Pacific Mail Steamship Company for $92,000 in the spring of 1851. Sold by the Pacific Mail and entered service on the Sacramento River. Broken up at San Francisco in 1888.

Arago

Wooden side-wheel steamer; 4 decks, 3 masts, round stern, no head; 2,240 tons; 290 ft. × 40 ft. × 31 ft. 6 in. (1855); 2,370 $\%_{100}$ tons (1865); two oscillating engines built by the Novelty Iron Works (Stillman, Allen and Company), one engine forward and one abaft the shaft; diameter of cylinders 5 ft. 5 in., length of stroke 10 ft.

Built by Westervelt and Sons under the superintendence of William Skiddy. Launched January 27, 1855. Operated between New York and Le Havre by the New York and Havre Steam Navigation Company from 1855 until 1861. Chartered by the Quartermaster's Department, War Department, in 1862, 1863, and 1865 at $1,000 to $1,200 per day. Made one voyage from New York to Aspinwall for the North American Steamship Company in 1868. Operated briefly in transatlantic service in the same year by Ruger Brothers. Sold to the Peruvian government in 1869.

Ariel

Wooden side-wheel steamer; 2 decks, 3 masts, round stern, no head; 1,295 $^{28}\!\%_5$ tons; 252 ft. 6 in. × 32 ft. 6 in. × 16 ft. 3 in. (1855); 1,736 $^{39}\!\%_{100}$ tons; 252 ft. × 32.6 ft. × 20.8 ft. (1865); single-beam engine built by the Allaire Works; diameter of cylinder 6 ft. 3 in., length of stroke 12 ft.; diameter of paddle wheels 33 ft.; face of paddles 8 ft.; 2 return-flue boilers.

Designed with a straight stem and no bowsprit or billethead, the upper part of the cutwater being ornamented merely with a little gilt scrollwork. Her lines were round, and ended in a round stern, decorated with a gilt eagle supporting the shield of the United States. At the time of her completion, the *Ariel's* hull was painted black, with a narrow red streak around her, and the upper works were cream color. Her paddle boxes were open and ornamented with an eagle on the wing. The upper deck was surrounded by a low net rail, and had a long house containing the smoking room, and aft of it the rooms of the officers, a few staterooms, and the companionway to the main saloon below. On the deck below, the dining saloon was forward, with the main saloon amidships and the ladies' cabin aft, with staterooms opening into them from either side. The steamer had berths for 284 cabin passengers.

Built by Jeremiah Simonson, New York. On the stocks as early as June, 1854, but not launched until March 3, 1855. Built to run with the *North Star* on Vanderbilt's Independent Line from New York to Aspinwall, connecting with the *Uncle Sam* and *Yankee Blade* on the Pacific. Began her service with one voyage from New York to Aspinwall for the United States Mail Steamship Company in July and August, 1855, and then entered the New York–Southampton–Le Havre service of Vanderbilt. Continued to operate in the transatlantic trade until 1859 and, in November of that year, entered Vanderbilt's service from New York to Aspinwall. She continued intermittently in this service until the summer of 1865. Chartered by the Quartermaster's Department, War Department, in 1861, 1862, 1864, and 1865 for $1,100 to $555 per day. On December 7, 1862, the *Ariel*, southbound from New York to Aspinwall, was captured off Cape Maysi, Cuba, by the C.S.S. *Alabama*. Since Captain

Semmes of the *Alabama* was unable to care for the passengers and crew of the *Ariel* aboard his ship, he allowed her to continue her voyage. After the Civil War, she was placed in transatlantic service for a short time by Ruger Brothers. In 1873 she was operating between Yokohama and Hakodate for the Pacific Mail Steamship Company and on October 27 of that year she struck a sunken reef about 110 miles from Yokohama and sank in twenty minutes.

Arizona

Wooden side-wheel steamer; 3 decks, 2 masts, round stern, billethead; 2,793 44/100 tons; 323.8 ft. × 44.8 ft. × 41 ft.; vertical-beam engine built by the Novelty Iron Works; diameter of cylinder 8 ft. 9 in., length of stroke 12 ft.; diameter of paddle wheels 46 ft.; face of buckets 12 feet.

Built by Henry Steers at Greenpoint, Long Island, for the Pacific Mail Steamship Company and launched January 19, 1865. Entered the service of the Pacific Mail between New York and Aspinwall on March 1, 1866. Continued in this through June, 1869. Broken up at San Francisco in 1877.

Atlantic

Wooden side-wheel steamer; 3 decks, 3 masts, round stern, full-length figure-head; 2,849 66/95 tons; 284 ft. × 45 ft. 11 in. × 22 ft. 11½ in. (1850); 2,667 98/100 tons (1865); average draft 19 ft.; 2 side-lever engines designed and built by the Novelty Iron Works; boilers by John Faron; diameter of cylinders 7 ft. 11 in., length of stroke 9 ft.; diameter of paddle wheels 35 ft.; speed 12 knots; cost $764,000.

Built by William H. Brown, New York, in 1848–1849 for the New York and Liverpool United States Mail Steamship Company (Collins Line). Operated between New York and Liverpool by the Collins Line from 1849 to 1858. Laid up at New York during 1858 and 1859. Purchased by the North Atlantic Steamship Company and sailed between New York and Aspinwall from October 20, 1859, to March 11, 1860. She made one voyage between New York and Aspinwall for the Panama Railroad in 1863, and one for the Pacific Mail Steamship Company in 1865. Chartered by the Quartermaster's Department, War Department, in 1861, 1862, 1863, 1864, and 1865 at $1,000 to $2,000 per day. Between 1866 and 1870 she operated for the North American Lloyd Company between New York, Southamptom, and Bremen. The *Atlantic* was broken up for her metal at Cold Spring Harbor, New York, in September, 1871.

Baltic

Wooden side-wheel steamer; 3 decks, 3 masts, round stern; 2,723 8/95 tons; 282 ft. 6 in. × 45 ft. × 22 ft. 6 in. (1850); 2,644 44/100 tons (1865); 2 side-lever engines built by the Allaire Iron Works; boilers by John Faron; diameter of cylinders 7 ft. 11 in., length of stroke 10 ft.; diameter of paddle wheels 36 ft.; speed 12 knots; cost $790,000.

Built by Brown and Bell, New York, in 1850 for the New York and Liverpool United States Mail Steamship Company (Collins Line). Entered the New York–Liverpool service of the Collins Line in 1850 and continued in it until 1858. She was then laid up until October 5, 1859, when she sailed from New

York for Aspinwall for the North American Steamship Company, which had purchased her. In 1860 she made the voyage from Aspinwall to New York in the record time of six days, twenty-one hours. The *Baltic* completed her last voyage in this service on March 27, 1860. She was chartered by the Quartermaster's Department, War Department, in 1861, 1862, 1863, 1864, and 1865 at $1,000 to $2,000 per day. The *Baltic* made one voyage from New York to Aspinwall for the Pacific Mail Steamship Company in 1865. Between 1866 and 1870, she was operated by the North American Lloyd between New York, Southampton, and Bremen. She was sold to Boston owners about 1870, her machinery was removed, and as a sailing ship she made several fast passages from San Francisco to Europe with cargoes of wheat. Sold to a German firm, the Baltic was badly strained in a gale between Bremen and Boston and was broken up at Boston about 1880.

Brother Jonathan

Wooden side-wheel steamer; 2 decks, 2 masts, round stern, billethead; 1,359 5%5 tons; 220 ft. 11 in. × 36 ft. × 13 ft. 10 in. (1851); 1,180 90⁄100 tons (1865); hull of white oak, live oak, locust, and cedar; floors of white oak 14 in. thick; designed with sharp ends, hollow lines, taffrail formed like an eagle with 9-ft. spread of wings; engines built by the Morgan Iron Works; diameter of cylinders 6 ft., length of stroke 11 ft.; diameter of paddle wheels 33 ft.; berths for 365 passengers as built; main saloon 70 ft. long with 12 staterooms on each side, each with two doors, one opening into saloon, and one on deck; cost $190,000.

Built by Perine, Patterson and Stack at Williamsburg, New York, for Edward Mills, who superintended construction. Launched November 2, 1850. Sailed between New York and Chagres for Mills in 1851 and 1852. Sold by Mills to Cornelius Vanderbilt in March, 1852. Underwent extensive repairs, in which her guards were raised and built up solid and her passenger capacity increased to 750. Cleared New York for San Francisco on May 14, 1852. Operated for Cornelius Vanderbilt between San Francisco and San Juan del Sur from 1852 until 1856. After 1856, the *Brother Jonathan* operated in the local coastwise service, owned by John T. Wright and the California Steam Navigation Company. She was extensively rebuilt at San Francisco in 1861. On July 30, 1865, she struck a sunken rock off St. George's Point, eight or ten miles north of Crescent City, and went down in forty-five minutes.

Cahawba

Wooden side-wheel steamer; 3 decks, 3 masts, round stern, alligator head; 1,643 15%5 tons; 250 ft. 3 in. × 37 ft. × 26 ft. 4 in.; one vertical-beam engine built by the Allaire Iron Works; diameter of cylinder 6 ft. 3 in., length of stroke 11 ft.; diameter of paddle wheels 31 ft.

Built in 1854 by William Collyer, New York, for S. T. Rogers. Operated between New York, Mobile, and New Orleans by Livingston, Crocheron and Company. Made one voyage from New York to San Juan de Nicaragua for C. A. Whitney in the summer of 1856. Chartered by the Quartermaster's Department, War Department, in 1861, 1862, and 1863 at $500 to $800 per day. Purchased by the Quartermaster's Department, War Department, May 1, 1864, for $135,000. Sold at public auction June 2, 1865, to Arthur Leary for $16,550.

California

Wooden side-wheel steamer; 2 decks, 3 masts, round stern, sharp tuck, billet-head; 1,057 64⁄95 tons; 199 ft. 2 in. × 33 ft. 6 in. × 20 ft.; side-lever engine; diameter of cylinder 1 ft. 5 in., length of stroke 8 ft.; cost $200,082.

Built by William H. Webb, New York, for the Pacific Mail Steamship Company. Keel laid January 4, 1848. Launched May 19, 1848. Cleared New York for Valparaiso, Panama, and San Francisco October 6, 1848. Arrived San Francisco February 28, 1849. Operated regularly between San Francisco and Panama from 1849 to 1854. In use as a spare steamer at San Francisco in 1856. Sent to Panama as a reserve steamer in 1857. Made voyages from San Francisco to Panama for the Pacific Mail in 1860, 1861, and 1866. The *California* was sold to Holladay and Brenham's California, Oregon and Mexico Steamship Company, but returned to the ownership of the Pacific Mail in 1872. In 1874, she was sold to Goodall, Nelson and Perkins, who operated her in the local coastwise service from San Francisco until the end of 1875, when her engines were removed and her hull sold to N. Bichard. Rigged as a bark, she was engaged in the coal-and-lumber trade until she was wrecked near Pacasmayo, Peru, in late December, 1894, or early January, 1895, with a cargo of lumber from Port Hadlock, Washington.

Carolina

Wooden twin-screw steamer; 2 decks, 3 masts, round stern, carved head; 544 68⁄95 tons; 149.7 ft. × 27.9 ft. × 14 ft.; 2 direct-acting engines; diameter of cylinders 3 ft. 8 in., length of stroke 3 ft.

Built by Charles and William Cramp, Philadelphia, in 1849 for S. H. Reynolds. Completed in December, 1849, and went into dry dock immediately to be coppered and have her upper cabin extended, since she had been purchased by the Pacific Mail Steamship Company and was being fitted for the San Francisco–Panama service. Sailed from New York for San Francisco on January 9, 1850. Arrived San Francisco May 7, 1850. Operated on the San Francisco–Panama line until the end of 1851. Sold for service in China in 1854.

Central America, see *George Law*

Champion

Iron side-wheel steamer; 3 decks, 2 masts, round stern, no figurehead; 1,419 15⁄95 tons; 235 ft. × 35 ft. × 18 ft. (1859); 1,452 66⁄100 tons (1865); draft 12 ft.; double-beam engine built by Harlan and Hollingsworth; diameter of cylinders 3 ft. 6 in., length of stroke 10 ft.; 2 boilers 24 ft. 4 in. × 9 ft., 28 lbs. pressure. First iron ship of any size to be built in the United States. Hull plates of wrought iron ½ to ⅞ in. thick. Four water-tight compartments. Upper deck had two tiers of staterooms entered only from deck outside. Ninety-six staterooms in main cabin containing sleeping accommodations for 388 cabin passengers; room for 350 steerage passengers; total passenger capacity, 900. Schooner-rigged. Cost $154,000.

Built by Harlan and Hollingsworth, Wilmington, Delaware, in 1859 for Cornelius Vanderbilt. Sailed from New York for San Francisco on October 23, 1859. Arrived San Francisco via Rio de Janeiro and Lota on January 1, 1860. Made two voyages from San Francisco to Panama for Vanderbilt's Atlantic and Pacific Steamship Company. Cleared San Francisco for New York April 3, 1860. The *Champion* operated from New York to Aspinwall for the Atlantic and Pacific Steamship Company from 1860 until the end of 1864. Chartered by the Quartermaster's Department, War Department, in 1864 and 1865 for $464 and $638 per day. Collided with British bark *Lady Octavia* on November 8, 1879, when thirty-five miles from the Delaware Capes. Sank in five minutes.

Cherokee

Wooden side-wheel steamer; 3 decks, 3 masts, sharp tuck, round stern, billet-head; 1,244 $89\frac{1}{95}$ tons; 210 ft. 8 in. × 35 ft. 4 in. × 17 ft. 8 in.; average draft 9 ft. 8½ in.; side-lever engine of about 500 h.p. built by the Novelty Iron Works; diameter of cylinder 6 ft. 3 in., length of stroke 8 ft. Averaged fifteen miles per hour on her trial trip with an ordinary gauge of steam.

Built by William H. Webb, New York, for the New York and Savannah Steam Navigation Company. Keel laid February 14, 1848. Launched June 12, 1848. Sailed on her first voyage to Savannah on October 3, 1848. Purchased by Howland and Aspinwall for their New York–Chagres line, and operated on it beginning December 13, 1849. The *Cherokee* burned at her dock at the foot of Warren Street, New York, on the evening of August 27, 1853. The steamer was scuttled to save her from complete destruction and was floated again on August 31, 1853. She was found not to be burned below the lower deck, and her engine was not damaged. A large part of her cargo was salvaged. She did not reënter the Chagres service. Owned by United States Mail Steamship Company in 1855.

China

Wooden side-wheel steamer; 3 decks, 3 masts, round stern, plain head; 3,836 $12\frac{2}{100}$ tons; 360 ft. × 47.4 ft. × 22.9 ft.; draft 20 ft. 4½ in.; vertical-beam engine built by the Novelty Iron Works; diameter of cylinder 8 ft. 9 in., length of stroke 12 ft.; 1,500 h.p.; built to carry 500 first- and second-cabin passengers, and 800 in the steerage.

Built by William H. Webb, New York, for the Pacific Mail Steamship Company's transpacific line. Originally to have been named *Celestial Empire*. Keel laid January 13, 1866. Launched December 8, 1866. Cleared New York for Panama and San Francisco July 1, 1867, and arrived at San Francisco, having brought passengers from Panama, on September 20, 1867. Entered the transpacific service. Purchased from the Pacific Mail by Henry Villard in 1883. Became a receiving ship for smallpox patients in 1884 and was broken up in 1886.

City of New York

Wooden screw steamer; 2 decks, 3 masts, round stern, spread-eagle head; 574 $7\frac{2}{95}$ tons; 166 ft. × 27 ft. × 18 ft.; two-cylinder engine built by Hogg and Delamater; diameter of cylinders 1 ft. 6 in., length of stroke 1 ft. 6 in.

Built by Capes and Allison, Hoboken, New Jersey, in 1851–1852. Made a single voyage from New York to Chagres in February–April, 1852. Miller and Lord (her chief owners) were agents southbound, and Palmer, Haight and Company were agents northbound. Chartered by the Quartermaster's Department, War Department, in 1861 at $10,000 per month, later in the same year at $4,500 per job, and in 1862 at $300 per day. Wrecked off Hatteras Inlet, June, 1862.

Colorado

Wooden side-wheel steamer; 3 decks, 3 masts, round stern, no head; 3,357 $22\!/\!95$ tons; 314 ft.×45 ft.×31 ft. 9 in. [*sic*] (1865); 3,728 $3\!/\!100$ tons; 340 ft.×45.6 ft.×22.6 ft. (1865); 3,727 $80\!/\!100$ tons (1867); draft 17 ft. 6 in.; vertical-beam engine by the Novelty Iron Works; diameter of cylinder 8 ft. 9 in., length of stroke 12 ft.; cost about $1,000,000; 52 staterooms on the main deck; berths for 1,500 in the steerage. In 1865, the *Colorado* was armed with two 20-pound field pieces on her quarters, two 30-pounders forward, besides Sharp's rifles, revolvers, muskets, pikes, and axes. She was originally brig-rigged, but when she was altered in San Francisco in 1866 to enter the China service, a mizzen-mast was added, and she was ship-rigged. At the same time, the outer tier of staterooms was taken from the main deck, and her guards reduced from 10–12 ft. to 2–3 ft.

Built by William H. Webb, New York, for the Pacific Mail Steamship Company. Keel laid June 6, 1863. Launched May 21, 1864. Sailed from New York for San Francisco via Rio de Janeiro, Callao, and Panama on April 1, 1865. The *Colorado* was in the San Francisco–Panama service after the summer of 1865 through June, 1869, with the exception of occasional trips on the China line, which she inaugurated on January 1, 1867. Sold by the Pacific Mail in 1878 and broken up in 1879.

Columbia

Wooden side-wheel steamer; 3 decks, 3 masts, round stern, eagle head; 777 $24\!/\!95$ tons; 193 ft.×29 ft.×19 ft. 5 in.; side-lever engine built by the Novelty Iron Works; diameter of cylinder 4 ft. 9 in., length of stroke 5 ft.; diameter of paddle wheels 22 ft.; face of buckets 8 ft.; schooner-rigged; cost $169,043. Built with a solid bottom, double floors, and iron braced diagonally. Light deck above main deck for promenading. Dining saloon 70 ft. long with a range of staterooms along each side. Forward of this were the engine room, pantry, galley, officers' mess, and sleeping quarters for officers and engineers. The lower cabins aft and forward could accommodate 150 passengers in berths.

Built by Westervelt and Mackay, New York, for the Pacific Mail Steamship Company in 1850. Sailed from New York for San Francisco on October 15, 1850. The *Columbia* was intended for the mail service between San Francisco and Astoria, but the stress of business on the Pacific coast led to her occasional employment between San Francisco and Panama during the period from 1851 to 1854. Her sale to Chinese owners was announced March 11, 1862, and she sailed from San Francisco for Shanghai under British colors on April 17, 1862.

Columbus

Wooden screw steamer; 2 decks, 3 masts, scroll figurehead; 460 25⁄95 tons; 148.8 ft. × 25.6 ft. × 12.8 ft.; side-lever engine built by Rainey, Neafie and Company, Philadelphia; diameter of cylinder 4 ft. 1 in., length of stroke 5 ft.; 87 h.p.

Built by Reeves and Brothers at Allowaystown, New Jersey, in 1848. Entered service between Philadelphia and Charleston, S.C., in February, 1848. Sent to the Pacific by George Law, Marshall Roberts, and others for service between San Francisco and Panama. Sailed from New York February 12, 1850. Arrived at Rio de Janeiro March 11, 1850. Arrived at San Francisco June 6, 1850. Sold to the Pacific Mail Steamship Company early in 1851 for $120,000. Operated by her new owners in the San Francisco–Panama service until 1854. In the latter year, she was chartered for a short time by the United States Navy. Sold to the Panama Railroad Company and operated in its local service on the west coast of Central America. Lost at Punta Remedios, Central America, December 9, 1861.

Commodore Stockton

Wooden side-wheel steamer; 2 decks, 3 masts, carved eagle on stern, scroll head; 435 70⁄95 tons; 153.7 ft. × 24.4 ft. × 12.2 ft.

Built by Davis and Burton, Philadelphia, in 1850 for R. F. Loper. Came from Philadelphia to San Francisco in 171 days. Advertised to sail from San Francisco for Panama on June 12, 1851, for J. Howard and Son's Empire City Line to connect with Vanderbilt's steamers on the Atlantic. Sailed from Panama for San Francisco June 30, 1851, with over 100 passengers, but returned two days later, having sprung a leak. When passage money was not returned, the passengers mutinied. She was then running for Edward Mills. In 1852, when operating for the Independent Line, she put into Acapulco in distress and was condemned. Her purchase by Valparaiso owners was announced in February, 1853. She was placed under the Chilean flag and her name changed to *Caupolican.*

Constitution (1st)

Wooden screw steamer; 2 decks, 3 masts; 530 35⁄95 tons; 167 ft. × 26 ft. × 12.8 ft.; draft 11 ft.; two direct-acting engines designed and built by I. P. Morris and Company, Philadelphia; cylinders above cranks; diameter of cylinders 2 ft. 10 in., length of stroke 2 ft. 10 in.; diameter of propeller 10 ft. 4 in.; 70 h.p.

Built in Philadelphia in 1849–1850 for Richard F. Loper and others. Sailed from New York for San Francisco in June, 1850. Made two voyages between San Francisco and Panama for the Empire City Line in 1851, and in 1852 made one voyage on the same route for the Pacific Mail Steamship Company. The *Constitution* made a voyage to the Hawaiian Islands before sailing from San Francisco for Puget Sound on July 8, 1857, to enter mail service between Olympia and Bellingham Bay. She returned to San Francisco, however, on July 13, having begun to leak badly. At that time, she was owned by Hunt and Scranton. Engines removed and rebuilt as a bark, 1860.

Constitution (2nd)

Wooden side-wheel steamer; 3 decks, 2 masts, round stern, no head; 3,315 $\frac{36}{95}$ tons; 342 ft. 6 in. × 44 ft. 8 in. × 22 ft. 4 in. (1861); 3,575 $\frac{36}{100}$ tons (1865); vertical-beam engine built by the Novelty Iron Works; diameter of cylinder 8 ft. 9 in., length of stroke 12 ft.; diameter of paddle wheels 40 ft.; face of paddles 18 ft.

Built by William H. Webb, New York, for the Pacific Mail Steamship Company. Keel laid December 8, 1860. Launched May 25, 1861. Chartered by the Quartermaster's Department, War Department, in 1861 and 1862 at $2,500 per day. Sailed from New York for San Francisco on June 19, 1862. Served between San Francisco and Panama from 1862 through June, 1869. Broken up at San Francisco in 1879.

Cortes

Wooden side-wheel steamer; 3 decks, 2 masts, round stern, billethead; 1,117 $\frac{38}{95}$ tons; 220 ft. 6 in. × 22 ft. 6 in. × 16 ft. 10 in.; double walking-beam engines built by the Morgan Iron Works; diameter of cylinders 3 ft. 6 in., length of stroke 10 ft.; built to carry 100 cabin and 600 steerage passengers; cost $198,000.

Built by Westervelt and Mackay, New York, for Davis, Brooks and Company. Launched March 28, 1852. Originally christened *Saratoga* and intended to run with the *Roanoke* from New York to Richmond. Sailed from New York for San Francisco July 10, 1852. Operated between San Francisco and Panama by the New York and San Francisco Steamship Line from the end of 1852 until the summer of 1853, when she was purchased by Cornelius Vanderbilt, and operated in his service from San Francisco to San Juan del Sur until March, 1855. In 1858 and 1859, she was sailing between San Francisco and Panama for the New York and California Steamship Company, and in 1860 on the same route for the Atlantic and Pacific Steamship Company. In 1860, the *Cortes* was purchased by the Pacific Mail Steamship Company and entered its Panama service in the last month of that year. In February, 1861, she was sold to Flint and Holladay, having just previously been in the Pacific Mail's Oregon service, and she was chartered by her new owners for service in China, sailing from San Francisco for Shanghai on April 14, 1862. The *Cortes* burned at Shanghai in 1865.

Costa Rica

Wooden side-wheel steamer; 2 decks, 2 masts, round stern, no head; 1,950 $\frac{11}{95}$ tons; 269 ft. × 38 ft. 10 in. × 27 ft. (1864); 1,917 $\frac{43}{100}$ tons (1865); vertical-beam engine built by the Allaire Iron Works; diameter of cylinder 6 ft. 9 in., length of stroke 12 ft.

Built by Jeremiah Simonson at Greenpoint, Long Island, in 1863, for Cornelius Vanderbilt. Originally called *Commodore*. Operated as the *Costa Rica* for Vanderbilt between New York and Aspinwall from July, 1864, until the summer of 1865, when she was purchased by the Pacific Mail Steamship Company, continuing on the same route until the spring of 1866. The *Costa Rica* sailed from New York for Hong Kong, Shanghai, and Yokohama via the Cape of Good Hope on April 1, 1867. She served on the Yokohama-Shanghai branch line of the Pacific Mail from 1867 until she was sold to the Mitsubishi Mail Steamship Company in 1875 and was renamed *Genaki Maru*. She was surveyed at Shanghai as late as 1879.

Crescent City

Wooden side-wheel steamer; 2 decks, 3 masts, round stern, no galleries, billet-head; 1,291 tons; 233 ft. 7 in. × 33 ft. 11 in. × 22 ft. 8 in.; engine and boilers designed and built by T. F. Secor and Company; side-lever engine; diameter of cylinder 6 ft. 8 in., length of stroke 9 ft.; diameter of paddle wheels 33 ft. 6 in.; 600 h.p.; 5 lifeboats.

Built by William H. Brown, New York, in 1847–1848 for Isaac Newton, Charles Stoddart, J. P. Whitney and Company, and J. Howard and Son for service between New York and New Orleans. Entered the New York–Chagres service December 23, 1848, for J. Howard and Son. Purchased by Charles Morgan and associates in January, 1849, but continued to be operated by the Howards. Passed under the control of the Pacific Mail Steamship Company in October, 1850, and early in 1851 was sold to the United States Mail Steamship Company for $187,500. She ran regularly from New York to Chagres until the summer of 1852 and made a single voyage in 1853. The *Crescent City* was lost on a reef in the Gulf of Mexico in 1856.

Dakota

Wooden side-wheel steamer; 3 decks, 2 masts, round stern, scroll head; 2,135 4⁄100 tons; 270 ft. × 40 ft. × 20.2 ft.; vert.-beam engine; nominal h.p., 850.

Built by Henry Steers, Greenpoint, New York, in 1865–1866 for William H. Webb. Originally named *Nicaragua*. Launched June 28, 1865. Made one voyage from New York to Aspinwall for the North American Steamship Company in August, 1868. Brought to the Pacific, and served briefly on William H. Webb's San Francisco–Australia line in 1873. Purchased by the Pacific Mail Steamship Company in 1873. Broken up in 1886.

Daniel Webster

Wooden side-wheel steamer; 2 decks, 3 masts, round tuck, scroll head; 1,035 49⁄95 tons; 223 ft. 4 in. × 31 ft. × 18 ft. 6 in.; engine built by the Allaire Iron Works; diameter of cylinder 4 ft. 8 in., length of stroke 10 ft.; 2 boilers 24 ft. × 9 ft., 34 lbs. pressure; built with 31 staterooms and accommodations for 116 passengers.

Built by William H. Brown, New York, for Cornelius Vanderbilt. Launched September 20, 1851. Sailed on her first voyage from New York to San Juan de Nicaragua for Vanderbilt on November 22, 1851. Continued to operate from New York and New Orleans to San Juan and later to Aspinwall for Vanderbilt and Charles Morgan until 1859. Chartered to the Quartermaster's Department, War Department, in 1861, 1862–1863, and 1863–1865 at $25,000 per job, and $400 to $900 per day. Went down October 3, 1866, en route to Mobile. Passengers taken off by the steamer *George Cromwell*.

Ecuador

Iron, paddle steamer; 323 tons gross, 271 tons net; 120.7 ft. × 21.5 ft. × 15 ft.; 150 h.p.

Built by Tod and McGregor, Glasgow, for the Pacific Steam Navigation Company in 1845 for the Callao–Guayaquil–Panama service. Made one voyage from Panama to San Francisco in July and August, 1850, with 96 passengers. Sold by the Pacific Steam Navigation Company in 1850.

El Dorado

Wooden side-wheel steamer; 3 decks, 3 masts, round stern, billethead; 1,049 $^{88}\!/_{95}$ tons; 228 ft. 4 in. × 30 ft. 10 in. × 23 ft.; average draft 12 ft.; 2 beam engines designed and built by Cunningham, Belknap and Company, New York; diameter of cylinders 4 ft. 2 in., length of stroke 10 ft.; diameter of paddle wheels 29 ft. 4 in.

Built by Thomas Collyer, New York. Launched December 2, 1850. Owned by Captain J. J. Wright. Purchased by Howland and Aspinwall, and sold again before completion to the United States Mail Steamship Company. Originally named *Caribbean*. Began operation in 1851 on the New Orleans–Chagres run, after one voyage from New York to Chagres with laborers for the Panama Railroad in March, 1851. Operated between New York and Chagres for the United States Mail Steamship Company from December, 1851, until 1853. The *El Dorado* was broken up in 1857, and her engines placed in the *Moses Taylor*.

Empire City

Wooden side-wheel steamer; 3 decks, 3 masts, round stern, dragon head; 1,751 $^{21}\!/_{95}$ tons; 238 ft. 8 in. × 39 ft. 4 in. × 24 ft. 4 in.; 1 side-lever engine built by T. F. Secor and Company; diameter of cylinder 6 ft. 3 in., length of stroke 9 ft.; estimated cost $220,000, of which $62,000 was for the engine.

Modeled for speed and very strong. Planking boarded edgewise. The hurricane deck extended the entire length and breadth of the steamer—a novelty in an ocean vessel—being supported by stanchions from the bulwarks and forming a canopy for the promenade deck below. She was said to be the first ocean vessel to have a deck house extending from stem to stern. From the stern forward, it contained a ladies' cabin or reception room, the galley, a social hall 35 ft. long in which men might smoke, and the forecastle. On the main deck, the waiters' quarters were forward, then the dining saloon off which opened staterooms with two berths each, then the pantry, and then the after saloon. The rooms opening off the latter apartment contained four berths each, and had large windows with glass an inch thick.

Built by William H. Brown, New York. Keel laid August 13, 1848. Launched March 10, 1849. Laid down for Isaac Newton, but sold on the stocks, in January, 1849, to Charles Morgan and associates. Sailed from New York for Chagres on her first voyage on July 17, 1849, for the Empire City Line, of which Charles Morgan was chief owner and J. Howard and Son were agents. She came under the control of the Pacific Mail Steamship Company in October, 1850, and early in 1851 was sold to the United States Mail Steamship Company for $225,000. She continued to run from New York to Chagres for her new owners until 1856, and in 1860 she was still operating for them from New York to New Orleans by way of Havana. She was chartered by the Quartermaster's Department, War Department, in 1861 at $25,000 for the job, and in 1861, 1862–1863, 1863, and 1864 at $775 to $1,000 per day. Purchased by the War Department on January 27, 1865, for $225,000 from Marshall O. Roberts, who had bought her at auction from the United States Mail Steamship Company for $12,000. In 1868, she was in use on quarantine duty in New York Harbor.

Ericsson

Wooden side-wheel steamer; 3 decks, 2 masts, round stern, no head; $1,902 \, 20/95$ tons; 253 ft. 6 in. × 39 ft. 8 in × 26 ft. 6 in. (1853); $1,545 \, 25/100$ tons (1865).

Intended to test John Ericsson's plan for driving a ship by hot air instead of steam. Original caloric engine had 4 cylinders, diameter 11 ft. 4 in., length of stroke 6 ft. With the failure of this engine, she was fitted with 2 inclined engines. Diameter of cylinders 5 ft. 2 in., length of stroke 7 ft. 8 in.

Built in 1852 by Perine, Patterson and Stack, Williamsburg, New York. She made one voyage across the Atlantic for the Collins Line, and to Bremen. In 1859 she belonged to Hargous and Company and was laid up at New York. Chartered to the Quartermaster's Department, War Department, in 1861, 1862, 1863, 1864, and 1865 at $700 to $1,200 per day. In 1865, she made three voyages from New York to San Juan de Nicaragua for the Central American Transit Company. Her engines were removed, and she was fitted as a sailing vessel in 1867. She was registered as late as 1873.

Falcon

Wooden side-wheel steamer; 1 deck, 3 masts, round stern, sharp tuck, billet-head; $891 \, 17/95$ tons; 244 ft. 2 in. × 30 ft. 2 in. × 21 ft. 5 in.; 2 inclined engines built by Hogg and Delamater, New York, for the *Iron Witch* and transferred to the *Falcon;* diameter of cylinders 5 ft., length of stroke 5 ft.; diameter of paddle wheels 32 ft.; 262 h.p.

Built by William H. Brown, New York, in 1848 for a group of New York and Boston businessmen. Sailed on her first voyage from New York to New Orleans via Savannah and Havana September 10, 1848. Purchased by the United States Mail Steamship Company and sailed from New York for Chagres on December 1, 1848. Remained in service from New York and New Orleans to Chagres until 1852. Converted into a towboat in 1857. By 1859, her engines had been removed, and she was serving as a quarantine hulk at Hoffman's Island.

Fremont

Wooden side-wheel steamer; 2 decks, 3 masts, round stern, carved head; $559 \, 39/95$ tons; 162 ft. × 27 ft. × 13 ft. 5 in.; 2 oscillating engines; diameter of cylinders 3 ft. 4 in., length of stroke 2 ft. 4 in.; cost $98,424.

Built in Philadelphia in 1850 by T. Birely. Purchased by the Pacific Mail Steamship Company when new and sent from New York to San Francisco in 1851, reaching the latter port on July 29. After the spring of 1852, the *Fremont* entered the coastwise service of the Pacific Mail between San Francisco and the Columbia, having previously been engaged in the Panama service. In February, 1861, the *Fremont* was sold to Flint and Holladay for their coastwise service.

Fulton

Wooden side-wheel steamer; 4 decks, 2 masts, round stern, plain head; 2,307 $^{93}\!/_{95}$ tons; 287 ft. 6 in. × 40 ft. 10 in. × 32 ft. (1863); 2,061 $^{25}\!/_{100}$ tons (1865); 2 oscillating engines built by the Morgan Iron Works; diameter of cylinders 5 ft. 5 in., length of stroke 10 ft.; 2 iron boilers.

Built by Smith and Dimon, New York. Laid down in 1852 or 1853 and completed in 1855. Operated in the transatlantic service by the New York and Havre Steam Navigation Company from 1856 until 1861. Chartered by the Quartermaster's Department, War Department, in 1862 and 1863–1865 at $950 to $1,500 per day. Made two voyages from New York to Aspinwall for the North American Steamship Company in the spring and summer of 1868. Returned to the transatlantic service for a short time and was sold to be broken up in March, 1870.

General Warren

Wooden screw steamer; 1 deck, 2 masts, square stern, billethead; 309 $^{13}\!/_{95}$ tons; 148 ft. × 23 ft. 6 in. × 9 ft. 4 in.; 2 high-pressure engines; diameter of cylinders 1 ft. 6 in., length of stroke 2 ft.

Built at Portland, Maine, in 1844, George Knight, Jr., owner. Was in New York in 1850 and was sent to the Pacific coast, arriving at San Francisco on July 20, 1851, thirty-one days from Panama. She entered the coastwise service north of San Francisco and was wrecked on Clatsop Spit, Columbia River, January 31, 1852.

George Law, later Central America

Wooden side-wheel steamer; 3 decks, 3 masts, round stern, no head; 2,141 $^{5}\!/_{95}$ tons; 278 ft. 3 in. × 40 ft. × 32 ft.; 2 oscillating engines built by the Morgan Iron Works; diameter of cylinders 5 ft. 5 in., length of stroke 10 ft.

Built in New York by William H. Webb for the United States Mail Steamship Company. Keel laid March 25, 1852. Launched October 28, 1852. Entered the New York–Aspinwall service on October 20, 1853. Name changed to *Central America* in July, 1857, since George Law, who had been a director of the company at the time of her construction, was no longer connected with it. Foundered at sea in a severe gale between Havana and New York on September 12, 1857. The blame for the *Central America's* loss seemed to lie with the engine-room force rather than with any structural defect or weakness in the hull. The fires were allowed to go down, and the ship lost headway, falling into the trough of the sea, where she was literally beaten to pieces. About 423 lives and $8,000,000 in gold were lost with the ship.

Georgia

Wooden side-wheel steamer; 3 decks, 4 masts, round stern, flying-horse's head; 2,727 $^{42}\!/_{95}$ tons; 248 ft. × 48 ft. 8 in. × 33 ft.; average draft 15 ft.; 2 side-lever engines built by T. F. Secor and Company; diameter of cylinders 7 ft.

6 in., length of stroke 8 ft.; diameter of paddle wheels 36 ft.; 681 nominal h.p.; hull sharp forward and full aft. Stem and figurehead in one piece, the figurehead representing the wild horse of Mazeppa. In order to give added strength, the rails were not cut for gangways, and the spar deck was fastened on with screws so that on a week's notice she could be converted for naval purposes. Her engines, which were 20 ft. abaft the center of the ship, were entirely below decks and therefore better protected.

Built by Smith and Dimon, New York, for the United States Mail Steamship Company. Launched September 6, 1848. Entered the New York–Chagres service on January 28, 1850, and continued to operate to the Isthmus until February, 1854. She was laid up in New York from 1854 until 1859. In the latter year she was valued at $100,000. Condemned.

Gold Hunter

Wooden side-wheel steamer; 1 deck, 3 masts, round stern, no head; 436$\frac{29}{95}$ tons; 172 ft. 6 in. × 25 ft. 6 in. × 10 ft. 4 in.; double engined.

Built by A. J. Westervelt, New York, for William Skiddy. Launched September 5, 1849. Cleared New York for San Francisco December 17, 1849, but returned to port two days later. Arrived at San Francisco from Panama April 29, 1850. It was expected that she would enter service on the Sacramento River, for which she had been constructed. Made one voyage to Acapulco in 1850, and two voyages to Tehuantepec, Nicaragua, and Panama in 1851, the last-named for Cornelius Vanderbilt. Purchased by the United States government in 1852, and became the *Active*, of the Coast and Geodetic Survey. Purchased for Holladay and Brenham's California, Oregon and Mexico Steamship Company in 1860 or 1861 and was engaged in coastwise service north of San Francisco until she was lost en route from San Francisco to Victoria on June 5, 1870, striking a rock about twenty-two miles north of Cape Mendocino in a dense fog. Her passengers and about half her cargo were taken off.

Golden Age

Wooden side-wheel steamer; 3 decks, 3 masts, round stern, full-length male head; 2,181$\frac{74}{95}$ tons; 272 ft. 10 in. × 41 ft. 10 in. × 25 ft. 1 in. (1856); 1,869$\frac{56}{100}$ tons (1865); vertical-beam engine built by the Morgan Iron Works; diameter of cylinder 6 ft. 11 in., length of stroke 12 ft.; cost $400,000.

Built by William H. Brown, New York, in 1853. Laid down as the *San Francisco*. Intended on completion for service between Australia and Panama. Sailed from New York on September 30, 1853, and went via Liverpool, the Cape of Good Hope, King George's Sound (Australia), and Melbourne, to Sydney. Operated in coastwise service in Australia while coal was being shipped to Tahiti for her use. Sailed from Sydney May 12, 1854, and arrived at Panama June 17, having called at Tahiti and coaled during a six days' stay. Purchased at Panama by the Pacific Mail Steamship Company in August, 1854, and entered the service between San Francisco and Panama in October of the same year. She remained on this run through 1869. Later transferred to the Yokohama–Shanghai branch line of the Pacific Mail. Sold to the Mitsubishi Mail Steamship Company in 1875 and renamed *Hiroshima Maru*. Remained in service as late as 1882.

Golden City

Wooden side-wheel steamer; 3 decks, 2 masts, round stern, no head; 3,373 $^{56}/_{95}$ tons; 343 ft. × 45 ft. 1 in. × 23 ft. (1863); 3,589 $^{6}/_{100}$ tons (1865); mean draft 18 ft.; vertical-beam engine built by the Novelty Iron Works; diameter of cylinder 8 ft. 9 in., length of stroke 12 ft.; diameter of paddle wheels 40 ft.; 1,800 h.p. Built with watertight compartments fore and aft, dividing her into three sections. Fourteen lifeboats, twelve of which were of Ingersoll's pattern, 28 ft. long. Fifty-six double staterooms.

Built by William H. Webb, New York, for the Pacific Mail Steamship Company. Keel laid June 23, 1862. Launched January 24, 1863. Cleared New York for San Francisco August 13, 1863. Operated between San Francisco and Panama for the Pacific Mail Steamship Company from November, 1863, through 1869. Lost on the coast of Lower California on February 10, 1870.

Golden Gate

Wooden side-wheel steamer; 3 decks, 3 masts, round stern, round tuck, spread-eagle head; 2,067 $^{35}/_{95}$ tons; 269 ft. 6 in. × 40 ft. × 22 ft.; mean draft 10 ft. 2 in.; two oscillating engines built by the Novelty Iron Works; diameter of cylinders 7 ft. 1 in., length of stroke 9 ft.; diameter of paddle wheels 32 ft.; 640 h.p.; cost $482,844.

Built by William H. Webb, New York, for the Pacific Mail Steamship Company. Keel laid July 1, 1850. Launched January 21, 1851. Entered the San Francisco–Panama service in November, 1851. Her passage from Panama to San Francisco of eleven days, four hours stood as a record until 1855. She remained in this service for the Pacific Mail until she burned at sea and was beached on the coast a short distance north of Manzanillo, Mexico, on July 27, 1862, with a loss of 223 lives and $1,400,000 in treasure.

Golden Rule

Wooden side-wheel steamer; 2 decks, 3 masts, round stern, scroll head; 2,767 $^{63}/_{95}$ tons; 304 ft. × 43 ft. 6 in. × 24 ft. (1864); 2,107 $^{28}/_{100}$ tons (1865); draft 14 ft.; vertical-beam engine built by the Morgan Iron Works; diameter of cylinder 6 ft. 9 in., length of stroke 12 ft.; diameter of paddle wheels 30 ft. Topsail schooner rig.

Built by Henry Steers at Greenpoint, Long Island, and launched as the *Retribution* on June 3, 1863. Constructed for Cornelius Vanderbilt but sold before launching to Marshall O. Roberts. Entered the New York–Aspinwall service of the Central American Transit Company in July, 1864, and after one voyage was transferred to the New York–San Juan de Nicaragua run. On May 30, 1865, while en route from New York to San Juan, the *Golden Rule* was wrecked on Roncador Reef. All the pasengers and about half the baggage and stores were taken off safely, but the steamer broke up on the reef.

Goliah

Wooden side-wheel steamer; 1 deck, no masts, round stern, no head; 333 $^{52}/_{95}$ tons; 145 ft. × 25 ft. × 9 ft. 9 in. (1849); 612 $^{84}/_{95}$ tons; 185 ft. × 28 ft. 6 in. × 12 ft. 6 in. (1854); vertical-beam engine built by T. F. Secor; diameter of cylinder 4 ft. 2 in., length of stroke 8 ft.; 250 indicated h.p.

Built in 1848 by William H. Webb, New York, as a tug. Sold by Webb and sent to California, arriving on January 21, 1851, at San Francisco, 244 days from New York and 24 days from Panama. Operated as a passenger steamer on the Sacramento River as the *Defender*. In 1854, she was rebuilt and enlarged, and after the summer of that year she operated in the local coastwise service north and south of San Francisco under the name *Goliah* for J. T. Wright. She later operated as a towboat in San Francisco Bay, and still later she was engaged in the same work on Puget Sound. She was dismantled and burned in 1899.

Granada

Wooden side-wheel steamer; 2 decks, 2 masts, round stern, billethead; 1,058 $^{91}/_{95}$ tons; 228 ft. × 31 ft. × 15 ft. 6 in.; vertical-beam engine; diameter of cylinder 5 ft. 5 in., length of stroke 10 ft.; cost $175,000.

Built by Jeremiah Simonson, New York, in 1855. Entered service between New York, New Orleans, and Aspinwall for the United States Mail Steamship Company in 1857, and remained in it until the spring of 1859. In 1860 she was operating for the same owners between New York and New Orleans via Havana. Later in that year, she was sent around to San Francisco by Marshall O. Roberts, and went ashore south of Fort Point, San Francisco, on October 13, 1860. The hull was sold on October 18, 1860.

Great Republic

Wooden side-wheel steamer; 3 decks, 3 masts, round stern, plain head; 3,881 $^{83}/_{100}$ tons; 360.3 ft. × 47.4 ft. × 22.8 ft.; vertical-beam engine built by the Novelty Iron Works; diameter of cylinder 8 ft. 9 in., length of stroke 12 ft. Divided into five watertight compartments by four bulkheads. Built to carry 250 cabin and 1,200 steerage passengers, with 2,000 tons of cargo, and 1,500 tons of coal. Twelve metal lifeboats fitted with masts and sails. Armed with five 20-pounders and two 30-pound Parrott guns.

Built by Henry Steers at Greenpoint, Long Island, for the Pacific Mail Steamship Company in 1866 and 1867. Cleared New York for Japan via Panama and San Francisco on May 18, 1867, and arrived at Panama on July 16, direct from New York. Made one voyage from Panama to San Francisco, sailing July 22 and arriving August 2, 1867. Entered the San Francisco–Hong Kong service, for which she was built, September 3, 1867. Sold to P. B. Cornwall of San Francisco in 1878 and was placed in the San Francisco–Portland service. The *Great Republic* was wrecked on Sand Island, Columbia River Bar, April 19, 1879.

Guiding Star

Wooden side-wheel steamer; 3 decks, 2 masts, round stern, no head; 2,384 38⁄95 tons; 300 ft. 6 in. × 40 ft. 6 in. × 33 ft. (1864); 2,595 73⁄100 tons (1865); vertical-beam engine from the *Mississippi;* diameter of cylinder 6 ft. 9 in., length of stroke 12 ft.

Built by Roosevelt, Joyce and Waterbury, New York. Launched August 13, 1864. Owned by the New York Mail Steamship Company and placed on the New York–Havana–New Orleans run in September, 1864. Operated to Bremen for the North American Lloyd in 1867. Made six voyages from New York to Aspinwall for the North American Steamship Company in 1868. Chartered in 1869 and 1870 by Ruger Brothers for service to Copenhagen. Broken up at Cold Spring, Long Island, in October, 1874.

Henry Chauncey

Wooden, side-wheel steamer; 3 decks, 2 masts, round stern, plain head; 2,656 67⁄100 tons; 319.45 ft. × 43 ft. × 20.08 ft.; mean draft 14 ft. 5 in.; vertical-beam engine built by the Novelty Iron Works; diameter of cylinder 8 ft. 9 in., length of stroke 12 ft. Capacity 250 first-cabin passengers, 250 second-cabin passengers, 300 steerage, 668 tons of cargo. Carried ten metal lifeboats besides the captain's gig.

Built by William H. Webb, New York, for the Pacific Mail Steamship Company. Keel laid October 10, 1863. Launched October 18, 1864. Entered the New York–Aspinwall service of the Pacific Mail on November 1, 1865. She remained on this run through 1869. The *Henry Chauncey* burned at sea off the coast of North Carolina near Body Island on August 16, 1871, en route from New York to Kingston and Aspinwall. The passengers and crew were all taken off, but the mails and freight were lost. The hull was rebuilt, and she was finally sold to be broken up to Elbert Stannard on July 18, 1877, for $19,000.

Hermann

Wooden side-wheel steamer; 3 decks, 3 masts, square stern, billethead; 1,734 45⁄95 tons; 234 ft. 11 in. × 39 ft. 6 in. × 31 ft. 7 in.; mean draft 19 ft. 6 in.; 2 side-lever engines built by the Novelty Iron Works; diameter of cylinders 6 ft., length of stroke 10 ft.; diameter of paddle wheels 36 ft.; 474 h.p.; cost $410,000.

Built by Westervelt and Mackay, New York, for the Ocean Steam Navigation Company in 1847–1848. Entered the New York–Bremen service on March 21, 1848, and remained in it until 1857. Sold to the California, New York and European Steamship Company, for which Henry Randall was agent, in August, 1858. She sailed from New York on August 23, 1858, and arrived at San Francisco via Panama on November 27. In February or March, 1859, she was sold to J. T. Wright for $40,000 and made one trip to the Northwest coast, after which she was said to have been "bought off" by the Pacific Mail. In the winter of 1862–1863 she made one voyage from San Francisco to Panama for the People's Line. On August 14, 1866, the *Hermann* was auctioned off to T. J. L. Smiley for $17,000, and by him she was sold to the Pacific Mail. She proceeded to Mare Island on November 14, 1866, to be refitted for the voyage to Yokohama, where the Pacific Mail planned to use her as a store ship and spare steamer. On March 1, 1867, the *Hermann* sailed for Yokohama. On February 13, 1869, while en route from Yokohama to the Straits of Sangar, she was wrecked on Point Kwatzu with a loss of about 330 lives.

Illinois

Wooden side-wheel steamer; 2 decks, 3 masts, round stern, round tuck, no head; 2,123 $^{65}/_{95}$ tons; 266 ft. 6 in. × 40 ft. 10 in. × 22 ft.; draft in ballast 17 ft.; two oscillating engines built by the Allaire Iron Works; diameter of cylinders 7 ft. 1 in., length of stroke 9 ft.; diameter of paddle wheels 33 ft.; 640 h.p.; berths for 500 passengers; cost $480,000.

Built by Smith and Dimon, New York, for the United States Mail Steamship Company in 1851. Originally laid down for the Pacific Mail Steamship Company. Entered the New York–Chagres service of the United States Mail Steamship Company on August 26, 1851, and remained in it until the spring of 1859, with several long periods of inactivity. She was sold at auction in February, 1860, to Cornelius Vanderbilt, who placed her on his New York–Havre line in the spring of that year. The price paid for her was $25,000. Chartered to the Quartermaster's Department, War Department, in 1861, 1862–1863, and 1864 at $1,000 to $1,600 per day. From October, 1863, until June, 1864, the *Illinois* ran again between New York and Aspinwall for Marshall O. Roberts. After the Civil War, she served as a quarantine ship at Hoffman's Island in lower New York Harbor until about 1900.

Independence (1st)

Wooden side-wheel steamer; 2 decks, 2 masts, round stern, no head; 613 $^{50}/_{95}$ tons; 211 ft. 6 in. × 27 ft. 10 in. × 10 ft. 9 in. Engine built by E. Coffee.

Built by William H. Brown, New York, for Cornelius Vanderbilt. Launched December 25, 1850, with engine on board and steam up. Sailed from New York for San Francisco January 13, 1851. Arrived at San Francisco with passengers from San Juan del Sur on September 17, 1851. She remained in this service until wrecked on Margarita Island, Lower California, on February 16, 1853, en route from San Juan del Sur to San Francisco. One hundred twenty-five lives were lost.

Independence (2nd)

Wooden side-wheel steamer; 2 decks, 2 masts, round stern, round tuck, no head; 1,376 $^{57}/_{95}$ tons; 223 ft. 5 in. × 36 ft. × 18 ft. 3 in.; fitted for 500 passengers.

Built by Capes and Allison, Hoboken, New Jersey, for Lauchlan McKay. Launched with engine aboard and steam up on December 20, 1851. Sold to L. A. Heath December 30, 1851. Intended to run between New York and Texas, but placed on the New York–Chagres route. Sailed from New York for Chagres on December 29, 1851 for E. Mills. Said to have been lost at sea, but no more definite information available concerning her.

Isthmus

Wooden side-wheel steamer; 1 deck, 2 masts, square stern, billethead; 337 $50\!/_{95}$ tons; 155 ft. 9 in. × 24 ft. 5½ in. × 10 ft.; inclined engine built by Hogg and Delamater; diameter of cylinder 3 ft. 4 in., length of stroke 8 ft.; diameter of paddle wheels 21 ft. 6 in.; nominal h.p. 69.

Built by Bishop and Simonson, New York, as the *Aurora,* in 1846–1847. Sold to the United States Navy on January 6, 1847, for $65,000 and renamed *Scorpion.* Served in the Gulf of Mexico during the Mexican War, and sold at auction at Brooklyn to Marshall O. Roberts on October 18, 1848, for $14,500. Sent by Roberts from New York to Chagres with passengers in December, 1848, and then entered the New Orleans–Chagres service. She was rebuilt in 1849 and was sent to the Pacific, arriving at San Francisco May 4, 1850. She operated between San Francisco and Panama for George Law until April, 1851, when she was purchased by the Pacific Mail for $102,000. She made occasional trips to Panama for her new owners until late in 1853. In December, 1853, she was placed in the San Francisco–San Diego service, and in January, 1854, she was purchased by Heiser and Company and renamed *Southerner.* She was purchased by Captain J. T. Wright in October, 1854, for $32,000. In attempting to cross the Columbia River Bar in December, 1854, she sprang a leak, and though she tried to run for Puget Sound, she was forced ashore about sixty miles south of Cape Flattery on December 26, 1854. Passengers and crew were taken off, but the ship was a total loss.

James Adger

Wooden side-wheel steamer; 2 decks, 3 masts, round stern, round tuck, spread-eagle head; 1,151 $28\!/_{95}$ tons; 215 ft. × 33 ft. 6 in. × 21 ft. 3 in.

Built by William H. Webb, New York, in 1852 for M. C. Mordecai of Charleston, South Carolina. Made one voyage from Aspinwall and San Juan de Nicaragua to New York for Spofford, Tileston and Company in January, 1857. Purchased by the U. S. Navy on July 26, 1861, for $85,000. Sold by the Navy to James B. Campbell on October 9, 1866, for $32,000. Broken up in Boston Harbor in 1878.

Japan

Wooden side-wheel steamer; 3 decks, 3 masts, round stern, plain head; 4,351 $72\!/_{100}$ tons; 362 ft. × 49 ft. × 23 ft.; loaded draft 18 ft.; vertical-beam engine built by the Novelty Iron Works; diameter of cylinder 8 ft. 9 in., length of stroke 12 ft.; built of white oak, live oak, cedar, and hacmatac; promenade deck 40 ft. above the water at the bow.

Built by Henry Steers, Greenpoint, Long Island, for the Pacific Mail Steamship Company. Launched December 17, 1867. Sailed from New York for Yokohama via Panama and San Francisco on April 11, 1868. Made the run from New York to Panama in sixty-three days including a stop of four days at Lota, Chile, for coal. Sailed from Panama June 19, 1868, and arrived at San Francisco July 3. Entered the San Francisco–Hong Kong service of the Pacific Mail, in which she remained until she was burned at sea between Yokohama and Hong Kong on December 17–18, 1874.

John L. Stephens

Wooden side-wheel steamer; 3 decks, 2 masts, round stern, no head; 2,182 $^{92}\!/_{95}$ tons; 274.3 ft. × 41 ft. × 17.3 ft. (1852); 1,995 $^{44}\!/_{100}$ tons (1865); beam over guards 65 ft. 6 in.; mean draft 12 ft.; one oscillating engine built by the Novelty Iron Works; diameter of cylinder 7 ft. 1 in., length of stroke 9 ft.; diameter of paddle wheels 32 ft.; 640 h.p. Fitted with Pierson's Patent Steam Condenser to supply fresh water for the boilers. It was estimated that this would effect a saving of 50 per cent. Coal capacity 450 tons. Tanks for 20,000 gals. fresh water. On the upper deck were 350 berths, built fore and aft with wide gangways. The ship was provided with an extensive suite of baths for passengers with instant hot and cold water. There were two steerage decks, the lower or berth deck having 550 single berths built athwartship with ample ventilating apparatus between them. The *John L. Stephens* was brigantine-rigged, and carried eight large lifeboats.

Built by Smith and Dimon, New York, for the Pacific Mail Steamship Company. Launched September 21, 1852. She cleared New York for San Francisco on December 17, 1852, and arrived at her destination with passengers from Panama on April 3, 1853. She continued to operate between San Francisco and Panama for the Pacific Mail until October of 1860. In 1864 she began making voyages between San Francisco and the Columbia River and was still in this service for the Oregon Steamship Company in 1876. In 1878 she was sold at San Francisco to Sisson, Wallace and Co., who sent her to Karluk, Alaska, for use as a floating cannery. On her return, she was retired from service and broken up the following year.

Lafayette

Wooden screw steamer; 2 decks, 3 masts, round stern, flying-dragon head; 1,059 $^{2}\!/_{95}$ tons; 210 ft. × 32 ft. 6 in. × 19 ft.; two direct-acting engines built by Hogg and Delamater, New York; diameter of cylinders 4 ft. 2 in., length of stroke 3 ft. 8 in.; diameter of propeller 14 ft.; 164 h.p.

Built by Perine, Patterson and Stack, Williamsburg, New York, for J. G. Williams. Launched on January 18, 1851. Made one voyage from Philadelphia to Europe and then, owned by Charles Stoddert, was placed on the New York–Chagres run. She sailed from New York on her first voyage on August 28, 1851, and was burned at Chagres on September 11, 1851.

McKim

Wooden side-wheel steamer; 1 deck, 3 masts, no gallery, scroll head; 244 $^{17}\!/_{95}$ tons; 175 ft. × 23 ft. × 9 ft. (1844); 2 decks, 3 masts, square stern, billethead; 376 $^{77}\!/_{95}$ tons; 129 ft. 6 in. × 23 ft. 2 in. × 11 ft. 7 in. (1854).

Built as the *John S. McKim* at Allowaystown, New Jersey, in 1844. Sold to the Quartermaster's Department, War Department, 1846. Returned to private ownership in 1849 and arrived at San Francisco from New Orleans and Panama on October 3 of that year. She then entered service on the Sacramento River. She made another voyage to Panama and northbound was condemned at Acapulco in the summer of 1851, her passengers being obliged to continue to San

Francisco as best they could. She must have been repaired, as she arrived at San Francisco on July 31, 1853, sixty-two days from Panama. Broken up at San Francisco in 1858.

Montana

Wooden side-wheel steamer; 3 decks, 2 masts, round stern, plain head; 2,676 82/100 tons; 318 ft. × 42.5 ft. × 20.6 ft.; beam over guards 72 ft.; vertical-beam engine built by the Novelty Iron Works; diameter of cylinder 8 ft. 9 in., length of stroke 10 ft.; diameter of paddle wheels 43 ft.

Built by Webb and Bell at Greenpoint, Long Island, for the Pacific Mail Steamship Company. Launched February 25, 1865. The *Montana* entered the San Francisco–Panama service of the Pacific Mail in October, 1866, and remained in it through 1869. She was broken up in November, 1877.

Monumental City

Wooden screw steamer; 737 46/95 tons; 180 ft. × 30 ft. × 15 ft.;* mean draft 12 ft.; two oscillating engines designed and built by Murray and Hazlehurst, Baltimore; diameter of cylinders 3 ft. 8 in., length of stroke 3 ft.; diameter of propeller 12 ft.; 119 nominal h.p. Built with accommodations for about 250 first- and second-cabin passengers. Flush promenade deck. Bark-rigged.

Built at Baltimore in 1850, A. A. Chapman, owner. Sailed on her trial trip on November 14, 1850. Made two voyages from San Francisco to Panama for the Empire City Line in the fall of 1851 and the spring of 1852, and one voyage from San Francisco to San Juan del Sur in the spring of 1852 for Cornelius Vanderbilt. She was the first steamer to cross the Pacific, sailing from San Francisco on February 17, 1853, and arriving at Sydney, via Tahiti, on April 23. She entered the coastwise trade between Sydney and Melbourne, but was wrecked off Malacoutta Bay, near Twofold Bay, on May 15, 1853, en route from Melbourne to Sydney, with a loss of thirty-three lives. She was owned at that time by Peter Stroebed.

Moses Taylor

Wooden side-wheel steamer; 3 decks, 2 masts, round stern, plain head; 1,372 56/95 tons; 246 ft. × 34 ft. × 17 ft. (1858); 1,354 tons (1865); engines from *El Dorado;* built to carry 600 passengers; staterooms on the upper deck for 100 passengers; cost $250,000.

Built by William H. Webb, New York, for Marshall O. Roberts. Keel laid January 10, 1857; launched August 1, 1857. The *Moses Taylor* sailed on her first voyage from New York to Aspinwall for the United States Mail Steamship Company on January 5, 1858. She continued in this service until September, 1859, when she was withdrawn. Sold at auction to Cornelius Vanderbilt on February 27, 1860, for $25,000. Brought to the Pacific and operated from San Francisco to San Juan del Sur by the People's Line from November, 1862 until August, 1863, and then from San Francisco to Panama until May, 1864. In

---

* The registry record for the *Monumental City* is missing in the file at the National Archives, and therefore only the tonnage given here is based upon official figures.

September, 1864, the *Moses Taylor* began running for the Central American Transit Company from San Francisco to San Juan del Sur, and continued for this company and its successor, the North American Steamship Company, until May, 1868. Between 1871 and 1873, she operated on William H. Webb's San Francisco–Honolulu–Australia line. She was purchased by the Pacific Mail Steamship Company in 1873, and was converted into a store ship in 1875. She had the nickname of *"Rolling Moses,"* although contemporary accounts state that this was undeserved.

Nebraska

Wooden side-wheel steamer; 3 decks, 2 masts, round stern, scroll head; 2,143 $^{82}\!/_{100}$ tons; 269 ft. × 40 ft. × 19 ft.; vertical-beam engine built by the Etna Iron Works; diameter of cylinder 7 ft. 1 in., length of stroke 12 ft; diameter of paddle wheels 33 ft.

Built by Henry Steers, Greenpoint, Long Island, for the Central American Transit Company. Originally was to have been named *Leona.* Launched October 26, 1865, as the *Managua.* Her name was changed to *Nebraska* before completion. Made one voyage from New York to Aspinwall for Webb's North American Steamship Company in the fall of 1867. Sailed from New York for San Francisco on January 8, 1868, and arrived, via Rio de Janeiro, Lota, and Panama, on March 27. The *Nebraska* operated between San Francisco and Panama for the North American Steamship Company until the fall of 1868. In 1871–1873, she served on Webb's line from San Francisco to Honolulu and Australia. She was purchased by the Pacific Mail Steamship Company in 1875, and was owned by Goodall, Nelson and Perkins in the following year. She was broken up at San Francisco in 1878.

Nevada

Wooden side-wheel steamer; 3 decks, 2 masts, round stern, no head; 1,691 $^{17}\!/_{100}$ tons; 281 ft. × 40 ft. × 16.3 ft. (1865); 2,143 $^{82}\!/_{100}$ tons (1866); vertical-beam engine; diameter of cylinder 7 ft. 1 in., length of stroke 12 ft.

Built at Brooklyn by Jeremiah Simonson. Launched March 18, 1865, as the *Paou Shan,* owned by Captain Thomas W. Dearborn. Registered October 9, 1866, with Thomas Dexter as owner. Sold to William H. Webb and name changed to *Nevada* on November 9, 1866. Sailed from New York on her trial trip on May 9, 1867. Made three voyages from New York to San Juan de Nicaragua for the North American Steamship Company in 1867. Sailed from New York for San Francisco on September 28, 1867, and arrived, via Lota and Panama, on December 15, 1867. The *Nevada* operated from San Francisco to Panama for the North American Steamship Company from December, 1867, until October, 1868. She served on Webb's San Francisco–Honolulu–Australia line from 1871 to 1873. In 1873, she was purchased by the Pacific Mail Steamship Company, which placed her on its Yokohama-Shanghai branch line. She was sold to the Mitsubishi Mail Steamship Company in 1875 and renamed *Saikio Maru.*

New Orleans

Wooden side-wheel steamer; 1 deck, 3 masts, square stern, eagle head; 761 $^{65}\!\!/_{95}$ tons; 209 ft. × 30 ft. × 12 ft.; vertical-beam engine built by T. F. Secor and Company, New York; diameter of cylinder 4 ft. 4 in., length of stroke 11 ft.; diameter of paddle wheels 32 ft.; nominal h.p. 131; accommodations for 160 cabin and 400 steerage passengers.

Built at New York in 1848. She was owned by the United States government early in 1849. On October 10, 1849, she was enrolled with G. Godfrey as owner. The *New Orleans* sailed from New York for San Francisco on February 5, 1850, and operated for the Empire City Line between San Francisco and Panama between September, 1850, and December, 1852. She sailed from San Francisco for Sydney on March 10–11, 1853, via Nukahiva, Tahiti, Tongatabu, Moreton Bay, and Port Jackson, arriving at the last-named port on May 14–15, 1853. The *New Orleans* was purchased by the Melbourne Steam Packet Company for 7,000 pounds and renamed *Governor General*. Later she was sold to the Australasian Steam Navigation Company and was operated on the coast of Australia until 1861, when she was purchased by owners in China.

New World

Wooden side-wheel steamer; 1 deck, 2 masts, square stern, scroll head; 525 $^{66}\!\!/_{95}$ tons; 216 ft. 2 in. × 27 ft. × 9 ft. 3 in.; vertical-beam engine; diameter of cylinder 3 ft. 10 in., length of stroke 10 ft. 1 in.

Built by William Furness at New York for William H. Brown. Launched with steam up on February 10, 1850. Sailed from New York for San Francisco on February 16, 1850. Called at Panama and carried 217 passengers from there to San Francisco, arriving on July 11, 1850. The *New World* entered the trade between San Francisco and Sacramento, remaining in it until 1864, when she was sold to the Oregon Steam Navigation Company and was operated on the Columbia River until 1868, and then was sent north for service on Puget Sound. She was broken up at San Francisco in 1878.

New York

Wooden side-wheel steamer; 3 decks, 2 masts, round stern, no head; 2,217 $^{43}\!\!/_{100}$ tons; 292.6 ft. × 41.7 ft. × 26.5 ft.; vertical-beam engine built by the Allaire Iron Works; diameter of cylinder 7 ft. 6 in., length of stroke 12 ft.; diameter of paddle wheels 35 ft.; 1,800 h.p.; bunker capacity 600 tons; built with accommodations for 200 first-cabin, 170 second-cabin, and 500 steerage passengers.

Built by Jeremiah Simonson, at Greenpoint, Long Island, for Cornelius Vanderbilt. Launched June 16, 1864. She entered service between New York and Aspinwall for Vanderbilt in September, 1865. After two voyages, she was sold to the Pacific Mail Steamship Company and continued on the same run from December, 1865, until April, 1867. With the opening of the Pacific Mail's transpacific service, the *New York* was sent to the Far East as a spare steamer, sailing from New York on August 2, 1867, by way of the Cape of Good Hope. She was employed on the Yokohama–Shanghai branch line of the Pacific Mail until 1875, when she was sold to the Mitsubishi Mail Steamship Company and by her new owners was renamed *Tokio Maru*. She was surveyed at Shanghai as late as 1878.

North America

Wooden side-wheel steamer; 2 decks, 4 masts, round stern, no head; 1,440 $^{29}\!\!/_{95}$ tons; 260 ft. 6 in. × 33 ft. 9 in. × 20 ft. 6 in.; engine built by the Morgan Iron Works; diameter of cylinder 5 ft., length of stroke 12 ft.

Built at New York by Lawrence and Sneeden. Launched September 14, 1850. At the time of her launching, the *North America* was said to be intended for the San Francisco–Panama run, but as late as February, 1851, she was owned by the Norwich and New London Steamboat Company and between February and June of that year she operated between New York and Chagres. Sailing from New York on June 24, 1851, she arrived at San Francisco via Panama on October 2. She entered the service of the Vanderbilt Independent Line between San Francisco and San Juan del Sur and was wrecked on February 27, 1852, when thirty miles south of Acapulco, northbound.

North Star

Wooden side-wheel steamer; 3 decks, 2 masts, round stern, no head; 1,867 $^{60}\!\!/_{95}$ tons; 262 ft. 6 in. × 38 ft. 6 in. × 28 ft. (1853); 2,004 $^{25}\!\!/_{100}$ tons (1865); two vertical-beam engines built by the Allaire Iron Works; diameter of cylinders 5 ft., length of stroke 10 ft.; diameter of paddle wheels 34 ft.; cost $285,400.

Built by Jeremiah Simonson, Greenpoint, Long Island, in 1853 for Cornelius Vanderbilt. The *North Star* was used by Vanderbilt as a private yacht for an excursion to Europe in 1853. She entered the New York–Aspinwall service for Vanderbilt in February, 1854, and from September of 1854 until January, 1855, she was operated for the United States Mail Steamship Company. In 1855, she was withdrawn to enter Vanderbilt's transatlantic service, returning to the New York–Aspinwall run for Vanderbilt in June, 1859. She was chartered by the Quartermaster's Department, War Department, in 1862, 1864, and 1865 at $1,200 to $641 per day. Between these tours of duty, she carried on her voyages to Aspinwall until February, 1865. The *North Star* was broken up at New London, Connecticut, in 1866.

Northern Light

Wooden side-wheel steamer; 3 decks, 3 masts, round stern, no head; 1,767 $^{91}\!\!/_{95}$ tons; 253 ft. 6 in. × 38 ft. 2 in. × 22 ft. 6 in. (1852); 2,056 $^{53}\!\!/_{100}$ tons (1865); draft at sea 14 ft.; two direct-acting lever-beam engines built by the Allaire Iron Works; diameter of cylinders 5 ft., length of stroke 10 ft.; diameter of paddle wheels 33 ft.; cost $290,000. The hull was built of live oak, locust, and cedar, with round lines, not flat or hollow. Her stem was straight, without head or cutwater, but finished at the top with gold scrollwork, while the stern was round and undecorated except for her name in gilt letters. The hull was painted dark green, with red and white lines at the guard streaks. She was built with accommodations for 250 first-class, 150 second-class, and 400 to 500 steerage passengers. The first-class dining saloon was on the main deck, amidships, and extended entirely across the vessel with dimensions of 40 ft. × 36 ft., having no staterooms on either side to interfere with ventilation. She was brigantine-rigged.

Built by Jeremiah Simonson, New York, for Cornelius Vanderbilt, and launched October 25, 1851. She entered Vanderbilt's service from New York to San Juan de Nicaragua on May 5, 1852, and continued in it until February, 1856. In September, 1857, she was placed on the New York–Aspinwall line of the United States Mail Steamship Company, where she remained until December of the same year. After making a single voyage from New York to Aspinwall for Vanderbilt in March, 1858, she was not placed on this run again until March, 1859, when she served for Vanderbilt again. She was chartered by the Quartermaster's Department, War Department, in 1862–1863, 1864, and 1864–1865 at $1,200 to $792 per day. In 1864, she was sold to Russell Sturgis and in 1867 was chartered by Ruger Brothers to open the service of their New York and Bremen Steamship Company, serving for these operators in 1868 and 1869. The *Northern Light* was sold October 1, 1870, for $25,000. She was owned by Henry F. Hammill in 1871. Broken up in 1875.

Northerner

Wooden side-wheel steamer; 2 decks, 3 masts, square stern, round tuck, billet-head; 1,102 $^{93}/_{95}$ tons; 203 ft. 6 in. × 32 ft. 4 in. × 21 ft. 7½ in.; average draft 12 ft.; side-lever engine built by the Novelty Iron Works; diameter of cylinder 5 ft. 10 in., length of stroke 8 ft.; diameter of paddle wheels 31 ft.; 208 nominal h.p.

Built by William H. Brown, New York, and launched in 1847. Intended for Spofford, Tileston and Company's service between New York and Charleston. Made one voyage from New York to Chagres via Charleston and Havana in March and April, 1849, for Spofford, Tileston. She was then sent to San Francisco, arriving August 15, 1850. After making one voyage to Panama for the Empire City Line, the *Northerner* was purchased by the Pacific Mail Steamship Company in December, 1850. She remained in the Pacific Mail's San Francisco–Panama service until May, 1853, after which she was employed as a spare steamer. Still later, the *Northerner* was placed on the route from San Francisco to the Columbia River and Puget Sound. On January 5, 1860, when northbound from San Francisco, she struck Blunt's Reef, about twenty miles south of the entrance of Humboldt Bay. The ship was beached, but with a loss of thirty-eight lives in the wreck.

Ocean Queen

Wooden side-wheel steamer; 3 decks, 3 masts, round stern, eagle head; 2,801 $^{9}/_{95}$ tons; 327 ft. × 42 ft. × 22 ft. 6 in. (1859); 2,715 $^{30}/_{100}$ tons (1865); draft 16 ft.; vertical-beam engine built by the Morgan Iron Works; diameter of cylinder 7 ft. 6 in., length of stroke 12 ft.; diameter of paddle wheels 38 ft.; cost $450,000.

Built by J. A. Westervelt and Sons, New York. Launched April 8, 1857. She was ostensibly constructed for Charles Morgan and Sons, but actually for the San Francisco–Nicaragua line of Morgan and Garrison. Originally christened

Queen of the Pacific, but when she was purchased by Vanderbilt before completion, she was renamed *Ocean Queen*. Until 1861, she was employed on Vanderbilt's transatlantic service. She was chartered by the Quartermaster's Department, War Department, in 1861–1862 at $2,000 per day. The *Ocean Queen* entered Vanderbilt's New York–Aspinwall service in October, 1862, and continued in it after her purchase by the Pacific Mail in 1865 until after June, 1869. In 1870, she made one voyage for Ruger Brothers from New York to France, Prussia, and Denmark. She was broken up in 1874. At that time she was owned by John Roach.

Ohio

Wooden side-wheel steamer; 3 decks, 4 masts, round stern, flying-serpent head; 2,432 $27/95$ tons; 246 ft. × 46 ft. × 32 ft. 9 in.; draft 15 ft.; two side-lever engines built by T. F. Secor and Company; diameter of cylinders 7 ft. 6 in., length of stroke 8 ft.; diameter of paddle wheels 36 ft.; 681 nominal h.p. Underwater body of oak, with upper streaks of locust, cedar, and live oak. Hull full forward and sharp aft. Stem and figurehead in one piece with the figurehead carved to represent a dragon's head with a sea serpent's tail 40 ft. long. On the taffrail were the parted coats of arms of the states of Ohio and Georgia. Rigged as a barkentine. Stateroom accommodations for 250 first-cabin and permanent berths for 80 steerage. Cost $450,000.

Built by Bishop and Simonson, New York, for the United States Mail Steamship Company. Launched August 12, 1848. Entered the service from New York to Chagres via Charleston, Savannah, Havana, and New Orleans on September 20, 1849. Withdrawn from service in the spring of 1854 and laid up at New York until at least 1859. She was broken up in 1860.

Ontario

Wooden screw steamer; 2 decks, 2 masts, round stern; 417 $25/95$ tons; 139 ft. 6 in. × 25 ft. 3 in. × 17 ft. 7 in. (1850).

Built at Rochester, New York, in 1846. Rebuilt at Buffalo in 1850. Made a single voyage from New York to Chagres in December, 1850–March, 1851. Southbound she carried only freight, but returning she brought fourteen passengers, coming via San Juan de Nicaragua. She was converted into a church in 1856.

Oregon

Wooden side-wheel steamer; 2 decks, 3 masts, round stern, dragon head; 1,099 $9/95$ tons; 202 ft. 9 in. × 33 ft. 10 in. × 20 ft. (1848); 1,052 $82/100$ tons (1865); one side-lever engine built by the Novelty Iron Works; diameter of cylinder 5 ft. 10 in., length of stroke 8 ft.; diameter of paddle wheels 26 ft.; 208 nominal h.p.; bark-rigged; cost $198,504.

Built by Smith and Dimon, New York, for the Pacific Mail Steamship Company. Launched August 5, 1848. Sailed from New York December 8, 1848, for San Francisco via Rio de Janeiro, Valparaiso, Callao, Paita, and Panama. Running time from New York to Panama fifty-five days, eight hours. Arrived San Francisco April 1, 1849. In regular service between San Francisco and

Panama until 1855. Made one voyage in 1856 with freight only. The *Oregon* was then placed on the line between San Francisco and the Columbia River and was engaged in that service when she was sold to Holladay and Flint in 1861. In 1869, her engine was removed, and she was converted into a bark for use in the lumber trade. The *Oregon* was sunk in the Straits of Juan de Fuca in collision with the bark *Germania* in 1880.

Oregonian

Wooden side-wheel steamer; 2 decks, 2 masts, round stern, plain head; 1,914 45/100 tons; 275.5 ft. × 42.4 ft. × 21.3 ft.; loaded draft 11 ft. 11 in.; vertical-beam engine built by the Allaire Iron Works; diameter of cylinder 6 ft. 10 in., length of stroke 12 ft.; diameter of paddle wheels 35 ft.; cost $400,000.

Built by Lawrence and Foulkes at Williamsburg, New York, in 1866. The *Oregonian* was designed for the San Francisco–Portland service and built for the Oregon Steam Navigation Company. She arrived at San Francisco on December 2 or 3, 1866, sixty-eight days from New York direct. Owing to the decline of the Oregon trade, the ship was offered for sale immediately. On January 22, 1867, she was purchased by the North American Steamship Company, and in November of that year she was placed on its line between San Francisco and Panama. The *Oregonian* was withdrawn in 1868, with the end of coastwise service by the North American Steamship Company. She was purchased by the Pacific Mail Steamship Company and placed on its Yokohama–Shanghai branch line. In 1876, she was sold to the Mitsubishi Mail Steamship Company.

Orizaba

Wooden side-wheel steamer; 3 decks, 2 masts, round stern, plain head; 1,450 62/95 tons; 246 ft. × 35 ft. × 18 ft. 4 in. (1858); 1,355 64/95 (1854); 1,334 12/100 (1865); vertical-beam engine built by the Morgan Iron Works; diameter of cylinder 5 ft. 5 in., length of stroke, 11 ft.; diameter of paddle wheels 32 ft.; cost $241,000. Total sleeping accommodations for 1,028. Fifty-six first-cabin staterooms, 30 of which were on deck, with 26 opening into the mail saloon. The second cabin was divided into 35 staterooms, which was an innovation on the Pacific at the time of the *Orizaba's* arrival, and in the steerage there were berths for 590, and standees for 60 more. The ship had an icehouse with a capacity of 30 tons, and tanks for 18,000 gallons of fresh water. She carried four large lifeboats and two quarter-boats.

Built by Jacob A. Westervelt and Company, New York. Launched January 14, 1854. The *Orizaba* was built for the New York–New Orleans–Vera Cruz line of Morgan and Harris. She made two voyages from New York to San Juan de Nicaragua in April and May, 1856, under the agency of C. A. Whitney but owned by Vanderbilt. In the same year, the *Orizaba* was sent to the Pacific and arrived at San Francisco October 30, 1856, sixty-one steaming days from New York via Rio de Janeiro, Lota, Valparaiso, Talcahuana, and San Juan del Sur. She operated for Vanderbilt's Nicaragua Steamship Company until February, 1857, and after April, 1858, sailed from San Francisco to Panama for C. K.

Garrison's New York and California Steamship Company. The *Orizaba* was purchased by the Pacific Mail in 1860 and began service for her new owners with her departure from San Francisco for Panama on June 1, 1861. She continued in this trade until April, 1864. On April, 1865, she was sold to the California Steam Navigation Company and was placed on the San Francisco–Portland–Victoria run. She was acquired by Holladay and Brenham in 1867 and was purchased from them in 1872 by the Pacific Mail. In 1875, the *Orizaba* was sold by the Pacific Mail to Goodall, Nelson and Perkins. Through all these changes of ownership, the steamer remained in the coastwise service north and south of San Francisco. She was broken up in 1887.

Orus

Wooden side-wheel steamer, 1 deck, no mast, square stern, sharp tuck, billet-head; 210 61/95 tons (1842); 247 26/95 tons (1845); 158 ft. 7 in. × 21 ft. 6 in. × 7 ft. 6 in. (1845).

Built at New York in 1842. Lengthened, 1845. Operated between New York and Red Bank on the Shrewsbury River. Purchased by Howland and Aspinwall in 1848 and sent from New York to Chagres with passengers on December 22, 1848. Intended for service on the Chagres River, but since she proved to be too large for this, the *Orus* was used as a tender and tug for steamers anchoring off the mouth of the river. Purchased by Vanderbilt for service on the San Juan River in Nicaragua late in 1849.

Pacific

Wooden side-wheel steamer; 2 decks, 3 masts, round stern; 1,003 84/95 tons; 225 ft. 6 in. × 30 ft. 4 in. × 19 ft. (1850); 875 99/100 tons (1865); vertical-beam engine built by the Archimedes Iron Works; diameter of cylinder 5 ft. 10 in., length of stroke 10 ft.; cost $100,000.

Built by William H. Brown, New York. Launched September 24, 1850, with her engines installed and steam up, so that her wheels turned as soon as she was water borne. Built for Major Albert Lowry and Captain Jarvis, who intended her for the San Francisco–Panama service. At first, she was placed temporarily on the New Orleans–Chagres service of the United States Mail Steamship Company in place of the *Falcon*. On her first trip to Havana, she made 360 miles in twenty-four hours, which was said to be the best day's run hitherto attained by an ocean steamer. Sailed from New York for San Francisco on March 19, 1851, and arrived July 2. The *Pacific* entered the service between San Francisco and Panama for Vanderbilt, having just been purchased by him; in September, 1851, she began running for him to San Juan del Sur and continued in this trade until September, 1855. After being laid up for some time, she entered the San Francisco–Columbia River service in 1858 for the Merchants' Accommodation Line. On July 18, 1861, she sank in the Columbia River near Coffin Rock, en route from Portland to Astoria. She was raised, repaired, and returned to service. In 1863, the *Pacific* was owned by S. J. Hensley of the Oregon and San Diego Steamship Line. She was purchased by Holladay and Brenham, probably in 1867, and was sold by them to the Pacific Mail in 1872. Her new owners placed her on the San Francisco–San Diego "branch" service until she was sold to Goodall, Nelson and Perkins in 1875. The *Pacific* was sunk in collision with the ship *Orpheus* near Cape Flattery on November 4, 1875, going down with a loss of over 250 lives.

Panama

Wooden side-wheel steamer; 2 decks, 3 masts, round stern; 1,087 $^{31}\!/_{95}$ tons; 200 ft. 4 in. × 33 ft. 10½ in. × 20 ft. 2 in. (1848); 887 $^{93}\!/_{100}$ tons (1865); mean draft 9 ft. 6 in.; one side-lever engine; diameter of cylinder 5 ft. 10 in., length of stroke 8 ft.; diameter of paddle wheels 26 ft.; 208 nominal h.p.; cost $211,356.

Built by William H. Webb, New York, for the Pacific Mail Steamship Company. Keel laid February 21, 1848. Launched July 29, 1848. Sailed from New York for San Francisco December 1, 1848, but returned under sail on December 25, having broken her cylinder and cylinder top. Repairs completed, she sailed a second time for San Francisco on February 15, 1849, arriving June 4. The *Panama* was in regular service between San Francisco and Panama for the Pacific Mail from 1849 until 1853, made a single voyage in 1854, and in 1856 and 1857 was spare steamer at Panama for the Pacific Mail. From 1858 until February, 1861, she was employed between San Francisco, the Columbia River, and Puget Sound. In February, 1861, she was sold to Holladay and Flint. The *Panama* was presented to the Mexican government in 1868 by Holladay and Brenham, armed with two 30-pounder Parrott guns and four 12-pound long guns, as part of an agreement in relation to a mail contract. She was placed in commission as the revenue and transport steamer *Juarez*.

Philadelphia

Wooden side-wheel steamer; 2 decks, 3 masts, round stern, figurehead; 897 $^{68}\!/_{95}$ tons; 190.8 ft. × 31.5 ft. × 15.7½ ft. (1850); lengthened in 1851; 1,238 $^{10}\!/_{95}$ tons; 231 ft. × 33 ft. 4 in. × 18 ft. 3 in.;* two side-lever engines built by Marrick and Towne, Philadelphia; diameter of cylinders 4 ft. 8 in.; length of stroke 6 ft. 9 in.; diameter of paddle wheels 27 ft.; 252 nominal h.p.; cost $180,000.

Built by Vaughn and Lynn, Philadelphia, in 1849. Purchased by Howland and Aspinwall January 29, 1850, for $190,000 to be placed on the run between New York and Chagres. Purchased in January, 1851, by the United States Mail Steamship Company for $187,500. She was lengthened by her new owners and placed in the New Orleans–Chagres service. She continued to operate on this run at least until 1860. Chartered by the Quartermaster's Department, War Department, in 1861 and 1862 at $1,000 to $800 per day. Broken up in 1866.

Pioneer

Wooden screw steamer; 3 decks, 3 masts, round stern, round tuck, full-length-man figurehead; 1,833 $^{17}\!/_{95}$ tons; 218 ft. 4 in. × 42 ft. 6 in. × 29 ft.; mean draft 19 ft.; two vertical direct-action trunk engines (cylinders over cranks); diameter of cylinders 7 ft. ½ in., diameter of trunks 3 ft. 3 in., length of stroke 4 ft. 3 in.; diameter of propeller 16 ft.

---

* The dimensions after lengthening are not based on official figures.

Built by Jacob Bell, New York, for Captain Asa Eldridge. Launched April 3, 1851. Purchased by Spofford, Tileston and Company in 1852. She made one voyage from New York to Liverpool and one from New York to Chagres in January and February, 1852. The *Pioneer* sailed from New York for San Francisco on March 19, 1852, via Rio de Janeiro and Panama. She was purchased by Vanderbilt after leaving New York but was lost in San Simeon Bay, August 17, 1852, without having reached San Francisco. The hull was later salvaged.

Prometheus

Wooden side-wheel steamer; 3 decks, 3 masts, round stern, serpent head; 1,207 $^{61}\!\!/_{95}$ tons; 230 ft. 6 in. × 33 ft. × 20 ft. 2 in.; two vertical-beam engines; diameter of cylinders 3 ft. 6 in., length of stroke 10 ft.

Built by Jeremiah Simonson, New York, for Cornelius Vanderbilt. Launched August 3, 1850. Built for the service between New York and San Juan de Nicaragua, and inaugurated it with her sailing of December 26, 1850. The *Prometheus* continued to operate between New York and San Juan for Vanderbilt and later for Charles Morgan, until September, 1854, when she was placed on the line between New Orleans and San Juan. The date at which she was condemned and withdrawn from service is not clear.

Republic

Wooden side-wheel steamer; 2 decks, 3 masts, square stern, figurehead; 852 $^{47}\!\!/_{95}$ tons; 200 ft. 10 in. × 29 ft. 9 in. × 14 ft. 10½ in.; mean draft 11 ft. 9 in.; two oscillating engines built by Murray and Hazlehurst, Baltimore; diameter of cylinders 4 ft. 6 in., length of stroke 6 ft.; diameter of paddle wheels 25 ft.; 225 nominal h.p.; cost $210,000.

Built at Baltimore in 1849 for the Baltimore Steam Packet Company, G. S. Norris being listed as owner. Sailed on her first trip to Charleston on September 29, 1849. Early in 1850, she was sold to Howland and Aspinwall [*sic*] for $135,000. She was sent to the Pacific coast, arriving at Panama on July 15, 1850, ninety-three days from New York via Rio de Janeiro and Valparaiso. She now entered the service between Panama and San Francisco for George Law. Sold to the Pacific Mail Steamship Company in January, 1851, for $197,000, and entered its service in May of that year. She was employed by her new owners chiefly in the local coastwise service north and south of San Francisco with occasional trips to Panama as late as 1855. At the time of her sale to Holladay and Flint in 1861 the *Republic* was employed on the line between San Francisco and Oregon. In 1864 her engines were removed and placed in the *Del Norte,* and in May, 1866, the caulked and patched hull of the *Republic* was towed to Acapulco to serve as a coal hulk and supply ship for the California, Oregon and Mexican Steamship Company.

Rising Star

Wooden side-wheel steamer; 3 decks, 3 masts, round stern, plain head; 2,726 $^{66}\!\!/_{100}$ tons; 303.54 ft. × 43.66 ft. × 23 ft.; vertical-beam engine built by the Etna Iron Works; diameter of cylinder 8 ft. 4 in., length of stroke 12 ft.

Built by Roosevelt, Joyce and Waterbury, New York, in 1865, for the New York Mail Steamship Company. She was sold to the Pacific Mail and operated between New York and Aspinwall from December, 1866, through 1869. The *Rising Star* was sold to John Roach in February, 1875, for $40,000. It has been suggested that this was in part payment for one of the Pacific Mail's new steamers. Broken up in 1877.

S.S. Lewis

Wooden screw steamer; 3 decks, 3 masts, square stern, billethead; 1,103 77⁄95 tons; 216.9 ft. × 32.6 ft. × 16.3 ft.; deckhouse 130 ft. long; geared-beam engine built by J. T. Sutton and Company, Philadelphia; 2 cylinders, diameter 5 ft., length of stroke 3 ft. 4 in.; 500 nominal h.p.; built of white oak, iron fastened.

Built at Philadelphia by Captain R. F. Loper, hull by Birely and Sons, for the New England Ocean Steamship Company, Herndon and Company's Boston–Liverpool line. Launched June 12, 1851. Christened *Samuel S. Lewis*. Sailed from Philadelphia for Boston September 13, 1851. On the failure of the New England Ocean Steamship Company, the ship was purchased by Vanderbilt, who sent her to the Pacific coast. She sailed from New York March 5, 1852, and arrived at San Francisco on July 7, one hundred and twenty-six days from New York, and twenty-six days from Panama. She operated between San Francisco and San Juan del Sur for Vanderbilt's Independent Line until she was lost three miles north of Bolinas on April 3, 1853, bound from San Juan del Sur to San Francisco. All her passengers were taken off, but the ship was a total loss.

Sacramento

Wooden side-wheel steamer; 2 decks, 2 masts, round stern, scroll head; 2,647 55⁄95 tons; 304 ft. × 42 ft. 6 in. × 29 ft. 2 in. (1864); 2,682 92⁄100 tons (1865); beam over guards 66 ft.; mean draft when launched 7 ft. 1 in.; vertical-beam engine built by the Novelty Iron Works; diameter of cylinder 8 ft. 4 in., length of stroke 12 ft.

Built by William H. Webb at Webb and Bell's yard, Greenpoint, Long Island, for the Pacific Mail Steamship Company. Launched May 8, 1863. Cleared New York for San Francisco June 14, 1864, and arrived via Callao and Panama on September 7. The *Sacramento* was engaged in the Pacific Mail's service between San Francisco and Panama from that time through 1869. She was wrecked on Geronimo Island, Lower California, on December 5, 1872, but with no loss of life.

St. Louis

Wooden side-wheel steamer; 2 decks, 3 masts, round stern, no head; 1,621 14⁄95 tons (1854); 1,771 91⁄100 tons; 266.4 ft. × 35.6 ft. × 15.9 ft. (1865); two vertical-beam engines built by the Morgan Iron Works; diameter of cylinders 4 ft. 2 in., length of stroke 10 ft.; cost $271,000.

Built by Jacob A. Westervelt, New York, for the Pacific Mail Steamship Company. Launched February 1, 1854. Although intended for service in the Pacific, the *St. Louis* was chartered to the New York and Havre Steam Navigation Company in place of the *Franklin*, sailing from New York for Havre on August 1, 1854. Made occasional voyages from New York to Aspinwall in the years 1855–1859, being used as a spare steamer, having been sold to the United States Mail Steamship Company in August, 1855, for $250,000. The *St. Louis* began fitting for a voyage to the Pacific in 1860, the rumor being that her owner, Marshall O. Roberts, intended to use her on a line between Panama and Valparaiso with the *Moses Taylor*. She sailed from New York for San Francisco on November 22, 1860, and arrived February 9, 1861, via Rio de Janeiro, Lota, and Panama. She had returned to the ownership of the Pacific Mail by this time and operated between San Francisco and Panama until 1866. She was dismantled at Panama in 1878.

San Francisco (1st)

Wooden side-wheel steamer; 3 decks, 2 masts, round stern, no head; 2,272 $14/95$ tons; 281 ft. 5 in. × 41 ft. × 24 ft. 10 in.; two oscillating engines built by the Morgan Iron Works; diameter of cylinders 5 ft. 5 in., length of stroke 8 ft.; diameter of paddle wheels 25 ft.; each engine 1,000 h.p.; staterooms for 350 cabin passengers; berths for 1,000 steerage; licensed to carry 1,600 passengers.

Built by William H. Webb, New York, for the Pacific Mail Steamship Company. Keel laid February 5, 1853. Launched June 9, 1853. Sailed from New York for San Francisco on December 21, 1853, with Companies A, B, D, G, H, I, K, and L of the Third Regiment, United States Artillery: 500 men and 21 women and children aboard in all. Encountered severe gales in the Atlantic, was disabled, and lay helpless and foundering from December 23, 1853, until January 5, 1854. About two hundred lives were lost before those on board were taken off and the ship abandoned.

San Francisco (2nd)

Wooden side-wheel steamer; 2 decks, 2 masts, round stern, plain head; 1,137 $15/100$ tons; 219 ft. × 35.5 ft. × 21.5 ft.; one side-lever engine built by Merrick and Son, Philadelphia; diameter of cylinder 6 ft. 8 in., length of stroke 8 ft.; maximum speed 9.5 knots per hour; brig-rigged.

Built at Philadelphia in 1853 by J. W. Lyon as the *Keystone State*. Owned by the Ocean Steam Navigation Company. Chartered, then sold to the United States Navy in 1861. Cost to Navy $125,000. Served as a gunboat during the Civil War. Sold at auction to Marshall O. Roberts September 15, 1865, for $54,000. Renamed *San Francisco* and entered service between New York and San Juan de Nicaragua for the North American Steamship Company in October, 1866. She continued in this until March, 1868. She was burned for her metal at Boston in 1879.

Santiago de Cuba

Wooden side-wheel steamer; 2 decks, 2 masts, round stern, no head; 1,567 $11/95$ tons; 229 ft. × 38 ft. × 19 ft. (1861); 1,627 $44/100$ tons (1865); draft 15 ft.; vertical-beam engine built by the Neptune Iron Works; diameter of cylinder 5 ft. 6 in., length of stroke 11 ft.; maximum speed 14 knots, average speed 8 knots; hull built of white oak; brigantine-rigged.

Built by Jeremiah Simonson at Greenpoint, Long Island, in 1861 for Valiente and Company for service between New York and Santiago. Purchased by the

Navy Department September 6, 1861, for $200,000 and served as a gunboat during the Civil War. Sold at auction at Philadelphia on September 21, 1865, for $108,000. Acquired by Marshall O. Roberts, who altered her for passenger traffic by the addition of mess houses, a cabin and spar deck. In November, 1865, she entered the service between New York and San Juan de Nicaragua for the Central American Transit Company. After August, 1866, she continued on the same route for the North American Steamship Company, changing her terminus to Aspinwall from December, 1867, until withdrawn in October, 1868. She made one voyage from New York to Havre in 1870, and in 1877 she was converted into a screw steamer at New York. Her beam engine was placed in the excursion steamer *Columbia* of the Rockaway Line. In 1886 she was converted into a barge and renamed *Marion*.

Sarah Sands

Iron screw steamer; 4 masts; bark-rigged, fourth mast being forward; 1,400 tons; 215 ft. × 32 ft. × 19 ft. 6 in.; height of spar deck 7 ft. 6 in.;* oscillating engine directly connected with the propeller shaft; diameter of cylinder 4 ft. 2 in., length of stroke 3 ft.; diameter of propeller 14 ft.; 200 nominal h.p.; bunker capacity 300 tons; clencher-built, and double riveted. Watertight compartments on lower, main, and spar decks. The forward cabin ran the full width of the ship, making possible three rows of tables, seating seventy in all.

Built by James Hudson and Company at Brunswick Dock, Liverpool, England. Launched September, 1846. Sands and Company were the largest owners of the ship in 1847. She sailed on her first voyage from Liverpool to New York on January 20, 1847, arriving February 10. Continued to operate across the Atlantic until December, 1849, when she was chartered by the Empire City Line and sent to San Francisco, where she arrived June 5, 1850. After operating from San Francisco to Panama for the Empire City Line until October, 1850, the *Sarah Sands* was purchased by the Pacific Mail, which operated her until July, 1851. She was sold, crossed to Australia, and returned to England, where she was again engaged in the Liverpool–New York service in April, 1852. The *Sarah Sands* also sailed between England and Canada before she was chartered by the British government for trooping service in the Crimean War. In 1857, while carrying troops to India, she was gutted by fire, but remained afloat and reached Mauritius in November, 1857. There her engines were removed, and she returned to England under sail. She was wrecked near Bombay in 1858.

Senator

Wooden side-wheel steamer; 754 87/95 tons; 219 ft. 5 in. × 30 ft. 4 in. × 12 ft. 2 in. (1848); 901 69/100 tons (1865); vertical-beam engine built by R. Duncan and Company; diameter of cylinder 4 ft. 2 in., length of stroke 11 ft.; 450 h.p.; schooner-rigged.

Built by William H. Brown, New York, in 1848. Operated by James Cunningham of East Boston, for whom she was built, from Boston to Portland, Belfast, Bangor, and Saint John, New Brunswick. Purchased by Lafayette Maynard

---

* Tonnage and dimensions are not based on official records.

late in 1848, and after serving for a short time on Long Island Sound early in 1849, she sailed from New York for San Francisco on March 10, 1849. Calling at Rio de Janeiro, San Carlos de Acud, and Valparaiso, the *Senator* reached Panama on September 14, 1849. She sailed from Panama on October 4 with 520 passengers, and arrived at San Francisco on October 27. From that time until 1854 the *Senator* ran between San Francisco and Sacramento. In 1854 she was purchased by the California Steam Navigation Company, and from 1855 until 1882 she plied between San Francisco and San Diego, calling at intermediate ports. In the course of these years, she was owned by S. J. Hensley, Holladay and Brenham, the Pacific Mail Steamship Company, and Goodall, Nelson and Perkins. In 1882, the engines of the *Senator* were removed, and she was temporarily rigged as a barkentine in 1884 for the voyage to New Zealand, where she was to become a coal barge.

Sierra Nevada

Wooden side-wheel steamer; 2 decks, 3 masts, round stern, flying-eagle head; $1,256\,7\%_{95}$ tons; 223 ft. 2 in. × 34 ft. 2 in. × 17 ft. 1 in. (1852); $1,394\,87\!/_{100}$ tons (1865); two vertical-beam engines built by the Morgan Iron Works; diameter of cylinders 3 ft. 6 in., length of stroke 10 ft.; accommodations for 570 steerage passengers; cost $210,000.

Built by William Collyer, New York, and launched as the *Texas* on October 25, 1851, S. Dayton, owner. Intended for Charles Morgan's New Orleans–Texas service. Operated from New York to Chagres from February until October, 1852, by the Empire City Line. Originally advertised for this line as the *Quartz Rock*. Made trial trip as *Sierra Nevada* on February 7, 1852. Purchased by Vanderbilt and sent to San Francisco, where she arrived March 23, 1853. Immediately entering the San Francisco–San Juan del Sur service, she remained in it until March, 1857. Purchased by the Pacific Mail in 1860, and placed in the San Francisco–Oregon service. In February, 1861, the *Sierra Nevada* was sold to Holladay and Brenham. She was wrecked on a reef seventy-five miles south of Monterey on October 17, 1869.

Sonora

Wooden side-wheel steamer; 3 decks, 2 masts, round stern, no head; $1,616\,7\%_{95}$ tons; 269 ft. × 36 ft. 2 in. × 24 ft.; two vertical-beam engines built by the Morgan Iron Works; diameter of cylinders 4 ft. 2 in., length of stroke 10 ft.; cost $302,000.

Built by J. A. Westervelt and Company, New York, for the Pacific Mail Steamship Company. Launched October 1, 1853. Cleared New York for San Francisco on March 11, 1854, and arrived May 31. The *Sonora* was placed in the San Francisco–Panama service and remained in it until May, 1863. She made a single voyage to Panama with troops in 1865. In 1868 she was dismantled and broken up on the beach at Sausalito.

Star of the West

Wooden side-wheel steamer; 3 decks, 2 masts, round stern, no head; $1,172\,53\%_{95}$ tons; 228 ft. 4 in. × 32 ft. 8 in. × 24 ft. 6 in.; two vertical-beam engines built by the Allaire Iron Works; cost $250,000.

Built by Jeremiah Simonson, New York, for Vanderbilt. Launched June 17, 1852. Originally laid down as the *San Juan*. Entered the service between New York and San Juan de Nicaragua for Vanderbilt on October 20, 1852, and continued in it for Charles Morgan after July, 1853, until March, 1856. She began running from New York to Aspinwall for the United States Mail Steamship Company in June, 1857. When that company withdrew from the New York–Aspinwall service in September, 1859, the *Star of the West* was placed on the New York–Havana–New Orleans line. She was chartered by the Navy Department to carry reinforcements to Fort Sumter in January, 1861, and was afterward sent to Texas to bring north a force of United States troops. When she was under charter to the Quartermaster's Department, War Department, her owners received $1,000 per day. She was seized by the Confederates, who turned her into a receiving ship at New Orleans. In order to prevent her falling into Union hands upon the capture of New Orleans in 1862, the *Star of the West* was burned.

Tennessee (1st)

Wooden side-wheel steamer; 2 decks, 3 masts, round stern, billethead; 1,275 $\frac{1}{95}$ tons; 211 ft. 10 in. × 35 ft. 8 in. × 22 ft.; draft 12 ft.; side-lever engine built by the Novelty Iron Works; diameter of cylinder 6 ft. 3 in., length of stroke 8 ft.; diameter of paddle wheels 31 ft.; 239 nominal h.p. Sharp ends but full amidships with bottom inclining to be flat, making her draft light and securing less variation between light and loaded. Built with accommodations for 200 passengers, but enlarged in 1849 to carry 200 cabin and 350 steerage passengers.

Built by William H. Webb, New York, for the Savannah Steam Navigation Company. Keel laid June 20, 1848. Launched October 25, 1848. Intended for service between New York and Savannah in connection with the *Cherokee* and sailed on her first voyage March 22, 1849. In October, 1849, the *Tennessee* was purchased by the Pacific Mail for $200,000 and sailed for San Francisco December 6, 1849. She arrived at Panama on March 12, 1850, in fifty-seven days' running time from New York, via Rio de Janeiro and Valparaiso, and reached San Francisco April 14. The *Tennessee* operated for the Pacific Mail between Panama and San Francisco until she went aground in a dense fog at Tagus Beach, Bolinas Bay, about four miles north of the entrance of San Francisco Bay on March 6, 1853. Her passengers, mail, and baggage were taken off, but the ship broke up.

Tennessee (2nd)

Wooden side-wheel steamer; 2 decks, 2 masts, round stern, carved head; 1,149 $\frac{21}{95}$ tons; 210 ft. × 33 ft. 11 in. × 16 ft. 11½ in.

Built at Baltimore in 1853–1854 for J. Hooper. Operated between New York and San Juan de Nicaragua for Vanderbilt in October, 1853, and for Charles Morgan and Sons on the same route from December, 1856, to April, 1857, with a single voyage in the summer of 1857 on which she brought back to New York deserters from Walker's army. Captured at New Orleans by Farrugut in 1862 and converted into a warship. Renamed *Mobile* September 1, 1864. Sold at auction at New York to Russell Sturgis March 30, 1865, for $25,000. Renamed *Republic* and lost in October, 1865.

Texas

Wooden side-wheel steamer; 2 decks, 2 masts, round stern, scroll head; 1,151 $^{92}\!/_{95}$ tons; 216 ft. × 35 ft. × 17 ft. 6 in. (1852); 637 $^{10}\!/_{95}$ tons (1852, New Orleans).

Built by Thomas Collyer, New York, in 1851–1852, Charles Morgan, owner. Operated from New York to San Juan de Nicaragua for Vanderbilt and Charles Morgan from September, 1856, until April, 1857. Abandoned in sinking condition off Texas coast October 5, 1868.

Uncle Sam

Wooden side-wheel steamer; 3 decks, 3 masts, round stern, no head; 1,433 $^{44}\!/_{95}$ tons; 235 ft. 6 in. × 35 ft. 8 in. × 22 ft.; engine built by the Allaire Iron Works; diameter of cylinder 5 ft. 6 in., length of stroke 11 ft.; diameter of paddle wheels 32 ft. Built to carry 800 pasengers. Cost $160,000.

Built by Perine, Patterson and Stack, Williamsburg, New York, for Edward Mills. Launched September 28, 1852. Operated by Mills from New York to Aspinwall from December, 1852, until May, 1853. Sent to the Pacific and sailed between San Francisco and Panama for the Independent Opposition Line from September, 1853, until September, 1854, when she was sold to Vanderbilt and placed on his Nicaragua Steamship Company line between San Francisco and San Juan del Sur. She made her last voyage for Vanderbilt in March, 1856. In May and June, 1856, the *Uncle Sam* made a voyage to Panama for unnamed operators, and then was not employed on the route again until she began to sail for the New York and California Steamship Company in May, 1859, on the Panama route. In January of 1860 she made one voyage for the Atlantic and Pacific Steamship Company, and by August of that year she had been purchased by the Pacific Mail and was operating for them. She made her last voyage to Panama in December, 1861. In February, 1866. the *Uncle Sam* was sold by the Pacific Mail to James S. Hermann and Company of Panama, who loaded her with barrels of beef, pork, wine, and ship's bread, and although she cleared for Chile, it was suspected that her cargo was destined for Spanish men-of-war off the west coast of South America. The *Uncle Sam* was lost in 1876.

Unicorn

Wooden side-wheel steamer; 650 tons; 162 ft. × 23 ft. × 16 ft.;* double engine; 250 h.p.; accommodations for 101 passengers.

Built at Greenock, Scotland, in 1838. Operated between Liverpool and Glasgow. Purchased by the British and North American Steamship Company (Cunard Line), and sailed from Liverpool for Halifax and Boston on May 16, 1840, as the pioneer of the service. Operated in the Cunard's intermediate

---

* Tonnage and dimensions not based on official figures.

service between Quebec, Pictou, and Halifax from 1840 until 1846. Sent from New York to California by Cunard, sailing April 23, 1849. Chartered by the Pacific Mail before arrival in San Francisco, December 1, 1849. Purchased by the Pacific Mail in 1850. Operated occasionally between San Francisco and Panama until April, 1853, when, having been sold, she was sent from Panama to Australia, later returning to England. The *Unicorn* was said to have ended her days as a steam corvette in the Portuguese navy.

Union (1st)

Wooden screw steamer; 2 decks, 3 masts, carved eagle on stern, scroll head; 593 $\frac{49}{95}$ tons; 180 ft. × 26.2 ft. × 13.1 ft.; mean draft 11 ft.; two direct-acting engines with cylinders over cranks built by Rainey, Neafie and Company; diameter of cylinders 2 ft. 10 in., length of stroke 2 ft. 10 in.; diameter of propeller 10 ft.; 70 nominal h.p.

Built at Philadelphia in 1849–1850. Richard F. Loper, owner; E. Lincoln, Samuel W. Reynolds, Ernest Zachrisson, and James Marks were part owners by the end of 1850. Cleared New York for San Francisco October 31, 1850, arriving April 2, 1851. She made two voyages to Panama for the People's Line. When she was sailing for the Independent Line, the *Union* was wrecked on July 5, 1851, at San Quentin, about six miles from Rosario, Lower California, when southbound for Panama. The ship went aground in the night owing to the negligence of the intoxicated crew, and though all passengers, crew, and treasure were safely landed, the ship broke up.

Union (2nd)

Wooden side-wheel steamer; 1 deck, 3 masts, round stern, flying-eagle head; 1,200 $\frac{59}{95}$ tons; 215 ft. × 34 ft. × 22 ft.; draft when ready for sea 13 ft.; two side-lever engines built by the Allaire Iron Works; diameter of cylinders 5 ft., length of stroke 7 ft.; diameter of paddle wheels 29 ft.; 313 nominal h.p.; sharp stem, small bowsprit, figurehead formed by a gilt eagle about to take flight, stern decorated with coat of arms. On deck were the dining saloon for officers, and rooms of the captain, doctor, and purser. On deck aft was a saloon surrounded by staterooms. On the main deck were the dining saloon and the main aft saloon with a row of staterooms on each side. Topgallant forcastle with bunks for the crew and promenade deck with a large number of skylights for the saloons.

Built by William H. Webb, New York, for Spofford and Tileston. Keel laid April 19, 1850. Launched September 9, 1850. Built for the run between New York and New Orleans. Made three voyages from New York to Aspinwall in the spring and summer of 1853. Sold to foreign owners in 1856.

United States

Wooden side-wheel steamer; 2 decks, 3 masts, round stern, billethead; 1,216 $\frac{37}{95}$ tons; 230 ft. × 33 ft. 2 in. × 19 ft. 8 in.; vertical-beam engine built by the Morgan Iron Works; diameter of cylinder 5 ft., length of stroke 12 ft.

Built by Thomas Collyer, New York, in 1851 as the *Bienville*. Owned by

Henry W. Johnson and others. Chartered to the New York and Galway Line in November, 1851. Operated between New York and Chagres from January, 1852, until February, 1853. Sold to Cuban owners in 1855 and renamed *Mexico*.

Washington

Wooden side-wheel steamer; 3 masts, square stern, figurehead; 1,640 $^{71}\!/_{95}$ tons; 230 ft. 5 in. × 38 ft. 8½ in. × 27 ft.; mean draft 19 ft. 6 in.; two side-lever engines built by the Novelty Iron Works; diameter of cylinders 6 ft., length of stroke 10 ft.; diameter of paddle wheels 34 ft. 8 in.; 474 nominal h.p.; cost $390,000.

Built by Westervelt and Mackay, New York, for the Ocean Steam Navigation Company. Launched January 30, 1847. Operated in the transatlantic service from 1847 until 1857, when the line was withdrawn owing to non-renewal of the subsidy. Sold to the California, New York and European Steamship Company, of which Henry Randall was agent, in August, 1858. Made two voyages from New York to San Juan de Nicaragua and Aspinwall for J. P. Yelverton in November, December, and January, 1858–1859. The *Washington* was sold to the Pacific Mail Steamship Company in 1860 and was sent to San Francisco, arriving on October 24 of that year. Being unfitted for the Panama service, the *Washington* made only two voyages in it before being laid up. Sold to Charles Hare, she was towed to Rincon Point, San Francisco, to be broken up in January, 1864. It was reported that her good timbers were to be used to build a 1,100-ton screw steamer, which was to be fitted with the engine of the Russian *Novik*, wrecked at Point Reyes.

Western Metropolis

Wooden side-wheel steamer; 2 decks, 2 masts, round stern, no head; 2,269 $^{69}\!/_{95}$ tons (1863); 2,092 $^{89}\!/_{100}$ tons; 284 ft. × 41 ft. × 23.3 ft. (1865). Engine perhaps brought from a Great Lakes steamer. Diameter of cylinder 6 ft. 2 in., length of stroke 12 ft.

Built in 1863 by F. T. Tucker, Brooklyn. L. Brown, owner. Made one voyage to San Juan de Nicaragua for the Central American Transit Company in February and March, 1865. Chartered to the Quartermaster's Department, War Department, in 1865 at $650 and $850 per day. Converted into a sailing vessel in 1878.

William Penn

Wooden screw steamer; 2 decks, 3 masts, square stern, billethead; 613 $^{16}\!/_{95}$ tons; 183 ft. × 26.4 ft. × 13.2 ft.

Built by Birely and Son, Philadalphia, in 1851. S. W. Reynolds, owner. Intended to operated between Philadelphia and Boston with the *Benjamin Franklin*, but this did not prove profitable. She made one voyage from New York to San Juan de Nicaragua and Chagres for Palmer and Company in March, 1852. Chartered to the French government in 1854. Sold to English owners in 1856.

Winfield Scott

Wooden side-wheel steamer; 3 decks, 3 masts, round stern, round tuck, man's bust figurehead; 1,291 5⁄95 tons; 225 ft. × 34 ft. 8 in. × 29 ft. 2 in.; draft 14 ft.; two side-lever engines built by the Morgan Iron Works; diameter of cylinders 5 ft. 6 in., length of stroke 8 ft.; 370 nominal h.p.; bunker capacity 300 tons; cargo capacity 400 tons; built of white oak, live oak, locust, cedar, and Georgia yellow pine. Double iron braced. The figurehead was a bust of Winfield Scott, placed in a niche at the stem. No bowsprit. The stern was ornamented with an American eagle and coat of arms. She was built with accommodations for 165 cabin and 150 steerage passengers. The dining saloon was 96 ft. long, and could seat over one hundred. At its after end was a private companionway and boudoir for ladies, and at the forward end were pantries and the main semi-circular companionway. On either side were staterooms which were lighted and ventilated from the sides and from the deck above. Between these rooms were corridors with lights and ventilators to throw light and air into the saloon. The drawing room was lighted and ventilated in the same manner. It had state-rooms on either side, leaving a room 80 ft. long by 14 ft. wide, with sofas on either side extending the whole length. At the after end, 18 ft. could be shut off by folding doors for ladies or families, while a semicircular companionway led from this room to the dining saloon and on deck. The forward saloon was similarly arranged for cabin passengers, except that in the after cabin, the berths were of Baker's patent variety, which supposedly always remained horizontal. The steerage accommodations were below.

Built by Westervelt and Mackay, New York, under the superintendence of Captain William Skiddy. Launched October 27, 1850. Charles Augustus Davis, Sidney Brooks, Theodore Dehan, Jacob A. Westervelt, Philip Woodhouse, William Skiddy, and Francis Skiddy, owners. The *Winfield Scott* was intended for service between San Francisco and Panama. Arriving at San Francisco April 28, 1852, she operated for the Independent Line until the end of that year, and for the New York and San Francisco Steamship Company from February until April, 1853. She was purchased by the Pacific Mail Steamship Company in July, 1853, and was lost on Anacapa Island when southbound for Panama on December 2 of that year. She struck in a dense fog, and though passengers, mail, and treasure were safely landed, the ship filled and sank.

Yankee Blade

Wooden side-wheel steamer; 3 decks, 3 masts, round stern, no figurehead; 1,767 38⁄95 tons; 274 ft. 5 in. × 34 ft. × 21 ft. 7 in.; engine built by the Allaire Iron Works; diameter of cylinder 6 ft. 4 in., length of stroke 12 ft.

Built by Perine, Patterson and Stack, Williamsburg, New York, in 1853. Owned by Edward Mills and made a single voyage from New York to Aspinwall for his Independent Opposition Line in December–January, 1853–1854. Sailed from New York for the Pacific on February 2, 1854, and arrived at San Fran-cisco May 4. Operated between San Francisco and Panama for the Independent Opposition Line and the Independent Steamship Company until she was wrecked, southbound, on Point Arguello, October 1, 1854. With her were lost thirty lives and $153,000 in specie.

APPENDIX II

PASSENGERS BY THE ISTHMIAN ROUTES, 1848–1869

THE FIGURES listed in the following table have been compiled from contemporary newspaper reports of departures and arrivals as printed in New York, Panama, and San Francisco. Since every voyage was not completely reported, the totals should be taken as only approximate. Even when the number of passengers on a particular steamer or a list of passengers was published, there are instances in which it seems clear that only first- and second-cabin passengers were considered, with the large number of steerage passengers omitted. A list of several hundred individual names is too often ended with the baffling phrase, "and many others." It was deemed sounder to leave the totals at an assured minimum rather than to venture into the field of conjecture for the production of a possible maximum figure.

Satisfactory official records are not available. The figures in parentheses are Custom House figures for San Francisco in the scattered years for which they are to be found in newspapers or elsewhere. For the arrivals, 1849–1850, Willard B. Farwell, "Cape Horn and Co-operative Mining," *Century Magazine*, n.s., XX, 593; for 1852, *San Francisco Prices Current and Shipping List*, December 31, 1852; for 1853, *ibid.*, December 30, 1853; for 1855, *ibid.*, June 29, October 4, November 3, and December 4, 1855, and January 3, 1856; for 1856, San Francisco *Mercantile Gazette and Shipping Register*, January 3, 1857; for 1857, *ibid.*, January 4, 1858; for 1858, *ibid.*, April 3, July 3, and October 4, 1858, and January 4, 1859; for 1859, San Francisco *Mercantile Gazette and Prices Current*, January 4, 1860; for 1860, *ibid.*, January 10, 1861; for 1861, *ibid.*, January 10, 1862; for 1862, *ibid.*, January 9, 1863; for 1863, *ibid.*, January 12, 1864; for 1864, *ibid.*, January 12, 1865; for 1867, J. Ross Browne, *Resources of the Pacific Slope* ... (New York, 1869), p. 291. In the tabulation which follows, the larger figure for each year, whether from Custom House, tabulation, or other source, is used since it seems clear that the figures are almost certainly minimal in each instance.

PASSENGERS, 1848–1869

Year	New York-San Francisco			San Francisco-New York		
	Number of Passengers			Number of Passengers		
	Via Panama	Via Nicaragua	Total	Via Panama	Via Nicaragua	Total
1848	335	......	335	......	......	......
1849	4,624	......	6,489	1,629	......	1,629
	(6,489)					
1850	11,229	......	13,809	7,770	......	7,770
	(13,809)					
1851	15,464	1,930	17,395	14,189	3,171	17,360
1852	21,263	10,563	34,794	11,845	5,921	17,766
	(24,231)			(11,549)	(4,988)	
1853	17,014	9,687	27,076	10,232	10,396	27,076
	(15,502)	(10,062)		(10,533)	(10,228)	
1854	18,445	13,063	31,508	10,808	9,248	20,056
1855	15,412	11,237	26,705	10,397	7,750	18,147
	(15,210)	(11,293)		(9,795)	(7,288)	
1856	18,090	4,523	22,613	12,245	3,530	17,778
	(17,233)	(4,148)		(12,468)	(5,310)	
1857	13,343	250	17,887	11,627	408	13,286
	(17,637)	(18)		(12,367)	(919)	
1858	20,596	......	24,621	8,030	......	10,411
	(24,621)			(10,408)	(3)	
1859	23,567	......	26,907	17,682	......	19,030
	(26,907)			(19,030)		
1860	16,257	......	20,092	11,213	......	11,213
	(20,092)			(10,084)		
1861	17,765	......	19,314	6,671	......	7,967
	(19,314)			(7,967)		
1862	17,328	562	18,865	5,959	500	7,861
	(18,303)			(7,361)		
1863	15,237	831	22,847	8,470	1,649	11,962
	(22,016)			(10,313)		
1864	20,643	295	24,589	12,671	1,625	14,923
	(23,573)	(1,016)		(12,627)	(2,252)	
1865	13,150	3,265	16,415	16,506	3,369	19,875
1866	22,889	3,612	26,501	12,450	4,757	17,207
1867	20,540	6,162	27,573	10,355	1,434	14,695
	(20,782)	(6,791)		(10,074)	(4,340)	
1868	38,680	1,715	40,395	18,243	3,975	22,218
1869 (to June 30)	12,744	......	12,744	4,724	......	4,724
Total	409,997	71,192	479,774	232,138	63,560	295,698

TREASURE SHIPMENTS FROM SAN FRANCISCO BY WAY OF THE ISTHMIAN ROUTES, 1849–1869*

Year	Via Panama	Via Nicaragua
1849	$ 4,140,200.00	. . . .
1850	26,573,000.00	. . . .
1851	33,407,240.00	$ 195,060.00
1852	37,076,629.00	119,071.00
1853	40,233,915.00	14,713,915.00
1854	27,033,944.00	20,890,944.00
1855	21,974,999.62	9,266,000.38
1856	43,540,621.00	1,018,679.00
1857	45,448,200.00	. . . .
1858	45,446,200.00	. . . .
1859	42,493,700.00	. . . .
1860	36,504,300.00	. . . .
1861	36,741,400.00	. . . .
1862	38,722,900.00	. . . .
1863	41,511,100.00	. . . .
1864	45,760,900.00	. . . .
1865	35,114,300.00	111,275.00
1866	37,323,400.00	. . . .
1867	30,724,700.00	. . . .
1868	27,129,500.00	. . . .
1869 (to June 30)	12,679,600.00	. . . .
Total†	$710,753,857.62	$46,314,942.38

* Based upon figures published in San Francisco newspapers, treasure shipments having been reported with the sailing of each steamer.
† Total treasure shipped from San Francisco by both routes in the period 1849–1869 was $757,068,800.00.

APPENDIX IV

BUILDERS OF STEAMERS SERVING ON THE ISTHMIAN ROUTES, 1848–1869

Port	Builder	Number of steamers	Total number of steamers
New York*	Bell	1	
	Bishop and Simonson.....	3	
	Brown, William H.	11	
	Brown and Bell..........	1	
	Capes and Allison........	2	
	Collyer, Thomas	5	
	Furness, William	1	
	Lawrence and Foulkes	1	
	Lawrence and Sneeden....	1	
	Perine, Patterson and Stack	5	
	Roosevelt, Joyce and Waterbury	2	
	Simonson, Jeremiah	10	
	Smith and Dimon	5	
	Steers, Henry	7	
	Tucker, F. T.	1	
	Webb, William H.	16	
	Webb and Bell	2	
	Westervelt, Jacob A.	6	
	Westervelt and Mackay ...	5	
	Builder unknown	2	87
Philadelphia	Birely	3	
	Cramp, Wharles and William	1	
	Davis and Burton	1	
	Lynn, J. W.	1	
	Vaughn and Lynn	1	
	Builder unknown	3	10
Baltimore	Builder unknown	3	3
Allowaystown, New Jersey	Reeves and Brothers	1	1
Glasgow, Scotland	Tod and McGregor	1	1
Greenock, Scotland	Builder unknown	1	1
Liverpool, England	James Hudson and Co. ...	1	1
Niagara-on-the-Lake, Ontario ..	Builder unknown	1	1
Portland, Maine	Builder unknown	1	1
Rochester, New York	Builder unknown	1	1
Wilmington, Delaware	Harlan and Hollingsworth.	1	1

* Including Brooklyn, Greenpoint, Hoboken, Williamsburg, etc.

108

ENGINE BUILDERS FOR STEAMERS ON THE ISTHMIAN ROUTES, 1848–1869

Place	Builder	Number of engines	Total number of engines
New York	Archimedes Iron Works...	1	
	Allaire Iron Works.......	14	
	Coffee, E.	1	
	Cunningham, Belknap and Co.	1	
	Duncan, R.	1	
	Etna Iron Works.........	2	
	Hogg and Delamater.....	4	
	Morgan Iron Works......	15	
	Neptune Iron Works......	1	
	Novelty Iron Works......	22	
	Secor, T. F.	2	64
Philadelphia	Marrick and Towne......	1	
	Merrick and Son.........	1	
	Morris, I. P., and Co......	1	
	Rainey, Neafie and Co. ...	2	
	Sutton, J. T.	1	6
Baltimore	Murray and Hazlehurst ...	1	1
Wilmington	Harlan and Hollingsworth.	1	1
			72

NOTES

ABBREVIATIONS IN NOTES

B.L.   Bancroft Library, University of California, Berkeley.

H.L.   Henry E. Huntington Library, San Marino.

H.U.L.   Treasure Room, Harvard University Library, Cambridge.

N.R.L.   Office of Naval Records and Library, United States Navy Depart-
            ment, Washington, D.C.

P.O.L.   Library, United States Post Office Department, Washington, D.C.

NOTES TO CHAPTER I

OPENING THE PANAMA ROUTE

[1] *Niles' Weekly Register*, XXX (August 26, 1826), 447; J. Fred Rippy, *Rivalry of the United States and Great Britain over Latin America (1808–1830)* (Baltimore, 1929), p. 222.

[2] *New York Journal of Commerce*, November 28, 1829; Robert Greenhlagh Albion, *Square-Riggers on Schedule: the New York Sailing Packets to England, France, and the Cotton Ports* (Princeton, 1938), p. 62.

[3] Cave Johnson to George R. Ward, July 14, 1847, Cave Johnson to the Secretary of State, July 14, 1847, *in* C. Johnson, Letter Book, R 2, Postmaster General, March 31, 1847, to May 17, 1848, P.O.L.

[4] George Henry Preble, *A Chronological History of the Origin and Development of Steam Navigation* (Philadelphia, 1883), pp. 327–328; William Wheelwright, *Statements and Documents Relative to the Establishment of Steam Navigation on the Pacific; with Copies of Decrees of the Governments of Peru, Bolivia, and Chile, Granting Exclusive Privileges to the Undertaking* (London, 1838); Arthur C. Wardle, *Steam Conquers the Pacific; a Record of Maritime Achievement, 1840–1940* (London, 1940), pp. 13–66.

[5] Royal Mail Steam Packet Co., *A Link of Empire, or 70 Years of British Shipping; Souvenir of the 70th Year of Incorporation of the Royal Mail Steam Packet Company* (London, 1909), p. 2; T. A. Bushell, *"Royal Mail"; a Centenary History of the Royal Mail Line, 1839–1939* (London, 1939), pp. 86–89.

[6] *New York Herald*, November 11, 1848, January 31, 1849.

[7] *Treaties and Conventions Concluded between the United States of America and Other Powers, since July 4, 1776. With Notes Showing What Treaties or Parts of Treaties Have Been Abrogated, and Decisions thereupon*, 41st Cong., 3rd sess., S. Doc. 36 (Washington, 1871), p. 187.

[8] Cave Johnson [Advertisement for Mail Service to Europe and the Gulf of Mexico under Act of March 3, 1845], Washington, October 4, 1845, *in* Mail Routes (Appendix . . . Mails to Europe . . .), New York, 1845–1849 (cited hereafter as Mails to Europe), facing p. 361, P.O.L. Offers might stipulate an alternative point of origin at Charleston, Pensacola, or New Orleans.

[9] Kendall broke up his offer into sections, proposing to carry out the New York–Chagres service for $16,000 annually; from Panama to the mouth of the Columbia via the Hawaiian Islands for $42,000, including Callao for an additional $2,000; from the Hawaiian Islands to Canton for $25,000 a year, if an overland mail were established to Oregon. He offered to carry a mail agent free of charge, to start the service from any port on the Atlantic coast of the United States, and to call at one port on the west coast of Mexico between Panama and Oregon. (*Ibid.*, pp. 365–367.)

[10] *Ibid.*

[11] Amos Kendall to Cave Johnson, June 24, 1846, *in* C. Johnson, Letter Book, Q 2, Postmaster General, March 17, 1846, to March 30, 1847, P.O.L.

[12] Cave Johnson to G. W. Hopkins, June 26, 1846, *ibid.*

[13] *Congressional Globe*, 29th Cong., 1st sess., p. 1199.

[14] *Ibid.*, pp. 184, 692, 831–833, 1128, 1199; *ibid.*, 2nd sess., pp. 183, 480; *New York Herald*, February 25, 1847.

[15] 9 *U. S. Stat. at L.* (1851), 200–201.

[16] Mails to Europe, P.O.L., pp. 369–371.

[17] *Ibid.; Postmaster General's Report, 1847*, 30th Cong., 1st sess., Ex. Doc. 1 (Washington, 1848), pp. 1323–1328.

[18] 5 *U. S. Stat. at L.* (1850), 748–750.

[19] John H. Morrison, *History of American Steam Navigation* (New York, 1903), p. 408.

[20] *Congressional Globe*, 29th Cong., 1st sess., p. 966.

[21] *Ibid.*, 2nd sess., pp. 275, 324, 367, 422–423, 440, 478, 572, 574.

[22] *New York Herald*, March 5, 1847; David Budlong Tyler, *Steam Conquers the Atlantic* (New York and London, 1939), pp. 138, 146–147; *Congressional Globe*, 29th Cong., 2nd sess., pp. 440, 478, 574.

[23] 9 *U. S. Stat. at L.* (1851), 187–188.

[24] *New York Herald*, March 6, 1847.

[25] *Ibid.*, March 23, 1847.

[26] Cave Johnson to James Gadsden, April 9, 1847, Cave Johnson to James Gadsden, April 23, 1847, *in* C. Johnson, Letter Book, R 2, P.O.L.

[27] *New York Times*, January 17, 1881; David Budlong Tyler, *op. cit.*, p. 144.

[28] U. S. Circuit Court, *Sloo* vs. *Law and Others* (New York, 1849), pp. 3–8.

[29] J. Y. Mason to A. G. Sloo, August 20, 1847, *in* General Letter Book, no. 38, March 15, 1847, to October 2, 1847, Navy Department, N.R.L., p. 418; *Sloo* vs. *Law and Others*, p. 9.

[30] Robert Greenhalgh Albion, "Law, George," *Dictionary of American Biography* (New York, 1933), XI:39–40; *New York Herald*, February 9, 1852, June 2 and 5, 1855.

[31] Robert Greenhalgh Albion, "Roberts, Marshall Owen," *Dictionary of American Biography* (New York, 1935), XVI:11–12; *New York Herald*, July 17, 1841.

[32] *New York Herald*, January 4, 20, and February 13, 1850.

[33] *Ibid.*, March 7, 1848.

[34] *Ibid.*, March 23 and 24, 1848.

[35] John Y. Mason to J. M. Woodward, April 23, 1847, *in* General Letter Book, no. 38, N.R.L., p. 117.

[36] C. Morris to J. Y. Mason, Washington, July 20, 1848, *in* Captains' Letters, January–December, 1848, N.R.L., no. 118.

[37] Edward E. Dunbar, *The Romance of the Age; or the Discovery of Gold in California* (New York, 1867), pp. 49–54.

[38] C. Morris to J. Y. Mason, Washington, July 20, 1848, *in* Captains' Letters, January–December, 1848, N.R.L., no. 118; John Y. Mason to J. M. Woodward, Navy Department, June 17, 1847, *in* General Letter Book, no. 38, N.R.L., p. 238.

[39] J. Y. Mason to C. H. Todd, Navy Department, June 17 and 30, 1847, *ibid.*, pp. 238, 272–273.

[40] J. Y. Mason to C. H. Todd, Navy Department, July 15, 1847, *ibid.*, pp. 314–315.

[41] Edward E. Dunbar, *op. cit.*, pp. 49–54.

[42] C. Morris to J. Y. Mason, Washington, July 20, 1848, Captains' Letters, January–December, 1848, N.R.L., no. 118.

[43] J. Y. Mason to A. Harris, Navy Department, July 26, 1847, *in* General Letter Book, no. 38, N.R.L., p. 343.

[44] Agreement signed by Arnold Harris, Washington, July 7, 1847, notarized, *in* Miscellaneous Letters, June, 1848, N.R.L.

[45] J. Y. Mason to A. Harris, Navy Department, July 31, 1847, *in* General Letter Book, no. 38, N.R.L., p. 368.

[46] J. Y. Mason to Arnold Harris, Navy Department, August 7, 1847, *ibid.*, p. 388.

[47] J. Y. Mason to Arnold Harris, Navy Department, September 23, 1847, *ibid.*, p. 491.

⁴⁸ J. Y. Mason to Arnold Harris, Navy Department, November 6, 1847, *ibid.*, no. 39, October 4, 1847, to April 26, 1848, N.R.L., p. 62.

⁴⁹ J. Y. Mason to Joseph Bryan, agent for A. Harris, Navy Department, November 10, 1847, *ibid.*, p. 65.

⁵⁰ S. Ex. Doc. 50, ser. no. 619, pp. 54–55.

⁵¹ *Ibid.*, p. 55; J. Y. Mason to William H. Aspinwall, Navy Department, November 16, 1847, *in* General Letter Book, no. 39, October, 1847, to April 28, 1848, N.R.L., p. 85; J. Y. Mason to William H. Aspinwall, Navy Department, November 22, 1847, *ibid.*, p. 92.

⁵² J. Y. Mason to J. M. Woodward, Navy Department, November 13, 16, 1847, General Letter Book, no. 39, N.R.L., pp. 79, 84.

⁵³ J. Y. Mason to G. H. Todd, Navy Department, November 24, 1847, *ibid.*, p. 102.

⁵⁴ William H. Aspinwall to [John Y. Mason], February 7, 1848, *in* Miscellaneous Letters, February, 1848, N.R.L., no. 133; William H. Aspinwall to J. Y. Mason, June 21, 1848, *ibid.*, June, 1848, N.R.L., no. 133.

⁵⁵ William H. Aspinwall to Messrs. Robinson, Bissell and Co., June 13, 1850, *in* Presid't to A. Robins[on], B[issell] & Co., December, 1848, to November, 1850 (hereafter cited as Aspinwall-Robinson Letter Book), collection of Daulton Mann, New York.

⁵⁶ Richard J. Purcell, "Aspinwall, William Henry," *Dictionary of American Biography* (New York, 1928), I:396; Robert Greenhalgh Albion, *The Rise of New York Port [1815–1860]* (New York, 1939), pp. 174–175, 246; [Moses Yale Beach], *The Wealth and Biography of the Wealthy Citizens of New York* (10th ed.; New York, 1846), p. 2.

⁵⁷ Alfred Robinson, Statement of recollections on early years of California made by Alfred Robinson for Bancroft Library, 1878 (hereafter cited as Robinson, Statement), B.L., pp. 25–26.

⁵⁸ *New York Herald*, May 19, 1848.

⁵⁹ Cave Johnson to John Y. Mason, Secretary of the Navy, January 18, 1848, *in* C. Johnson, Letter Book, R 2, P.O.L.

⁶⁰ Cave Johnson to C. Gilliam, Agent for the Post Office Department, Oregon City, May 30, 1848, *ibid.*, S 2, May 18, 1848, to January 24, 1849, P.O.L.

⁶¹ Cave Johnson to J. Y. Mason [Post Office Department], May 31, 1848, *ibid.*

⁶² J. Y. Mason to Wm. H. Aspinwall, New York, Navy Department, June 10, 1848, *in* General Letter Book, no. 40, April 27, 1848, to November 20, 1848, N.R.L., pp. 114–116.

⁶³ *New York Herald*, April 2, 5, and 13, 1848.

⁶⁴ [Moses Yale Beach], *op. cit.*, p. 16.

⁶⁵ Pacific Mail Steamship Co., *Charter of the Pacific Mail Steam Ship Company, with its Amendments Inclusive of May 1st, 1866* (New York, 1867).

⁶⁶ Pacific Mail Steamship Co., *Report of Committee, October 12, 1854* (New York, 1854), pp. 12–13

⁶⁷ Navy Departments, Contracts, Transportation of Mail, April 20, 1847–October 5, 1860, N.R.L., pp. 1–8.

⁶⁸ C. Morris to John Y. Mason, Bureau of Construction and Repair, March 29, 1847, *in* Bureaux' Letters, January to June, 1847, N.R.L., no. 87.

⁶⁹ William Skiddy to J. Y. Mason, New York, February 4, 1848, *in* Miscellaneous Letters, February, 1848, N.R.L., no. 15.

⁷⁰ George Law to J. Y. Mason, New York, October 5, 1848, *ibid.*, October, 1848, N.R.L., no. 25.

⁷¹ 32nd Cong., 1st sess., S. Doc. 50, pp. 55–56.

⁷² See Appendix I.

[73] William H. Aspinwall to J. Y. Mason, New York, September 19, 1848, *in* Miscellaneous Letters, September, 1848, N.R.L., no. 125.

[74] J. Y. Mason to Isaac McKeever, Navy Department, September 21, 1848, *in* Officers, Ships of War, no. 42, June 12, 1848, to April 16, 1849, N.R.L., p. 200.

[75] I. McKeever, W. L. Hudson, T. Hartt to John Y. Mason, Navy Yard, New York, September 28, 1848, *in* Commandants of Navy Yards, New York, 1848, N.R.L., no. 125.

[76] J. Y. Mason to M. C. Perry, Navy Department, November 20, 1848, *in* Officers, Ships of War, no. 42, N.R.L., pp. 296–297.

[77] M. C. Perry to J. Y. Mason, New York, December 6, 1848, *in* Captains' Letters, January–December, 1848, N.R.L., no. 196.

[78] *New York Herald*, June 14, 1848.

[79] *Ibid.*, June 17, 1848.

[80] *Ibid.*, July 17, 1848.

[81] *Congressional Globe*, 30th Cong., 1st sess., p. 954.

[82] *New York Herald*, July 21, 1848.

[83] *Congressional Globe*, 30th Cong., 1st sess., pp. 964–965.

[84] *New York Herald*, July 22, 1848; *Congressional Globe*, 30th Cong., 1st sess., pp. 982–983.

[85] *Statutes at Large and Treaties of the United States of America, December 1, 1845, to March 3, 1851* (Boston, 1851), IX: 267–268.

[86] 32nd Cong., 1st sess., S. Doc. 50, pp. 56–58; P. M. Wetmore to John Y. Mason, Navy Agent's Office, New York, October 4, 1848, *in* Navy Agents and Storekeepers, 1848, N.R.L., no. 162.

NOTES TO CHAPTER II

PIONEER YEARS, 1849–1851

[1] J. Y. Mason to Robert C. Schenck, January 11, 1847, *in* General Letter Book, no. 37, September 25, 1846, to March 15, 1847, N.R.L., p. 266.

[2] *New York Herald*, February 27, 1847.

[3] Arthur B. Stout, "Journal," quoted at length in *First Steamship Pioneers* (San Francisco, 1874), p. 88; J. Y. Mason to William H. Aspinwall, September 21, 1848, *in* General Letter Book, no. 40, April 27, 1848, to November 20, 1848, N.R.L., p. 373; *New York Herald*, October 6 and 7, 1848; William Skiddy to J. Y. Mason, October 25, 1848, *in* Navy Agents and Storekeepers, 1848, N.R.L.

[4] John Haskell Kemble, *The Genesis of the Pacific Mail Steamship Company* (San Francisco, 1934), pp. 15–18.

[5] *New York Herald*, November 30, December 1, 2, and 27, 1848, January 6 and February 18, 1849.

[6] Kemble, *op. cit.*, pp. 26–27.

[7] J. Y. Mason to George Law, September 20, 1848, *in* General Letter Book, no. 40, N.R.L., p. 404.

[8] J. Y. Mason to Messrs. George Law, Marshall O. Roberts, Navy Department, October 31, 1848, *ibid.*, p. 469.

[9] J. Y. Mason to George Law, Navy Department, November 21, 1848, *ibid.*, no. 41, November 21, 1848, to June 30, 1849, N.R.L., p. 7; J. Y. Mason to George Law, Navy Department, December 2, 1848, *ibid.*, p. 13; *New York Herald*, December 1 and 2, 1848.

[10] Hubert Howe Bancroft, *History of California* (San Francisco, 1888), VI: 113–116.

¹¹ *New York Herald*, March 4, 1849.

¹² *Ibid.*, January 16, 1849; Alfred Robinson, Statement of recollections of California, B.L., p. 23.

¹³ William H. Aspinwall to Alfred Robinson, December 8, 1848, *in* Aspinwall-Robinson Letter Book, collection of Daulton Mann, New York.

¹⁴ *New York Herald*, March 4, 1849.

¹⁵ *Ibid.*, February 15, 1849.

¹⁶ Victor M. Berthold, *The Pioneer Steamer "California," 1848–1849* (Boston and New York, 1932), pp. 37–42, 47–50.

¹⁷ *San Francisco Alta California*, February 1, 1849.

¹⁸ *Ibid.*, March 1, 1849.

¹⁹ Berthold, *op. cit.*, p. 63; R. H. Pearson, "Memoir," *San Francisco Daily Evening Bulletin*, March 3, 1868.

²⁰ *New York Herald*, March 25, 1849.

²¹ *Ibid.*, May 29, 1849.

²² Pearson, "Memoir."

²³ *New York Herald*, February 18, 1849.

²⁴ M. Hall McAllister, "Diary," in *Re-union of the Pioneer Panama Passengers on the Fourth of June, 1874* (San Francisco, 1874), pp. 13–17; *New York Herald*, June 26, 1849.

²⁵ *New York Herald*, February 15 and 18, 1849.

²⁶ *Ibid.*, April 8 and 10, 1849.

²⁷ *Ibid.*, November 15, 1848.

²⁸ John T. Little, Statement of events in the first years of American occupation of California, B.L., p. 3; *New York Herald*, June 26, 1849.

²⁹ *New York Herald*, February 16, 18, April 8, 10, and May 10, 1849.

³⁰ *Ibid.*, April 10, 1849.

³¹ *Panama Echo*, April 6, 1850, quoted in *San Francisco Daily Pacific News*, April 30, 1850.

³² *San Francisco Alta California*, July 19, 1849.

³³ *Ibid.*, December 22, 1849.

³⁴ George Law, M. O. Roberts, E. Crosswell, *United States Mail Steamships* (New York, 1850), pp. 4–7, 19–20.

³⁵ William H. Aspinwall to Jonathan Meredith, New York, January 10, 1848 [*sic*], *in* Jonathan Meredith Papers, Manuscripts Division, Library of Congress. From internal evidence, the date could not be 1848 and is in all probability 1849.

³⁶ *New York Herald*, April 6 and 24, 1849.

³⁷ *Ibid.*, October 11 and December 6, 1849. For details of the construction of ships mentioned see Appendix I.

³⁸ *The Panama Echo*, March 16, 1850.

³⁹ *San Francisco Herald*, November 20, 1851.

⁴⁰ William H. Aspinwall to Alfred Robinson, New York, December 8, 1848, March 19 and April 19, 1849, *in* Aspinwall-Robinson Letter Book.

⁴¹ William Ballard Preston to William H. Aspinwall, Navy Department, January 2, 1850, S. Ex. Doc. 50, ser. no. 619, p. 61.

⁴² William Ballard Preston to William H. Aspinwall, Navy Department, May 20, 1850, *in* General Letter Book, no. 43, January 24, 1850, to July 27, 1850, N.R.L., p. 389.

⁴³ William H. Aspinwall to William Ballard Preston, June 4, 1850, S. Ex. Doc. 50, ser. no. 619, pp. 172–173.

⁴⁴ William Ballard Preston to William H. Aspinwall, Navy Department, June 8, 1850, *in* General Letter Book, no. 43, N.R.L., p. 389.

[45] Samuel Thurston to William B. Preston, June 8, 1850, S. Ex. Doc. 50, ser. no. 619, p. 174.

[46] N. K. Hall to William A. Graham, Post Office Department, September 30, 1850, *in* N. K. Hall, Letter Book, U 2, Postmaster General, July 21, 1850, to April 23, 1852, P.O.L. The interests hostile to the people of Oregon could hardly be other than the Hudson's Bay Company, recently moved from Fort Vancouver on the Columbia to its new headquarters on the North Pacific, Fort Victoria at the southern tip of Vancouver Island.

[47] Two letters, William A. Graham to William H. Aspinwall, Navy Department, October 1, 1850, *in* General Letter Book, no. 44, July 27, 1850, to February 10, 1851, N.R.L., pp. 189–191.

[48] *San Francisco Daily Alta California,* December 10, 1850.

[49] J. Collamer to Thomas J. Rush, Post Office Department, June 27, 1850, *in* J. Collamer, Letter Book, T 2, Postmaster General, January 25, 1849, to July 20, 1850, P.O.L.

[50] William H. Aspinwall to Messrs. Robinson, Bissell and Co., New York, June 13, 1850, *in* Aspinwall-Robinson Letter Book.

[51] *Congressional Globe,* 31st Cong., 1st sess., pp. 2047–2049, 2050–2053.

[52] *San Francisco Daily Alta California,* December 9, 10 and 12, 1850.

[53] *Congressional Globe,* 31st Cong., 2nd sess., pp. 769–770, 832; S. Ex. Doc. 50, ser. no. 619, pp. 182–183.

[54] S. Ex. Doc. 50, ser. no. 619, pp. 145–148.

[55] *Ibid.,* p. 184; William A. Graham to William H. Aspinwall, Navy Department, March 21, 1851, *in* General Letter Book, no. 45, February 10, 1851, to September 19, 1851, N.R.L., p. 101.

[56] Pacific Mail Steamship Co., *Charter;* William H. Aspinwall to Messrs. Robinson, Bissell and Co., New York, June 13, 1850, *in* Aspinwall-Robinson Letter Book.

[57] William H. Aspinwall to Alfred Robinson, May 5, 1849, *ibid.*

[58] William H. Aspinwall to Alfred Robinson, December 8, 1848, *ibid.*

[59] William H. Aspinwall to Robinson, Bissell and Co., November 13, 1850, *ibid.*

[60] *New York Herald,* July 11, 1850.

[61] *Ibid.,* December 24, 1848, and January 28, 1849.

[62] *San Francisco Pacific News,* September 25, 1849. See Appendix I.

[63] *New York Herald,* November 7, December 13 and 14, 1849.

[64] *San Francisco Alta California,* June 6, 1850. See Appendix I.

[65] J. Collamer to J. Howard and Son, Post Office Department, November 10, 1849, and J. Collamer to A. W. Thompson, Post Office Department, November 13, 1849, *in* J. Collamer, Letter Book, T 2, P.O.L.

[66] William H. Aspinwall to Messrs. Robinson, Bissell and Co., New York, October 28, 1850, *in* Aspinwall-Robinson Letter Book.

[67] *Panama Herald,* August 4 and 7, 1851.

[68] *New York Herald,* January 1, 25, and 31, 1852.

[69] *Ibid.,* June 12, 1849.

[70] *Ibid.,* November 5, 1849.

[71] *Ibid.,* November 30, December 16 and 18, 1849.

[72] *Ibid.,* January 25, 1850.

[73] Frederick Henry Wolcott, Diary, 1849–1854, Manuscripts Division, New York Public Library, Vol. I, entry for Tuesday, January 29, 1850.

[74] New York Superior Court, *William Heilman* vs. *Marshall O. Roberts* (New York, 1861), pp. 22–23.

[75] *New York Herald,* October 29, 1850.

[76] William H. Aspinwall to Alfred Robinson, or if absent to Gilmor Meredith, New York, May 13, 1850, *in* Aspinwall-Robinson Letter Book.

[77] *Heilman* vs. *Roberts*, pp. 18–43; *New York Herald*, March 14 and April 1, 1851.

[78] *San Francisco Alta California*, April 7 and May 9, 1849.

[79] *San Francisco Tri-Weekly Alta California*, January 9, 11, and 14, 1850.

[80] *San Francisco Daily Alta California*, January 29, 1850.

[81] *Ibid.*, February 21, 1850.

[82] *New York Herald*, February 7, 1850.

[83] *Ibid.*, March 5, 1849.

[84] William H. Aspinwall to Alfred Robinson, or if absent to Gilmor Meredith, New York, May 13, 1850, *in* Aspinwall-Robinson Letter Book.

[85] William H. Aspinwall to Messrs. Robinson, Bissell and Co., New York, October 28, 1850, *ibid.*

[86] Samuel W. Comstock to Alfred Robinson, New York, November 13, 1849, *ibid.*

[87] *New York Herald*, November 14, 1848.

[88] *Ibid.*, December 11, 1848.

[89] *Ibid.*, August 21, 1849; M. O. Roberts to H. J. Hartstene, New York, August 27, 1849, *in* Roberts Letter Book, November 30, 1848—October 16, 1849, Naval History Society, New York.

[90] *New York Herald*, September 15, 1849.

[91] *Ibid.*, July 28, 1849.

[92] *Ibid.*, September 23, 1849.

[93] *Ibid.*, March 3, 1850.

[94] *Ibid.*

[95] *Panama Echo*, March 16, 1850.

[96] *New York Herald*, October 10, 1850.

[97] Samuel W. Comstock to Messrs. Robinson, Bissell and Co., New York, September 28, 1850, *in* Aspinwall-Robinson Letter Book.

[98] *New York Herald*, February 25, 1851.

[99] *Panama Star*, September 16, 1851.

[100] *New York Herald*, November 15, 1848.

[101] *San Francisco Alta California*, July 19, 1849.

[102] *New York Herald*, November 30, 1849; San Francisco *Supplement to the Pacific News*, January 5, 1850; *Panama Echo*, March 16, 1850.

[103] *San Francisco California Daily Courier*, November 1 and 11, 1850.

[104] *San Francisco Daily Herald*, January 4 and April 28, 1851.

[105] *New York Herald*, June 20, 1851.

[106] *San Francisco Daily Herald*, June 30, 1851.

[107] *San Francisco Daily Alta California*, October 26, 1851.

[108] *New York Herald*, December 20, 1849.

[109] *San Francisco Daily Alta California*, July 12 and 13, 1850.

[110] *Ibid.*, November 1 and 11, 1850.

[111] *New York Herald*, April 5, 1851; M. O. Roberts to J. R. Jennings, New York, April 14, 1851, *in* Roberts Letter Book, August 6, 1850—September 27, 1853, Naval History Society, New York.

NOTES TO CHAPTER III

BATTLE OF THE TITANS, 1851–1860

[1] John T. Sullivan, *Report of Historical and Technical Information Relating to the Problem of Interoceanic Communication by way of the American Isthmus* (Washington, 1883), p. 212.

[2] *Ibid.*, pp. 122–123.

[3] Hubert Howe Bancroft, *Chronicles of the Builders of the Commonwealth* (San Francisco, 1891), V:392.

[4] *New York Herald*, December 14, 1849, and January 9, 1850.

[5] Bancroft, *op. cit.*, V:392; Alvin F. Harlow, "Vanderbilt, Cornelius," *Dictionary of American Biography* (New York, 1936), XIX:171; Wheaton J. Lane, *Commodore Vanderbilt; an Epic of the Steam Age* (New York, 1942), pp. 91–94.

[6] *New York Herald*, July 9, 1850; *San Francisco Alta California*, August 29, 1850.

[7] *San Francisco California Courier*, August 26, 1850; *San Francisco Daily Herald*, January 9, 1851; *San Francisco Daily Alta California*, May 27, August 31, September 1, and December 28, 1851.

[8] S. Ex. Doc. 50, ser. no. 619, pp. 163–164.

[9] Cornelius Vanderbilt by D. B. Allen to William A. Graham, March 17, 1851, *ibid.*, pp. 162–163.

[10] William A. Graham to Cornelius Vanderbilt, Navy Department, March 19, 1851, *in* General Letter Book, no. 45, February 10, 1851, to September 18, 1851, N.R.L., p. 99.

[11] *San Francisco Daily Alta California*, July 4, 1851.

[12] Gilmor Meredith to Jonathan Meredith, Grass Valley, December 10, 1851, *in* Jonathan Meredith Papers, Manuscripts Division, Library of Congress.

[13] *New York Herald*, November 8, 1851.

[14] *Ibid.*, November 30 and December 2, 1851.

[15] *Ibid.*, December 1, 1851.

[16] *Panama Herald*, December 22, 1851.

[17] *New York Herald*, January 31, 1851.

[18] *Ibid.*, February 4 and 16, 1852.

[19] *Ibid.*, March 9, 1852.

[20] *Ibid.*, December 21, 1851, and March 8, 1852.

[21] *Ibid.*, March 8, 1852.

[22] *Ibid.*, March 16, 1852.

[23] *Ibid.*, September 15, 1852.

[24] *Ibid.*, October 8, 1852.

[25] *Ibid.*, January 13, 1853.

[26] *Panama Star*, February 19, 1853.

[27] Pacific Mail Steamship Co., *Proceedings at Meeting of Stockholders of Pacific Mail Steamship Co., Held June 28, 1855* (New York, 1855), pp. 5–7.

[28] *New York Herald*, September 10, 1853.

[29] *San Francisco Prices Current and Shipping List*, February 9, 1853.

[30] John Overton Choules, *The Cruise of the Steam Yacht "North Star": a Narrative of the Excursion of Mr. Vanderbilt's party to England, Russia, Denmark, France, Spain, Italy, Malta, Turkey, Madeira, etc.* (Boston, 1854), *passim;* Harlow, "Vanderbilt," *Dictionary of American Biography*, XIX:171; H. W. Howard Knott, "Garrison, Cornelius Kingsland," *ibid.*, VII:167–168; Lane, *op. cit.*, pp. 102–110.

[31] Pacific Mail Steamship Co., *Report of Two Committees of Stockholders, 1855* (New York, 1855), p. 19; *San Francisco Daily Alta California*, August 17, 1853.

[32] *New York Herald*, September 8 and 10, 1853.

[33] *Ibid.*, September 28, 1853.

[34] *San Francisco Daily Alta California*, May 7, 1853.

[35] *Ibid.*, May 10 and June 18, 1853.

[36] *Ibid.*, September 1, 1854.

[37] *Panama Weekly Herald*, October 17, 1853.

[38] *Put's Original California Songster. Giving in a Few Words What Would Occupy Volumes, Detailing the Hopes, Trials and Joys of a Miner's Life* (San Francisco, 1868), pp. 43–44.

[39] See Appendix I.

[40] *New York Herald*, May 29, November 8, November 11, December 16, 1853, and February 2, 1854; *San Francisco Daily Alta California*, February 18 and March 5, 1854.

[41] *New York Herald*, February 28, 1854.

[42] *Ibid.*, May 18 and June 6, 1854.

[43] *Ibid.*, April 10, 1854.

[44] *Ibid.*, June 12, 1854.

[45] *Ibid.*, September 1, 1854; *San Francisco Daily Alta California*, October 2 and 3, 1854; *Congressional Globe*, 35th Cong., 1st sess., p. 2844.

[46] *San Francisco Daily Alta California*, October 4, 1854.

[47] Pacific Mail Steamship Co., *Report of Two Committees of Stockholders, 1855*, p. 19; *New York Herald*, September 11, 1854.

[48] *San Francisco Daily Alta California*, January 17, 1855.

[49] *New York Herald*, March 14 and 17, 1855; Pacific Mail Steamship Co., *Proceedings at Meeting of Stockholders, 1855*, p. 9.

[50] *New York Herald*, April 6 and June 19, 1855.

[51] *Ibid.*, June 23, 1855.

[52] *Ibid.*, June 30, September 12, and October 16, 1855.

[53] *Ibid.*, November 22, 1855.

[54] *San Francisco Daily Alta California*, January 5, 1853.

[55] *Ibid.*, 1853–1855, *passim*.

[56] See Appendix II.

[57] *San Francisco Daily Alta California*, December 19, 1855.

[58] *Ibid.*, January 5 and 31, 1856.

[59] *New York Herald*, January 7, 1856.

[60] Hubert Howe Bancroft, *History of Central America* (San Francisco, 1887), pp. 328, 338, 341; Harlow, "Vanderbilt," p. 171; Lane, *op. cit.*, pp. 116–119.

[61] *New York Herald*, March 18, 1856.

[62] *Ibid.*, March 31, 1856.

[63] *San Francisco Daily Alta California*, March 5 and April 19, 1856.

[64] Bancroft, *Chronicles of the Builders*, V:398–399; Harlow, "Vanderbilt," p. 171; Lane, *op. cit.*, pp. 121–124; *San Francisco Daily Alta California*, August 15, 1856.

[65] *New York Herald*, June 6, 1856.

[66] *San Francisco Daily Alta California*, November 20, 1856.

[67] *Ibid.*, February 15, 1857.

[68] *New York Herald*, March 26 and 28, 1854, February 7, 1857.

[69] *Ibid.*, May 16, 1857.

[70] Bancroft, *Central America*, III:360–361; idem, *Chronicles of the Builders*, V:400–401; Lane, *op. cit.*, pp. 130–131.

[71] *The Prospectus of the California and New York Steamship Company* (San Francisco, 1857), pp. 3–8; *New York Herald*, April 9, 1857; *San Francisco Daily Alta California*, April 18, May 3, 11, and July 7, 1857.

[72] Bancroft, *Chronicles of the Builders*, V:403.

[73] *San Francisco Daily Evening Bulletin*, March 3, 4, and 5, 1858.

[74] *San Francisco Prices Current and Shipping List*, June 12, 1857.

[75] *San Francisco Daily Alta California*, September 16, 1857.

[76] *San Francisco Daily Evening Bulletin*, December 31, 1857.

[77] *New York Herald*, October 26 and November 13, 1858; *San Francisco Daily Alta California*, December 4, 1858.

[78] *New York Herald*, February 5, 6, and 10, 1858.

[79] *San Francisco Daily Evening Bulletin*, February 15, 1858.

[80] *Ibid.*, March 31, 1858.

[81] *Congressional Globe*, 35th Cong., 1st sess., p. 2844; *San Francisco Daily Evening Bulletin*, March 31, 1858.

[82] *San Francisco Daily Evening Bulletin*, April 1, 1858.

[83] *Ibid.*, April 2, 1858; *San Francisco Daily Alta California*, April 5, 1858.

[84] *San Francisco Daily Evening Bulletin*, April 2, 1858; *San Francisco Daily Alta California*, April 15, 1858.

[85] Paul Neff Garber, *The Gadsden Treaty* (Philadelphia, 1923), pp. 41–61.

[86] 10 *U. S. Stat. at L.* (1853), 1035–1036.

[87] Bancroft, *Chronicles of the Builders*, V:389.

[88] Aaron V. Brown to William H. English, Chairman of the Post Office Committee, Post Office Department, May 20, 1858, *in* A. V. Brown, Letter Book, X 4, Postmaster General, March 23, 1857, to April 2, 1859, P.O.L.

[89] Aaron V. Brown to William H. English, Post Office Department, May 24, 1858, *ibid.*

[90] United States Postmaster General, *Report of the Postmaster General for the Year 1859* (Washington, 1859), p. 51; Pacific Mail Steamship Co., Cash Book, January 1st, 1858, to December 9th, 1858, G; Cash Book, December 10th 1858, to December 31st, 1859, H.L., *passim;* Bancroft, *Chronicles of the Builders*, V: 389–390.

[91] *Prospectus of the People's California Steamship Co., New York and San Francisco, 1858* (New York, 1858), pp. 1–3, 8; Bancroft, *Chronicles of the Builders*, V:409.

[92] *New York Herald*, June 29 and September 29, 1858.

[93] *New York Herald*, October 8, 9, 14, and 25, 1858.

[94] *San Francisco Daily Alta California*, January 27, 1859; *Panama Star and Herald*, February 1, 1859; *San Francisco Prices Current and Shipping List*, February 12, 1859; *New York Herald*, February 15, 1859; *Harper's Magazine*, Vol. III., no. 112 (February 19, 1859), p. 2.

[95] *New York Herald*, February 13, 1859.

[96] *Ibid.*, May 13, 1859.

[97] J. Holt to Isaac Toucey, Post Office Department, March 28, 1859, *in* A. V. Brown, Letter Book, X 4, P.O.L.; J. Holt to Isaac Toucey, Post Office Department, April 9, 1859, and J. Holt to Howell Cobb, Post Office Department, May 7, 1859, *in* J. Holt, H. King, Letter Book, X 5, Postmaster General, March 18, 1859, to May 6, 1861, P.O.L.

[98] United States Postmaster General, *Report of the Postmaster General for the Year 1859* (Washington, 1859), p. 23.

[99] *New York Herald*, February 15, 1859.

[100] *Ibid.*, May 11 and 13, June 2, and September 5, 1859; *Panama Star and Herald*, July 14, 1859.

[101] *New York Herald,* May 13 and 16, 1859.

[102] *Ibid.,* May 13, 1859.

[103] *Ibid.,* May 16, 1859.

[104] *Ibid.,* June 21, 1859.

[105] *San Francisco Daily Alta California,* November 17, 1857.

[106] *New York Herald,* July 10 and 12, 1859.

[107] *Panama Star and Herald,* September 17, 1859.

[108] *New York Herald,* October 3 and 5, 1859; *San Francisco Daily Alta California,* November 27, 1859.

[109] *New York Herald,* September 5, 1859; *San Francisco Daily Alta California,* September 3, 1859.

[110] *New York Herald,* October 4 and 5, 1859.

[111] *Ibid.,* October 3, 5, and 6, 1859.

[112] *San Francisco Daily Alta California,* September 21, 1859.

[113] J. C. Dobbin to Messrs. George Law, Marshall O. Roberts, and Bowes R. McIlvaine, assignees of Albert G. Sloo, Navy Department, February 13, 1854, *in* General Letter Book, no. 50, January 17, 1854, to August 4, 1854, N.R.L., p. 69.

[114] J. C. Dobbin to M. O. Roberts, Navy Department, September 18, 1854, and J. C. Dobbin to M. O. Roberts, Navy Department, September 27, 1854, *ibid.,* no. 51, August 4, 1854, to February 15, 1855, N.R.L., pp. 117, 140–141.

[115] J. C. Dobbin to M. O. Roberts, Navy Department, *ibid.,* no. 52, February 15, 1855, to August 17, 1855, N.R.L., pp. 38–39.

[116] *San Francisco Daily Alta California,* November 19, 1857.

[117] *New York Herald,* September 20, 1853–May 11, 1857, *passim.*

[118] *Ibid.,* June 26, 1853.

[119] *Ibid.,* January 7, 1860; *San Francisco Daily Alta California,* May 6 and 14, 1854.

[120] John P. Kennedy to William H. Aspinwall, Navy Department, November 30, 1852, and John P. Kennedy to William H. Aspinwall, Navy Department, December 3, 1852, *in* General Letter Book, no. 47, April 19, 1852, to December 3, 1853, N.R.L., pp. 294, 501; J. C. Dobbin to W. H. Aspinwall, Navy Department, October 29, 1853, *ibid.,* no. 49, June 28, 1853, to January 17, 1854, N.R.L., pp. 309–310.

[121] *Panama Star and Herald,* February 4, 1856.

[122] J. C. Dobbin to W. H. Aspinwall, Navy Department, June 15, 1854, *in* General Letter Book, no. 50, N.R.L., p. 384.

[123] *San Francisco Daily Alta California,* January 11 and 12, 1856.

[124] Pacific Mail Steamship Co., *Charter; Bill of Complaint, Affidavits, &c., and Opinion of Mr. Justice Blatchford, in the Suit of Brown, Hargreaves, et al., vs. Atlantic Mail Steamship Company, et al.* (New York, 1867), p. 2; *New York Herald,* February 8 and March 14, 1856.

[125] Pacific Mail Steamship Co., *Report of Committee, 1854,* p. 12.

[126] *San Francisco Daily Alta California,* January 3, 1856; *New York Herald,* March 6, 1856.

[127] Pacific Mail Steamship Co., *Proceedings at Meeting of Stockholders, 1855,* pp. 5–7; *Report of Committee, 1854,* p. 21.

[128] *New York Herald,* May 25, 1857; Pacific Mail Steamship Co., *Fourth Annual Report, 1858* (New York, 1859), p. 6; *Fifth Annual Report, 1859* (New York, 1859), p. 8.

[129] *New York Herald,* May 16, 1860.

[130] *Ibid.,* June 23, 1858.

[131] *Ibid.,* February 4, 1853—January 3, 1860, *passim.*

[132] *Ibid.*, September 26, 1858.

[133] *Ibid.*, January 6, 1853.

[134] *Ibid.*, June 26, 1862.

[135] *Ibid.*, September 27, 1858.

[136] *Ibid.*, July 12, August 20, August 22, and October 5, 1859.

[137] *Ibid.*, December 12, 1859.

[138] *Ibid.*, November 11, 1859; *Panama Star and Herald*, February 18, 1860.

[139] *New York Herald*, November 11, 21, 26, 29, 30, and December 1, 1859.

[140] *Ibid.*, December 2, 3, and 5, 1859.

[141] *Ibid.*, February 16, 18, 19, 20, and 22, 1860; *Panama Star and Herald*, March 1 and June 2, 1860.

[142] *Panama Star and Herald*, June 28, 1860.

[143] *New York Herald*, March 1, 1860; *San Francisco Daily Alta California*, April 17 and July 20, 1860.

NOTES TO CHAPTER IV

THE CLOSING YEARS, 1860–1869

[1] Theodore T. Johnson to unknown correspondent in office of Pacific Mail Steamship Co., San Francisco, June 3, 1863, H.L.; see Appendix I.

[2] Fessenden Nott Otis, *Illustrated History of the Panama Railroad; together with a Traveller's Guide and Business Man's Hand-Book for the Panama Railroad and its Connections with Europe, the United States, the North and South Atlantic and Pacific Coasts, China, Australia, and Japan, by Sail and Steam* (New York, 1862), p. 150.

[3] Charles Toll Bidwell, *Isthmus of Panama* (London, 1865), p. 95.

[4] *San Francisco Daily Alta California*, July 14, 1860.

[5] *Panama Star and Herald*, June 30, 1864.

[6] *Ibid.*, August 4, 1864, and September 16, 1865.

[7] *Ibid.*, November 15, 1864.

[8] *New York Herald*, February 6, 1865.

[9] *Ibid.*, June 6, 1862, and August 13, 1863.

[10] *Ibid.*, 1860–1862, *passim*.

[11] *Ibid.*, May 19, 20, 21, and 22, 1860.

[12] *Ibid.*, October 17, 1860.

[13] *Ibid.*, November 15 and 18, 1860; *San Francisco Daily Alta California*, December 1, 1860.

[14] *Panama Star and Herald*, December 29, 1860.

[15] *New York Herald*, January 30 and May 17, 1861.

[16] *Ibid.*, November 14, 1861, and 1861–1862, *passim*.

[17] *Ibid.*, 1862–1863, *passim*.

[18] *San Francisco Daily Evening Bulletin*, April 28, 1863.

[19] *Ibid.*

[20] *New York Herald*, September 18, 1863.

[21] [Brown Brothers and Co.] to Messrs. Brown and Brown, [New York], November 25, 1859, *in* Brown Brothers Letters, Manuscripts Division, New York Public Library, LXXXVIII:82.

[22] Pacific Mail Steamship Co., *Bill of Complaint*, pp. 5–8.

[23] *Idem, Charter; Bill of Complaint*, pp. 2–4.

[24] *New York Herald*, August 23 and 31, 1865.

[25] Pacific Mail Steamship Co., *Bill of Complaint*, pp. 9–12; *New York Herald,* September 20, 1865; *Panama Star and Herald,* October 12 and 16, 1865; *San Francisco Daily Evening Bulletin,* September 23, 1865.

[26] *New York Herald,* 1864–1865, *passim;* Anon., "Pacific Mail," *Harper's Weekly,* August 2, 1873, p. 2.

[27] *Panama Star and Herald,* January 11, 1866.

[28] *New York Herald,* October 8, 1865; *Panama Star and Herald,* January 11, 1866.

[29] *San Francisco Daily Evening Bulletin,* March 28, 1868, and March 1, 1869.

[30] *Ibid.,* April 19, 1867; also 1860–1869, *passim; San Francisco Steamer Bulletin,* July 10 and October 8, 1867, January 9, 1868.

[31] Pacific Mail Steamship Co., *Charter; New York Herald,* November 20, 1866.

[32] *San Francisco Bulletin,* November 21, 1866.

[33] William Swinton, *How the "Ring" ran Pacific Mail: A Story of Wall Street* (New York, 1867), p. 7; Anon., "Pacific Mail," *Harper's Weekly,* August 2, 1873, p. 2; *New York Herald,* November 22, 1866, February 27, 1867, and 1866–1867, *passim.*

[34] *Ibid.,* 1868–1869, *passim.*

[35] Pacific Mail Steamship Co., *Bill of Complaint,* pp. 13–39; William Swinton, *op. cit.,* pp. 7–11; *New York Herald,* November 18, 20, 21, and December 3, 1867.

[36] J. Holt to William Pennington, Pos Office Department, February 13, 1860, *in* J. Holt, H. King, Letter Book, X 5, Postmaster General, March 18, 1859, to March 6, 1861, P.O.L.

[37] J. Holt to D. L. Yulee, Post Office Department, June 20, 1860, *ibid.*

[38] *New York Herald,* July 6, 1860.

[39] *Ibid.,* July 12, 1860.

[40] *Ibid.,* July 11, 1860.

[41] Letter Book, No. 9, J. A. J. Creswell, Post Office Department [March 12, 1869—January 20, 1874], P.O.L.

[42] J. Holt to William Pennington, Post Office Department, December 29, 1860; Horatio King to John A. Dix, Post Office Department, February 25, 1861, and Horatio King to R. M. T. Hunter, Post Office Department, February 25, 1861, *in* J. Holt, H. King, Letter Book, X 5, P.O.L.

[43] *San Francisco Daily Alta California,* June 26, 1861.

[44] *Ibid.,* June 19, 1862; *San Francisco Daily Evening Bulletin,* January 16, 1865; W. Dennison to D. C. McRuer, Post Office Department, June 11, 1866, *in* W. Dennison, Letter Book, No. 7, Post Office Department, October 1, 1864, to July 6, 1866, P.O.L.

[45] Pacific Mail Steamship Co., *Seventh Annual Report* (New York, 1861), p. 7.

[46] Foreign mail transportation: New York and San Francisco via Panama.

Fiscal year	Compensation
1861–1862	$17,267.16
1862–1863	11,343.77
1863–1864	31,098.58
1864–1865	18,595.81
1865–1866	24,888.58
1866–1867	26,742.00
1867–1868	27,343.87
1868–1869	7,997.74

(United States Postmaster General, *Annual Reports, 1862–1869,* Washington, 1862–1869.)

[47] W. Dennison to W. T. Otto, Post Office Department, February 1, 1866, *in* W. Dennison, Letter Book, No. 7, P.O.L.

[48] *San Francisco Daily Evening Bulletin*, May 8, 1865.

[49] *Ibid.*, April 3, 1869.

[50] *New York Herald*, July 24 and 26, 1860.

[51] *San Francisco Daily Alta California*, October 22, 1860; [*Granada*, Log, New York–New Orleans–Aspinwall–San Francisco, May 8, 1859—October 14, 1860.] Entries for October 13–18, 1860, MS, Naval History Society Library, New York.

[52] *Panama Star and Herald*, June 3, 1862.

[53] *New York Herald*, August 21, 1862; *San Francisco Daily Evening Bulletin*, September 8, 1862.

[54] *San Francisco Evening Bulletin*, October 17, 1862.

[55] *Ibid.*, December 9 and 20, 1862.

[56] *Ibid.*, June 13 and December 22, 1863.

[57] *Ibid.*, February 2, March 2, 22, and 28, April 12 and 22, July 12, September 2 and 21, November 2, December 2 and 13, 1864; *New York Herald*, December 18, 1864.

[58] *San Francisco Daily Evening Bulletin*, August 30, 1864.

[59] *Panama Star and Herald*, March 7, 1865.

[60] *New York Herald*, August 16 and December 5, 1865.

[61] *New York Tribune*, January 23, 25, 27, and February 15, 1866; *Panama Star and Herald*, January 30, 1866; Pacific Mail Steamship Co., *Report of Louis McLane, President pro. tem., to the Board of Directors of the Pacific Mail Steamship Co.* (New York, 1867), p. 6.

[62] *New York Tribune*, January 27, 1866; *Panama Star and Herald*, January 30, 1866.

[63] *New York Tribune*, January 24, 1866.

[64] *San Francisco Daily Evening Bulletin*, March 14, 1866.

[65] *New York Herald*, November 13 and 14, 1867; Pacific Mail Steamship Co., *Report of Louis McLane, 1867*, p. 7.

[66] H. H. Bancroft, *Chronicles of the Builders* (San Francisco, 1891), V:418; *New York Herald*, May 29, 1868.

[67] *New York Herald*, January 16, 1868; *Panama Star and Herald*, March 3, 1868.

[68] A most interesting letter relating to the North American S.S. Co. exists in the W. S. Ladd Papers at Reed College. It is addressed to "Friend R." and is unsigned and undated. Seemingly written from New York between February and October, 1868, it is evidently the work of someone high in the company, though not Webb himself. Possibly it was written by Moses Taylor. The "Friend R." may refer to I. W. Raymond, San Francisco agent of the company, or to William Chapman Ralston, banker, who was interested in it.

The letter gives the capital stock of the North American S.S. Co. as only $1,600,000, owned entirely by Webb and a few of his friends. Although it speaks boldly of the prospects of the company, it is evident that help is being sought. The plan proposed is that the State of California or the City of San Francisco be induced to appropriate $1,000,000 in currency to be used in expanding the stock of the company. The point is made that, as long as the competition continues, Californians will have the benefit of low rates and immigration also will be stimulated, thus justifying the investment of public funds. It is suggested that with some judicious rate raising, stock in the company can be made to pay 12 per cent, and perhaps an agreement for increased rates may be made with the Pacific Mail—all after the money has been appropriated, of course. The writer suggests that, if arrangements for funds can be made in California, he and "Friend R." will make $50,000 from the transaction, but if nothing can be done, "Destroy this letter & say nothing I have written." (W. S. Ladd Papers, Reed College Library, Portland, Oregon.)

[69] *Panama Star and Herald,* October 22, 1868.

[70] *New York Herald,* January 10 and June 15, 1869.

[71] *Panama Star and Herald,* December 16, 1862.

[72] *Ibid.,* December 13, 1862; *New York Herald,* December 28, 1862.

[73] *Panama Star and Herald,* December 18, 1862.

[74] *New York Herald,* December 31, 1862.

[75] *Panama Star and Herald,* February 7 and 17, 1863.

[76] *Ibid.,* January 6, 1863.

[77] *New York Herald,* March 7, 1863.

[78] *Panama Star and Herald,* May 26, 1864.

[79] *New York Herald,* October 4, 1864.

[80] *San Francisco Daily Evening Bulletin,* January 17, 1865.

[81] *San Francisco Daily Alta California,* March 9, 1861. The *Levant* was never heard from after her sailing from Honolulu.

[82] *Ibid.,* June 29, 1861.

[83] *Panama Star and Herald,* June 18, 1864.

[84] J. B. Montgomery, Flag Officer commanding Pacific Squadron, to Commander David McDougal, commanding U.S. steamer *Wyoming,* U.S. Flag Ship *Lancaster,* Bay of Panama, August 9, 1861, and J. B. Montgomery, Flag Officer commanding Pacific Squadron, to Captain Robert Ritchie, commanding U.S. steamer *Saranac,* U.S. Flag Ship *Lancaster,* Bay of Panama, August 29, 1861, *in* Pacific Squadron, November, 1860, to December, 1861, N.R.L., Vol. II, nos. 210 and 239.

[85] Brainerd Dyer, "Confederate Naval and Privateering Activities in the Pacific," *Pacific Historical Review,* Vol. III, No. 4 (December, 1934), pp. 433–443; *Panama Star and Herald,* November 12, 15, and 17, 1864, and June 2, 1866.

[86] *San Francisco Daily Evening Bulletin,* August 3 and 10, 1865.

[87] Thomas Woodbine Hinchliff, *Over the Sea and Far Away, Being a Narrative of Wanderings round the World* (London, 1876), pp. 174–194.

NOTES TO CHAPTER V

THE PANAMA STEAMERS

[1] See Appendix I.

[2] *New York Herald,* July 10 and 22, 1849.

[3] See Appendixes I and IV; also Robert Greenhalgh Albion, *The Rise of New York Port* [*1815–1860*] (New York and London, 1939), pp. 148–151, 278–293.

[4] See Appendixes I and V.

[5] See Appendix I.

[6] *New York Herald,* January 24, 1850.

[7] William H. Webb, "Certificate of Ships Constructed," II:125–125a, Webb Institute of Naval Architecture.

[8] Engineer's Log, Pacific Mail Steamship Co.'s S.S. *Oregon,* Voyages 1–10, 1848–1851 (April 14, July 14, 1849), M. H. De Young Memorial Museum, San Francisco.

[9] Kemble, *Genesis of the Pacific Mail* (San Francisco, 1934), pp. 24–25.

[10] *San Francisco Daily Alta California*, June 14, 1849; Richard H. Pearson, "Memoir," *San Francisco Daily Evening Bulletin*, March 3, 1868.

[11] Engineer's Log of *Oregon*, April 12, 13, 17, 21, 26, 28, May 3, 5, 1849; Pearson, "Memoir."

[12] Stout, "Journal," in *First Steamship Pioneers* (San Francisco, 1874), pp. 99–100.

[13] *New York Herald*, July 23, 1849.

[14] Engineer's Log of *Oregon*, October 18, 1849, and January 9, 1851.

[15] *New York Herald*, December 22, 1853.

[16] William H. Aspinwall to Alfred Robinson, New York, May 22, 1849, *in* Aspinwall-Robinson Letter Book, collection of Daulton Mann, New York.

[17] *New York Herald*, March 14, 1852.

[18] *Ibid.*, September 20, 1849.

[19] *Ibid.*, July 22, 1849.

[20] *San Francisco Daily Alta California*, April 12 and May 14, 1853.

[21] *New York Herald*, December 22, 1853; *Panama Star and Herald*, September 16, 1865.

[22] *Panama Star and Herald*, August 13, 1864.

[23] Willam H. Aspinwall to Messrs. Robinson, Bissell and Co., New York, July 13, 1850, *in* Aspinwall-Robinson Letter Book.

[24] *New York Herald*, May 30, 1848.

[25] *San Francisco Daily Evening Bulletin*, February 25, 1858.

[26] New York Superior Court, *Heilman* vs. *Roberts*, pp. 57–75.

[27] *San Francisco Daily Alta California*, October 9, 1851.

[28] Gilmor Meredith to Jonathan Meredith, Grass Valley, December 10, 1851, *in* Jonathan Meredith Papers, Manuscripts Division, Library of Congress.

[29] Pacific Mail Steamship Co., Journal, September 1st, 1853, to July 31st, 1856, H.L.

[30] *Idem*, Cash Book, December 10, 1858, to December 31, 1859, Journal, May 1, 1861, to January 31, 1863. Cash Book, October 8, 1868, to July 30, 1869, H.L.

[31] *Idem, Report of Two Committees of Stockholders, 1855*, p. 18.

[31a] M. O. Roberts to Paradise Lawranson and Co., New York, August 13 [1850], George Law to J. A. Jennings [New York], November 12 [1852] *in* Roberts Letter Book, August 6, 1850—September 27, 1853, Naval History Society, New York.

[32] Pacific Mail Steamship Co., Journal, February 10th, 1851, to June 2nd, 1852, and June 5th, 1852, to August 31st, 1853, H.L.

[33] *Idem, Report of Committee, 1854*, p. 5.

[34] *Idem, Report of Two Committees of Stockholders, 1855*, p. 45.

[35] *Idem*, Journal, August 1, 1856, to September 25, 1858, September 26, 1858, to December 31, 1859, and May 1, 1861 to January 31, 1863, H.L.

[36] *Idem*, Cash Book, October 9, 1868, to July 30, 1869, H.L.

[37] Elisha Oscar Crosby, Memoirs and reminiscences of E. O. Crosby, H.L.

[38] Pacific Mail Steamship Co., *Report of Committee, 1854*, pp. 17–18.

[39] *New York Herald*, May 25, 1857.

[40] Pacific Mail Steamship Co., *Fourth Annual Report, 1858* (New York, 1858), pp. 4–5; *Fifth Annual Report, 1859* (New York, 1859), pp. 6, 8.

[41] William H. Aspinwall to Alfred Robinson, New York, May 26, 1849, *in* Aspinwall-Robinson Letter Book.

[42] J. Y. Mason to A. G. Sloo, Navy Department, December 22, 1847, *in* General Letter Book, no. 39, October 4, 1847, to April 26, 1848, N.R.L., p. 165; James Findlay Schenck to William Ballard Preston, New York, September 7, 1849, *in* Officers' Letters, September, 1849, N.R.L.

[43] David D. Porter to William Ballard Preston, Washington, July 5, 1849, *in* Officers' Letters, July, 1849, N.R.L.

[44] J. C. Dobbin to George Law, Navy Department, April 2, May 13 and 30, 1853, *in* General Letter Book, no. 48, December 6, 1852, to June 28, 1853, N.R.L., pp. 317, 405, 442.

[44a] *Georgia, Illinois,* Logs, *passim;* M. O. Roberts to J. A. Jennings [New York], November 12 [1852], *in* Roberts Letter Book, August 6, 1850—September 27, 1853, Naval History Society, New York.

[45] William H. Aspinwall to Alfred Robinson, New York, December 22, 1848, *in* Aspinwall-Robinson Letter Book.

[46] Kemble, *op. cit.,* p. 23.

[47] *Ibid.,* pp. 26, 30.

[48] William H. Aspinwall to William Ballard Preston, New York, May 22, 1849, *in* Miscellaneous Letters, May, 1849, N.R.L.

[49] William Ballard Preston to William H. Aspinwall, Navy Department, June 7, 1849, *in* General Letter Book, November 21, 1848, to June 30, 1849, N.R.L., p. 468.

[50] *San Francisco Daily Evening Bulletin,* August 27, 1862.

[51] Pearson, "Memoir"; William H. Aspinwall to Alfred Robinson, New York, April 19, 1849, *in* Aspinwall-Robinson Letter Book.

[52] William H. Aspinwall to Alfred Robinson, New York, May 22, 1849, and William H. Aspinwall to Messrs. Robinson, Bissell and Co., New York, July 13, September 13, and October 12, 1850, *ibid.*

[53] Samuel W. Comstock to Alfred Robinson, New York, March 16, 1850, *ibid.*

[54] W. W. Vanderbilt, Statement of W. W. Vanderbilt, *in* Miscellaneous statements on California history, B.L., p. 32.

[55] Samuel W. Comstock to Alfred Robinson, New York, January 2, 1850, *in* Aspinwall-Robinson Letter Book.

[56] *San Francisco Shipping List and Prices Current,* February 17 and July 30, 1852.

[57] Pacific Mail Steamship Co., *Report of Committee, 1854,* p. 23.

[58] *Idem,* Cash Books, 1852–1869, H.L., *passim.*

[59] *San Francisco Daily Alta California,* June 3, 1860.

[60] *Panama Star and Herald,* November 10, 1860.

[61] *Ibid.,* September 25, 1860.

[62] *Ibid.,* August 14 and 19, October 28, 1862.

[62a] M. O. Roberts to S. F. Potter, New York, March 2, 1850, *in* Roberts Letter Book, December 11, 1848—August 3, 1850, *Georgia, Illinois,* Logs, *passim,* Naval History Society, New York.

[63] William H. Aspinwall to Alfred Robinson, New York, May 5, 1849, *in* Aspinwall-Robinson Letter Book.

[64] William H. Aspinwall to Alfred Robinson, New York, May 22, 1849, *ibid.*

[65] Samuel W. Comstock to Alfred Robinson, New York, February 16, 1850, *ibid.*

[66] William H. Aspinwall to Alfred Robinson, New York, April 2, 1849, *ibid.*

[67] *Panama Star and Herald,* August 9, 1855.

[68] Notaria publica, No. 1, del circuito de Panamá, protocolo numero 2, año 1853, instrumentos del 41 al 101, volume serial no. 0188, instrumento no. 87, Archivo de Panamá, pp. 262–265.

[69] *Panama Star and Herald,* October 30, 1855, and March 25, 1862.

[70] *Ibid.,* February 22, and April 8, 1856, September 11, October 23, and December 9, 1858, January 18, 1862.

[71] *Ibid.,* March 27, 1862.

[72] John B. Peirce to Mrs. John B. Peirce, Acapulco, April 2, 1850, *in* Letters, 1850–1852, H.U.L.; *New York Herald*, July 12, 1850.

[73] William H. Aspinwall to John Van Dewater, New York, June 13, 1850, *in* Aspinwall-Robinson Letter Book.

[74] William H. Aspinwall to Alfred Robinson, New York, May 25, 1849, and William H. Aspinwall to Alfred Robinson, London, October 5, 1849, *ibid.*

[75] *San Francisco Daily Alta California*, February 5, 1850.

[76] *Ibid.*, June 27, 1850.

[77] *Ibid.*, November 30, 1852.

[78] Pacific Mail Steamship Co., *Report of Committee, 1854*, pp. 8, 22.

[79] *San Francisco Daily Alta California*, October 31, 1857.

[80] Pacific Mail Steamship Co., *Report of Two Committees of Stockholders, 1855*, p. 13.

[81] *San Francisco Daily Alta California*, June 3, 1856.

[82] Pacific Mail Steamship Co., *Fourth Annual Report, 1858* (New York, 1858), p. 6.

[83] *San Francisco Daily Alta California*, May 8, 1858.

[84] *San Francisco Daily Evening Bulletin*, May 13, 1868, and February 3, 1869.

[85] J. C. Dobbin to W. H. Aspinwall, Navy Department, February 6, 1856, *in* General Letter Book, no. 53, August 18, 1855, to March 20, 1856, N.R.L., pp. 396–397.

[86] William H. Aspinwall to Messrs. Robinson, Bissell and Co., New York, October 28, 1850, *in* Aspinwall-Robinson Letter Book.

[87] *San Francisco Daily Alta California*, May 7 and 13, 1854.

[88] *Ibid.*, October 4 and 18, 1857.

[89] Anon., *A Sketch of the Route to California, China and Japan via the Isthmus of Panama* (San Francisco and New York, 1867), p. 84.

[90] Cave Johnson to J. Y. Mason, Post Office Department, May 24, 1848, *in* C. Johnson, Letter Book, S 2, May 18, 1848, to January 24, 1849, P.O.L.

[91] G. Simpson to William H. Aspinwall, Lachine, October 13, 1848, *in* Aspinwall-Robinson Letter Book.

[92] *California Star and Californian*, December 9, 1848.

[93] Samuel W. Comstock to Alfred Robinson, New York, January 14, 1850, *in* Aspinwall-Robinson Letter Book.

[94] William H. Aspinwall to Messrs. Robinson, Bissell and Co., New York, June 13, 1850, *ibid.*

[95] William H. Aspinwall to Messrs. Robinson, Bissell and Co., New York, October 12, 1850, *ibid.*

[96] William H. Aspinwall to Alfred Robinson, New York, March 19, 1849, *ibid.*

[97] William H. Aspinwall to Alfred Robinson, New York, May 26, 1849, *ibid.*

[98] New York Superior Court, *Heilman* vs. *Roberts*, p. 115.

[99] *Ibid.*, p. 113.

[100] *Ibid.*, p. 136.

[101] *Panama Star*, April 8, 1851; *San Francisco Daily Pacific News*, April 3, 1851.

[102] *San Francisco Daily Alta California*, July 9, 1853.

[103] *Panama Star*, December 14, 1853.

[104] Pacific Mail Steamship Co., *Report of Committee, 1854*, p. 14.

[105] *Idem, Proceedings at a Meeting of Stockholders, June 28, 1855* (New York, 1855), p. 7.

[106] *Idem, Fourth Annual Report, 1858* (New York, 1858), p. 6; *Fifth Annual Report, 1859* (New York, 1859), p. 8.

[107] *New York Herald*, January 6, 1850.

[108] *San Francisco Daily Alta California*, January 24, 1854.

[109] *Ibid.*, December 17, 1853.

[110] *Ibid.*, February 15, 1854.

[111] *Ibid.*, February 15 and 16, 1854.

[112] *New York Herald*, February 7–12, 14–18, 21–25, 1854; W. B. Cooper, *Incidents of Shipwreck; or the Loss of the San Francisco* (Philadelphia, 1855).

[113] *New York Herald*, January 6, 1854.

[114] *Ibid.*, September 19–27, October 6, and November 30, 1857.

[115] *Put's Golden Songster. Containing the Largest and Most Popular Collection of California Songs Ever Published* (San Francisco, 1858), pp. 7–8.

[116] *New York Herald*, August 20, 1851.

[117] *San Francisco Prices Current and Shipping List*, April 15 and 29, 1853.

[118] *Ibid.*

[119] *Ibid.*, April 29, 1853; *San Francisco Daily Alta California*, December 7, 1853.

[120] *San Francisco Prices Current and Shipping List*, October 14, 1854.

[121] *New York Herald*, June 25, 1865.

[122] *San Francisco Daily Alta California*, August 7–8, 1862.

[123] *San Francisco Daily Evening Bulletin*, January 9, 1863.

NOTES TO CHAPTER VI

THE VOYAGE

[1] M. O. Roberts to M. C. Mordecai, New York, January 27, 1849, M. O. Roberts to John H. Richmond, New York, June 13, 1849, M. O. Roberts to Cohen, Morris and Co., New York, September 14, 1849, M. O. Roberts to Joseph F. Schenck, New York, September 20, 1850, *in* Roberts Letter Book, November 30, 1849—October 16, 1849; *Georgia*, Log, April 19–21, 1849, and *passim*, Naval History Society, New York.

[1a] *San Francisco Daily Alta California*, October 2, 1857.

[2] *San Francisco Daily Evening Bulletin*, October 25, 1865.

[3] *New York Herald*, January 29, 1849.

[4] Levi Stowell, Diary of Levi Stowell for the year 1849, Borel Collection, Stanford University Library, entry for February 20, 1849.

[5] John B. Peirce to Mrs. John B. Peirce, Steamer *Cherokee*, at sea, off Santo Domingo, February 23, 1850, *in* Letters, 1850–1852, H.U.L.

[6] Gilmor Meredith to Emma Meredith, Steamship *California*, at sea, July 22, 1851, *in* Jonathan Meredith Papers, Manuscripts Division, Library of Congress.

[7] *New York Herald*, November 11, 1863.

[8] Samuel H. Willey, Personal memoranda of Samuel H. Willey, B.L., pp. 8–9.

[9] Philip Hone to Jonathan Meredith, New York, November 14, 1849, *in* Jonathan Meredith Papers, Manuscripts Division, Library of Congress.

[10] *New York Herald*, November 11, 1863.

[11] *Ibid.*, April 6, 1854.

[12] *Ibid.*, November 11, 1863.

[13] Stowell, Diary.

[14] Theodore T. Johnson, *Sights in the Gold Region and Scenes by the Way* (Dublin, 1851), pp. 110–111.

[15] *New York Herald*, November 27, 1863.

[16] *San Francisco Daily Alta California,* June 19, 1850.

[17] Gilmor Meredith to Jonathan Meredith, San Francisco, November 1, 1849, *in* Jonathan Meredith Papers, Manuscripts Division, Library of Congress.

[18] *San Francisco Daily Alta California,* May 13, 1862.

[19] *San Francisco Daily Evening Bulletin,* November 21, 1868.

[20] Stowell, Diary, entries for January 30 and 31, February 8, 1849.

[21] W., "By Sea and Land to California," *Littell's Living Age* (Boston), XXI (April–June, 1849):164–165.

[22] Crosby, Memoirs, p. 10.

[23] Albert Williams, Memoir, H.L., p. 17.

[24] John B. Peirce to Mrs. John B. Peirce, Steamer *Cherokee,* at sea, February 21, 1850, *in* Letters, 1850–1852, H.U.L.

[25] John B. Peirce to Mrs. John B. Peirce, Steamer *Cherokee,* at sea, off Santo Domingo, February 23, 1850, *ibid.*

[26] George Gordon, *The Safety of Steamship Passengers on Ocean Routes. A Letter to the Honorables J. P. Benjamin, Wm. M. Gwin, E. D. Baker, and J. W. Nesmith, Senators of the United States, en route for New York, on board the P.M.S.S. Company's Steamship Sonora, November, 1860* (1860), pp. 13–14.

[27] *Panama Star and Herald,* May 19, 1860.

[28] *New York Herald,* November 11, 1863.

[29] *Panama Star and Herald,* October 13, 1864.

[30] United States Department of State, Index, Despatches from Consuls, New Granada, Ecuador, Peru, Bolivia, Chile, October 31, 1853—May 25, 1870, No. 17, National Archives, pp. 140–144.

[31] *Panama Star and Herald,* July 21, August 13 and 16, 1864.

[32] San Francisco *Supplement to the Pacific News,* November 3, 1849.

[33] William H. Aspinwall to Messrs. Robinson, Bissell and Co., New York, July 13, 1850, *in* Aspinwall-Robinson Letter Book, collection of Daulton Mann, New York.

[34] Stowell, Diary, entries for February 1, 19, 21, and 26, 1849.

[35] Pearson, "Memoir."

[36] Anon., "Notes of a Journey in the Isthmus of Panama and California," *Hogg's Instructor* (Edinburgh, 1851), VII:122.

[37] *Ibid.,* p. 122; Henry Sturdivant, Journal of Henry Sturdivant from Dec. 8, 1849, of Cumberland, Maine, H.L., p. 11.

[38] Samuel W. Comstock to Alfred Robinson, New York, January 2, 1850, *in* Aspinwall-Robinson Letter Book.

[39] William H. Aspinwall to Messrs. Robinson, Bissell and Co., New York, September 13, 1850, *ibid.*

[40] George Sherman, "Voyage to California and to Oregon," H.L., p. 2.

[41] Henry H. Peters, Diary: New York to San Francisco, 1850, Manuscripts Division, New York Public Library, pp. 38, 40.

[42] John B. Peirce to Mrs. John B. Peirce, Acapulco, April 12, 1850, *in* Letters, 1850–1852, H.U.L.

[43] George E. Schenck, Statement of George E. Schenck on the Vigilance Committee, 1856, B.L., pp. 11–13.

[44] Bayard Taylor, *Eldorado, or, Adventures in the Path of Empire; Comprising a Voyage to California, via Panama; Life in San Francisco and Monterey; Pictures of the Gold Region, and Experiences of Mexican Travel* (New York, 1850), I:32.

[45] John B. Peirce to Mrs. John B. Peirce, Acapulco, April 2, 1850, in Letters, 1850–1852, H.U.L.

[46] Taylor, *op. cit.,* pp. 32–33.

[47] *Panama Star*, June 30, 1853.

[48] *San Francisco Daily Evening Bulletin*, December 7, 1865.

[49] *Panama Star and Herald*, September 5, 1861.

[50] Charles Toll Bidwell, *Isthmus of Panama* (London, 1865), p. 113.

[51] *Panama Star and Herald*, December 19, 1861.

[52] New York Superior Court, *Heilman vs. Roberts*, pp. 225, 227–228.

[53] Peters, Diary, p. 40.

[54] Thomas Craig Smith, "Travels of Matthew Maus," *in* Sketches of Californian pioneers, written or dictated by themselves for Bancroft's Pacific Library, San Francisco, B.L., p. 2.

[55] *San Francisco Daily Alta California*, February 13, 1853.

[56] *New York Herald*, February 26, 1855.

[57] *Weekly Panama Star and Herald*, April 9, 1855.

[58] *New York Herald*, May 29, 1857; *San Francisco Daily Alta California*, August 20, 1858.

[59] *Panama Star and Herald*, September 15, 1860.

[60] *Ibid.*, November 10, 1860.

[61] *Ibid.*, August 19 and September 5, 1863.

[62] *Ibid.*, August 4, 1864.

[63] *Ibid.*, December 22, 1859, and October 13, 1864.

[64] *San Francisco Daily Alta California*, January 28, 1853.

[65] William H. Aspinwall to Messrs. Robinson, Bissell and Co., New York, August 28, 1850, *in* Aspinwall-Robinson Letter Book.

[66] Stowell, Diary, entries for February 2 and 13, 1849.

[67] Gilmor Meredith to Emma Meredith, Steamship *California*, at sea, July 22, 1851, *in* Jonathan Meredith Papers, Manuscripts Division, Library of Congress.

[68] John B. Peirce to Mrs. John B. Peirce, Acapulco, April 2, 1850, *in* Letters, 1850–1852, H.U.L.

[69] Peters, Diary, p. 39.

[70] *San Francisco Daily Alta California*, March 21, 1861.

[71] M. Hall McAllister, "Diary," *Re-union of the Pioneer Panama Passengers on the Fourth of June, 1874* (San Francisco, 1874), pp. 13–17.

[72] Leonard W. Hayes, "Diary of a Forty-niner," Essex Institute, Salem, pp. 1–3.

[73] *Bound Home, or the Gold Hunter's Manual* (New York, 1852).

[74] *Put's Golden Songster. Containing the Largest and Most Popular Collection of California Songs Ever Published* (San Francisco, 1858), p. 29.

NOTES TO CHAPTER VII

THE ISTHMIAN LINK

[1] See page 3 of the present work.

[2] *Panama Star*, February 11, 1851.

[3] Hubert Howe Bancroft, *California Inter Pocula* (San Francisco, 1888), p. 161.

[4] *New York Herald*, January 25 and 31, 1849.

[5] *Panama Star*, February 11, 1851; *New York Herald*, February 17, 1852.

[6] *Panama Star*, February 11, 1851.

[7] E. L. Autenrieth, *A Topographical Map of the Isthmus of Panama, together with a Separate and Enlarged Map of the Lines of Travel, and a Map of the City of Panama . . . with a Few Accompanying Remarks for the Use of Travellers* (New York, 1851), pp. 6–10.

[8] George E. Schenck, Statement of George E. Schenck on the Vigilance Committee of 1856, B.L., pp. 3–4.

[9] *Panama Star,* February 11, 1851.

[10] *New York Herald,* March 30, 1849.

[11] *Ibid.,* March 31, 1849.

[12] *Ibid.,* July 28 and September 28, 1849.

[13] *Panama Echo,* March 16, 1850; *Georgia,* Log, March 12, 14, June 26, 1850, Naval History Society, New York.

[14] *New York Herald,* July 16 and August 23, 1850; *Panama Star,* September 13, 1850.

[15] *New York Herald,* August 23, 1850.

[16] *Panama Star,* October 18, 1850; *New York Herald,* December 15, 1850, and January 22, 1851.

[17] *New York Herald,* October 29, 1850.

[18] *Panama Star,* February 11 and March 14, 1851.

[19] *New York Herald,* August 7, 1851.

[20] *Ibid.,* August 23 and October 29, 1850.

[21] Autenrieth, *op. cit.,* p. 9.

[22] Theodore T. Johnson, *Sights in the Gold Region* (Dublin, 1851), pp. 49–57.

[23] Bancroft, *op. cit.,* p. 174.

[24] *New York Herald,* January 31, 1849.

[25] *Ibid.,* January 25, 1849.

[26] *Ibid.,* March 25 and 30, 1849.

[27] *Ibid.,* March 31, 1849.

[28] *Panama Star,* February 11, 1851.

[29] *Ibid.,* May 18, 1853.

[30] Autenrieth, *op. cit.,* p. 9; *Panama Star,* February 11, 1851.

[31] *Panama Herald,* October 4, 1853.

[32] *New York Herald,* October 29, 1853.

[33] *Panama Weekly Star,* January 23, 1854.

[34] *Ibid.*

[35] *New York Herald,* August 7, 1850; *Panama Star,* December 31, 1850.

[36] Henry Tracy to M. O. Roberts, Panama, August 8, 1850, *in* New York Superior Court, *Heilman* vs. *Roberts,* pp. 232–235.

[37] Henry Tracy to M. O. Roberts, Chagres, September 11, 1850, *ibid.,* pp. 239–244.

[38] *New York Herald,* October 7, 1851.

[39] Hubert Howe Bancroft, *History of Central America* (San Francisco, 1887), III:519; *Weekly Panama Star and Herald,* March 19, 1855.

[40] *Panama Star,* October 18 and November 15, 1850.

[41] *Panama Herald,* August 18 and 20, 1853; *Panama Weekly Star,* October 31, 1853.

[42] William H. Sidell, Journal of Panama Survey, 1849, Canal Zone Library, Balboa Heights, I:97.

[43] *Panama Star and Herald,* September 10, 1868.

[44] *New York Herald,* June 26, 1849.

[45] *Ibid.,* May 25, 1850.

[46] *Ibid.,* June 20, 1851.

[47] *Ibid.,* September 28, 1849.

[48] *Ibid.,* April 27, 1850; *Panama Herald,* February 16, 1852.

[49] *Panama Star and Herald,* September 10, 1868; Samuel H. Willey, Personal memoranda, B.L., pp. 60–68.

[50] *Panama Star and Herald,* January 11, 1853.

[51] *Ibid.*, September 10, 1868.

[52] Ernesto J. Castillero R., *El Ferrocarril de Panamá y su Historia* (Panama, 1932), pp. 1–4.

[53] F. N. Otis, *Panama Railroad* (New York, 1861), p. 17.

[54] *New York Herald*, October 14, 1852.

[55] William Nelson to James Buchanan, U. S. Consulate, Panama, March 24, 1848, *in* Consular Letters, Panama, April 7, 1823—December 20, 1850, No. 1, National Archives, Division of Department of State; Otis, *op. cit.*, p. 17.

[56] *Memorial of W. H. Aspinwall, John L. Stephens, and Henry Chauncey, in reference to the Construction of a Railroad across the Isthmus of Panama*, 30th Cong., 2nd sess., [Senate] Misc. Doc. 1, December 11, 1848 (Washington, 1848), pp. 1–4.

[57] *Congressional Globe*, 30th Cong., 1st sess., p. 40.

[58] *New York Herald*, December 19, 1848.

[59] *Ibid.*, December 23, 1848.

[60] Report 26, *Railroad across the Isthmus of Panama*, January 16, 1849, 30th Cong., 2nd sess., H. R. 721 (Washington, 1849), pp. 1, 7, 20.

[61] *Congressional Globe*, 30th Cong., 2nd sess., p. 382.

[62] *Ibid.*, pp. 398–402, 411–415, 457–463.

[63] William H. Aspinwall to Alfred Robinson, New York, March 14, 1849, *in* Aspinwall-Robinson Letter Book, collection of Daulton Mann, New York.

[64] *Congressional Globe*, 30th Cong., 2nd sess., pp. 130–131.

[65] *Contract between the Republic of New Granada and the Panama Railroad Co.* (New York, 1856), pp. 5, 7, 9, 11, 13, 15, 17, 25, 29, 31, 33, 51; Otis, *op. cit.*, pp. 17–18.

[66] *New York Herald*, November 18 and 21, 1859.

[67] *Contract between the United States of Colombia and the Panama Railroad Co.* (New York, 1867), pp. 5, 9, 11, 21, 23, 29, 31, 39.

[68] *New York Herald*, December 13, 1848.

[69] Panama Railroad Co., *Act of Incorporation* (New York, 1849), p. 1.

[70] *New York Herald*, June 29, 1849.

[71] *Ibid.*, June 16, 1849, and January 13, 1855.

[72] *Ibid.*, July 3, 1849.

[73] *Ibid.*, January 19 and 24, 1849; Sidell, Journal of Panama survey, Canal Zone Library, Balboa Heights, C. Z., I: 1, 3; Otis, *op. cit.*, p. 21.

[74] Sidell, Panama survey, I: 74, 75, *passim; New York Herald*, June 20, 25, and 26, 1849.

[75] *Ibid.*, July 14, 1849.

[76] Otis, *op. cit.*, pp. 24–25.

[77] Panama Railroad Co., Minutes of Executive Committee, March 12, 1850, Office of the Panama Railroad Co., New York.

[78] Otis, *op. cit.*, pp. 26–28.

[79] *Panama Star*, September 27, 1850; *New York Herald*, February 12, 1851.

[80] *New York Herald*, March 9, 1851.

[81] *Panama Star*, January 28, 1851; *Panama Herald*, May 19, 1851.

[82] *New York Herald*, July 6, 1851.

[83] *Panama Herald*, September 8 and November 17, 1851.

[84] *Panama Herald*, December 15, 1851; *New York Herald*, December 22, 1851.

[85] *New York Herald*, February 18, April 13, 1852; *Panama Herald*, February 23, 1852.

[86] *Panama Herald*, May 28, 1852; *New York Herald*, April 13, May 3 and 5, June 13, July 16, 1852.

[87] *Panama Herald*, March 9, 1852.

[88] *Ibid.*

[89] *New York Herald*, June 13, 1852.

[90] *Ibid.*, July 31, 1852.

[91] *Panama Star*, November 8, 1853.

[92] *New York Herald*, October 12, 1853.

[93] *Panama Star*, November 8, 1853.

[94] Otis, *op. cit.*, p. 34.

[95] *Panama Herald*, June 8 and December 7, 1852.

[96] *Ibid.*, March 12, 1852; *New York Herald*, January 7, 1860.

[97] *Panama Herald*, March 9, 1852, March 11, September 29, 1853; *Panama Star*, March 11 and 12, 1853; Otis, *op. cit.*, pp. 34–35.

[98] *Panama Star*, October 7, 1851.

[99] *New York Herald*, June 30, 1853.

[100] *Panama Herald*, June 21 and August 18, 1853.

[101] *Panama Star*, November 26, 1853.

[102] *Panama Weekly Star*, January 30, 1854.

[103] *Weekly Panama Star and Herald*, July 17 and October 2, 1854; *Panama Star and Herald*, November 14, 1854.

[104] *Aspinwall Daily Courier*, February 24, 1855.

[105] *Weekly Panama Star and Herald*, February 12, 1855.

[106] *New York Herald*, January 29, February 6 and 26, 1855.

[107] *Ibid.*, March 2, 1855.

[108] *Panama Star and Herald*, February 17 and 20, 1855; *Aspinwall Daily Courier*, February 24, 1855.

[109] George M. Totten to Gouverneur Kemble, Aspinwall, November 15, 1854, *Weekly Panama Star and Herald*, December 25, 1854.

[110] Sidell, Panama survey, I:7, 11–12, 29, 46–47, II:195–196.

[111] *Panama Star*, September 27, 1850.

[112] *New York Herald*, October 29, 1850.

[113] *Ibid.*, January 17, 1851.

[114] *Ibid.*, June 7, 1851.

[115] *Panama Weekly Star*, June 13, 1853; *Panama Star*, June 14, 1853.

[116] *New York Herald*, August 8, 1853; see also p. 194 of the present work.

[117] *New York Herald*, September 20, 1853.

[118] *Ibid.*, October 12, 1853; *Panama Star*, November 10, 1853.

[119] Panama Railroad Co., *Communication of the Board of Directors* (New York, 1853), pp. 17–18.

[120] *Panama Herald*, January 12, 1854; *Panama Weekly Herald*, April 3, 1854.

[121] *Panama Weekly Herald*, August 21 and September 4, 1854; Otis, *op. cit.*, pp. 35–36.

[122] *Panama Weekly Star*, April 17, 1854.

[123] *New York Herald*, March 2, 1855.

[124] *Ibid.*, May 4, 1858.

[125] Sidell, Panama survey, I:4, 61–62, 68–71, 73.

[126] *Panama Star*, January 14, 1851.

[127] *New York Herald*, February 12, 1851.

[128] *Ibid.*, February 9, 1851.

[129] *Ibid.*, August 24, 1852.

[130] *Ibid.*, June 13, 1853; *Panama Herald*, June 30, 1853.

[131] Panama Railroad Co., *Communication of the Board of Directors* (New York, 1855), pp. 14–15.

[132] *Ibid.*, pp. 23–24; *New York Herald*, January 13 and March 2, 1855.

[133] *Panama Star and Herald*, January 3, 1856.

[134] Otis, *op. cit.*, p. 137.

[135] *Ibid.*, pp. 137–140; *Panama Weekly Star and Herald*, February 12, April 9 and 23, 1855; *Panama Star and Herald*, March 20, 1855.

[136] C. T. Bidwell, *Isthmus of Panama* (London, 1865), p. 136.

[137] Panama Railroad Co., Minutes of the Board of Directors, August 16, 1855, Office of the Panama Railroad Co., New York, *passim; Panama Star and Herald*, March 25, 1858.

[138] William H. Aspinwall to Jonathan Meredith, New York, June 10, 1851, *in* Jonathan Meredith Papers, Manuscripts Division, Library of Congress.

[139] *New York Herald*, January 13, 1855.

[140] *An Act to Amend the Act Entitled "An Act to Incorporate the Panama Rail Road Company"* (New York, 1855), p. 1.

[141] *New York Herald*, December 30, 1852.

[142] Panama Railroad Co., *Communication of Board of Directors, 1855*, pp. 10–11; *New York Herald*, January 13, 1855.

[143] *New York Herald*, July 11, 1857, January 19 and February 4, 1858, January 8, 1859, June 24, 1860; notices and clippings pasted in collection (A) of pamphlets, circulars, newspaper clippings, maps, etc., relating to the Panama Railroad Company, the shipping in the West Indies and the Pacific Mail Company, mounted in a scrapbook, New York Public Library, pp. 20–21.

[144] *New York Herald*, 1851–1869, *passim*.

[145] Panama Railroad Co., *Communication of Board of Directors, 1855*, pp. 10–11.

[146] *Panama Star and Herald*, May 14, 1867.

[147] Journal, from October 19, 1848, to March 6, 1849, Vol. 21, Post Office Department, Cave Johnson, P.M.O., P.O.L., p. 7.

[148] *New York Herald*, April 10, 1849.

[149] *Ibid.*, May 28, 1849.

[150] J. Collamer to John M. Clayton, Post Office Department, November 28, 1849, and J. Collamer to A. B. Corwine, Post Office Department, December 6, 1849, *in* J. Collamer, Letter Book, T 2, Postmaster General, January 25, 1849, to July 20, 1850, P.O.L.

[151] *Panama Star*, May 13 and July 29, 1851; *Panama Herald*, November 17, 1851.

[152] J. Collamer to John M. Clayton, General Post Office, April 8 and June 11, 1850, *in* J. Collamer, Letter Book, T 2, P.O.L.; Letter Book, No. 9, J. A. J. Creswell, Post Office Department, March 12, 1869—January 20, 1874, P.O.L.

[153] Letter Book, No. 9, J. A. J. Creswell, P.O.L.; *Report of the Postmaster General, December 4, 1852* (Washington, 1853), p. 636; Panama Railroad Co., *Letter from the Directors to the Senate and House of Representatives* (New York, 1856), pp. 3–7; *New York Herald*, November 30, 1851.

[154] *Report of the Postmaster General respecting the Operations and Conditions of the Post Office Department during the Fiscal Year Ending June 30, 1861* (Washington, 1861), p. 81; W. Dennison to W. T. Otto, Post Office Department, February 1, 1866, *in* W. Dennison, Letter Book, No. 7, October 1, 1864, to July 6, 1866, P.O.L.; *The Annual Report of the Postmaster General of the United States for the Fiscal Year 1867* (Washington, 1867), p. 64.

[155] *New York Herald*, June 6, 1850.

[156] United States Department of State, Index, Despatches from consuls, Mexico, New Granada, Venezuela, Ecuador, December 28, 1828—December 19, 1853, No. 5, and Despatches from consuls, New Granada, Ecuador, Peru, Bolivia, Chile, October 31, 1853—May 25, 1870, No. 17, National Archives.

[157] *Panama Weekly Star*, March 27, 1854.

[158] *Panama Weekly Star and Herald,* March 26 and April 16, 1855.

[159] *Panama Star and Herald,* February 21, April 17 and 19, 1856; *New York Herald,* April 30, 1856.

NOTES TO CHAPTER VIII

SIGNIFICANCE OF THE PANAMA ROUTE

[1] M. C. Perry to William Ballard Preston, New York, April 9, 1850, *in* Captains' Letters, January–December, 1850, N.R.L.; William Skiddy to Charles W. Skinner, New York, April 27, 1850, *in* Mail Steamers, 1847–1850, Class 2, A. D., Subject files, N.R.L.

[2] *Congressional Globe,* 30th Cong., 2nd sess., pp. 406–408, 428–429.

[3] *Ibid.,* 31st Cong., 1st sess., pp. 1072, 1858; Anon., *A Few Suggestions respecting the United States Mail Service* (1850), pp. 7–9.

[4] Anon., *A Few Suggestions respecting the United States Mail Service,* p. 24.

[5] Sen. Ex. Doc. 1, series no. 549, p. 432.

[6] *Ibid.,* 50, series no. 619, pp. 51–54.

[7] *New York Herald,* January 28 and 30, 1850.

[8] Abstract of Log of U.S.S. *Portsmouth,* 2nd, N.R.L.; J. C. Dobbin to W. H. Aspinwall, Navy Department, April 10 and 13, July 6, 1854, *in* General Letter Book, no. 50, January 17, 1854, to August 4, 1854, N.R.L., pp. 211, 223, 437; J. C. Dobbin to W. H. Aspinwall, Navy Department, November 18, 1854, *ibid.,* no. 51, August 4, 1854, to February 15, 1855, N.R.L., p. 362; J. C. Dobbin to W. H. Aspinwall, Navy Department, July 5, 1855, *ibid.,* no. 52, February 15, 1855, to August 17, 1855, N.R.L., pp. 415–416; J. C. Dobbin to W. H. Aspinwall, Navy Department, October 9, 1855, *ibid.,* no. 53, August 18, 1855, to March 20, 1856, N.R.L., p. 127.

[9] J. Collamer to Thomas J. Rusk, General Post Office, February 4, 1850, *in* J. Collamer, Letter Book, T 2, Postmaster General, January 25, 1849, to July 20, 1850, P.O.L.

[10] J. Collamer to Thomas J. Rusk, Post Office Department, June 27, 1850, *ibid.;* Sen. Ex. Doc. 50, ser. no. 619, p. 12.

[11] *Regulations for the Government of the Post Office Department* (Washington, 1847), pp. 34–35.

[12] Cave Johnson to S. York Atlee, Post Office Department, November 18, 1848, *in* C. Johnson, Letter Book, R 2, extra, Postmaster General, 1848–1849, P.O.L.

[13] *New York Herald,* May 25, 1850; *Panama Star,* September 20 and December 31, 1850, January 7, 1851.

[14] *San Francisco Daily Alta California,* October 13, 1852; *Panama Star,* November 12, 1853.

[15] M. O. Roberts to S. R. Hobbie, New York, October 25, 1849, M. O. Roberts to J. Collamer, New York, November 13, 1849, *in* Roberts Letter Book, December 11, 1848—August 3, 1850, Naval History Society, New York; N. K. Hall to Thomas Corwin, Post Office Department, February 20, 1851, N. K. Hall to William H. Aspinwall, Post Office Department, July 24, 1851, N. K. Hall to W. V. Brady, Post Office Department, August 7 and 19, 1851, N. K. Hall to Hugh Maxwell, Post Office Department, August 29, 1851, *in* N. K. Hall, Letter Book, U 2, Postmaster General, July 21, 1850, to April 23, 1852, P.O.L.

[16] *New York Herald,* February 25, March 14, 1862; *San Francisco Daily Alta California,* February 19, 1862; *Panama Star and Herald,* March 8 and 18, 1862.

[17] William H. Aspinwall to Messrs. Robinson, Bissell and Co., New York, September 13, 1850, *in* Aspinwall-Robinson Letter Book, collection of Daulton Mann, New York.

[18] *California Daily Courier,* October 19, 1850.

[19] See Appendix II.

[20] Figures of any sort for the overland emigration to California in the period under consideration are notably lacking. For the year 1849, Bancroft estimated a total immigration into California of approximately 81,000, of whom 33,000 were Americans traveling overland and 23,000 came by sea from the United States; of these last only 4,624 were listed as coming by Panama. For estimating the emigration after 1849, the official census figures have been taken as indicating the general trend. At the beginning of 1849, the population of California was roughly 21,000, in 1860 it was 379,994, and in 1870 it was 560,247. Owing to the small number of women in California prior to 1860, the birth rate may be taken as lower than the death rate, while for the whole period, these figures are considered as approximately balancing. This would mean that the net gains of 348,994 between 1849 and 1860 and of 180,253 between 1860 and 1870 indicate the amount of immigration. In estimating the immigration by way of Panama, it has been considered that the total number of passengers coming to California to remain might be reached by subtracting the total of eastbound passengers by Panama from the total of westbound passengers. This gives the figure of 60,595 as coming in the decade 1849–1859, and 87,969 between the beginning of 1860 and June 30, 1869. The figures for passage to California by Cape Horn fell off rapidly after the first years. In 1852 there were 3,346; in 1854, 1,263; in 1856, 39; in 1857, 33; and in 1860, 627. The whole subject of emigration to the Pacific coast between 1849 and 1869 remains to be studied carefully, but on the basis of the figures given above, the estimates given for travelers coming by the Panama route would seem to be reasonably correct.

The following sources were used in the analyses of the emigration to California in this period: Hubert Howe Bancroft, *History of California* (San Francisco, 1888), VI:159; J. D. B. De Bow, *Statistical View of the United States . . . Seventh Census* (Washington, 1854), p. 394; Jos[eph] C. G. Kennedy, *Preliminary Report on the Eighth Census, 1860* (Washington, 1862), p. 8; Francis A. Walker, *A Compendium of the Ninth Census (June 1, 1870)* (Washington, 1872), p. 8; *San Francisco Prices Current and Shipping List,* December 31, 1852, December 30, 1853, January 4, 1858; *San Francisco Mercantile Gazette and Prices Current,* January 4, 1860. Figures for passengers by the Panama route are based on Appendix II.

[21] Richard Lambert, compiler, *Legislature of California, 1852, List of Names of the State Officers, Members of the Legislature, Officers of the Senate and House of Representatives of the Third Session, Held in the City of Sacramento* (Sacramento, 1852).

[22] New York Superior Court, *Heilman vs. Roberts,* p. 126; *San Francisco Daily Alta California,* March 4, 1860.

[20] See Appendix III.

[24] William H. Aspinwall to Alfred Robinson, New York, May 22, 1849, *in* Aspinwall-Robinson Letter Book.

[25] Samuel W. Comstock to Alfred Robinson, New York, December 1 and 13, 1849, *ibid.*

[26] *Panama Star and Herald,* August 12, 1861.

BIBLIOGRAPHY

BIBLIOGRAPHY

BIBLIOGRAPHICAL AIDS

United States Library of Congress. *A List of Books (with References to Periodicals) on Mercantile Marine Subsidies.* Third ed., with additions. Washington, 1906.

————. *Additional References Relating to Mercantile Marine Subsidies.* Reprint of 1911 ed. Washington, 1923.

————. *List of References on the Pacific Mail Steamship Company.* Washington, 1916.

MANUSCRIPT SOURCES

Archivo de Panamá, Panama.

Notaria publica, No. 1, del circuito de Panamá, protocolo numero 2, año 1853, instrumentos del 41 al 101.

Bancroft Library, University of California, Berkeley.

Chapin, E. R., and others. Sketches of Californian pioneers, written or dictated by themselves for Bancroft's Pacific Library, San Francisco.

Connor, John W. Statement of a few recollections on early California by John W. Connor for Bancroft Library.

Dean, Peter. Statement of occurrences in California by Peter Dean for Bancroft Library.

Hawley, David N. Statement of David N. Hawley.

Hayes, Benjamin. "Emigrant Notes."

Henshaw, Joshua S. Statement of historical events in California in early times after American occupation, by Joshua S. Henshaw (a 49er).

Larkin, Thomas Oliver. Documents for the history of California.

Little, John T. Statement of events in the first years of American occupation of California. Related by John T. Little for Bancroft Library.

Low, Frederick F. Observations of F. F. Low on early California.

Ord, Edward O. C. Personal diary of a trip from New York to San Francisco, 1850.

Roach, Philip A. Statement of historical facts on California by Hon. Philip A. Roach for Bancroft Library.

Roberts, M. R. "Navigation in California."

Robinson, Alfred. Statement of recollections on early years of California made by Alfred Robinson for Bancroft Library.

Schenck, George E. Statement of George E. Schenck on the Vigilance Committee of 1856.

Stout, Arthur B. Log of the Steamship *California.* October 6, 1848, to February 28, 1849. [Log carried only as far as December 1, 1848.]

Vanderbilt, W. W. Statement of W. W. Vanderbilt, *in* Miscellaneous statements on California history.

Willey, Samuel H. Personal memoranda of Samuel H. Willey.

Williams, Henry B. "Pacific Mail Steamship Company."

Williams, Henry F. Statement of recollections on early days of California by a pioneer of 1849.

Williams, S. H. Letter Book.

Borel Collection, Stanford University Library, California.

Stowell, Levi. Diary of Levi Stowell for the year 1849.

Canal Zone Library, Balboa Heights, Canal Zone.

Sidell, William H. [Journal of Panama survey, January 9, 1849, to June 23, 1849.] 2 vols.

Collection of Daulton Mann, New York City.

Pacific Mail Steamship Company. Presid't to A. Robins[on], B[issell], & Co. Dec. 1848, to Nov. 1850. [Photostat in Henry E. Huntington Library.]

Essex Institute, Salem, Massachusetts.

Bailey, Rensselaer. From New York to San Francisco in 1849 A.D. Logbook of Rensselaer Bailey, Clintonsville, New York. [Transcript.]

Heyes, Leonard W. "Diary of a Forty-niner."

Harvard University Library, Treasure Room, Cambridge, Massachusetts.

Peirce, John B. Letters, February 21, 1850, February 23, 1850, April 2, 1850, April 12, 1850.

Henry E. Huntington Library, San Marino, California.

Crosby, Elisha Oscar. Memoirs and reminiscences of E. O. Crosby.

Pacific Mail Steamship Company. [Cash Books, July 1, 1852, to December 31, 1859, and October 9, 1868, to July 30, 1869.] 7 vols.

———. [Journals, February 10, 1851, to December 31, 1859, May 1, 1861, to January 31, 1863, and January 1, 1869, to June 30, 1871.] 7 vols.

———. [Ledgers, September 1, 1853, to May 31, 1855, August 1, 1856, to January 1, 1859, and January 1, 1860, to June 30, 1871.] 4 vols.

———. [Waybills, January 1, 1861, to June 23, 1862.]

Sherman, George. "Voyage to California and to Oregon."

Sturdivant, Henry. Journal of Henry Sturdivant from Dec. 8, 1849, of Cumberland, Maine.

Williams, Albert. Memoir.

Library of Congress, Manuscripts Division, Washington, D.C.

Jonathan Meredith Papers. Vols. XVI–XIX.

Library, United States Post Office Department, Washington, D.C.
Journal, from October 19, 1848, to March 6, 1849. Vol. 21. Post Office Department. Cave Johnson, P.M.G.

[Letter Books, March 17, 1846, to April 23, 1852, September 14, 1852, to October 20, 1855, October 24, 1856, to January 20, 1874.] 16 vols.

Mail Routes (Appendix . . . Mails to Europe . . .) New York, 1845–1849.

M. H. De Young Memorial Museum, San Francisco, California.
[Engineer's Log, Pacific Mail Steamship Company's Steamer *Oregon*, Voyages 1–10, 1848–1851.]

National Archives, Washington, D.C.
Bureau of Marine Inspection and Navigation, Department of Commerce.
Record of Enrollments, 1841–1869. Nos. 13–35. 23 vols.
———. Record of Registers, 1841–1869. Nos. 9–17. 9 vols.
———. Ship Enrollments.
———. Ship Registers.
Department of State.
Index. Despatches from consuls. Mexico, New Granada, Venezuela, Ecuador, December 28, 1828—December 19, 1853, No. 5.
Index. Despatches from consuls. New Granada, Ecuador, Peru, Bolivia, Chile. October 31, 1853—May 25, 1870. No. 17.

Navy Department.
Abstract of log of U.S.S. *Portsmouth*, 2nd [1854].
Bureaux' Letters, Jan.–June, 1847.
Captains' Letters, January, 1848—December, 1855. 11 vols.
Commandants of Navy Yards. New York. 1848.
Commanders' Letters, July–December, 1855, April, 1856—March, 1857. 6 vols.
Congress' Letters, January, 1849—December 23, 1854. 3 vols.
Contracts. Transportation of Mail. April 20, 1847—October 5, 1860. Navy Department.
Executive Letters, January, 1847—June, 1852, January, 1853—June, 1855, January, 1858—June, 1858, 1859, supplemental volumes 1846–1849. 17 vols.
General Letter Books, September 25, 1846—November 11, 1857. 20 vols.
Journal kept on board U.S.S. *Portsmouth*, 1852–1855.
Mail Steamers, 1847–1850. Class 2, A.D., Subject Files.
Miscellaneous Letters, January, 1848—September, 1858. 72 vols.
Navy Agents and Storekeepers, 1848.
Navy Agents' and Storekeepers' Letters, 1850.
Navy Agents' Letters, 1849, 1851. 2 vols.

Officers' Letters, January, February, April, July, August, September, November, 1849, February, April, July, September, October, 1850, January, April, September, December, 1851, February, October, December, 1852, October, 1853. 20 vols.

Officers, Ships of War, no. 42, June 12, 1848, to April 16, 1849.

Pacific Squadron, November, 1860—October 25, 1864. 2 vols.

Naval History Society Library, New York Historical Society, New York City.

[*America*, Log, New York–Panama, November 1—December 31, 1863.]

[*Empire City*, Log, New York–Havana–New Orleans, January 9, 1852—January 3, 1853.]

[*Georgia*, Log, New York–New Orleans–Chagres and Aspinwall, January 29, 1850—July 31, 1851.] 3 vols.

[*Granada*, Log, New York–New Orleans–Aspinwall–San Francisco, May 8, 1859—October 14, 1860.]

[*Illinois*, Log, New York–Aspinwall, February 20, 1855—November 25, 1856.]

[*Moses Taylor*, Log, New York–Aspinwall, January 5, 1858—May 26, 1859.]

[*Ohio*, Log, New York–Aspinwall, January 20, 1853—March 26, 1854.]

[*Philadelphia*, Log, New Orleans–New York, January 2–19, 1855.]

[*Republic*, Log, New York–San Francisco, 1850–1852.]

[*St. Louis*, Log, New York–Aspinwall, October 7, 1858—April 12, 1859.]

Roberts, Marshall Owen. [Letter Books, November 30, 1848—October 16, 1849, November 30, 1848—July 27, 1850, December 11, 1848—August 3, 1850, August 6, 1850—September 27, 1853.] 4 vols.

United States Mail Steamship Company. [Drafts. Blank check book with stubs March 13, 1851—June 16, 1853.]

———. [Blank receipts for passage from Panama to San Francisco with stubs July 27, 1850—March 26, 1851.]

———. [Blank receipts for passage from New York in the *Georgia*.]

———. [Package of blank tickets and passage contracts for United States Mail Steamship Company and competing lines.]

———. Voyage stores. U.S. Mail S.S. Co., 1854 and 1855.

New York Public Library, Manuscripts Division, New York City.

Brown Brothers' Letters. Vol. 88.

Peters, Henry H. Diary: San Francisco to New York via Panama, 1851; New York to San Francisco via Nicaragua, 1852; San Francisco to New York via Panama, 1853–1854.

Wolcott, Frederick Henry. Diary, 1849–1854. Vol. I.

Panama Railroad Company, Office of the, New York City.

Minutes of the Board of Directors. 12 vols. 1849–1903.

Minutes of the Executive Committee. 11 vols. 1849–1903.

University of California at Los Angeles, Library, Los Angeles, California.
Lancey, Thomas Crosby. Journal, 1846–1849. 3 vols.

Webb Institute of Naval Architecture, New York City.
Webb, William H. Certificates of Ships Constructed. 2 vols.

PRINTED SOURCES

OFFICIAL

Congressional Globe, 29th to 31st, 35th Congresses. Washington, 1845–1851, 1859.

DAVIS, CHARLES H. *Report on Interoceanic Canals and Railroads between the Atlantic and Pacific Oceans.* Washington, 1867.

Executive Documents, 30th Congress, 1st session, no. 8. Washington, 1848.

List of the Post Offices in the United States, with the Names of Postmasters on the 1st of July, 1855, also, the Principal Regulations of the Post Office Department. Washington, 1855.

Mails. Reports of the Secretary of the Navy and the Postmaster-General, Communicating, in Compliance with a Resolution of the Senate, Information in relation to the Contracts for the Transportation of Mails by Steamship between New York and California, March 23, 1852. 32nd Congress, 1st session, *Senate Executive Document,* 50. Washington, 1852.

Message of the President to Congress, Dec. 24, 1849. 31st Congress, 1st session, *Senate Document,* no. 1, Washington, 1850.

PETERS, RICHARD, ed. *The Public Statutes at Large of the United States of America, from the Organization of the Government in 1789 to March 3, 1845.* 5 vols. Boston, 1845–1854.

Railroad across the Isthmus of Panama. Report of T. Butler King, Committee on Naval Affairs on the Memorial of W. H. Aspinwall, John L. Stephens, Henry Chauncey, January 16, 1849. 30th Congress, 2nd session, Report no. 26, to accompany bill H.R. 721. Washington, 1849.

Regulations for the Government of the Post Office Department. Washington, 1847.

Report of Postmaster General, 1847–1869. 23 vols. Washington, 1848–1870.

Report of the Secretary of the Navy, December 6, 1847. Washington, 1847.

Revision of the Laws relating to the Post Office Department . . . Prepared . . . for the Committee on Post Office and Post Roads. Washington, 1863.

State of New York. No. 9. In Senate, January 12, 1855. Report of the Committee on Commerce and Navigation, relative to the Panama Railroad. Albany, 1855.

Statutes at Large and Treaties of the United States of America. Vols. IX–XIV, December 1, 1845—March, 1867. Boston, 1851–1868.

WARE, JOSEPH A. comp. *The Postal Laws and Regulations, Published by Authority of the Postmaster General.* Washington, 1866.

SEMIOFFICIAL AND PRIVATE

Anonymous. *A Few Suggestions respecting the United States Steam Mail Service.* 1850.

————. *A Sketch of Events in the Life of George Law, Published in Advance of his Autobiography, also, Extracts from the Public Journals.* New York, 1855.

————. "A Trip around Cape Horn by the Steamer *Tennessee*," *Journal, Franklin Institute.* No. 49, May, 1850.

————. *A Sketch of the Route to California and Japan via the Isthmus of Panama. A Useful and Amusing Book to every Traveller.* San Francisco, 1867.

————. *Festival in Celebration of the Twenty-fifth Anniversary of the Arrival of the Steamer California at San Francisco, February 28, 1849, Given by the Society of "First Steamship Pioneers," February 28, 1874.* San Francisco, 1874.

————. *Memorial to the Hon. Senate and the House of Representatives of the United States in Congress Assembled.* 1851.

————. "Notes of a Journey in the Isthmus of Panama and California," *Hogg's Instructor.* Vol. VII, n. s., pp. 110–112, 130–133, 173–175. Edinburgh, 1851.

————. "Pacific Mail," *Harper's Weekly.* August 2, 1873, New York.

————. *Pacific Mail. A Review of the Report of the President.* "Wherefore rejoice: What conquest brings he home?" New York, 1865.

————. "The Pacific Steam Quarrel," *Harper's Magazine.* Vol. III, no. 112, February 19, 1859. New York.

————. *Re-union of the Pioneer Panama Passengers on the Fourth of June, 1874, Being the Twenty-fifth Anniversary of the Arrival of the Steamship Panama at San Francisco.* San Francisco, 1874.

ASPINWALL, WILLIAM HENRY. *First Annual Report of the Pacific Mail Steamship Co., May, 1855.* New York, 1855.

ASPINWALL, WILLIAM HENRY, STEPHENS, JOHN L., CHAUNCEY, HENRY. *Memorial of Wm. H. Aspinwall, John L. Stephens, and Henry Chauncey in reference to the Construction of a Railroad across the Isthmus of Panama.* 30th Congress, 2nd session [Senate], Misc. Doc. 1, December 11, 1848. Washington, 1848.

AUTENRIETH, E. L. *A Topographical Map of the Isthmus of Panama, together with a Separate and Enlarged Map of the Lines of Travel, and a Map of the City of Panama. With a Few Accompanying Remarks for the Use of Travellers.* New York, 1851.

BANCROFT, HUBERT HOWE. *California Inter Pocula.* San Francisco, 1888.

BARTOL, B. H. *A Treatise on the Marine Boilers of the United States.* Philadelphia, 1851.

BATES, (Mrs.) D. B. *Incidents on Land and Water, or Four Years on the Pacific Coast. Being a Narrative of the Burning of the Ships Nonantum, Humayoon and Fanchon, together with Many Startling and Interesting Adventures on Sea and Land.* 4th edition. Boston, 1858.

BIDWELL, CHARLES TOLL. *Isthmus of Panama.* London, 1865.

Bound Home, or the Gold Hunter's Manual: a Newspaper Published on board the Pacific Mail S.S. Co.'s Steamship "Northerner." Capt. Henry Randall, on her Late Trip from San Francisco to Panama, March 2, 1852. Peppergrass, Hot-Korn, and Co., Publishers and Proprietors. S. C. Peppergrass. F. A. Hot-Korn, George W. Baggs, Editors. New York, 1852.

BURNETT, PETER H. *Recollections and Opinions of an Old Pioneer.* New York, 1880.

California and New York Steamship Company. *The Prospectus of the California and New York Steamship Company.* San Francisco, 1857.

Claims Commission of the United States of America and the United States of Colombia. *Before the Claims Commission of the United States of America and the United States of Colombia. Claims of the Panama Railroad Company, the Pacific Mail Steamship Company, and the U.S. Mail Steamship Company. Supplementary Brief. S. S. Cox, Counsel.* Washington, 1866.

COLE, (Mrs.) CORNELIUS. "To California via Panama in 1852," *Annual Publications of the Historical Society of Southern California.* Vol. IX, part 3 (1914), pp. 163–172. Los Angeles, 1914.

COOPER, W. B. *Incidents of Shipwreck; or the Loss of the San Francisco.* Philadelphia, 1855.

DAVIS, WILLIAM HEATH. *Seventy-five Years in California.* San Francisco, 1929.

DUNBAR, EDWARD E. *The Romance of the Age; or the Discovery of Gold in California.* New York, 1867.

EMMONS, GEORGE F. *The Navy of the United States, from the Commencement, 1775 to 1853; with a Brief History of Each Vessel's Service and Fate as Appears upon Record. Compiled by Lieut. George F. Emmons, U.S.N., from the Most Reliable Sources, under the Authority of the Navy Department. To which Is Added a List of Private Armed Vessels, Fitted out under the American Flag, Previous and Subsequent to the Revolutionary War, with Their Services and Fates; also a List of the Revenue and Coast Survey Vessels, and the Principal Ocean Steamers Belonging to the Citizens of the United States in 1850.* Washington, 1853.

FABENS, JOSEPH. *A Story of Life on the Isthmus.* Putnam's Semimonthly Library for Travelers and the Fireside. 1853.

GORDON, GEORGE. *The Safety of Steamship Passengers on Ocean Routes. A Letter to the Honorables J. P. Benjamin, Wm. M. Gwin, E. D. Baker, and J. W. Hosmith, Senators of the United States, en route for New York, on board the P.M.S.S. Company's Steamship Sonora, November, 1860.* 1860.

HINCHLIFF, THOMAS WOODBINE. *Over the Sea and Far Away, Being a Narrative of Wanderings round the World.* London, 1876.

HOLDEN, C. W. "Notes of Hand," *Holden's Dollar Magazine*. Vol. III, no. 6 (June, 1849), Vol. IV, no. 1 (July, 1849). New York, 1849.

HOLINSKI, ALEXANDRE. *La Californie et les routes interocéaniques*. 2d ed. Brussels, 1853.

JOHNSON, THEODORE T. *Sights in the Gold Region and Scenes by the Way*. New York, 1849.

LAW, GEORGE, ROBERTS, M. O., CROSSWELL, E. *United States Mail Steamships. Facts Respectfully Submitted to the Consideration of the Congress of the United States*. New York, 1850.

New York Public Library. *Collection (A) of Pamphlets, Circulars, Newspaper Clippings, Maps, etc., relating to the Panama Rail-Road Company, the Shipping in the West Indies and the Pacific Mail Company, Mounted in a Scrapbook*. 185— to 187—.

New York Superior Court. *William Heilman* vs. *Marshall O. Roberts*. New York, 1861.

O'CONNOR, CHARLES, EVARTS, WILLIAM M., LOWREY, GROSVENOR. *Opinions of Charles O'Connor, William M. Evarts, and Grosvenor Lowrey, Given to the Pacific Mail Steamship Company, and the Central American Transit Co. upon Certain Statutes of the State of California, Requiring Revenue Stamps upon Passage Tickets*. New York, 1866.

ORAN. "Tropical Journeyings," *Harper's New Monthly Magazine*. Vol. XVIII (January, 1859). New York, 1859.

OTIS, FESSENDEN NOTT. *Illustrated History of the Panama Railroad; together with a Traveller's Guide and Business Man's Hand-Book for the Panama Railroad and its Connections with Europe, the United States, the North and South Atlantic and Pacific Coasts, China, Australia, and Japan by Sail and Steam*. New York, 1862.

————. *Isthmus of Panama. History of the Panama Railroad; and of the Pacific Mail Steamship Company. Together with a Traveller's Guide and Business Man's Hand-Book for the Panama Railroad, and the Lines of Steamships Connecting it with Europe, the United States, the North and South Atlantic and Pacific Coasts, China, Australia, and Japan*. New York, 1867.

Pacific Mail Steamship Company. *Additional Regulations for the Company's Steamers. November, 1872*. New York, 1872.

————. *Bill of Complaint, Affidavits, &c., and Opinion of Mr. Justice Blatchford, in the Suit of Brown, Hargreaves, et al., vs. Atlantic Mail Steamship Company, et al.* New York, 1867.

————. *Charter of the Pacific Mail Steam Ship Company, with Its Amendments Inclusive of May 1st, 1866*. New York, 1867.

————. *Fourth Annual Report of the Pacific Mail Steamship Company, 1858. May 12, 1858*. New York, 1858.

————. *Fifth Annual Report of the Pacific Mail Steamship Company, May 23, 1859*. New York, 1859.

————. *Freight and Passenger Tariff No. 5. Pacific Mail Steam Ship Company. 1870.* New York, 1870.

————. *Instructions to Captains, Pacific Mail Steam Ship Company.* New York, 1872.

————. *The Memorial of the Pacific Mail Steamship Company to the Senate and Assembly of the State of California.* San Francisco, 1868.

————. *Proceedings at Meeting of Stockholders of Pacific Mail Steamship Company, held June 28, 1855.* New York, 1855.

————. *Report of Louis McLane, President pro. tem. to the Board of Directors of the Pacific Mail Steamship Company.* New York, 1867.

————. *Report of the Committee Appointed to Investigate the Affairs of the Pacific Mail Steamship Company, October 12, 1854.* New York, 1854.

————. *Report of the President to the Stockholders, February, 1868.* New York, 1868.

————. *Reports of Two Committees of Stockholders Appointed at the Annual Meeting, May, 1855, of the Pacific Mail Steamship Company's Stockholders, and Made at an Adjourned Meeting, Held 20th June, 1855.* New York, 1855.

————. *Report of the Committee Appointed to Investigate the Affairs of the P. M. S. S. Co., Oct. 12, 1854.* New York, 1854.

————. *Seventh Annual Report, May, 1861.* New York, 1861.

————. *Sixth Annual Report of the Pacific Mail Steamship Company, May, 1860.* New York, 1860.

————. *Statement of 28th June, 1855, from Mr. William H. Aspinwall, President of the Pacific Mail Steamship Company in Answer to the Reports from Two Committees Appointed by Stockholders, 24th May, 1855; with Replies to Attacks on Committee's Reports by Hon. Abijah Mann, Jr., Chairman of the First Committee, and Mr. Theodore Dehon, Chairman of the Second Committee.* New York, 1855.

Panama Railroad Company. *A letter from the Directors of the Panama Railroad Company, Addressed to the Senate and House of Representatives of the United States, in Reply to the Remarks of the Postmaster-General, Contained in his Report to the President, and Presented to Congress, December 3, 1856.* New York, 1856.

————. *Act of Incorporation, Panama R.R. Co., 1849.* New York, 1849.

————. *Communication of the Board of Directors of the Panama Railroad Company to the Stockholders, together with the Report of the Chief Engineer to the Directors.* New York, 1853.

————*Communication of the Board of Directors of the Panama Railroad Company to the Stockholders; together with the Report of the Chief Engineer to to the Directors, and an Appendix, Containing Tables of Grades, Tangents, and Curves of the Panama Railroad, and Observations upon the Levels of the Atlantic and Pacific Oceans.* New York, 1855.

————. *Contract between the Republic of New Granada and the Panama Railroad Company.* New York, 1856.

————. *Contract between the United States of Colombia and the Panama Railroad Company.* New York, 1867.

————. *Panama Rail-Road Company.* New York, 1849.

————. *Panama Rail-Road Time Table and Train Rules. 1871.* 1871.

————. *Statement for the Year Ending December 31st, 1856.* New York, 1857.

————. *Statement for the Year Ending December 31st, 1857.* New York, 1858.

————. *Statement for the Year Ending December 31st, 1858.* New York, 1859.

————. *Statement for the Year Ending December 31st, 1859.* New York, 1860.

————. *Statement for the Year Ending December 31st, 1860.* New York, 1861.

————. *Statement for the Year Ending December 31st, 1861.* New York, 1862.

————. *Statement for the Year Ending December 31st, 1862.* New York, 1863.

————. *Statement for the Year Ending December 31st, 1863.* New York, 1864.

PARKER, WILLIAM H. *Remarks on the Navigation of the Coasts between San Francisco and Panama, by Wm. H. Parker, Commander, Pacific Mail Steam Ship Company, San Francisco, June 1st, 1871. Second Edition, with an Appendix.* San Francisco, 1873.

PEARSON, RICHARD H. "Memoir," *San Francisco Daily Evening Bulletin.* March 3, 1868.

People's California Steamship Company. *Prospectus of the People's California Steamship Company, New York and San Francisco, 1858.* New York, 1858.

PRATT, JULIUS H. "To California by Panama in '49," *The Century Illustrated Monthly Magazine.* Vol. XLI (n. s., Vol. XIX) (November, 1890–April, 1891), pp. 901–917.

ROBINSON, ALFRED. *Life in California during a Residence of Several Years in the Territory Comprising a Description of the Country and the Missionary Establishments, with Incidents, Observations, etc. with an Appendix Bringing forward the Narrative from 1846 to the Occupation of the Territory by the United States.* San Francisco, 1891.

ROBINSON, TRACY. *Panama: a Personal Record of Forty-Six Years.* New York and Panama, 1907.

RYAN, WILLIAM REDMOND. *Personal Adventures in Upper and Lower California in 1848–9.* 2 vols. London, 1850.

SEYMOUR, (CAPTAIN). *The Isthmian Routes. A Brief Description of Each Projected Route, and of Those Now Existing, Showing the Capacity of Their Harbors, the Comparative Advantages of Each, and the Distance of Each from New York to San Francisco, from the Best Sources of Information and from Personal Observation and Survey over Each, in the Years from 1856 to 1861.* New York, 1863.

SHERMAN, WILLIAM TECUMSEH. *Memoirs.* New York, 1893.

SHUCK, OSCAR T., ed. *The California Scrap-Book: a Repository of Useful Information and Select Reading Comprising Choice Selections of Prose and Poetry, Tales and Anecdotes, Historical, Descriptive, Humorous, and Senti-*

mental Pieces, Mainly Culled from the Various Newspapers and Periodicals of the Pacific Coast. San Francisco, 1869.

STUART, CHARLES B. *The Naval and Mail Steamers of the United States.* New York and London, 1855.

SWINTON, WILLIAM. *How the "Ring" Ran Pacific Mail: a Story of Wall Street.* New York, 1867.

TAYLOR, BAYARD. *Eldorado, or, Adventures in the Path of Empire: Comprising a Voyage to California, via Panama; Life in San Francisco and Monterey; Pictures of the Gold Region, and Experiences in Mexican Travel.* 2 vols. 2d edition. New York, 1850.

TOMES, ROBERT. *Panama in 1855. An Account of the Panama Rail Road, of the Cities of Panama and Aspinwall, with Sketches of Life and Character on the Isthmus.* New York, 1855.

TROLLOPE, ANTHONY. "The Journey to Panama," in PROCTOR, ADELAIDE A., *The Victoria Regia: a Volume of Original Contributions in Poetry and Prose.* London, 1861.

United States Circuit Court. *In the Circuit Court for the United States, for The Second Circuit, and Southern District of New York. In equity, between Albert C. Sloo, a citizen of Ohio, complainant, and George Law, Marshall O. Roberts, Prosper M. Wetmore, Edwin Crosswell, and Bowes R. McIlvaine, citizens of the State of New York, defendants. Bill of equity. Daniel D. Lord, solicitor of complainant.* New York, 1849.

United States Mail Steamship Company. *Mail Service of the U.S. Mail Line of Steamers, between New York, Havana, New Orleans, & Aspinwall (Chagres) from October, 1850, to October, 1856.* New York, 1856.

W. "By Sea and Land to California," *Littell's Living Age,* XXI, 163.

WEBB, WILLIAM HENRY. *Plans of Wooden Vessels Selected as Types from One Hundred and Fifty of Various Kinds and Descriptions from a Fishing Smack to the Largest Clipper Ships and Vessels of War, Both Sail and Steam, Built by William H. Webb, in the City of New York, from the Year 1840 to the Year 1869 . . .* 2 vols. New York, 1897.

[WHEELER, O. C., WHEELER, (Mrs.) O. C., WILLIAMS, HENRY FAIRFAX]. *First Steamship Pioneers.* San Francisco, 1874.

WHEELWRIGHT, WILLIAM. *Statements and Documents Relative to the Establishment of Steam Navigation in the Pacific; with Copies of Decrees of the Governments of Peru, Bolivia, and Chile, Granting Exclusive Privileges to the Undertaking.* London, 1838.

WORTLEY, EMELINE STUART. *Travels in the United States, etc., during 1849 and 1850.* No date or place of publication.

NEWSPAPERS

Alta California. 1849–1869. San Francisco.
California Daily Courier. 1850. San Francisco.
California Star. 1847–1848. San Francisco.
California Star and Californian. 1848. San Francisco.

Courier. 1855. Aspinwall.
Daily Evening Bulletin. 1854–1869. San Francisco.
Daily Herald. 1850. San Francisco.
Daily Pacific News. 1851. San Francisco.
Daily Union. 1862. Sacramento.
Mercantile Chronicle. 1865–1868. Panama.
Mercantile Gazette and Prices Current. 1859–1865. San Francisco.
New York Herald. 1846–1869. New York.
Panama Echo. 1850. Panama.
Panama Herald. 1851–1854. Panama.
Panama Star. 1849–1854. Panama.
Panama Star and Herald. 1854–1869. Panama.
San Francisco Prices Current and Shipping List. 1852–1859. San Francisco.
San Francisco Shipping List and Prices Current. 1852. San Francisco.
The Mercantile Gazette and Shipping Register. 1856–1869. San Francisco.
Tribune. 1865–1869. New York.

SECONDARY WORKS

ALBION, ROBERT GREENHALGH. *Square-Riggers on Schedule: the New York Sailing Packets to England, France, and the Cotton Ports.* Princeton, 1938.

———, in collaboration with POPE, JENNIE BARNES. *The Rise of New York Port [1815–1860].* New York and London, 1939.

ANONYMOUS. "William H. Aspinwall," *Appleton's Cyclopaedia of American Biography.* Vol. I. New York, 1887.

BANCROFT, HUBERT HOWE. *Chronicles of the Builders of the Commonwealth.* Vol. V. San Francisco, 1891.

———. *History of California.* Vols. V–VII. San Francisco, 1890.

———. *History of Central America.* Vol. III. San Francisco, 1887.

———. *History of Oregon.* Vol. II. San Francisco, 1890.

BATES, WILLIAM W. *American Navigation; the Political History of Its Rise and Ruin and the Proper Means for Its Encouragement.* Boston and New York, 1902.

BERTHOLD, VICTOR M. *The Pioneer Steamer "California," 1848–1849.* Boston and New York, 1932.

BRADLEE, FRANCIS B. C. *Some Account of Steam Navigation in New England.* Salem, 1920.

BROWN, JOHN CROSBY. *A Hundred Years of Merchant Banking; a History of Brown Brothers and Company, Brown, Shipley & Company, and the Allied Firms.* New York, 1909.

BUSHELL, T. A. *"Royal Mail," a Centenary History of the Royal Mail Line, 1839–1939.* London [1939].

CASTILLERO R., ERNESTO J. *El Ferrocarril de Panamá y su historia.* Panama, 1932.

CHASE, PHILIP P. "On the Panama Route during the Gold Rush to California," Colonial Society of Massachusetts, *Transactions*, November, 1929—November, 1930, from the *Publications of the Colonial Society of Massachusetts*. Vol. XXVII. Boston, 1932.

CROFFUT, A. A. *The Vanderbilts and the Story of Their Fortune*. Chicago and New York, 1886.

CURTIS, WILLIAM ELROY. *Trade and Transportation between the United States and Latin America*. Senate Executive Document, No. 54. 51st Congress, 1st session. Washington, 1890.

DOLLAR, ROBERT. *One Hundred Thirty Years of Steam Navigation*. San Francisco, 1931.

DUNMORE, WALTER T. *Ship Subsidies; an Economic Study of the Policy of Subsidizing Merchant Marines*. New York and Boston, 1907.

ELDREDGE, ELWIN MARTIN. "Early Steam Navigation on the Pacific," *Pacific Marine Review*. July, 1921, pp. 398–399. San Francisco.

FERRIER, WILLIAM WARREN. *Origin and Development of the University of California*. Berkeley, 1930.

FRASER, J. P. MUNRO. *History of Solano County*. San Francisco, 1879.

GUINN, J. M. "Down in Panama," *Publications of the Historical Society of Southern California*. Vol. VI, part 2 (1904), pp. 115–121. Los Angeles.

———. "To California via Panama in the Early '60s," *ibid*. V (annual publications of 1900, 1901, 1902), 13–21. Los Angeles.

HASKINS, C. W. *The Argonauts of California*. . . . New York, 1890.

HITTELL, THEODORE H. *History of California*. Vol. III. San Francisco, 1898.

HOWLAND, F. *A Brief Genealogical and Biographical History of Arthur Henry and John Howland and Their Descendants*. New Bedford, 1885.

HUNT, ROCKWELL, DENNIS and AMENT, WILLIAM SHEFFIELD. *Oxcart to Airplane*. Los Angeles, 1929.

JOHNSON, ALLEN, and MALONE, DUMAS, eds. *The Dictionary of American Biography*. 20 vols. New York, 1928–1936.

KEMBLE, JOHN HASKELL. "Pacific Mail Service between Panamá and San Francisco, 1849–1851," *The Pacific Historical Review*. Vol. II, no. 4 (December, 1933), pp. 405–417. Glendale.

———. *The Genesis of the Pacific Mail Steamship Company*. San Francisco, 1934.

———. "The Panamá Route to the Pacific Coast, 1848–1869," *The Pacific Historical Review*. Vol. VII, no. 1 (March, 1938), pp. 1–13. Glendale.

———. "The *Senator;* the Biography of a Pioneer Steamship," *California Historical Society Quarterly*. Vol. XVI, no. 1 (March, 1937), pp. 61–70. San Francisco.

LANE, WHEATON J. *Commodore Vanderbilt; An Epic of the Steam Age*. New York, 1942.

LAWSON, WILL. *Pacific Steamers*. Glasgow, 1927.

LLOYD, J. T. *Reminiscences of the Two Vanderbilts, "Corneel" and "Bill."* Boston, 1887.

PARISH, JOHN CARL. "By Sea to California," *The Trans-Mississippi West; Papers Read at the Conference Held at the University of Colorado, June 18– June 21, 1928.* Edited by James F. Willard and Collin B. Goodykoontz. Boulder, 1930.

PARKER, H., and BOWEN, FRANK C. *Mail and Passenger Steamships of the Nineteenth Century; the Macpherson Collection with Iconographical and Historical Notes.* Philadelphia [1927].

PARKS, E. TAYLOR. *Colombia and the United States, 1765–1934.* Durham, 1935.

PREBLE, GEORGE HENRY. *A Chronological History of the Origin and Development of Steam Navigation.* Philadelphia, 1883.

RAINEY, THOMAS. *Ocean Steam Navigation and the Ocean Post.* New York and London, 1858.

RENNINGER, WARREN D. *Government Policy of Aid in American Shipbuilding from Earliest Times to the Present.* Philadelphia, 1911.

ROYAL MAIL STEAM PACKET COMPANY. *A Link of Empire, or 70 Years of British Shipping; a Souvenir of the 70th Year of the Incorporation of the Royal Mail Steam Packet Co.* London, 1909.

SCOVILLE, J. A. (WALTER BARRETT, *pseud.*) *The Old Merchants of New York.* 5 vols. in 3. New York, 1863–1866, and later editions.

SCROGGS, WILLIAM C. *Filibusters and Financiers; the Story of William Walker and His Associates.* New York, 1916.

SMITH, ARTHUR D. HOWDEN. *Commodore Vanderbilt; an Epic of American Achievement.* New York, 1927.

SULLIVAN, JOHN T. *Report of Historical and Technical Information Relating to the Problem of Interoceanic Communication by way of the American Isthmus.* Washington, 1883.

TYLER, DAVID BUDLONG. *Steam Conquers the Atlantic.* New York and London, 1939.

WARDLE, ARTHUR C. *Steam Conquers the Pacific; a Record of Maritime Achievement, 1840–1940.* London, 1940.

WILTSEE, ERNEST A. *Gold Rush Steamers [of the Pacific].* San Francisco, 1938.

WRIGHT, BENJAMIN C. *San Francisco's Ocean Trade Past and Future.* San Francisco, 1911.

WRIGHT, DORIS MARION. "An Introduction to the Study of the Population of California, 1848–1870." Unpublished master's thesis. Claremont Colleges Library.

WRIGHT, E. W., ed. *Lewis and Dryden's Marine History of the Pacific Northwest.* Portland, 1895.

INDEX

Abbey Taylor (brig), 195

Acapulco, 35, 36, 112, 113, 143, 147, 160; coal depot at, 134, 138, 139, 147

Accessory Transit Company, 59, 66; charter of, annulled, 74–75. *See also* Nicaragua Steamship Company; Nicaragua Transit Company

Acosta, Santos, 182

Adams and Company, 180

Adamson and Company, 171

Adriatic (steamer), 81, 84

Alabama (C.S.S.), 110–111 *passim*

Alaska (side-wheeler), 101, 116, 213

Allaire, James P., 119

Allen and Paxson, 52

Allen, Daniel B., 85, 96–97, 98

Allen, Edward, 176

Allen, Horatio, 183

Allen, William, 29

Alta California, 3, 7; discovery of gold in, 33

Alta California (newspaper), quoted, 35, 67, 68, 70, 72–73, 86, 87–88, 152

America (side-wheeler), 107, 111, 119, 214; steerage rate on, 108

American Atlantic and Pacific Ship Canal Company, 59, 77

Amonoosuck (bark), 195

Antelope (side-wheeler), 50, 51, 214; rates on, 55

Arabella (brig), 195

Arago (side-wheeler), 109, 117, 215

Arctic (steamer), 140

Ariel (side-wheeler), 82, 87, 96, 104, 105, 112, 131, 215; capture of, 110–111; criticism of, 162–163

Arizona (side-wheeler), 101, 216

Aspinwall (Colon) (replacing Chagres), 65, 69, 91; warships to be stationed at, 110; treasure left at, 111; supplies of coal kept at, 132, 137; opening of new port of, 166; Parédes' suggestion respecting, 186–187; growth of, 187; Vigilance Committee organized at, 198; resident mail agents at, 204

Aspinwall to New Orleans line, 101

Aspinwall, William Henry, 22–23, 33, 44, 48, 83, 90, 93, 98, 99, 127, 138, 139; mail contract assigned to, 20–

22, carried out by, 27–28; operated steamers on Pacific, 22–25; elected president of Pacific Mail, 25; quoted, 34, 39, 43, 51, 53, 54, 129, 180–181, 205–206, 208; letter from Postmaster General to, 42, and from Sec'y of Navy to, 42; agreement between Postmaster General, Sec'y of Navy, and, 44–45; director of North Atlantic Steamship Company, 84; resigned presidency of Pacific Mail, 90; favored coalition with Vanderbilt, 94; connected with Central American Transit Company, 108; letter of, to Sec'y of Navy, 128–129; instructions of, to Robinson, *see* Robinson, Alfred; recommendation of, 135; presented memorial to Congress, 179–180; and construction of railroad across Isthmus of Panama, 183; advice of, to Jonathan Meredith, 195–196; orders of, for voyage of *Oregon*, 205–206; on gold shipments, 208

Astor, John Jacob, 6

Astoria: founding of, 6; mail service to, 10, 23–24, 31, 41; recommended as terminus of mail line, 42 *passim*

Atlantic (side-wheeler), 81, 84, 92, 101, 117, 119, 216

Atlantic and Pacific Ocean Company, 2

Atlantic and Pacific Ship Canal Company, 77, 78

Atlantic and Pacific Steamship Company, 84, 92

Atlantic Mail Steamship Company, 96, 99–100, 102, 103; agreement between, and Pacific Mail, 100

Augusta (gunboat), 111–112 *passim*

Baldwin, J. L., 179, 184, 185

Baltic (side-wheeler), 81, 84, 92, 94, 101, 117, 216

Bancker, Captain Abraham, 171

Bartlett, Edwin, 25, 183

Beaver (steamer), 6

Benicia, California: base of operations for steamers, 134–136; sale of Pacific Mail property at, 136; coal on hand at, 139